Lecture Notes in Computer Science 16155

Founding Editors

Gerhard Goos
Juris Hartmanis

AF147711

The series Lecture Notes in Computer Science (LNCS), including its subseries Lecture Notes in Artificial Intelligence (LNAI) and Lecture Notes in Bioinformatics (LNBI), has established itself as a medium for the publication of new developments in computer science and information technology research, teaching, and education.

LNCS enjoys close cooperation with the computer science R & D community, the series counts many renowned academics among its volume editors and paper authors, and collaborates with prestigious societies. Its mission is to serve this international community by providing an invaluable service, mainly focused on the publication of conference and workshop proceedings and postproceedings. LNCS commenced publication in 1973.

Rudrapatna K. Shyamasundar · Huawei Huang ·
Songlin He · Junbin Fang · Liang-Jie Zhang
Editors

Blockchain –
ICBC 2025

8th International Conference
Held as Part of the Services Conference Federation, SCF 2025
Hong Kong, China, September 27–30, 2025
Proceedings

 Springer

Editors
Rudrapatna K. Shyamasundar
Indian Institute of Technology Bombay
Mumbai, Maharashtra, India

Huawei Huang 🔟
Sun Yat-sen University
Guangzhou, China

Songlin He 🔟
Southwest Jiaotong University
Chengdu, China

Junbin Fang
Jinan University
Guangzhou, China

Liang-Jie Zhang 🔟
Shenzhen University
Shenzhen, China

ISSN 0302-9743   ISSN 1611-3349 (electronic)
Lecture Notes in Computer Science
ISBN 978-3-032-06175-1   ISBN 978-3-032-06176-8 (eBook)
https://doi.org/10.1007/978-3-032-06176-8

This Springer imprint is published by the registered company Springer Nature Switzerland AG
The registered company address is: Gewerbestrasse 11, 6330 Cham, Switzerland

If disposing of this product, please recycle the paper.

Preface

The International Conference on Blockchain (ICBC) aims to provide an international forum for both researchers and industry practitioners to exchange the latest fundamental advances in the state-of-the-art technologies and best practices of blockchain, as well as emerging standards and research topics which will define the future of blockchain.

ICBC 2025 was a member of the Services Conference Federation (SCF). SCF 2025 had the following 10 collocated service-oriented sister conferences: 2025 International Conference on Web Services (ICWS 2025), 2025 International Conference on Cloud Computing (CLOUD 2025), 2025 International Conference on Services Computing (SCC 2025), 2025 International Conference on Big Data (BigData 2025), 2025 International Conference on AI & Multimodal Services (AIMS 2025), 2025 International Conference on Metaverse (METAVERSE 2025), 2025 International Conference on Internet of Things (ICIOT 2025), 2025 International Conference on Cognitive Computing (ICCC 2025), 2025 International Conference on Edge Computing (EDGE 2025), and 2025 International Conference on Blockchain (ICBC 2025).

This volume presents the accepted papers of the 2025 International Conference on Blockchain (ICBC 2025), held in Hong Kong, China during September 27-30, 2025. For this conference, each paper was single-blind reviewed by three independent members of the International Program Committee. After carefully evaluating their originality and quality, we accepted 16 papers from 29 submissions.

We are pleased to thank the authors whose submissions and participation made this conference possible. We also want to express our thanks to the Organizing Committee and Program Committee members, for their dedication in helping to organize the conference and reviewing the submissions. We owe special thanks to the keynote speakers for their impressive speeches.

Finally, we would like to thank operations team members Jing Zeng, Sheng He, Yishuang Ning, and Zhuolin Mei for their excellent work in organizing this conference. We look forward to your future great contributions as a volunteer, author, and conference participant in the fast-growing worldwide services innovations community.

August 2025

Rudrapatna K. Shyamasundar
Huawei Huang
Songlin He
Junbin Fang
Liang-Jie Zhang

Organization

Honorary Chair

Hai Jin   Huazhong University of Science and Technology, China

General Chair

Kai Lei   Peking University, China

Program Chairs

R. K. Shyamasundar   Indian Institute of Technology Bombay, India
Huawei Huang   Sun Yat-sen University, China
Songlin He   Southwest Jiaotong University, China
Junbin Fang   Jinan University, China

Application and Industry Track Chairs

Murugan Lakshmanan   Fidelity Investments, USA
Jianxin Huang   Ceprei Lianrui Information Technology Co., Ltd., China

Services Conference Federation (SCF 2025)

General Chairs

Ali Arsanjani   Google, USA
Wu Chou   Essenlix Corporation, USA

Coordinating Program Chair

Liang-Jie Zhang   Shenzhen University, China

CFO and International Affairs Chair

Min Luo   Services Society, USA

Operation Committee

Jing Zeng	China Gridcom Co., Ltd., China
Yishuang Ning	Tsinghua University, China
Sheng He	Kingdee International Software Group Co., Ltd., China
Zhuolin Mei	Jiujiang University, China

Steering Committee

Calton Pu (Co-chair)	Georgia Tech, USA
Liang-Jie Zhang (Co-chair)	Shenzhen University, China

ICWS 2025 Program Committee

Adel ElMessiry	WebDBTech, USA
Alexander Semenov	University of Florida, USA
Anusha Avyukt	University of Southern California, USA
Changhao Chenli	Indiana Institute of Technology, USA
Chao Wang	University of Science and Technology of China, China
Derek H. Sorensen	University of Cambridge, UK
François Charoy	Université de Lorraine, France
Haopeng Chen	Shanghai Jiao Tong University, China
Ji Liu	University of Sydney, Australia
Mike McBride	Futurewei Technologies, USA
Roberto Di Pietro	King Abdullah University of Science and Technology, Saudi Arabia
Sagar Suresh	A. P. Shah Institute of Technology, India
Venkata Suman Doma	Deloitte, USA
Xiangyu Li	Eastern Institute of Technology, Ningbo, China

Conference Sponsor – Services Society

The Services Society (S2) is a non-profit professional organization that has been created to promote worldwide research and technical collaboration in services innovations among academia and industrial professionals. Its members are volunteers from industry and academia with common interests. S2 is registered in the USA as a "501(c) organization", which means that it is an American tax-exempt nonprofit organization. S2 collaborates with other professional organizations to sponsor or co-sponsor conferences and to promote an effective services curriculum in colleges and universities. S2 initiates and promotes a "Services University" program worldwide to bridge the gap between industrial needs and university instruction.

The Services Sector accounted for 79.5% of the GDP of the USA in 2016. The Services Society has formed 5 Special Interest Groups (SIGs) to support technology- and domain-specific professional activities.

- Special Interest Group on Services Computing (SIG-SC)
- Special Interest Group on Big Data (SIG-BD)
- Special Interest Group on Cloud Computing (SIG-CLOUD)
- Special Interest Group on Artificial Intelligence (SIG-AI)
- Special Interest Group on Metaverse (SIG-Metaverse)

About the Services Conference Federation (SCF)

As the founding member of the Services Conference Federation (SCF), the first **International Conference on Web Services (ICWS)** was held in June 2003 in Las Vegas, USA. Meanwhile, the First International Conference on Web Services - Europe 2003 (ICWS-Europe 2003) was held in Germany in October 2003. ICWS-Europe 2003 was an extended event of the 2003 International Conference on Web Services (ICWS 2003) in Europe. In 2004, ICWS-Europe was changed to the European Conference on Web Services (ECOWS), which was held in Erfurt, Germany.

Sponsored by the Services Society and Springer, SCF 2018 and SCF 2019 were held successfully on June 25 – June 30, 2018, in Seattle, USA, and on June 25 – June 30, 2019, in San Diego, USA. SCF 2020 and SCF 2021 were held successfully online and in satellite sessions in Shenzhen, China. SCF 2022 and 2023 were held successfully on December 10–14, 2022 and on September 23–26, 2023, in Hawaii, USA. SCF 2024 was held successfully on November 16–19, 2024, in Bangkok, Thailand. To celebrate its 23rd birthday, SCF 2025 was held on September 27–30, 2025, in Hong Kong, China.

In the past 22 years, the ICWS community has expanded from Web engineering innovations to scientific research for the whole services industry. Service delivery platforms have been expanded to mobile platforms, the Internet of Things, cloud computing, and edge computing. The services ecosystem has gradually been enabled, value-added, and intelligence embedded through enabling technologies such as big data, artificial intelligence, and cognitive computing. In the coming years, all transactions with multiple parties involved will be transformed into blockchain and metaverse.

Based on technology trends and best practices in the field, the Services Conference Federation (SCF) will continue serving as the conference umbrella's code name for all services-related conferences. SCF 2025 defined the future of New ABCDE (AI, Blockchain, Cloud, BigData, & IOT) and entered the 5G for Services Era. **The theme of SCF 2025 was Services Agent.** We are very proud to announce that SCF 2025's 10 co-located theme topic conferences all centered around "services", with each focusing on exploring different themes (web-based services, cloud-based services, Big Data-based services, services innovation lifecycle, AI-driven ubiquitous services, blockchain-driven trust service ecosystems, industry-specific services and applications, and emerging service-oriented technologies).

- **Bigger Platform:** The 10 collocated conferences (SCF 2025) were sponsored by the Services Society, which is the world-leading not-for-profit organization (501(c)(3)) dedicated to the service of more than 30,000 worldwide Services Computing researchers and practitioners. A bigger platform means bigger opportunities for all volunteers, authors, and participants. Meanwhile, Springer provided sponsorship of the best paper awards and other professional activities. All the 10 conference proceedings of SCF 2025 were published by Springer and indexed in the ISI Conference

Proceedings Citation Index (included in Web of Science), Engineering Index EI (Compendex and Inspec databases), DBLP, Google Scholar, IO-Port, MathSciNet, Scopus, and ZBlMath.

- **Brighter Future:** While celebrating the 2025 version of ICWS, SCF 2025 highlighted the International Conference on AI and Multimodal Services (AIMS 2025) to build the fundamental infrastructure for enabling AIGC services ecosystems. It will also lead our community members to create their own brighter future.
- **Better Model:** SCF 2025 continued to leverage the invented Conference Blockchain Model (CBM) to innovate the organizing practices for all the 10 theme conferences. Senior researchers in the field are welcome to submit proposals to serve as CBM Ambassador for an individual conference to start better interactions during your leadership role in organizing future SCF conferences.

We look forward to your great contributions as a volunteer, author, and conference participant for the fast-growing worldwide services innovations community. If you would like to contribute to SCF 2026 as a leading volunteer or try the new Conference Blockchain Model, please feel free to contact us to become a conference volunteer. For other queries or questions, please feel free to visit our conference websites and find contact information on SCF 2026.

All the invited talks and paper presentations of SCF 2020, SCF 2021, and SCF 2022 are open to all Services Society community members for free. You can watch all presentations through SCF 365.

Contents

Unconditionally Safe Light Client 1
Niusha Moshrefi, Peiyao Sheng, Soubhik Deb, Sreeram Kannan,
and Pramod Viswanath

ZKP-StylePatch: Hybrid NFT Anti-counterfeit Framework 30
Tiantian Wu, Yixuan Shen, Fan Zhang, You Jiang, Lei Yao, Bin Zhou,
and Junbin Fang

A Blockchain-Based Range Proof Framework in Supply Chain 45
Jianyu Zou, Songlin He, Xukang Lyu, and Dongliang Chu

Regulated Blockchain Enabled Market for Internet of Things 59
Pengyu Liu, Enyuan Zhou, Song Guo, Zicong Hong, Wuhui Chen,
and Bin Xiao

Useful Proof of Work Consensus for Efficient Route Planning as Block
Mining 74
Yiheng Jiang, Yuwei Le, Rui Jiang, Xiaoyang Zhou, and Jiaheng Wang

Trusted Department Recommendation Based on Blockchain for Industrial
Chain Collaboration 89
Zhenchao Yan, Songlin He, Chase Wu, and Haohui Cai

MEVShield: A DeFi-Friendly Blockchain Scheme Based on Order
Protection 104
Ganwen Zheng, Wenjun Zhu, Shiyao Wang, and Jianan Hong

A Federated Blockchain-Enabled 6G Streaming Architecture: Protocol
Innovation and Trusted Ecology 117
Zihao Zhou, Kaibin Wei, and Tuo Song

Blockchain and Its Applications in the Automotive Industrial Value Chain 134
Tong Gu, Songlin He, Han Min, Xiaotong Chen, Zhenchao Yan,
Xukang Lyu, and Dongliang Chu

Why is it Challenging to Overcome, Minimize or Regulate MEV? 149
R. K. Shyamasundar

Design and Implementation of a Configurable Network Benchmarking
Framework for Blockchain Systems 170
    Huazheng Cheng, Xinwei Ning, Shengli Zhang, and Taotao Wang

A Novel Blockchain-Based Decentralized Drone Delivery Commercial
Platform: From Concept to Practice 185
    Shibing Xiao, Xinxin Luo, and Burong Deng

Blockchain-Based Business Model: Open Innovation Strategy for Smart
Edge Data Flow 198
    Xiaoqin Feng, Yiming Hong, Longyue Guo, Guoli Feng, and Huijie Chen

Evaluating Blockchain Platforms for Managing and Sharing Medical Data
Using NFTs and IPFS 213
    L. K. Bang, M. N. Triet, H. V. Khanh, and N. T. K. Ngan

Privacy-Preserving Transaction Chain Retrieval and Reconstruction
for Collaborative Supervision 227
    *Yuhan Yang, Qian Xu, Huajie Shen, Bo Yu, Wei He, Lijun Wei, Jing Wu,
    and Chengnian Long*

Lussa Platform: How AI and Blockchain Can Change the Gaming Industry 235
    Adel ELMessiry and Magdi El Messiry

Author Index 245

Unconditionally Safe Light Client

Niusha Moshrefi[1]([⊠]), Peiyao Sheng[2], Soubhik Deb[3], Sreeram Kannan[3],
and Pramod Viswanath[2]

[1] Princeton University, Princeton, USA
niusha@princeton.edu
[2] Witness Chain, Seattle, USA
psheng2@illinois.edu, pramodv@princeton.edu
[3] EigenLabs, Seattle, USA
{soubhik,sreeram}@eigenlabs.org

Abstract. Blockchain applications often rely on lightweight clients to
access and verify on-chain data efficiently without the need to run a
resource-intensive full node. These light clients must maintain robust
security to protect the blockchain's integrity for users of applications
built upon it, achieving this with minimal resources. Moreover, different
applications have varying security needs. This work focuses on addressing
these two key requirements and identifying the fundamental cost-latency
trade-offs to achieve tailored, optimal security for light clients.

Staking can provide *economic* guarantees (like in Proof-of-Stake
blockchains). In this paper, we formalize this *cryptoeconomic* security
to light clients, ensuring that the cost of corrupting the data provided to
light clients must outweigh the potential profit, then, propose an economically secure light client protocol. We further introduce "insured"
cryptoeconomic security to light clients, providing *unconditional* protection via the attribution of adversarial actions and the consequent slashing
of stakes. Moreover, the divisible and fungible nature of stake facilitates
programmable security, allowing for customization of the security level
according to the specific needs of different applications.

We implemented our light client in less than 1000 lines of Solidity
and TypeScript code [49] and evaluated their gas cost, latency, and computational overhead. For example, for a transaction valued at \$32k, the
light client can choose between zero cost with a latency of 5 h, or instant
confirmation with an insurance cost of \$7.45. Thus, the client can select
the optimal point on the latency-cost trade-off spectrum that best aligns
with its needs. Our light client requires negligible storage and minimal
computation, typically verifying only a few signatures (as few as one
in most cases).

Keywords: Light client · Blockchain · Ethereum · Economic security

1 Introduction

In PoS blockchains, validators secure the network by "locking" a certain amount
of stake (e.g., 32 ETH in Ethereum) to participate in the consensus protocols.

© The Author(s), under exclusive license to Springer Nature Switzerland AG 2026
R. K. Shyamasundar et al. (Eds.): ICBC 2025, LNCS 16155, pp. 1–29, 2026.
https://doi.org/10.1007/978-3-032-06176-8_1

The inherent nature of security in these PoS blockchains is *economic*: the greater the total stake, the more cost or loss needed to attack the consensus protocol (e.g., one third of the total stake, as in Ethereum PoS). Enforcing such costs relies on a feature called *accountable* security [1,2,31,35,36,38], which allows for the confiscating or "slashing" of stakes if validators sign conflicting states.

Full nodes in PoS blockchains play a critical role in maintaining the blockchain's integrity. They verify consensus signatures, replicate a full copy of transaction history, and execute state transitions. These tasks require significant resources and sophisticated hardware. For example, operating a full node for Ethereum demands at least 2TB of SSD storage [5]. In contrast, light clients prioritize resource efficiency, making them suitable for applications that only need to verify specific transactions and states, such as mobile wallets and cross-chain bridges [27,45]. Due to their limited resources, light clients sacrifice some degree of independence and immediacy in verifying blockchain security. They must communicate with full nodes to achieve the same level of security, particularly across three main areas: consensus (agreement on data inclusion), data availability (preventing censorship and downtime) and the validity of state transitions (ensuring state consistency). This paper explores the fundamental trade-offs between cost and latency of light clients required to achieve optimal security. We specifically focus on light clients that verify the consensus agreement and isolate the problem from state transition validation and data availability check, which are topics of independent interest [6,19–21].

Bitcoin introduces Simple Payment Verification (SPV) as its light client protocol. SPV enables light clients to verify the inclusion of a transaction in a specific block using a Merkle proof and the block header. Therefore, light clients need only download the block headers of the blockchain and can verify transaction finality by checking the depth of the block. In this context, the computational cost of consensus verification is relatively low for light clients in Bitcoin. However, in PoS blockchains like Ethereum, the consensus check is inherently more complex by design. It involves maintaining the whole validator set, tracking their stake changes and performing many signature checks for the consensus protocol. On the other hand, the security of PoW light clients relies on the assumption that the majority of full nodes are honest. In contrast, PoS blockchains derive their security economically through slashable stakes. The system rely on the rationality of consensus participants, aiming to ensure that the cost of attack exceeds any potential profit, which may vary in different contexts. Therefore, designing a light client protocol for PoS blockchains presents two essential requirements: (1) addressing the high cost of consensus verification, and (2) ensuring economic security and leveraging its dynamic nature.

To reduce the cost of verification, Ethereum's current light client protocol relies on a sync committee [16], composed of 512 randomly selected Ethereum validators, each staking 32 non-slashable ETH. However, this design exhibits significant security flaws. A dishonest supermajority within the sync committee could mislead light clients to accept invalid data without facing any penalties. Even if accountability were introduced through slashing, the combined stake of the sync committee remains negligible in comparison to the extensive Ethereum validator pool, which exceeds over 1 million validators as of January 2025 [43]. Consequently, this approach provides weak security for the light clients.

Furthermore, in the current design, light clients treat all transactions, whether worth a million dollars or a hundred dollars, with the same level of security. However, in the real world, security measures are naturally tailored based on the value at risk. For example, banks allocate more resources and scrutiny to safeguarding substantial deposits than they do for smaller checks. This principle should ideally extend to blockchain transactions, where the security guarantee provided by a light client should correspond to the transaction's value. For instance, if a light client is verifying the inclusion of a $100 transaction, it should require authentication supported by an amount of slashable stakes slightly higher than $100. In such a scenario, a rational validator staking this amount would lack the incentive to manipulate the data sent to that particular light client, as the potential loss from being slashed would outweigh the gain from the fraud.

In this paper, we decouple the security of the blockchain consensus from the security provided to light clients for accessing on-chain data. For light clients, there is no need to comprehensively verify the consensus of the entire network. Instead, we apply the same principles of *economic security* for PoS system to each light client and introduce *programmability* into this security framework: we ensure that the cost of corrupting a light client's verification process exceeds the potential profit from such corruption. This cost is tailored to the specific security needs of light clients, akin to the k-deep confirmation rule in Bitcoin. Consequently, each light client can independently balance its security level against the associated verification cost.

With security now programmable, individualized, and inherently economic, we introduce *insured security*. Economic security already guarantees that the stakes slashed from malicious validators always exceeds the potential gains. Thus, even if validators behave irrationally, the economic penalties are sufficient to cover any losses incurred. Insured security is designed to provide additional financial protection in the event of security breaches. Before processing a transaction, light clients are able to purchase insurance corresponding to the transaction's value. Validators involved in the light client protocol are held accountable for their commitments: if they sign incorrect data, they are penalized by having their stakes slashed, and the insured amount is then refunded to the light client from these funds.

Our Contribution. In this paper, we propose a light client protocol for PoS blockchains, denoted as LC$_{eco}$, featuring programmable economic security and optimal cost-efficiency. Its variant LC$_{ins}$ incorporates an insurance scheme to further provide unconditional protection for adversarial actions. The system offers the following advancements:

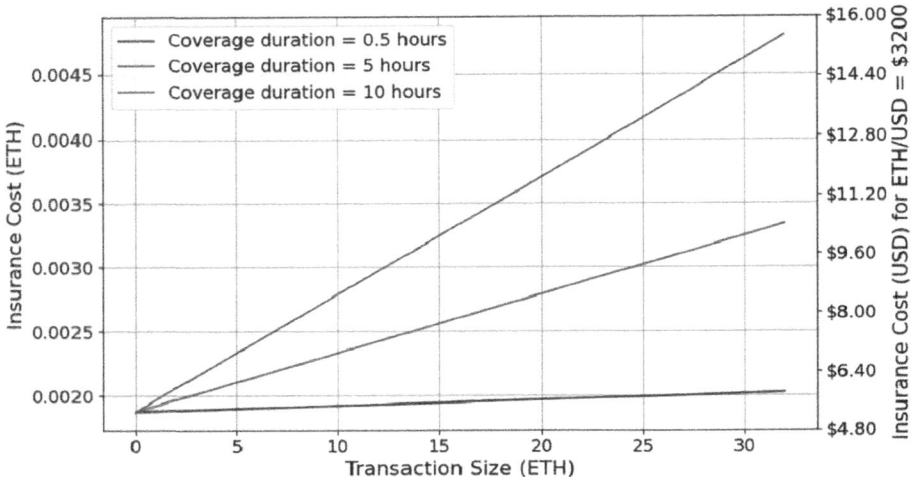

Fig. 1. Insurance cost vs. Transaction size (or covered value) for different insurance duration

Table 1. Comparison of our designs LC_{eco} and LC_{ins} with existing light client protocols.

-	Full PoS	Sync Committee	LC_{eco}	LC_{ins}
Computation cost	$V/32$	512	1	1
Storage cost	100 MB	30 KB	$<100B$	$<100B$
Latency	10 s	1 s	Few hours	2.8 ms
Security	Economic	Reputation-based	Economic	Insured
Programmability	×	×	✓	✓

- **Economic security.** We define economic security for light clients by making corruption economically infeasible for validators. In this protocol, light clients who want to verify specific on-chain states interact with a group of full nodes, known as *data providers*. These data providers validate and sign off on the legitimacy of the requested states, sending their confirmations to the light clients. The light clients then wait for some predetermined time to get ensured that the data providers are not slashed and the provided data is correct. During this waiting period, a network of full nodes, termed as *watcher network*, actively monitors for potential inconsistency between data providers' responses and on-chain data. This network guarantees that if any data provider signs an incorrect proof, at least one watcher will detect this error and alert the light client within the designated timeframe. Through this system, the protocol effectively ensures that the costs associated with misleading behavior exceed any potential profits, thus promoting honesty through economic incentives.
- **On-demand, programmable security.** Unlike traditional PoS blockchains that offer a uniform security level, our protocol allows light clients to cus-

tomize security measures based on their specific application needs. Leveraging stake-based voting, the group of data providers are chosen to ensure that the cumulative stakes exceed the desired security threshold – a minimum percentage of stake backing the data for specific applications. This approach provides each application with the granular control based on the risk assessments.

– **Insured security.** Our protocol further introduces an insured security feature, enabling light clients to purchase insurance against potential losses from adversarial actions. This insurance scheme provides dual benefits: firstly, it allows light clients to accept the data from providers immediately upon receipt, bypassing the waiting period. Secondly, in the case of security attack, it ensures that light clients do not incur financial losses. The insurance cost is calculated based on the coverage duration, the value protected, and the expected return rate for insurance stakers. Additionally, a constant gas cost is incurred for the inclusion and execution of the insurance payment transaction. The cost of insurance across various coverage durations is illustrated in Fig. 1. This scheme provides compensation for damages, protecting against irrational adversaries willing to incur significant penalties.

– **Optimal cost and latency.** Our protocol not only achieves programmable and optimal security guarantees but also significantly reduces the computational costs associated with consensus verification. Table 1 illustrates the performance comparisons between various protocols. Computation refers to the number of signatures required to be verified. For full PoS and sync committee, we assume all states are synchronized and only calculate the cost of verifying the consensus of a single block. Storage here is only for the consensus and not for storing the entire blockchain. For LC_{eco}, the latency is determined by the light client and typically spans a few hours. V is the total number of validators of PoS blockchain (it is greater than 1 million as of January 2025 for Ethereum [43]). The distribution of Ethereum transaction values indicates that over 85% of transactions are valued at less than 10 ETH [50], requiring only one data provider with a 32 ETH stake to secure them. Therefore, we focus our calculations on scenarios that rely on a single data provider. Our light client protocol with economic security optimizes both communication and computational efforts, although it does increase latency due to the optimistic verification path required to ensure security. By introducing insurance, the protocol achieves optimal performance across all metrics and offers enhanced financial guarantees in the event of attacks.

Implementation and Evaluations. We implemented our nodes in TypeScript using less than 700 lines of code, and the smart contract in Solidity using approximately 300 lines of code. Our implementation of the light client protocols is live on the Ethereum testnet Sepolia. We assume multiple data providers registered on the smart contract with 32 ETH worth of stake each, and the light client is connected to one honest watcher. Then, assess the light client design by the following metrics:

- Cost efficient: Light client incurs the cost of insurance if they opt in for it. The cost is proportional to the level of desired security for the light client.
- Fast confirmation: The light client gets instant confirmation for the data as soon as it is confirmed on Ethereum.
- Light computation: The computation cost for our design is minimal; few milliseconds for a light weight device.

The light client can select an optimal balance in the trade-off between latency and cost. It has the option to either confirm the inclusion of data after a delay at no cost(LC_{eco}), or pay a cost proportional to the delay to achieve instant confirmation(LC_{ins}). For a transaction valued at most \$32k, we calculate the cost to be as low as \$7.45 (0.02% of the covered value). In all cases, the light client maintains security equivalent to that of a full node.

Organization. In Sect. 2, we provide background on Proof-of-Stake (PoS) blockchains and light clients. Our model is introduced in Sect. 3. The protocol designs for economic security and insured security are presented in Sects. 4 and 5, respectively, along with their analyses. The evaluation of the protocol and details of our implementation are discussed in Sect. 6. Further discussion on the system design is provided in the last Sect. A.8.

2 Background

In this section, we introduce and define key terminology essential for understanding the protocol.

Ethereum uses Proof-of-Stake (PoS) as its consensus mechanism after the upgrade in Sep 2022. PoS means that the growth of the blockchain is guaranteed by participants who put some stake at risk to be slashed in case of their misbehavior.

In the Ethereum network, *validators* stake 32 ETH in a contract to be able to participate in the network, with a unique secret key and a public key serving as their identity. A validator's stake will get destroyed if it acts dishonestly. Each validator is linked to a *node*. Nodes can host various validators. Currently, Ethereum has more than 800,000 validators but less than 6000 nodes.

Ethereum operates with two crucial intervals: the *slot*, 12 s in duration, and the *epoch*, comprising 32 slots, equivalent to 6.4 min. One validator is randomly selected to be a block proposer in every slot. Then, other validators *attest* to the proposed block based on a random selection. Every active validator attests in every epoch, but not in every slot. Dishonest attestations by a validator leads to its stake being slashed.

A transaction gets *finalized* when it is part of a block that will not get out of the canonical chain without a large amount of ETH getting burned. On Ethereum, the first block in each epoch is a *checkpoint*. Validators vote for pairs of checkpoints that they consider to be valid. If a pair of checkpoints attracts votes representing at least two-thirds of the total staked ETH, the later checkpoint becomes *justified*, and the earlier checkpoint that was previously justified becomes *finalized*.

Moreover, on Ethereum, the inclusion of a transaction can be checked by verifying an inclusion proof. A block contains several fields including a `body` which has an `execution_payload`. It has a header called `execution_payload_header` that includes `transactions_root` using which transaction inclusion checks can be done efficiently.

3   Model

This section introduces the model used in our protocol design.

Blockchain. We assume a programmable blockchain with deterministic finalization rule for its blocks.

The parties involved in the system are: data providers, watchers and the light client. The parties, their relation and connections are shown in Fig. 2. All parties are computationally bounded to perform only polynomial-time computations.

Data Providers. Data providers operate full nodes and keep track of the latest state of the blockchain. They stake assets to provide services to verify the validity of states requested by light clients. The stakes are subject to potential slashing for misbehavior to ensure accountability. Each data provider has a publicly known cryptographic identity, referred to as a public key, which is linked to their stake. They sign all data sent to light clients with the secret key corresponding to their public key, enabling verification of data origin and integrity. We use m_{sk} to represent a message m signed by the data provider with secret key sk.

Data providers can join and stay in the system by maintaining a minimum amount of stake. Moreover, they can freely exit, reclaiming their remaining stake from the system after a withdrawal delay.

Data providers may act arbitrarily maliciously. All malicious data providers are governed by one adversary and can coordinate attacks. We assume the existence of at least one rational data provider to ensure liveness. A rational data provider aims to maximize their own utility, which is the monetary profit made in the currency of the stake they provide. Data providers can earn rewards on their stake in the protocol. The reward comes from the light clients who pay for and use their service.

Watchers. Watchers are full nodes connected to light clients to assist in data verification. Anyone can become a watcher to profit from monitoring and slashing misbehaving parties. Watchers receive data provided to the light clients by the data provider. When a watcher receives invalid data signed by a data provider, it is obligated to present on-chain evidence to slash the misbehaving provider's stake and alert the light client before the *challenge period* ends. The challenge period (denoted by T_{cp}) is a duration determined by light clients based on the value of the state it wants to check. A longer challenge period increases the light client's confidence that an honest watcher has verified its provided data. The challenge period has a maximum duration $maxT_{cp}$ determined by the system when initializing the protocol. For simplicity, we assume each light client connects to at least one honest watcher. Building a watcher network within rational model and designing normal path incentives is an independent topic of interest [42].

Light Client. Light clients are resource-constrained clients that aim to verify the inclusion of a state or transaction on the blockchain with minimal cost. Light clients are connected with a group of data providers and watchers during the verification process. They can not directly read data from blockchain, but can send transactions to on-chain contracts through the network diffusion functionality.

Light Client Bootstrapping. There exist a couple of ways for a client to access the latest finalized state of the blockchain. These methods are heavier in computation, but provide full node level security. For example, to use the full node protocol or zero-knowledge proofs.

4   Light Client with Economic Security

Alice runs a blockchain full node that provides data for Bob's wallet. She can attack Bob by refusing to pay him but still use his service. Alice creates and signs a payment transaction to Bob, but does not propagate it to be included in the blockchain. She privately mines a block including that transaction and gives it to Bob, so that in his wallet he gets convinced that he has received the money and the balance is updated. Then, Alice self-spends the money in her account on-chain, so that the signed transaction to Bob cannot be included in the blockchain later. This way, she uses Bob's service and Bob will never receive the payment.

Alice here could be a centralized data provider managing a specific wallet, or a corrupted majority of sync committee validators on Ethereum that happen to be selected at the same time.

This shows the low security of the light clients in the current system. In what follows, we introduce our light client protocol, LC_{eco}, which enables light clients to access on-chain data with economic security. Meaning that Alice in the above scenario would incur a higher cost than the profit received from Bob's service. Therefore, she would not be incentivized to perform such attack in the first place.

4.1   Protocol Overview

We first introduce our light client protocol, LC_{eco}, which enables light clients to access on-chain data with economic security. A light client queries specific data providers to verify the inclusion of a state or transaction on the blockchain, referred to throughout the paper as the *target state*. The process itself is known

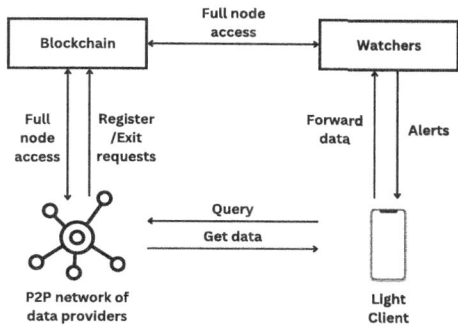

Fig. 2. System participants and their interactions.

as the *state inclusion check*. Data providers sign the block hash containing the target state along with any necessary proofs, and then send this information to the light client. The light client forwards all received data to connected watchers and waits for the challenge period to pass, during which it listens for alerts from watchers. If no alerts are received, the light client verifies the signatures and the proof, accepting the validity of the data. If watchers find inconsistencies between the data received from a light client and their view of the blockchain, they slash the data provider on-chain and alert the light client about the discrepancy.

A malicious or irrational data provider that provides an invalid proof for the light client gets slashed by the watchers. This is where the economic security comes in. A rational data provider never misbehaves in this protocol, since the penalty is more than the potential profit. Therefore, we expect the dispute path to happen very infrequently in the system.

4.2   Light Client

The light client first bootstraps and obtains the latest state of the blockchain. It extracts the latest set of data providers with their stakes. Then, it selects a group of data providers, ensuring the cumulative stakes exceed the value of its future request state. A higher total stake increases the light client's confidence in the accuracy of the data. However, this potentially necessitates more computation to verify proofs, presenting a trade-off that the light client must manage when choosing data providers.

The light client selects a challenge period duration T_{cp} that is the light client's estimate for how long it takes for an honest watcher to receive and verify the data. This depends on the watcher service the light client connects to and can vary from a few seconds to a few hours.

The light client generates a request (n_B, h_s) and sends it to the chosen data providers to verify that a target state s has been included in a committed block B. This request includes the block number n_B (same as block height) of the block containing the target state and the hash of the target state h_s.

Normal Path. The light client waits for responses from the data providers, then, forwards them to the connected watchers and monitors for any alerts. If no alerts are received once the challenge period elapses, the light client verifies the signatures of the data providers and the proof of state inclusion, then, proceeds to accept the data. The flow of normal path is depicted in Fig. 3.

If one or more data providers do not respond, the light client replaces them with another set of data providers. This has no cost for the light client except for the wait time. This is similar to the current situation with light clients requesting data from blockchain full nodes. If they don't respond, the light client changes its peers until it finds active ones.

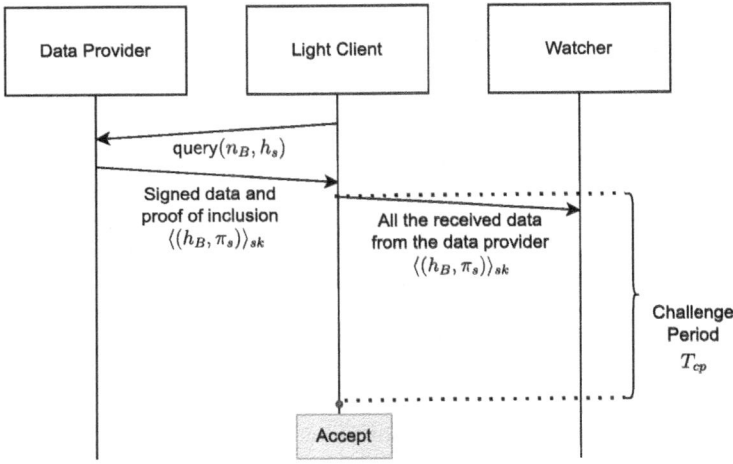

Fig. 3. The normal path for economic security. We have simplified this example, by supposing the light client has chosen only one data provider. Also, we only show the honest watcher here.

Dispute Path. If during the challenge period, the light client receives any alerts from watchers, it verifies the alert, discards all data from the implicated data provider, and restarts the protocol. Alerts include a proof of inclusion for the slashing event. The light client must bootstrap again to ensure that the slashing event actually occurred. The flow of the dispute resolution path is depicted in Fig. 4.

4.3   Data Providers

Data providers respond to requests from light clients by signing the target state if it has been included in a committed block. The response is denoted as $(h_B, \pi_s)_{sk}$,

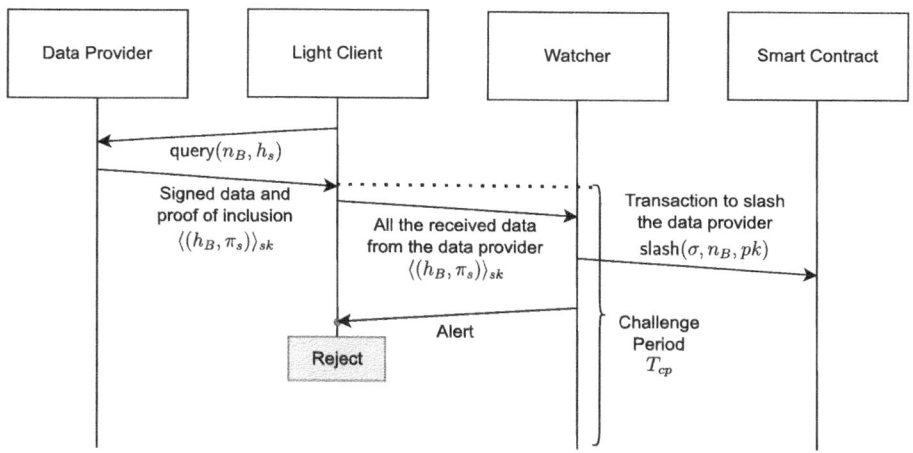

Fig. 4. The dispute resolution path for economic security. This simplified example assumes the light client has selected a single data provider and depicts only the honest watcher.

where h_B represents the hash of the requested block B and π_s is the inclusion proof of state s in B.

Data providers are free to join and leave the system. They form a set that is updated upon the execution of *register* and *withdraw* requests. We describe a method for keeping track of joining and leaving data providers that light clients can verify while updating their state each time they run the protocol. The data providers join and leave the system in epochs called *update epoch*. The details of how it works is explained in Appendix A.2.

4.4   Watchers

Watchers receive signed data from light clients, originally provided by data providers. They continuously verify that the signatures are from active data providers and confirm whether the data has been finalized on the blockchain.

If a signature fails to meet these criteria, the watcher sends a transaction (σ, n_B, pk) to the smart contract, providing the data provider's public key and the signature on the disputed data, along with the block number. If the data is proven incorrect or lacks finalization confirmation, the smart contract slashes the stakes of the offending data provider.

There are two cases where the data does not exist on the finalized chain and the watcher needs to slash the data provider: 1. It may be due to pending finalization 2. Because another block for that number has been finalized. The former can be confirmed via the blockchain's finalization rules, while the latter requires proving to the contract that a different block has been finalized by the Ethereum consensus. Under the assumption that Ethereum validators are honest and do not endorse conflicting blocks, such proof confirms malicious actions by the data provider, warranting a slash.

Following a successful slash, the watcher notifies the light client, including proof of the slashing event's inclusion on the blockchain.

Note that if the signature does not belong to any of the current active data providers with stake at risk, the watcher cannot perform an on-chain slashing. However, the watcher will promptly notify the light client of this situation. This occurs if, after the light client selects an active data provider to query and before the challenge period concludes, the data provider's entire stake is slashed for another query, rendering them inactive. So, the watcher has to alert the light client not to trust the data this data provider provides. In such cases, the watcher is required to provide the light client with proof of the recent slashing event that deactivated the data provider. The light client then verifies the inclusion of this slashing event before disregarding the data.

4.5   On-chain Smart Contract

An on-chain smart contract performs two key functions: first, it holds the stakes of data providers and decides when to slash them; second, it manages the entry and exit of data providers within the system. The smart contract maintains a list of public keys for all data providers, determining *active* and *leaving* data providers, along with their corresponding stakes.

The slashing conditions are implemented in the contract to enable on-chain verification of disputes raised by watchers, thus eliminating the need for trust in the watchers. Anyone can present proof to dispute a data provider.

4.6   Analysis

Safety. After receiving data from the data provider, the light client waits for the challenge period to see if it receives any alerts from the watchers. This guards against potential malicious behavior by the data provider who might manipulate data despite the risk of being slashed. If no alerts are received, the light client can trust the data. However, if any alerts are received and verified, the light client discards the data and restarts the process. The light client is secure against both rational and irrational data providers because data providers are economically disincentivized from deviating from the protocol, and watchers are in place to alert the light clients about any malicious data.

Note that our protocol aligns the light client with the state derived from the Ethereum consensus mechanism, but it does not safeguard against attacks targeting the consensus process itself. To counter potential consensus attacks on Ethereum that might affect the light client, an additional layer of verification through social consensus can be implemented.

Full Node Level Security. Our approach offers light clients the same level of security guarantees that Ethereum PoS provides to full nodes. On Ethereum, validators risk their stakes when they vote on proposed blocks. Misbehaving validators face slashing penalties. After a certain period, a block achieves finality, at which point full nodes accept it permanently. Similarly, in our light client protocol, data providers with stakes at risk can also be slashed for misbehavior. They sign the blockchain data they assert to be finalized. Once the challenge period (T_{cp}) has elapsed, the data is considered finalized from the light clients' perspective and is accepted permanently. In both scenarios, economic security is achieved.

Liveness. The system remains live as long as there is at least one rational data provider in the network. In this context, "liveness" means that no query goes unanswered indefinitely. Data providers are motivated to participate and act honestly within the protocol because their profits are proportional to their stake and the services they provide to light clients. This incentivization ensures that rational data providers stay engaged and responsive.

Efficiency. Many small transactions that collectively sum up to the stake of a single data provider can be handled at the same time by that data provider. All those light clients only need to verify a single signature. Even larger transactions could be verified by a light client by only checking a few signatures.

This programmable security aligns with what we observe in the real world, where many small transactions happening in banks or institutions do not need extra care and can proceed quite quickly. However, to move large amounts, additional time and care are required.

Challenge Period. From Sect. 3, our security model assumes the existence of at least one honest watcher who, during the challenge period T_{cp}, will examine the data forwarded by the light client. It's important to note that T_{cp} is not a global parameter; instead, each light client sets their own T_{cp} based on their specific security requirements and the watcher service they use. The longer the T_{cp} that a light client considers, the higher the likelihood that an honest watcher will review the data received from the data provider(s). Beyond a specific duration, increasing the challenge time no longer change the probability of an honest watcher verifying the data significantly. We incorporate this threshold in the protocol by setting a maximum value $maxT_{cp}$.

5   Light Client with Insured Security

In this section, we enhance the protocol to better serve light clients who require faster confirmation. To eliminate the waiting time associated with the challenge period and to compensate affected light clients connected to a malicious data provider, we introduce a new concept: *insured security*. This approach assigns a portion of the data providers' staked value to each query from a light client in the form of insurance. Then, should misbehavior occur, this insurance mechanism guarantees that the light client is compensated from the slashed staked value. This adaptation leads to the design of an insured light client protocol, $\mathsf{LC_{ins}}$, that offers unconditional safety. We will elaborate on this protocol in this section.

5.1   Protocol Overview

The light client first calculates the maximum potential loss from being misinformed about the state of the blockchain. It then purchases insurance for the determined amount and specifies a coverage duration. The light client initiates a transaction to buy the insurance and utilizes LC_{eco} to check its finalization.

In this design, stakes are specifically attributed to state check queries from light clients. This specific attribution allows for compensation to the light client if the data provider misbehaves and is subsequently slashed, ensuring economic safety even if data providers act unpredictably.

5.2   Light Client

The light client bootstraps as before, but this time, the active data provider set will include an additional attribute: the "attributable" stakes of each data provider, which represent the amount of stakes that have not been assigned to any existing insured requests. Before purchasing the insurance, the light client must determine two key parameters: the coverage amount and its duration.

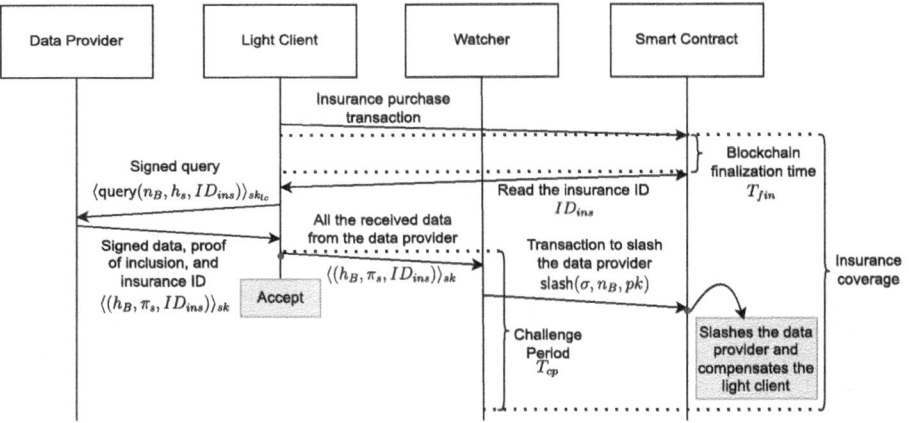

Fig. 5. The dispute resolution path for the insured security. We have simplified this example, by supposing the light client has chosen only one data provider. Also, we only show the honest watcher here.

The detailed explanation on coverage duration and coverage amount is in Appendix A.3.

Purchasing Insurance. After selecting the parameters, the light client makes an on-chain call to purchase insurance, specifying the chosen data providers, their stake portions summing to the predetermined threshold, and the desired coverage duration. The light client then waits for the blockchain's finality time to pass, and uses LC_{eco} to check the inclusion of the insurance payment transaction. Note that the insurance purchasing transaction might be reverted if there is insufficient available attributable stake. This situation could arise if the combined queries from different light clients exceed the available stake of a specific data provider in the previous block. The light client must verify whether the transaction was successful or reverted.

After successfully purchasing insurance, the protocol remains the same as LC_{eco}. The only change here is that the light client does not need to wait for the challenge period, allowing the data to be accepted immediately after signature verification. The flow of interactions in this design is depicted in Fig. 5.

The flow for watchers and data providers stay the same as LC_{eco}.

5.3   On-chain Smart Contract

Two new functions are essential to the smart contract to facilitate the insurance feature: buying insurance and claiming insurance. Additionally, modifications are necessary for handling withdrawal requests by data providers.

All the details of necessary functions is explained in Appendix A.4.

Table 2. Cost for applying each protocol for checking the inclusion of transactions with values 10 ETH(\$32k), 32 ETH(\$100k), 160 ETH(\$512k), and 320 ETH(\$1M) respectively for 1, 1, 5, and 10 providers. Computation is in terms of number of signature checks.

	LC_{eco}				LC_{ins}			
Number of data providers	1	1	5	10	1	1	5	10
Cost	\$0	\$0	\$0	\$0	\$7.45	\$10.68	\$29.38	\$52.76
Computation	1	1	5	10	1	1	5	10
Latency	5 h	5 h	5 h	5 h	2.8 ms	2.8 ms	13.2 ms	25.8 ms

5.4   Analysis

Scalability. In this design, the capacity of the system is defined as the sum of the total stakes of all rational data providers. Larger values for state checks cannot be processed by the system, ensuring full coverage. Subsequently, the maximum rate at which the system can insure value and support inclusion checks is limited to this total amount for a single challenge period.

Data Provider Incentives. Data providers earn rewards as a percentage of their staked value in the system. The annual percentage yield (APY) depends on the total insurance value purchased by all the light clients in a year. By determining a minimum APY for the data providers, we can calculate the pro-rata insurance cost for each user. The details of insurance cost calculation comes next.

Cost of Insurance. We observe a crucial relationship between the challenge period (T_{cp}) the light client waits for in LC_{eco} and the cost the light client incurs in LC_{ins} for purchasing insurance. If the light client prefers not to wait for the challenge period, it can opt to pay for insurance instead, thereby bypassing the wait entirely. The cost of this insurance is directly linked to the level of security the light client requires, which in turn determines the challenge period that the light client seeks to avoid. A higher security level necessitates a longer challenge period, meaning that the stakes need to be locked for a longer duration.

The details of the evaluation of costs is in Appendix A.5.

6   Evaluation

The main objective of our experimental evaluations is to: (1) Find the computational overhead. (2) Evaluate the latency before the light client can confirm the data. (3) Find the incurred cost.

In our scenario, we assume that every data provider registered on the smart contract has staked 32 ETH, equivalent to an Ethereum validator's stake. We have one light client aiming to verify a transaction valued at less than 32 ETH. This light client needs to query only a single data provider. For simplicity, the light client is connected to exactly one honest watcher. We explain the details of the experimental setup in appendix A.6.

Our experiments focus on both the economic security protocol LC_{eco} and the insured security protocol LC_{ins}, verifying the finalization of a block hash on the light client. We exclude the time and computation required to verify the Merkle proof of inclusion for its target state, as this is consistent across all light client protocols.

Computation. The computation required by the light client is consistent in both designs. In the economic design LC_{eco}, the light client begins verification after the challenge period elapses. In the insured design LC_{ins}, verification starts once the inclusion of the insurance payment transaction is confirmed. In both cases, the light client performs one signature verification check on the block hash, taking an order of milliseconds.

Latency. We varied transaction sizes in our experiments, requiring signatures from 1 to 5 data providers, and measured the latency. The results are depicted in Appendix A.7. In all cases, the delay is only a few milliseconds. Consequently, in our economic security design, latency is primarily influenced by the challenge period, as computation and communication delays are minimal.

The challenge period, configurable by the light client, typically spans several hours but could be reduced to minutes with a fast and reliable watcher network. In contrast, in insured security scenarios, latency depends solely on the time needed to complete signature verification, which scales linearly with the number of required provider signatures. Given that this process usually takes only milliseconds, we achieve instant confirmation.

We select a 5-hour challenge period as a reasonable example for a retail user with a relatively small transaction value (less than \$32k). This choice is based on empirical data, reflecting the average response time of watchers in current networks. Naturally, a faster watcher service could significantly reduce this challenge period.

Cost. In order to provide economic security, the light client incurs no additional costs in normal path. However, to provide insured security, the cost for the light client to purchase insurance is divided into two parts: the transaction gas fee and the insurance premium. The transaction gas cost for calling `buyInsurance()` with inputs from one data provider's address in our implementation is 200k. Additionally, there is the cost of the insurance itself, as calculated in the previous section for the expected stake return rate of $APY = 6\%$. Given the current ETH price of \$3200 and gas cost of 9.377 Gwei, the transaction gas fee amounts to \$6. The insurance premium costs \$1.45, totaling \$7.45 for buying insurance covering 10 ETH (\$32k) for 1500 blocks (approximately 5 h). We repeat the experiment for different transaction values and different number of data providers. Both the transaction cost and the insurance premium cost increase with the covered value. The results are summarized in Table 2.

We do not account for any gas costs for an honest watcher. In practice, using watcher services may incur costs comparable to a token swap operation on Uniswap [42]. Additionally, the cost incurred by a watcher for submitting a dispute on-chain is compensated from the slashed stake of the data provider implicated in that dispute.

7 Conclusion

In this paper, we have formalized the cryptoeconomic security for light clients and introduced programmable security options tailored to their needs. We presented two economically robust designs for a light client, focusing on Ethereum PoS. The first design is more cost-effective for the light client but introduces a higher latency. The second design allows the light client to trust the data almost instantaneously, albeit for a small fee. Importantly, in this design, the light client is compensated if the provided data proves incorrect. This work introduces the first economically safe light client protocol, serving as a pivotal component for various applications that need to verify transaction inclusions to secure the finalization of their payments. These received payments might be in exchange for services or goods provided to their counterparts, or can be the requests in applications like bridges that mint value upon verifying the finalization of a payment. In all cases, the applications can enjoy almost instant verification while being insured for the value of their payments.

A   Appendix

A.1   Related Work

Techniques for a lightweight client to verify consensus were originally discussed in the Bitcoin paper [11], known as Simplified Payment Verification (SPV). It allows clients to download only block headers and verify the existence of transactions through SPV proofs. While this method reduces the workload on the resource-limited client [22–24], it necessitates a frequent online presence to keep up with the main chain's growth. Clients inactive for long periods face the challenge of linearly verifying block headers upon reactivation [3]. To address the limitations of SPV, innovations like FlyClient [12] and Non-Interactive Proofs of Proof-of-Work (NiPoPoW) [13] leverage the inherent authentication of a chain's few suffix blocks, enabling the proof of these blocks to clients at a sublinear cost. However, their reliance on verifying PoWs restricts their applicability to PoS consensus models. To address the security and efficiency challenges in PoS bootstrapping, PoPoS [14] introduces a bisection game to effectively challenge adversarial Merkle trees of PoS epochs. [18] proposes a composable solution to create light clients for lazy blockchains [39,40]. Though they achieve minimal space and avoid requiring always-online clients to maintain stake distributions, the issue of enabling clients to go offline without incurring substantial costs for rejoining the network remains unaddressed.

In popular Ethereum wallets like MetaMask, the consensus client logic is handled by centralized infrastructure providers such as Infura [15]. These providers undoubtedly result in a lightweight and efficient user experience. However, the centralization of such services means that a compromised provider could potentially mislead users by altering payment and balance details or by censoring transactions. To improve security and accelerate bootstrapping, one of the most popular adoptions in Ethereum is a sync committee [16], which comprises 512 validators selected every 27 h, to sign block headers in the beacon chain. However, the lack of economic penalties for misbehavior among committee members still raises concerns about the reliability and security of this system. The introduction of a generic superlight client [17] for permissionless blockchains within a game-theoretic framework offers a new perspective. This model represents a special variant of multi-party computation under rational settings. However, it does not provide economic guarantees and fails to address the threat posed by malicious, irrational data providers. In contrast, our light client focuses on cryptoeconomic security. The concept of economic security paired with an insurance scheme was first explored in recent work named stakesure [7]. We apply this definition to establish a general framework that provides economic security and insured security that unconditionally protects the light client against malicious behaviors for PoS chains.

An alternative research approach focuses on the use of zero-knowledge proofs to create succinct proofs [34]. For example, Mina [25,26] and Plumo [32] effectively facilitate lightweight consensus verification through the use of recursive SNARK compositions [33] and SNARK-based state transition proofs. Halo [30] improves Plumo by removing the trusted setup. However, these methods impose a considerable computational burden on block producers for proof generation [29], and they do not address compensation for potential losses experienced by light clients. In the context of other PoS protocols like Tendermint [31] used in Cosmos, the role of the light client is explored within their Interblockchain Communication (IBC) protocol [27,28]. Notably, these implementations are specific to their respective platforms and are not directly applicable to Ethereum or various other PoS blockchains.

A.2   Update Epoch Length

We define *update epoch* for data providers, each consisting of B_u blocks, a value set during protocol initialization. The duration of update epoch, denoted by T_u ($T_u = B_u \times$ avg(block interval time) represents the minimum duration needed to process withdraw requests. We ensure T_u is significantly greater than the maximum challenge period ($T_u \gg maxT_{cp}$). Withdraw requests made within an update epoch take effect at the last block of the following epoch. Below, we detail how each type of request is executed:

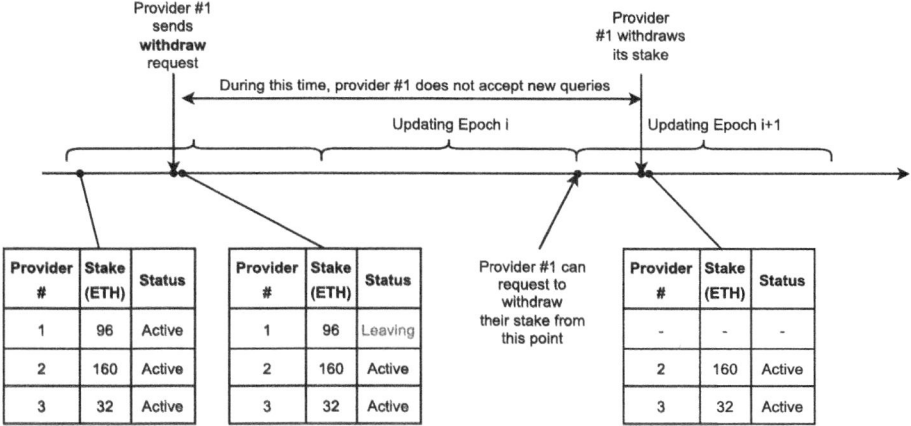

Fig. 6. This diagram illustrates the blockchain's growth and details the process by which a data provider exits the protocol.

1. **Register:** A new data provider who deposits more than the minimum required stake is immediately added to the *active* data provider list.

2. **Withdraw:** When a data provider decides to exit the system, their status immediately changes from *active* to *leaving*, and they cease protocol engagement. The actual withdrawal of their stake is only permitted after the end of the following update epoch. An example of this process is illustrated in Fig. 6.

A data provider labeled as leaving may still be slashed for past behavior but will no longer accept requests. This measure prevents data providers from acting maliciously and quickly withdrawing their stake to avoid penalties. The condition $T_u \gg maxT_{cp}$ ensures that all user challenge periods have expired for any requests made to a data provider before they are permitted to withdraw their stakes.

After bootstrapping, the light client acquires an initial list of data providers. To stay updated, it must refresh this list each time it validates a block in a new update epoch, since the set of data providers remains static throughout an update epoch. Lengthening the update epoch delays stake withdrawal for stakers, impacting those wishing to exit the system. However, this delay occurs only once for data providers who choose to leave. The advantage of extending update epochs is a reduction in the frequency of set transitions, which simplifies the verification process for light clients. Additionally, this updating mechanism enables light clients to predict the active data provider set for future blocks, ensuring they experience no delays due to changes in the network of data providers.

A light client that remains online to perform multiple state inclusion checks does not need to bootstrap for each verification. Assume the blockchain is in update epoch i, where $i \in \mathbb{N}$. If the light client has recently completed an inclusion check, it already has access to the active data provider set for epoch i. To prepare for epoch $i + 1$, it needs only the register and withdraw requests from epoch $i - 1$ to be applied to the set from epoch i. The light client uses these requests as the target state in our protocol and queries data providers to confirm their inclusion on the blockchain. Once the maximum challenge period from the start of epoch i elapses, all checks for epoch $i - 1$ are considered verified from the light client's perspective. Thus, the light client can anticipate the status of the data provider set for epoch $i + 1$ before the blockchain progresses to that point, avoiding delays related to data providers entering or exiting the network, and allowing it to select active data providers in advance.

A.3   Parameter Selection for Light Client with Insurance

Coverage Amount. The light client calculates the maximum potential profit that data providers could gain from corrupting the data as the coverage amount. Then to establish the desired level of security, the light client select the set of data providers, specify the proportion of their stakes needed for the insured request, whose total attributable stakes exceed the coverage amount.

A low-value transaction inclusion check might be sufficiently secured by a portion of the stake from a single data provider. However, a high-value bridge transaction might require backing from most of the staked assets by multiple data providers. In the former case, only one signature verification is necessary during the protocol execution while selecting more data providers for the same coverage amount incurs higher verification cost.

Coverage Duration. The light client sets a challenge period (T_{cp}) like before, which determines how long it will wait for alerts from watchers. Unlike in $\mathsf{LC_{eco}}$ where the light client would wait for the entire challenge period before accepting the target state, $\mathsf{LC_{ins}}$ provides immediate finality. That is, the light client will accept the target state as soon as it receives responses from data providers, but it will keep listening any potential alert from watchers for T_{cp}.

The light client determines a coverage duration for its insurance that is longer than T_{cp}. The light client wants to ensure that any detected misbehavior is covered during the insurance duration. Our protocol also allows the light client to cover multiple checks within the same insurance policy. In this case, setting must take into account the number of *independent state inclusion checks* denoted by n. The total coverage duration must extend beyond the point when T_{cp} has elapsed for each of these checks to ensure full coverage of all checks.

The coverage duration for a single transaction ($n = 1$) needs to be set to cover the total time elapsed from the moment the light client sends the insurance payment transaction to the point when challenge period ends, which includes the sum of the following parameters:

- Blockchain finality time (T_{fin}, for the insurance payment to get finalized)
- Locally selected challenge period (T_{cp}^0, to check the inclusion of the insurance payment transaction)
- Another locally selected challenge period (T_{cp}^1, to check the inclusion of the current transaction)
- Estimated communication delay times (Δ_{comm})
- Estimated computation and verification time (Δ_{comp})

Now suppose there are multiple transaction inclusions to check; the only additional delay is that the light client needs to wait for multiple challenge periods to cover all the independent inclusion checks. We denote the i-th check has challenge period T_{cp}^i. Then the coverage duration is:

$$T_{cov} \geq T_{fin} + \sum_{i=0}^{n} T_{cp}^i + \Delta_{comm} + \Delta_{comp} \tag{1}$$

In this paper, we assume $n = 1$ for simplicity without losing generality. For larger n, the same procedure needs to get repeated for each of the state inclusion checks.

A.4   Smart Contract for Insurance

Buying Insurance. When this function is invoked, it first validates the inputs (, and data providers' public keys) by checking the availability of attributable stakes from the selected data providers. If the stakes are sufficient and available, the contract allocates and locks them for the duration of the insurance, rendering it unavailable for other queries until the insurance expires. The smart contract assigns a unique ID to each purchased insurance, recording this ID along with the light client's public key, the involved data providers, and insurance parameters.

Claiming Insurance. Watchers trigger this function by submitting data signed by data providers that contradicts to on-chain states, including the relevant insurance ID. Upon receipt, the contract verifies the authenticity of the dispute and, if validated, slashes the data providers' stakes. It then allocates the slashed amount to the light client associated with the indicated insurance ID, thus compensating for any breach of security.

Withdrawal Request. Data providers can exit the system by submitting a withdrawal request. Upon receipt of such a request, the contract changes the provider's status from "active" to "leaving" and stops assigning new insurances to that provider's stake. However, under the insured protocol, portions of the provider's stake may be locked in active insurances that extend beyond the period of the withdrawal request. The provider must continue to serve these commitments until all associated insurances expire. Only after the expiration of the last active insurance can the provider fully disengage from the protocol, and the withdrawal of their stake can be processed at the end of the subsequent update epoch.

A.5   Insurance Cost Calculations

To evaluate the cost of insurance for light clients, let's consider a realistic example. Assume we have n data providers recognized by the smart contract as active for at least one block over the course of a year, which consists of B blocks. With an average block interval time of $12\,\mathrm{s}$ on Ethereum, this gives us $B = 2,628,000$ blocks per year.

If a node exits and then rejoins the system, it is counted as two separate data providers. Let S_i denote the total staked value for the i-th data provider. In return for staking, data providers earn rewards, representing the cost of their locked stakes. Assume an Annual Percentage Rate (APY) of 6% for data providers, as determined by market equilibrium.

We define u as the utilization ratio of the stakes. Utilization refers to the proportion of the stake locked on the contract to hold the corresponding data provider accountable for a specific query. This stake is locked when a user purchases insurance for a designated duration. The parameter u represents the average portion of the total stake utilized by users at any given time throughout the year:

$$u = \frac{\sum_{t=1}^{B} u_t}{B} \tag{2}$$

where

$$u_t = \frac{\sum_{i \in DP(b_t)} S_i^{lock}}{\sum_{i \in DP(b_t)} S_i} \tag{3}$$

where $DP(b_t)$ is the set of data providers with active status on the smart contract in block b_t and S_i^{lock} represents the locked stake of the i-th data provider. Now, we can define the cost of locking a unit of stake for one block, c, as follows:

$$c = \frac{APY}{Bu} \tag{4}$$

Light clients determine a coverage period T_{cov} and an insurance value V_{cov}. The cost of insurance required to be paid to the data providers is given by

$$p_{ins} = c \cdot T_{cov} \cdot V_{cov} \tag{5}$$

where a lower bound for T_{cov} is determined from inequality (1).

Knowing this, for example, to check a single transaction valued at 100 ETH, with a 5-hour challenge time (1500 blocks), and assuming $u = 0.75$, the cost of insurance would be:

$$p_{ins} = \frac{0.06}{2628000 \times 0.75} \times 1500 \times 100 = 0.004566 \text{ ETH} \tag{6}$$

This calculation does not include the gas cost of the transaction to purchase the insurance, which we evaluated in the experiments (Sect. 6).

A.6   Experiments

Our light client protocol's smart contract, implemented in Solidity with less than 300 lines of code, is deployed on the Ethereum testnet, Sepolia [46], which simulates the consensus mechanism of Ethereum. We developed the backend nodes in TypeScript, including the light client (approximately 350 lines), data providers (approximately 150 lines), and watcher nodes (approximately 200 lines). These nodes communicate over a local network via the HTTP protocol.

We initially set up two Sepolia full nodes, each on an AWS Lightsail instance with 16 GB RAM, 4 vCPUs, and 500 GB SSD. We use Geth [47] as the execution client and Prysm [48] as the consensus client. We then deploy the data provider and watcher nodes on separate instances, configuring their web3 provider to their respective local full nodes. This setup allows the nodes to access the latest blockchain data directly. The light client is deployed on a Lenovo ThinkPad X1 Carbon Laptop, featuring an Intel Core i7 processor, 16 GB RAM, and a 512GB SSD, though the actual hardware requirements are significantly lower.

A.7   Latency of Signature Verification

The measured latency of verifying the data provider signatures for the light client is depicted in Fig. 7.

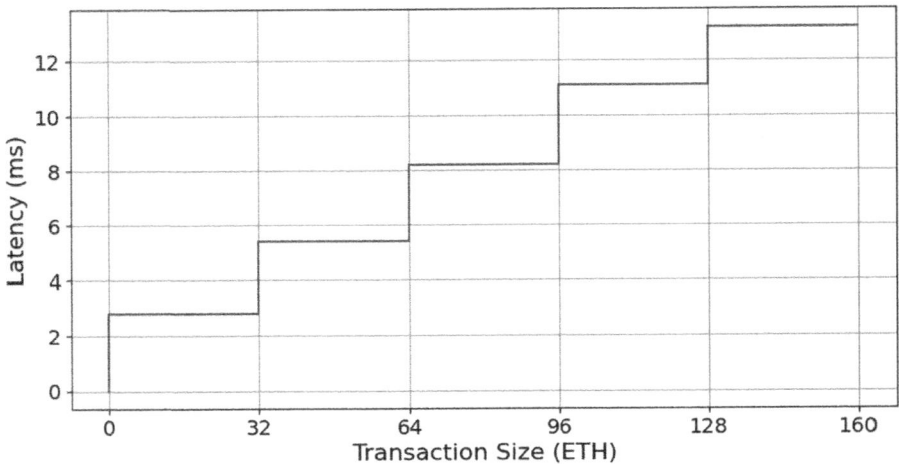

Fig. 7. Latency of verifying the data provider signatures for the light client.

A.8   Discussion

A.9   Diverse Staking

So far, we have assumed that data providers stake or re-stake ETH. This compels light clients to calculate the maximum loss value in ETH, even if their loss is in another token whose value changes rapidly in relation to ETH. This necessitates complex calculations for buying insurance and imposes some risks for the light client due to unpredictable market movements.

To address this, staking can be diversified in terms of the staked token. Data providers can stake other widely used tokens like stablecoins or wrapped Bitcoin, offering more options for light clients to buy insurance. This also enables more data providers to join the system as it allows them to be exposed to the price of their token of choice while staking. However, there may still be light clients using unsupported tokens or having more complex loss functions.

A.10   Trustless Watchers

In our protocol, we simplify the assumption to require the presence of at least one honest watcher to ensure the security of the light client. In practice, this assumption can be replaced by a decentralized, incentivized watchtower network. Recent work [42] introduced a protocol called "Proof of Diligence" to enhance rollup security, where a pool of rational actors, known as watchtowers, are incentivized to continuously verify rollup transactions. In our context, light clients can offer small rewards to incentivize watchtowers to diligently verify the correctness of responses generated by data providers. Conversely, dishonest or lazy behavior by watchtowers is penalized through slashing mechanisms. Since watchtowers also operate as full nodes, they are capable of detecting inconsistencies in the state and alerting the light client. The protocol is designed such that diligent watching is the only Nash equilibrium, thereby ensuring that cryptoeconomic security is maintained effectively.

A.11   Delegation

As mentioned before, the preference is to have fewer data providers with larger amounts of stake to expedite the verification process for the light client. However, to allow data providers with less valuable assets to join the protocol, delegation can be employed. This involves smaller data providers pooling their stake and delegating their data provision duties to a single node. This is not a new concept and has been utilized in various blockchain contexts.

In delegation, the reward is distributed among all stakers proportionally to their staked value, with some additional reward going to the operator node. Delegation is also beneficial for users who are unfamiliar with or lack access to the necessary resources for running a data provider node but have assets they wish to stake.

A.12   Proposed Block Guarantee

So far, we have only discussed the guarantee that a block has been finalized. On Ethereum, every proposed block will eventually become either an uncle block or finalized. Another useful guarantee that can be supported by this design is to ensure whether a block has been proposed in the blockchain. It might not yet be finalized, but since finalization in Ethereum takes roughly 13 min, to avoid this wait, a light client can use this new type of guarantee to access the data faster. The block might not get finalized later, but that happens with a very low probability. Such a guarantee is useful for low-value transactions that require low latency.

To add this feature to the system, the light client needs to add a flag to the query it sends to the data provider determining which type of guarantee it wants. Then, the data providers also need to include the same flag in their signed data so that when the watchers provide it on-chain, the smart contract knows which guarantee to check this data against.

The data provider that signs the block data will get slashed only if the signed block header was not ever proposed in the blockchain. To support this guarantee, we need to modify the design slightly. For watchers to be able to provide a proof to the smart contract that a data provider has signed incorrect data, they have to prove to the contract that a certain block has not been proposed in the blockchain at all. Meaning, it is neither finalized nor an uncle block. This can be done optimistically, requiring the data providers to provide inclusion proofs if disputed. The inclusion proofs can be in form of zero-knowledge proofs to reduce the cost of on-chain verification. Moreover, the watchers need to stake some assets in the system, with each watcher staking an amount greater than the gas fee of the call to provide the necessary proof in case of a dispute. This way, the watchers do not have incentive to dispute falsely.

Data providers need to submit on-chain inclusion proofs in case of a dispute. If the data provider has not misbehaved, there are two possibilities: either the block has become finalized, or it has become an uncle block. The proof for the latter case is to check the inclusion of the block in the state root of the latest block header. For the former, in addition to the inclusion proof, finality check is also needed. Here, we leverage the fact that uncle blocks are included in the state root commitment, as well as the finalized blocks.

A.13 Cost and Fee Management

The fee that the light clients pay for the insurance goes for the compensation of the data providers. Data providers get compensated proportional to the time and amount of the insurance they provide for the light clients.

Watchers also get compensated for the services they provide. They get a percentage of the slashed stake whenever they slash a data provider successfully. This way they stay incentivized to actively watch the data they receive from the light clients.

A.14 Data Availability

Since data providers operate full nodes and maintain the complete blockchain data, they are capable of supporting not only consensus verification services but also data availability checks. Previous studies [19–21] have designed efficient data structures for light nodes to verify data availability. Overall, there are two basic models: a "pull" model in which light clients randomly sample data from full nodes, and a "push" model in which block producer disperses different data chunks to data providers. The "pull" model can be directly adopted here under the same security assumption. Staked data providers are responsible for answering sampling requests from the light client. The light client then forwards data samples to an honest validator node until the validator can either reconstruct the block or provide an incorrect-coding proof. The fraud proof can be submitted on-chain to penalize malicious data providers. A related protocol [41] also examines the cryptoeconomic security for the data availability committee. Our light client protocol further offers insights into extending cryptoeconomic security to insured security, utilizing penalties to compensate for losses caused by data availability attacks.

References

1. Sheng, P., Wang, G., Nayak, K., Kannan, S., Viswanath, P.: BFT protocol forensics. In: Proceedings of the 2021 ACM SIGSAC Conference on Computer and Communications Security, CCS 2021. ACM (2021). https://doi.org/10.1145/3460120.3484566
2. Neu, J., Tas, E.N., Tse, D.: The Availability-Accountability Dilemma and its Resolution via Accountability Gadgets. Cryptology ePrint Archive, Paper 2021/628 (2021). https://eprint.iacr.org/2021/628

3. Lu, Y., Tang, Q., Wang, G.: Generic Superlight Client for Permissionless Blockchains. arXiv, vol. abs/2003.06552 (2020). https://api.semanticscholar.org/CorpusID:212725679

4. Kiayias, A., Lamprou, N., Stouka, A.-P.: Proofs of proofs of work with sublinear complexity. In: Clark, J., Meiklejohn, S., Ryan, P.Y.A., Wallach, D., Brenner, M., Rohloff, K. (eds.) FC 2016. LNCS, vol. 9604, pp. 61–78. Springer, Heidelberg (2016). https://doi.org/10.1007/978-3-662-53357-4_5

5. Ethereum.org. Run a Node (2025). https://ethereum.org/en/run-a-node/

6. Kalodner, H., Goldfeder, S., Chen, X., Weinberg, S.M., Felten, E.W.: Arbitrum: scalable, private smart contracts. In: 27th USENIX Security Symposium (USENIX Security 2018), pp. 1353–1370 (2018)

7. Deb, S., Raynor, R., Kannan, S.: STAKESURE: Proof of Stake Mechanisms with Strong Cryptoeconomic Safety. arXiv preprint arXiv:2401.05797 (2024)

8. Kiayias, A., Miller, A., Zindros, D.: Non-Interactive Proofs of Proof-of-Work. Cryptology ePrint Archive, Paper 2017/963 (2017). https://eprint.iacr.org/2017/963

9. Kiayias, A., Polydouri, A., Zindros, D.: The velvet path to superlight blockchain clients. In: Proceedings of the ACM SIGSAC Conference on Computer and Communications Security, pp. 205–218 (2021). https://doi.org/10.1145/3479722.3480999

10. Braithwaite, S., et al.: A Tendermint Light Client (2020)

11. Nakamoto, S.: Bitcoin: A Peer-to-Peer Electronic Cash System (2008). https://bitcoin.org/bitcoin.pdf

12. Bünz, B., Kiffer, L., Luu, L., Zamani, M.: Flyclient: super-light clients for cryptocurrencies. In: 2020 IEEE Symposium on Security and Privacy (SP), pp. 928–946. IEEE (2020)

13. Kiayias, A., Miller, A., Zindros, D.: Non-interactive proofs of proof-of-work. In: Bonneau, J., Heninger, N. (eds.) FC 2020. LNCS, vol. 12059, pp. 505–522. Springer, Cham (2020). https://doi.org/10.1007/978-3-030-51280-4_27

14. Agrawal, S., Neu, J., Tas, E.N., Zindros, D.: Proofs of Proof-of-Stake with Sublinear Complexity, arXiv preprint arXiv:2209.08673 (2022)

15. Infura Inc. Infura Documentation (2016). https://infura.io/docs

16. Ethereum Foundation: Ethereum 2.0 Specifications (2023). https://github.com/ethereum/eth2.0-specs

17. Lu, Y., Tang, Q., Wang, G.: Generic superlight client for permissionless blockchains. In: Chen, L., Li, N., Liang, K., Schneider, S. (eds.) ESORICS 2020. LNCS, vol. 12309, pp. 713–733. Springer, Cham (2020). https://doi.org/10.1007/978-3-030-59013-0_35

18. Tas, E.N., Zindros, D., Yang, L., Tse, D.: Light Clients for Lazy Blockchains, arXiv preprint arXiv:2203.15968 (2022)

19. Al-Bassam, M., Sonnino, A., Buterin, V.: Fraud and Data Availability Proofs: Maximising Light Client Security and Scaling Blockchains with Dishonest Majorities, arXiv preprint arXiv:1809.09044 (2019)

20. Yu, M., Sahraei, S., Li, S., Avestimehr, S., Kannan, S., Viswanath, P.: Coded merkle tree: solving data availability attacks in blockchains. In: Bonneau, J., Heninger, N. (eds.) FC 2020. LNCS, vol. 12059, pp. 114–134. Springer, Cham (2020). https://doi.org/10.1007/978-3-030-51280-4_8

21. Sheng, P., Xue, B., Kannan, S., Viswanath, P.: ACeD: scalable data availability oracle. In: Borisov, N., Diaz, C. (eds.) FC 2021. LNCS, vol. 12675, pp. 299–318. Springer, Heidelberg (2021). https://doi.org/10.1007/978-3-662-64331-0_16

22. Dorri, A., Kanhere, S.S., Jurdak, R., Gauravaram, P.: LSB: a lightweight scalable blockchain for IoT security and anonymity. J. Parallel Distrib. Comput. **134**, 180–197 (2019)
23. Frey, D., Makkes, M.X., Roman, P.L., Taïani, F., Voulgaris, S.: Bringing secure bitcoin transactions to your smartphone. In: Proceedings of the 15th International Workshop on Adaptive and Reflective Middleware, pp. 1–6 (2016)
24. Gervais, A., Capkun, S., Karame, G.O., Gruber, D.: On the privacy provisions of bloom filters in lightweight bitcoin clients. In: Proceedings of the 30th Annual Computer Security Applications Conference, pp. 326–335 (2014)
25. Bonneau, J., Meckler, I., Rao, V., Shapiro, E.: Coda: Decentralized Cryptocurrency at Scale, Cryptology ePrint Archive (2020)
26. Mina Foundation: Mina Documentation (2019). https://docs.minaprotocol.com/en
27. Goes, C.: The Interblockchain Communication Protocol: An Overview, arXiv preprint arXiv:2006.15918 (2020)
28. Braithwaite, S., et al.: A Tendermint Light Client, arXiv preprint arXiv:2010.07031 (2020)
29. Chatzigiannis, P., Baldimtsi, F., Chalkias, K.: SoK: blockchain light clients. In: International Conference on Financial Cryptography and Data Security, pp. 615–641. Springer (2022)
30. Bowe, S., Grigg, J., Hopwood, D.: Recursive Proof Composition Without a Trusted Setup, Cryptology ePrint Archive (2019)
31. Buchman, E.: Tendermint: byzantine fault tolerance in the age of blockchains. Ph.D. dissertation, University of Guelph (2016)
32. Gabizon, A., et al.: Plumo: towards scalable interoperable blockchains using ultra light validation systems. In: Proceedings of the 3rd ZKProof Workshop, London, UK, vol. 20 (2020)
33. Bitansky, N., Canetti, R., Chiesa, A., Tromer, E.: Recursive composition and bootstrapping for SNARKs and proof-carrying data. In: Proceedings of the Forty-Fifth Annual ACM Symposium on Theory of Computing, pp. 111–120 (2013)
34. Ben-Sasson, E., Chiesa, A., Tromer, E., Virza, M.: Scalable zero knowledge via cycles of elliptic curves. Algorithmica **79**, 1102–1160 (2017)
35. Tang, W., Sheng, P., Roy, P., Wang, X., Fanti, G., Viswanath, P.: Raft-Forensics: High Performance CFT Consensus with Accountability for Byzantine Faults, arXiv preprint arXiv:2305.09123 (2023)
36. Civit, P., Gilbert, S., Gramoli, V.: Polygraph: Accountable Byzantine Agreement, Cryptology ePrint Archive, vol. 2019, p. 587 (2019)
37. Stewart, A., Kokoris-Kogia, E.: GRANDPA: A Byzantine Finality Gadget, arXiv preprint arXiv:2007.01560 (2020)
38. Buterin, V., Griffith, V.: Casper the Friendly Finality Gadget, arXiv preprint arXiv:1710.09437 (2017)
39. Al-Bassam, M.: Lazyledger: A Distributed Data Availability Ledger with Client-Side Smart Contracts, arXiv preprint arXiv:1905.09274 (2019)
40. Bagaria, V., Kannan, S., Tse, D., Fanti, G., Viswanath, P.: Prism: deconstructing the blockchain to approach physical limits. In: Proceedings of the 2019 ACM SIGSAC Conference on Computer and Communications Security, pp. 585–602 (2019)
41. Tas, E.N., Boneh, D.: Cryptoeconomic security for data availability committees. In: International Conference on Financial Cryptography and Data Security, pp. 310–326. Springer (2023)

42. Sheng, P., Rana, R., Bala, S., Tyagi, H., Viswanath, P.: Proof of Diligence: Cryptoeconomic Security for Rollups, arXiv preprint arXiv:2402.07241 (2024)
43. Ethereum Validator Queue (2024). https://www.validatorqueue.com/
44. EigenLabs: EigenLayer (2023). https://www.eigenlayer.xyz/
45. Ethereum Foundation: Ethereum Wallets (2024). https://ethereum.org/en/wallets/
46. Etherscan Team: Sepolia Etherscan (2024). https://sepolia.etherscan.io/
47. Ethereum Foundation: go-ethereum (2024). https://github.com/ethereum/go-ethereum
48. Prysmatic Labs: Prysm (2024). https://github.com/prysmaticlabs/prysm
49. Unconditionally Safe Light Client (2024). https://github.com/ForSubmissionOnly/safe-light-client
50. Said, A., et al.: Detailed analysis of ethereum network on transaction behavior, community structure, and link prediction. PeerJ Comput. Sci. **7**, e815 (2021). https://doi.org/10.7717/peerj-cs.815.

ZKP-StylePatch: Hybrid NFT Anti-counterfeit Framework

Tiantian Wu[1], Yixuan Shen[1], Fan Zhang[1], You Jiang[1], Lei Yao[2],
Bin Zhou[1(✉)], and Junbin Fang[1(✉)]

[1] Jinan University, Guangzhou 510632, China
junbinfang@foxmail.com
[2] Shenzhen Yunanbao Technology Co., Ltd., Shenzhen 518000, China

Abstract. With the growth of decentralized finance (DeFi), non-fungible tokens (NFTs), particularly those based on artistic images, have become mainstream. However, copyright issues are increasingly severe, as forged or plagiarized artworks are minted and resold as NFTs, infringing creators' intellectual property rights. Despite progress in NFT copyright protection, detection remains post-minting, and the rise of AI-generated models has intensified image forgery and style plagiarism, which existing methods fail to address. We propose ZKP-StylePatch, comprising: (1) a model to detect the origin of artistic images, and (2) a zero-knowledge proof mechanism to verify model output integrity and authenticity. Using GenImage and a style-transferred NFT dataset, experiments show ZKP-StylePatch achieves 91.35% accuracy in detecting artwork authenticity.

Keywords: StyleTransfer · NFT · Zero-knowledge proof

1 Introduction

In recent years, non-fungible tokens (NFTs) have emerged as core digital assets in decentralized finance (DeFi), encompassing various categories including digital artworks, music, and games [1]. Especially in the field of digital art [2], NFTs provide strong copyright protection for digital artists through their indivisibility, irreproducibility, and uniqueness, thus gaining wide recognition among creators and collectors [3].

The copyright protection of NFTs primarily relies on the verification module during the minting process: When an NFT owner submits original data to a smart contract, the verification module checks the existence and format of metadata as well as the validity of the original data parameters [4], thereby ensuring the uniqueness of the submitted data and preventing duplicate minting. However, with the expansion of the NFT market, the existing protection mechanism has become inadequate in addressing emerging copyright infringement issues [5]. Attackers can introduce imperceptible perturbations to authentic NFT images, altering the token ID while maintaining visual integrity, thereby successfully bypassing the existence verification of the module to proceed with

R. K. Shyamasundar et al. (Eds.): ICBC 2025, LNCS 16155, pp. 30–44, 2026.
https://doi.org/10.1007/978-3-032-06176-8_2

minting. Current copyright infringement includes two types: NFT name counterfeit and NFT image counterfeit. NFT name counterfeit exploits the no-naming-restriction feature of blockchain to steal authentic NFT names or use confusingly similar names as their counterfeit NFT names [6,7], and NFT image counterfeit deceives buyers by copying authentic NFT image URLs or minting "counterfeit" NFTs visually similar to authentic ones [8,9].

Currently, NFT name counterfeiting can be effectively detected by similarity algorithms such as the Levenshtein distance [9], while NFT image counterfeiting is more covert but lacks effective detection means. Existing image counterfeiting detection methods adopt post-minting mechanisms [10,11]: After the original data is minted into NFT, the detection platform inspects the NFT images and delists counterfeit products. However, post-minting detection has two major defects: (1) The images may have been traded before minting, causing economic losses to creators; (2) Centralized detection platforms may collude with attackers, making it difficult to ensure the credibility of detection results. Therefore, it is crucial to implement pre-minting detection and introduce a trusted verification mechanism. Furthermore, the development of artificial intelligence technologies (image generation models [12] and style conversion tools [13]) has further aggravated the risk of image counterfeiting: On the one hand, if AI-generated images circulate at the price of human creations, it will squeeze the creative space of humans, and even lead to the disappearance of human-created NFTs in the market. On the other hand, using style conversion tools (such as AdaIN [14] and DiffStyle [15]) to imitate and plagiarize the styles of popular NFTs and sell the plagiarized works at high prices will directly infringe the copyrights of original creators. However, existing detection methods cannot identify AI-generated NFT images and style migration plagiarism.

In this paper, we propose a novel framework called **Zero-Knowledge Proof-StylePatch (ZKP-StylePatch)**, which implements pre-minting detection of forgery and plagiarism in original data, and ensure trustworthy verification of off-chain detection models. ZKP-StylePatch automatically detects and verifies the data before minting, assigning three types of labels: authentic images, forged images, and plagiarized images. It will trigger different actions based on the labels: invoking the standard minting function for "authentic images", triggering a minting function with the "AI-created" description for "forged images", and rejecting minting for "plagiarized images".

Specifically, for the detection of image forgery and plagiarism, we first utilize the "shredding" module of the StylePatch detection model to crop the original complete image into patches and randomly reassemble them. Subsequently, style features and frequency-domain features are extracted from all patches, and a weighted score is calculated to distinguish normal patches from abnormal ones. The results are then input into an MLP classifier to detect the category of the original image and assign labels. For the ZKP verification module, zero-knowledge proof files for the input, intermediate outputs, and final output of StylePatch are generated, packaged with the labels output by StylePatch, and submitted to the chain for input-output consistency verification to ensure the credibility of the off-chain detection model. We use two large-scale datasets: a widely used benchmark GenImage dataset [16] (2.66 million images) and a self-generated NFT_AIArt dataset (1.3 million image pairs). We compare our ZKP-StylePatch with 10 state-of-the-art models, and the results show that it achieves a detection accuracy of 91.35% in robust detection, outperforming current SOTA models.

In general, our contributions are summarized as follows:

(1) We propose a pre-minting off-chain detection model targeting image deepfake attackers for the first time.
(2) To address the trustworthiness issue of off-chain detection models, we introduce the ZKP-StylePatch framework, which integrates off-chain detection with proof file generation and on-chain verification with minting. This framework enables an automated detection and verification system from source image submission to minting completion.
(3) Experimental results demonstrate that ZKP-StylePatch achieves SOTA detection performance.

2   Related Work

2.1   Existing Detection Methods for NFT Image Forgery

The rapid growth of the NFT market has exacerbated image forgery and copyright infringement, undermining artists' rights and collectors' asset security. Existing detection methods primarily rely on post-mint strategies, as implemented by platforms like OpenSea, which use computer vision to identify plagiarism after NFTs are minted, delisting counterfeits upon detection [10,11]. These methods leverage perceptual hashing (e.g., aHash, dHash) for efficient visual fingerprinting [17], transformation-invariant feature extraction via SIFT and SURF [18], and deep learning models like Siamese Networks for semantic similarity analysis [19]. Additionally, another method is proactive defenses, such as digital watermarking, embed imperceptible ownership proofs to verify authenticity [8]. Despite their advancements, these approaches face three critical limitations: (1) Delayed Detection and Resource Inefficiency: Post-mint detection permits counterfeit NFTs to consume blockchain resources (e.g., gas fees) and risks financial losses for buyers due to delayed takedowns, with immutable on-chain records causing persistent data pollution. (2) Centralized Control: Platform-driven enforcement contradicts blockchain's decentralized ethos, introducing risks of inconsistent standards, opacity, and single points of failure. (3) Complex Rights Enforcement: Tracing and resolving on-chain counterfeits is resource-intensive and legally challenging for creators and buyers, hindering effective recourse (Fig. 1).

2.2   AI-Generated Image Detection Methods

With the rapid advancement of artificial intelligence in the field of generative art, AI can now effortlessly produce a large volume of images, often mimicking

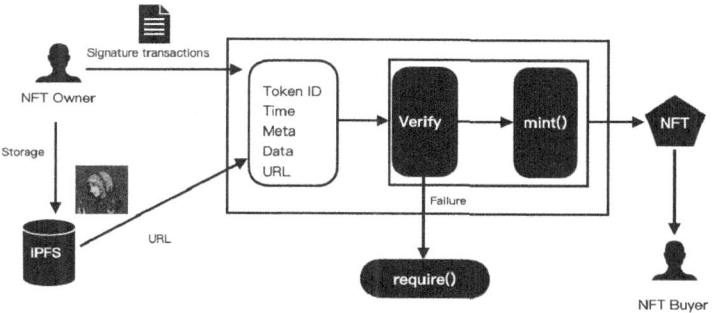

Fig. 1. The Process Of NFT Mint.

specific artistic styles or blending existing visual elements. This makes it increasingly difficult to determine the true origin and authenticity of digital artworks [20]. Detection methods are categorized into four types based on their principles and feature dimensions: (1) Local Feature and Noise Pattern Detection: CNNSpot [21] leverages ResNet-50 [22] for 99.6% accuracy on GAN-generated images but struggles with diffusion models. LNP [23] targets diffusion models like ADM with 99.2% accuracy, yet suffers a 20% performance drop under Gaussian blur. DIRE-G/D [24] attains 100% accuracy on Stable Diffusion via reconstruction error but falters on non-diffusion models. (2) Core Network Architecture Optimization: DeiT-S [25] offers data-efficient Transformers but lacks diffusion model robustness, while Swin-T [26] achieves 92% accuracy on Wukong datasets with high computational cost (<10 FPS), hindering real-time DeFi applications. (3) Hybrid Feature and Multimodal Fusion: Fusing [27] integrates CNNs and Transformers for a 12% performance boost in complex backgrounds, and UnivFD [28] reaches 95% accuracy across eight models via contrastive learning, though both falter against novel mechanisms like ADM's dynamic noise or VQDM's discrete tokens. AIDE [29] combines visual, noise, and semantic features for 60% mAP on COCO (3.5–4.6% above SOTA), but multi-task training causes instability. (4) Frequency-Domain and Texture Analysis: Zhang et al. [30] achieve >99% accuracy on GAN-generated images using Fourier transforms, less effective on low-frequency models. F3Net [31] improves Chameleon precision by 3.5% via frequency-spatial fusion, while GramNet [32] maintains <10% false positives but struggles with texture-enhanced models like GLIDE [33]. PatchCraft [34] emphasizes texture contrast, yet underperforms on style transfer models like CycleGAN [35]. These limitations highlight the need for adaptive, efficient models to counter evolving generative techniques in NFT authenticity detection. Therefore, developing a real-time detection model capable of identifying deepfake image types with strong generalization ability is of paramount importance.

2.3   The Generative Mdels for Style-Transferred Images

In recent years, style transfer techniques have witnessed rapid advancements within the domain of computer vision, giving rise to a variety of representative models such as Adaptive Instance Normalization (AdaIN [14]), Whitening and Coloring Transform (WCT), StyleGAN-NADA [13], and DiffStyle [15]. These approaches accomplish effective 0style migration by manipulating statistical attributes—such as mean and variance—within the feature space, blending style encodings, or performing stylized image synthesis based on diffusion modeling frameworks. Crucially, these methods preserve the semantic structure and content contours of the source image, instead emulating the target style through adjustments to color distributions, texture details, and spatial correlations. For instance, AdaIN achieves style transfer by normalizing the feature statistics of the content image to align with those of the style image, thereby producing outputs with consistent local texture patterns; WCT operates by applying more sophisticated transformations at the covariance matrix level, thereby modulating texture orientation and local frequency structures; concurrently, GAN- or diffusion-based style generators such as StyleGAN-NADA enhance perceptual realism while introducing intricate stylization details and artifacts within high-frequency components.

Building on the aforementioned methods, we propose StylePatch, a model based on frequency-domain and texture feature analysis. This model extracts style features and analyzes frequency distributions to output three label types corresponding to image categories. In Sect. 4, we evaluate the detection efficiency of existing models under the current task scenario. Detailed experimental results are presented in Table 1.

3   Method

The first section introduces StylePatch, a detection model designed to identify the origin of NFT source images. The second section presents the ZKP verification framework, which ensures consistency between the input and output of the detection model. Each part is elaborated in detail below.

3.1   The Architecture of StylePatch

StylePatch comprises four modules: an image processing module, a frequency-domain and style feature extraction module, a high-pass filter, and a classifier, as illustrated in Fig. 2.

Image Processing. In the image processing module, to disrupt the global semantic coherence of the image and emphasize local texture characteristics, the input image $I \in \mathbb{R}^{C \times H \times W}$ is partitioned into N fixed-size patches: $\mathcal{P}_i = \text{Crop}(I, i)$, $i = 1, 2, ..., N$, and the spatial arrangement of these patches is randomly permuted. Every patch Size is $\mathbb{R}^{C \times h \times w}$. This procedure effectively attenuates semantic content interference during discrimination, thereby compelling the model to concentrate predominantly on the image's fundamental structural and statistical attributes.

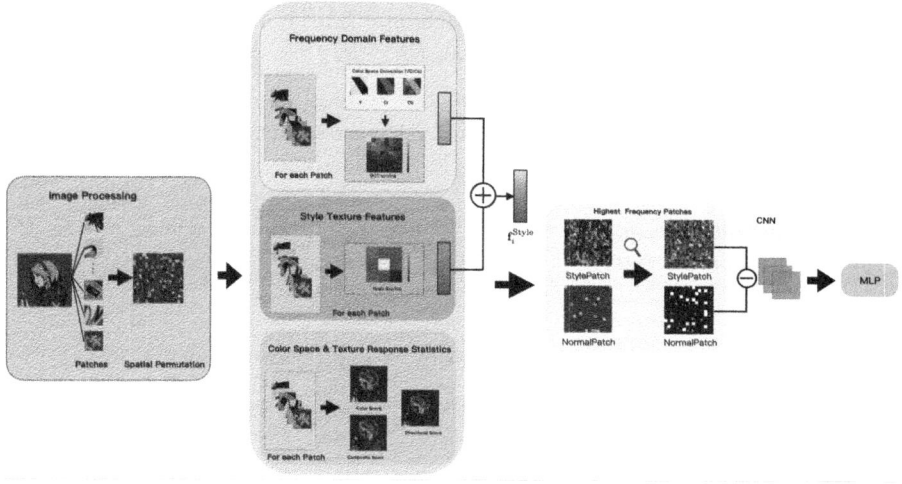

Fig. 2. Framework of the Proposed StylePatch.

Feature Extraction. Each patch is evaluated through frequency-domain and stylistic texture features:

- DCT Features: Patches are converted to YCrCb color space, and 2D DCT is applied per channel to extract mid-to-high frequency anomalies (e.g., brush-stroke effects). The top 8×8 coefficients per channel form $\mathbf{d}i \in \mathbb{R}^{192}$, with score:

$$s_i^{\text{DCT}} = \frac{1}{C} \sum_{c=1}^{C} \sum_{u,v} \left| F_i^{(c)}(u,v) \right|, \tag{1}$$

where $F_i^{(c)}(u,v) = \sum_{x=0}^{h-1} \sum_{y=0}^{w-1} \mathcal{P}_i^{(c)}(x,y) \cos\left[\frac{\pi(2x+1)u}{2h}\right] \cos\left[\frac{\pi(2y+1)v}{2w}\right]$.

- Gram Matrix Statistics: CNN feature maps $\Phi_i \in \mathbb{R}^{3 \times 1024}$ are used to compute the Gram matrix G_i, flattened to $\mathbf{g}_i \in \mathbb{R}^9$, with style intensity $s_i^{\text{Gram}} = \|G_i\|_F = \sqrt{\sum_{m,n} G_i(m,n)^2}$, capturing inter-channel texture correlations. Where G_i equals to $\frac{1}{H \cdot W \cdot C} \Phi_i \cdot \Phi_i^{\top}$, This score, combined with DCT features, forms the style feature vector $\mathbf{f}_i^{\text{Style}} = [\mathbf{g}_i, \mathbf{d}_i] \in \mathbb{R}^{C^2+192}$, with its L2 norm $\left\| \mathbf{f}_i^{\text{Style}} \right\|_2$ used in the composite score.

- Color Statistics: In Lab color space, mean and variance per channel yield $\mathbf{f}_i^{\text{Color}} = [\mu_i^{(L)}, \mu_i^{(a)}, \mu_i^{(b)}, \sigma_i^{(L)}, \sigma_i^{(a)}, \sigma_i^{(b)}] \in \mathbb{R}^6$, with score: $s_i^{\text{Color}} = \left\| \mathbf{f}_i^{\text{Color}} \right\|_2$.

Texture and Directional Features:

- Texture Metric: A custom texture metric s_i^{Tex} is computed on the grayscale patch $\mathcal{P}i^{\text{gray}} \in \mathbb{R}^{32 \times 32}$, quantifying local gradient variations to capture fine-grained structural complexity. Gradients are calculated along four directions:

horizontal (Δ_x), vertical (Δ_y), main diagonal ($\Delta d1$), and anti-diagonal (Δ_{d2}) The texture score is: $s_i^{\text{Tex}} = \sum_{x,y} |\Delta_x \mathcal{P}_i^{\text{gray}}(x,y)| + \sum_{x,y} |\Delta_y \mathcal{P}_i^{\text{gray}}(x,y)| + 1.2 \cdot \left(\sum_{x,y} |\Delta_{d1} \mathcal{P}_i^{\text{gray}}(x,y)| + \sum_{x,y} |\Delta_{d2} \mathcal{P}_i^{\text{gray}}(x,y)| \right)$, where the 1.2 weight amplifies diagonal contributions, emphasizing complex, non-orthogonal texture patterns often introduced by style transfer (e.g., cross-hatching or stippling).

- Directional filter responses yield $s_i^{\text{Dir}} = \frac{1}{K} \sum_{k=1}^{K} |R_i^{(k)}|_2^2$, where $R_i^{(k)}$ is the filtered grayscale image.

Composite Score and Reconstruction. A composite score:

$$s_i = \gamma((s_i^{\text{Tex}})^{0.7} + s_i^{\text{Color}}) + \beta |\mathbf{f}_i^{\text{Style}}|_2 + \delta s_i^{\text{Dir}}, \tag{2}$$

with $\mathbf{f}_i^{\text{Style}} = [\mathbf{g}_i, \mathbf{d}_i]$, $\alpha = 0.7$, $\beta = 0.4$, $\gamma = 0.2$, $\delta = 0.2$, ranks patches. Top 50% are StylePatch (complex textures), bottom 50% are NormalPatch (simpler features), reconstructed into two 512×512 images.

We propose a feature extraction module to analyze image patches, deriving frequency-domain and stylistic texture features to quantify texture complexity, edge density, and color variation. A composite score, computed via Eq. 2, ranks patch feature richness. Patches in the top 50% are classified as StylePatch, exhibiting intricate patterns and high visual complexity, while the bottom 50% are labeled NormalPatch, characterized by simpler features. These patches are reconstructed into feature-rich StylePatch and feature-poor Normal-Patch images for downstream tasks. Fourier transforms are applied to reconstructed images, followed by a high-pass filtering module that suppresses low-frequency components (e.g., smooth backgrounds) to highlight high-frequency residuals. These residuals capture latent traces, such as edge reconstruction errors from style transfer models, non-smooth transitions in image enhancement, and device encoding artifacts. We employ 30 different high-pass filters, covering a range of scales, orientations, and frequency bands to build a redundant yet robust residual feature representation. Equation gives the representation, $R_j^{\text{rich}} = H_j \odot F^{\text{rich}}$, $R_j^{\text{poor}} = H_j \odot F^{\text{poor}}$, and $F^{\text{rich}} = \mathcal{F}(\mathcal{I}^{\text{rich}})$, $F^{\text{poor}} = \mathcal{F}(\mathcal{I}^{\text{poor}})$, $\{H_j\}_{j=1}^{30}$. Finally, the filtered images are fed into a convolutional neural network to extract deep discriminative features, $\text{Concat}(f^{\text{rich}}, f^{\text{poor}})$, and $f^{\text{rich}} = \text{Conv}(R_j^{\text{rich}})$, $f^{\text{poor}} = \text{Conv}(R_j^{\text{poor}})$, which are then classified to determine the image's authenticity, The output is labeled 0, 1, or 2, where 0 represents the real image, 1 represents the image generated by the AI, and 2 represents the style migration image generated by the AI. This pipeline fundamentally relies on comparing the statistical differences in high-frequency features between texture-rich and texture-poor regions to ascertain whether an image has undergone style transfer or similar manipulations, thereby enabling effective detection of the provenance of NFT images.

3.2   The Pipline of ZKP-StylePatch

Zero-knowledge proofs (ZKPs), especially zk-SNARKs, efficiently and privately verify StylePatch model's image processing, mitigating off-chain collusion risks. ZKPs offer superior verification speed and low Ethereum Gas costs, ensuring robust, tamper-proof, and high-throughput on-chain verification for decentralized AI.

The verification process for zero-knowledge proofs (ZKPs) is designed as follows:

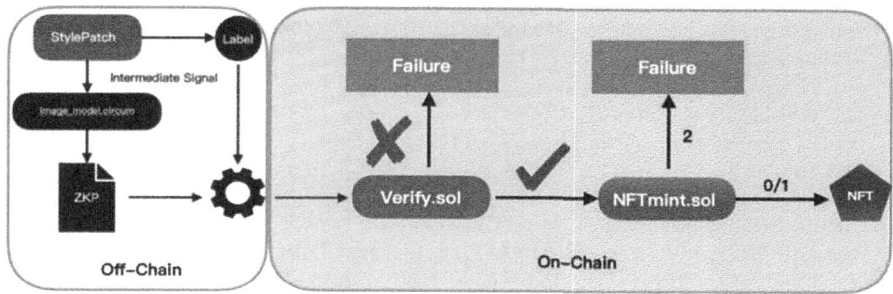

Fig. 3. Overview of the Proposed ZKP-StylePatch Framework.

Model Execution and Intermediate Output Generation. Users submit an image to the off-chain StylePatch model, which performs style feature extraction and texture scoring, generating intermediate outputs and three final classification labels. These intermediate outputs are crucial for zero-knowledge proof (ZKP) inputs, ensuring the entire computation, not just the final output, adheres to the model's definition.

Zero-Knowledge Proof Generation. The prover (model operator) uses zk-SNARK tools (e.g., circom, snarkjs) to represent StylePatch's computation as a circuit with mathematical constraints. Using the input image's hash, intermediate outputs, and final labels, the prover generates a compact ZKP file (a few hundred bytes), proving computation correctness without revealing sensitive data.

On-Chain Proof Submission and Verification. The prover submits the ZKP file, input image hash, and output labels to a smart contract. The contract uses a pre-configured verification key to execute the zk-SNARK verification algorithm (e.g., elliptic curve pairing checks), confirming proof validity in milliseconds with low Gas costs (approx. 300,000–600,000 on Ethereum).

Algorithm 1. ZKP-StylePatch Detection Pipeline

1: **Input:** Image $I \in \mathbb{R}^{C \times H \times W}$
2: Partition image: $\{P_i\} \leftarrow \text{Crop}(I, 32 \times 32)$
3: Shuffle patches: $\{P_i\} \leftarrow \text{Shuffle}(\{P_i\})$
4: **for** each patch P_i **do**
5:     $d_i \leftarrow \text{DCT}(P_i)$ ▷ Frequency features
6:     $g_i \leftarrow \text{Gram}(\phi(P_i))$ ▷ Texture features
7:     $f_i^{\text{style}} \leftarrow [g_i, d_i]$, $f_i^{\text{color}} \leftarrow [\mu(L, a, b), \sigma(L, a, b)]$
8:     $s_i^{\text{tex}} \leftarrow \text{GradientEnergy}(P_i)$, $s_i^{\text{dir}} \leftarrow \text{DirectionalFilter}(P_i)$
9:     Compute score: $s_i = \gamma \cdot ((s_i^{\text{Tex}})^\alpha + s_i^{\text{Color}}) + \beta \cdot \left\| f_i^{\text{Style}} \right\|_2 + \delta \cdot s_i^{\text{Dir}}$,
10: **end for**
11: Split patches by median s_i: `StylePatch` / `NormalPatch`
12: Reconstruct $I_{\text{rich}}, I_{\text{poor}}$
13: $F_{\text{rich}}, F_{\text{poor}} \leftarrow \text{FFT}(I_{\text{rich}}, I_{\text{poor}})$
14: **for** each high-pass filter H_j **do**
15:     $R_j^{\text{rich}} \leftarrow H_j \odot F_{\text{rich}}, R_j^{\text{poor}} \leftarrow H_j \odot F_{\text{poor}}$
16: **end for**
17: Extract features $f^{\text{rich}}, f^{\text{poor}}$ from CNN
18: Classification: Label $\in \{0, 1, 2\} \leftarrow \text{Classifier}([f^{\text{rich}}, f^{\text{poor}}])$
19: Generate ZK proof: $\pi \leftarrow \text{ZK\_Prove}(I_{\text{hash}}, \text{features}, \text{Label})$
20: On-chain verify: `Verify`(π) and trigger NFT minting

Verification Result Handling. Upon successful verification, the smart contract confirms untampered computation and consistent output labels, potentially recording results, triggering actions like token minting, and notifying parties. Failure results in the smart contract rejecting the operation, preventing untrustworthy on-chain records. If verification is successful, the minting contract is triggered: label 0 initiates NFT minting (function 1); label 1 triggers minting with an "AI-Generated" description (function 2); label 2 prevents minting. Algorithm 1 and Fig. 3 detail the framework.

4   Experimental Results

In this section, we comprehensively evaluate the detection efficiency of our method on state-of-the-art generative models. We also demonstrate the superiority of the proposed method by comparing it with multiple baselines.

4.1   Experimental Setup

Datasets. The dataset comprises two large-scale collections: GenImage [34] and NFT_AIArt. GenImage includes 2.66 million images (1.33 million real, labeled 0; 1.33 million AI-generated, labeled 1), with metadata on image sources and generation parameters, suited for authenticity detection and generative modeling. NFT_AIArt contains 1.3 million pairs of style-transferred images (labeled 2), derived from GenImage's real images using CNN, CycleGAN, and Diffusion models, adopting styles from Opensea projects (e.g., Azuki, CryptoPunks) for style migration and digital art research. All images are resized to 512×512 pixels and normalized to $[0, 1]$. The dataset is split into 70% training, 15% validation, and 15% test sets.

Baselines. We evaluated ten advanced detectors including: Spec [30], DeiT-S [25], Swin-T [26], CNNSpot [21], F3net [31], GramNet [32], DIRE [24], GenDet [36], Patchcraft [34], AIDE [29].

Implementation Details. First, input images were standardized to a resolution of 512×512 pixels using bilinear interpolation and normalized with mean and standard deviation for RGB channels. The pipeline segments images into non-overlapping 32×32 patches, extracting:: Gram matrices to capture inter-channel style correlations, DCT coefficients in the YCrCb color space, a custom texture metric, Lab color space statistics, and directional filter responses using seven high-pass filter sets to compute energy. These features are integrated into a composite texture complexity score as shown in Eq. 2. Patches are segmented into texture-rich and texture-poor regions based on the 50th percentile of this score, followed by random grid placement for image reconstruction. The model, a dual-path convolutional neural network with style-guided attention, was trained using the Adam optimizer (learning rate 0.001, $\beta_1 = 0.9$, $\beta_2 = 0.999$) for 500 epochs with a batch size of 16, employing cross-entropy loss and data augmentation including random horizontal flips and rotations. All tensor operations were performed on the ten NVIDIA RTX 4090 GPUs when available to ensure computational efficiency.

Metrics. To evaluate the performance of our three-class detection model, we mainly use the standard metrics: classification accuracy (Acc). These metrics provide a robust assessment of the model's ability to correctly classify instances.

4.2   Comparison to State-of-the-Art Model

Since current advanced models output only two classes—real images and AI-generated images-the classifier needs to be improved to enforce a three—class output: real images, AI-generated images, and style-transferred images. The model's performance can then be evaluated and compared accordingly. The model evaluation results are shown in Table 1.

Previous studies have analyzed model performance by incorporating image degradation augmentations, such as random JPEG compression and Gaussian blur, to improve robustness under low-quality image conditions and to evaluate model behavior when faced with degraded inputs. However, upon further analysis of the real-world data distribution in our task, we observed that images uploaded by users for NFT minting are generally of high quality, typically being high-resolution artworks without noticeable compression or degradation. This

Table 1. Comparison to State-of-the-art Model Across Various Models(%).

Method	Midjourney	SD v1.4	SD v1.5	GLIDE	YQDM	CycleGAN	Mean
Spec [30]	52.70	99.85	99.85	96.90	63.20	50.70	77.20
CNNSpot [21]	52.20	99.80	99.85	97.20	65.70	51.40	77.69
F3Net [31]	54.40	99.75	99.85	96.20	63.60	52.00	77.63
GramNet [32]	72.90	99.70	99.85	**99.70**	82.80	67.60	87.09
DeiT-S [25]	55.55	99.85	99.70	99.10	68.80	52.10	79.18
Swin-T [26]	57.70	99.85	99.85	**99.70**	69.20	55.45	80.29
DIRE [24]	62.40	99.80	99.80	96.45	77.10	62.40	82.99
GenDet [36]	79.00	99.80	99.80	93.75	83.70	72.20	88.04
PatchCraft [34]	79.08	**99.90**	99.90	96.85	85.06	72.20	88.83
AIDE [29]	79.38	99.74	**99.96**	96.85	**86.28**	72.66	89.14
StylePatch(Ours)	**84.70**	**99.90**	99.90	96.28	85.88	**80.24**	**91.35**

phenomenon can be attributed to the NFT market's preference for high-quality images, as low-quality images often fail to attract buyers, resulting in low or no transaction prices. Consequently, the likelihood of encountering significantly compressed or blurred images in practical deployment is low. Moreover, our model has demonstrated stable and strong detection performance on both the validation set and real-world test images without the use of degradation-based augmentations, indicating sufficient generalization capacity given the current high-quality image distribution. Therefore, considering practical requirements, training stability, and computational efficiency, we decided not to incorporate image degradation augmentations, avoiding unnecessary perturbations during model training. Based on the above analysis, we conclude that such augmentation strategies do not offer significant practical benefits for the current task.

4.3   Ablation Studies

To evaluate the effectiveness of the power transformation applied to texture metrics, we conducted an ablation study comparing the proposed non-linear transformation, $(s_i^{\text{Tex}})^{0.7}$, against a linear scaling approach. The texture metric, denoted as s_i^{Tex}, quantifies the local gradient variation within an image patch, reflecting the complexity or richness of the texture. However, the raw texture metric often exhibits a wide dynamic range, with extremely high values in highly textured regions and near-zero values in smooth regions. Directly incorporating these raw values into the composite score can lead to an imbalance, where texture dominates other features (e.g., color or orientation), compromising model robustness and generalization. The power transformation with an exponent less than 1 (e.g., 0.7) serves two primary purposes. First, it mitigates the impact of extreme values. For instance, a large texture value such as $s_i^{\text{Tex}} = 100$ is reduced to $(100)^{0.7} \approx 25.12$, while smaller values like $s_i^{\text{Tex}} = 1$ remain unchanged

$((1)^{0.7} = 1)$. This non-linear compression ensures a smoother contribution of texture metrics to the composite score, preventing outliers from disproportionately influencing the results. Second, the transformation balances the texture metric's contribution relative to other features in the composite score, fostering a more robust feature representation. In our experiments, we compared the performance of the model using the power transformation against a baseline with linear scaling of s_i^{Tex}. The results demonstrate that the power transformation significantly improves model stability and generalization, as evidenced by [insert metric, e.g., a 5% increase in classification accuracy]. This improvement is attributed to the reduced dominance of extreme texture values and the enhanced balance among feature contributions, validating the efficacy of the proposed non-linear approach over linear scaling.

In this section, we also conduct an in-depth analysis of how each module contributes to the performance of StylePatch. We progressively remove individual feature extraction modules to evaluate their impact on the overall model performance. Specifically, we assess the representational contributions of four key components: the Gram matrix-based style feature extraction module, the DCT module, the patch partitioning and reconstruction module, and the high-pass filter. Table 2 shows the model performance after removing each module.

Table 2. Module Configurations and Their Mean Performance.

Gram	DCT	PR	HPF	Mean
✗	✓	✓	✓	86.84
✓	✗	✓	✓	88.95
✓	✓	✗	✓	84.20
✓	✓	✓	✗	87.73
✓	✓	✓	✓	**91.35**

4.4 ZKP-Driven Secure and Transparent Evaluation

To ensure the verifiability and privacy protection of the StylePatch style evaluation process, we introduce a Zero-Knowledge Proof (ZKP) mechanism. This allows the intermediate signals generated by the model to be verified off-chain, and subsequently validated on-chain via smart contracts. Experimental results demonstrate that this module can reliably and efficiently generate valid proofs without revealing the original image content, thereby ensuring that the evaluation process remains verifiable, tamper-proof, and privacy-preserving. Table 3 presents the times for key operations in the ZKP-StylePatch framework. It includes the generation time of the proof file, which is less than 60 s, as well as the verification delay time, which is less than 100 ms.

Table 3. Times for ZKP Proof Generation and Verification.

Item	Time
Proof file generation time	<60 s
Verification delay time	< 100 ms

The integration of ZKP enables trustworthy publication of model predictions and supports secure, transparent, and practical on-chain asset generation based on style credibility.

5   Conclusion and Limitations

The rapid growth of the NFT market presents significant opportunities for digital artists but also introduces challenges like intellectual property infringement, especially with AI-generated and style-transferred artworks. The proposed ZKP-StylePatch framework offers a robust solution by detecting and verifying the provenance of NFT images. It integrates an off-chain detection model, StylePatch, with an on-chain zero-knowledge proof (ZKP) mechanism, ensuring high accuracy (91.35%) and tamper-proof verification. ZKP-StylePatch is a crucial advancement in protecting intellectual property within the NFT space, effectively detecting AI-generated content and securing on-chain verification. However, the study has limitations. It defines style transfer plagiarism as AI-generated works minted as NFTs but excludes human-created works inspired by existing NFT styles. This distinction arises from the subjective nature of human creativity, which often involves complex inspirations and personal expression, making plagiarism difficult to ascertain. Another limitation concerns ZKP's practicality. While ZKP ensures security and privacy by verifying detection model consistency without revealing sensitive information, its high computational complexity and resource consumption can hinder efficiency. This is particularly problematic in scenarios requiring high transaction volume or concurrent requests, potentially slowing detection and failing to meet real-time demands in platforms like DeFi or NFT marketplaces. Future research should focus on optimizing ZKP algorithms or combining them with more lightweight cryptographic technologies to enhance performance while maintaining security.

Acknowledgments. This work was supported by the Shenzhen Science and Technology Program (KJZD20230923114500002).

Disclosure of Interests. The authors have no competing interests to declare that are relevant to the content of this article.

References

1. Wlasinsky, O.: Literature review on the most popular of NFTS types. Int. J. Educ. Technol. Artif. Intell. **2**(1), 8–12 (2023)
2. Ante, L., Fiedler, I.: The new digital economy: how decentralized finance (DEFI) and non-fungible tokens (NFTS) are transforming value creation, ownership models, and economic systems (2024)
3. Vasan, K., Janosov, M., Barabási, A.-L.: Quantifying NFT-driven networks in crypto art. Sci. Rep. **12**(1), 2769 (2022)
4. Wang, Q., Li, R., Wang, Q., Chen, S.: Non-fungible token (NFT): overview, evaluation, opportunities and challenges. arXiv preprint arXiv:2105.07447 (2021)
5. Ma, K., Huang, J., He, N., Wang, Z., Wang, H.: SoK: on the security of non-fungible tokens. Blockchain Res. Appl. 100268 (2025)
6. OpenSea. Moonbirds collection (2023). https://opensea.io/collection/proofmoonbirds. Accessed 19 June 2025
7. Yuga Labs. Bored ape yacht club official website (2022). https://boredapeyachtclub.com/. Accessed 19 June 2025
8. Wang, F., Zhangjie, F., Zhang, X.: A self-defense copyright protection scheme for NFT image art based on information embedding. ACM Trans. Multimed. Comput. Commun. Appl. **21**(2), 1–23 (2024)
9. Das, D., Bose, P., Ruaro, N., Kruegel, C., Vigna, G.: Understanding security issues in the NFT ecosystem. In: Proceedings of the 2022 ACM SIGSAC Conference on Computer and Communications Security, pp. 667–681 (2022)
10. OpenSea. What is opensea's copymint policy (2025). https://support.opensea.io/en/articles/8867065-what-is-opensea-s-copymint-policy. Accessed 19 June 2025
11. OpenSea. An update on verification and copymint prevention (2025). https://opensea.io/blog/articles/an-update-on-verification-and-copymint-prevention. Accessed 19 June 2025
12. Goodfellow, I., et al.: Generative adversarial networks. Commun. ACM **63**(11), 139–144 (2020)
13. Gal, R., Patashnik, O., Maron, H., Bermano, A.H., Chechik, G., Cohen-Or, D.: Stylegan-nada: clip-guided domain adaptation of image generators. ACM Trans. Graph. (TOG) **41**(4), 1–13 (2022)
14. Huang, X., Belongie, S.: Arbitrary style transfer in real-time with adaptive instance normalization. In: Proceedings of the IEEE International Conference on Computer Vision, pp. 1501–1510 (2017)
15. Jeong, J., Kwon, M., Uh, Y.: Training-free style transfer emerges from H-space in diffusion models. arXiv preprint arXiv:2303.15403, vol. 3, no. 1 (2023)
16. Zhu, M., et al.: Genimage: a million-scale benchmark for detecting AI-generated image. Adv. Neural. Inf. Process. Syst. **36**, 77771–77782 (2023)
17. Kotzer, A., Naamneh, M., Rottenstreich, O., Reviriego, P.: Detection of NFT duplications with image hash functions. In: 2024 IEEE International Conference on Blockchain and Cryptocurrency (ICBC), pp. 1–7. IEEE (2024)
18. Lowe, G.: Sift-the scale invariant feature transform. Int. J. **2**(91–110), 2 (2004)
19. Roy, S.K., Harandi, M., Nock, R., Hartley, R.: Siamese networks: the tale of two manifolds. In: Proceedings of the IEEE/CVF International Conference on Computer Vision, pp. 3046–3055 (2019)
20. Foo, L.G., Rahmani, H., Liu, J.: AI-generated content (AIGC) for various data modalities: a survey. ACM Comput. Surv. **57**(9), 1–66 (2025)

21. Wang, S.Y., Wang, O., Zhang, R., Owens, A., Efros, A.A.: CNN-generated images are surprisingly easy to spot... for now. In: Proceedings of the IEEE/CVF Conference on Computer Vision and Pattern Recognition, pp. 8695–8704 (2020)
22. He, K., Zhang, X., Ren, S., Sun, J.: Deep residual learning for image recognition. In: Proceedings of the IEEE Conference on Computer Vision and Pattern Recognition, pp. 770–778 (2016)
23. Liu, B., Yang, F., Bi, X., Xiao, B., Li, W., Gao, X.: Detecting generated images by real images. In: European Conference on Computer Vision, pp. 95–110. Springer (2022)
24. Wang, Z., et al.: Dire for diffusion-generated image detection. In: Proceedings of the IEEE/CVF International Conference on Computer Vision, pp. 22445–22455 (2023)
25. Touvron, H., Cord, M., Douze, M., Massa, F., Sablayrolles, A., Jégou, H.: Training data-efficient image transformers & distillation through attention. In: International Conference on Machine Learning, pp. 10347–10357. PMLR (2021)
26. Liu, Z., et al.: Swin transformer: hierarchical vision transformer using shifted windows. In: Proceedings of the IEEE/CVF International Conference on Computer Vision, pp. 10012–10022 (2021)
27. Ju, Y., Jia, S., Ke, L., Xue, H., Nagano, K., Lyu, S.: Fusing global and local features for generalized AI-synthesized image detection. In: 2022 IEEE International Conference on Image Processing (ICIP), pp. 3465–3469. IEEE (2022)
28. Ojha, U., Li, Y., Lee, Y.J.: Towards universal fake image detectors that generalize across generative models. In: Proceedings of the IEEE/CVF Conference on Computer Vision and Pattern Recognition, pp. 24480–24489 (2023)
29. Yan, S., et al.: A sanity check for AI-generated image detection. arXiv preprint arXiv:2406.19435 (2024)
30. Zhang, X., Karaman, S., Chang, S.-F.: Detecting and simulating artifacts in GAN fake images. In: 2019 IEEE International Workshop on Information Forensics and Security (WIFS), pp. 1–6. IEEE (2019)
31. Qian, Y., Yin, G., Sheng, L., Chen, Z., Shao, J.: Thinking in frequency: face forgery detection by mining frequency-aware clues. In: Vedaldi, A., Bischof, H., Brox, T., Frahm, J.-M. (eds.) ECCV 2020. LNCS, vol. 12357, pp. 86–103. Springer, Cham (2020). https://doi.org/10.1007/978-3-030-58610-2_6
32. Liu, Z., Qi, X., Torr, P.H.S.: Global texture enhancement for fake face detection in the wild. In: Proceedings of the IEEE/CVF Conference on Computer Vision and Pattern Recognition, pp. 8060–8069 (2020)
33. Nichol, A., et al.: Glide: towards photorealistic image generation and editing with text-guided diffusion models. arXiv preprint arXiv:2112.10741 (2021)
34. Zhong, N., Xu, Y., Li, S., Qian, Z., Zhang, X.: Patchcraft: exploring texture patch for efficient AI-generated image detection. arXiv preprint arXiv:2311.12397 (2023)
35. Zhu, J.-Y., Park, T., Isola, P., Efros, A.A.: Unpaired image-to-image translation using cycle-consistent adversarial networks. In: Proceedings of the IEEE International Conference on Computer Vision (ICCV) (2017)
36. Zhu, M., et al.: Gendet: towards good generalizations for AI-generated image detection. arXiv preprint arXiv:2312.08880 (2023)

A Blockchain-Based Range Proof Framework in Supply Chain

Jianyu Zou[1], Songlin He[1,2(✉)], Xukang Lyu[3], and Dongliang Chu[3]

[1] Southwest Jiaotong University, Chengdu 610031, Sichuan, China
zoujy@my.swjtu.edu.cn, sohe@swjtu.edu.cn
[2] Manufacturing Industry Chain Collaboration Industrial Software Key Laboratory of Sichuan Province, Chengdu 610031, Sichuan, China
[3] Zhejiang New Rise Digital Technology Co., Ltd., Hangzhou 311899, China
{clu,chudongliang}@newrisedt.com

Abstract. In supply chain management, a common scenario lies in proving an entity's ability, e.g., a supplier needs to prove its supplying ability by revealing its commodity transactions often have quantity constraints (e.g., minimum order quantity and maximum supply capacity). However, traditional verification mechanisms require the trading participants to disclose their core business secrets, which poses significant risks of commercial privacy leakage. To meet the verification requirements of business constraints while strictly protecting the sensitive data of all participants, this study proposes a verifiable privacy protection protocol based on non-interactive zero-knowledge range proof and blockchain technology. The core innovation of this framework lies in enabling suppliers to generate and submit cryptographic proofs to purchasers (namely as a verifier) without revealing their exact production capacity, thereby efficiently and reliably proving their ability to meet specific transaction quantity requirements. In addition, the process is designed atop blockchain, which, acting as an infrastructure of supply chain, plays the role of recording immutable transactions of proofs and coordinating participants. Security analysis is performed and experiment is conducted to showcase the protocol's efficacy and efficiency.

Keywords: Supply Chain · Blockchain · Zero-Knowledge · Range Proof

1 Introduction

In global economic integration, supply chains are the key link between production, consumption, and global trade. It is not only a channel for the circulation of goods and services, but also profoundly affects the competitiveness of business activities. It is estimated that the global supply chain management market is valued at \$21.95 billion in 2023 and is expected to grow to approximately \$30.9 billion by 2026 [2]. Another forecast shows that the market will reach approximately \$89.57 billion by 2034 [32]. As data-driven and business processes become more refined, the number of participants involved in the supply chain, from raw

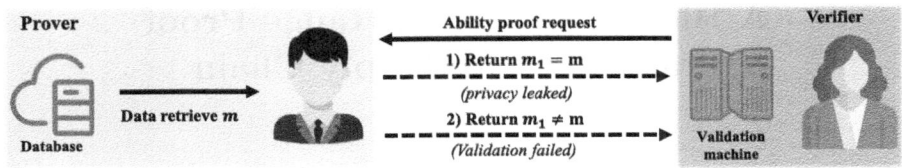

Fig. 1. Privacy and verification dilemmas in supply chain ability proof

material suppliers and manufacturers to logisticians, distributors, and financial institutions, has increased dramatically, making data interaction scenarios more complex and frequent than ever before. In the process of business interactions in supply chain, many application scenarios essentially share the same characteristic. For instance, suppliers need to provide their inventory levels (in numbers) to demonstrate their supply capabilities, or transactions are frequently governed by strict quantitative commitments [33] like minimum order quantity. This kind of ability proof is of key significance to ensure the advancement of business flow.

However, in the implementation of commitments, there are often serious obstacles in data collaboration between different participants, resulting in inefficient business execution [11]. The core challenge is how to balance the actual needs for data privacy protection and data egress. As depicted in Fig. 1, supply chain participants try to prove their ability by disclosing data in internal databases, which often leads to two problems, i.e., the lack of trusted third-party (TTP) [29] endorsement makes it difficult to ensure the credibility of the data, and the disclosure of raw data may also bring the risk of important information leakage. The traditional model forces partners to disclose sensitive, proprietary data, such as real-time inventory from suppliers or demand forecasts from buyers, which is in direct contradiction to the need for business privacy [36]. Consequently, from a supply chain management perspective [1], enabling reliable data disclosure while not compromising confidentiality is not only beneficial, but also a critical necessity for fostering robust and efficient commerce [31].

In addition, blockchain has emerged as a promising technology for coordinating the participants in the general supply chain, where blockchain plays the role of a trusted third-party instead of relying on any costly or hard-to-find intermediary. Blockchain provides the critical security guarantee such as fairness where all participants in the supply chain should obtain their well-deserved items. As a basic infrastructure for supply chain ecosystem, blockchain has witnessed its potential of future wide application [13,26,35,40]. Thus, our proposed ability proof protocol is also built atop blockchain, where blockchain can record the proof process via transactions, thus realizing traceability and accountability.

Contributions. Overall, the contributions can be summarized as follows.

– We sort out multiple business scenarios that require the range proof-based ability proof in the supply chain field, where the general supply chain are divided into different types such as marketing, after-sales and accessory.

- We propose a supply chain ability proof protocol Π_{SCAP} that allows a supply chain participant, as a prover, to prove its ability of completing a business while preserving the sensitive information. The proof process is built atop blockchain for traceability and accountability.
- We analyzed key indicators of agreement and conducted experiments to demonstrate the efficiency and efficacy of the proposed protocol.

2 Related Works

2.1 Blockchain and Smart Contracts

As a distributed ledger technology, blockchain has witnessed its wide application in many practical scenarios including Internet of Things (IoTs) [19,21], cyber security [17], content delivery [18,39] and contract signing [20]. With the inherent characteristics of immutability and transparency [10], blockchain provides a strong supporting framework for data interaction in the supply chain field, primarily through two mechanisms: (i) shared ledger for data integrity. It establishes a unified, tamper-evident ledger that dismantles data silos, creating a single source of truth that reduces reconciliation costs and trust overhead [25,26,35]; (ii) smart contracts for process automation. It automates business agreements and enforces rules without costly intermediaries, simplified complex workflows [4,13,28,37]. However, this foundational transparency of blockchain and smart contract state directly conflicts with the need for commercial confidentiality. Protecting sensitive transaction details from leakage is therefore the primary challenge hindering practical adoption.

2.2 Privacy Preservation in Supply Chain

In the supply chain field, privacy protection involves the data exchange of multiple participants, which can be divided into two categories from the perspective of protection purposes: (i) data privacy protection. Based on blockchain, Xu et al. [38] used the attribute encryption mechanism (MA-ABE) to solve the data privacy and security problem of single-authority ABE in the supply chain Internet of Things. Sarfaraz et al. [34] optimized the access control logic by integrating priority attributes into role-based access control, and realized data privacy protection from the dimension of permission control. (ii) data computation protection. Pibernik et al. [30] utilizes secure multi-party computation (SMPC) to enable joint decision-making and benefit sharing among supply chain members without disclosing private data. Based on the personalized differential privacy optimization method, Ma et al. [27] realized the privacy protection of the model parameters of collaborative optimization model parameters by different institutions in supply chain finance without directly exchanging sensitive data.

Zero-knowledge proof (ZKP) is a key technology in the field of privacy protection [3], which can prove the authenticity of a statement to the verifier without revealing any additional information related to the statement. Zero-knowledge

Table 1. The comparison of representative range proof algorithms.

Algorithm	Aggregation Capacity	Verifier Time (ms)	Prover Time (ms)	No Trusted Setup
Bulletproofs [7]	Yes (O(log(m·k)))	6.32–11.96	1.37–2.51	Yes
HashWires [8]	No	0.003–0.194	0.002–0.01	Yes
BFGW [6] + KZG	Yes	9.57–12.56	5.65–5.68	No (requires CRS)
Groth16 [16]	Limited	31.18–34.46	34.23–34.46	No (requires CRS)
Lattice-based [5]	No	N/A	N/A	Yes

† "Aggregation Capacity" refers to compressing multiple proofs into one.

range proof (ZKRP), which is a sub-class of ZKP's specific application, shows unique application value in the supply chain capability proof scenario. We comprehensively considered multiple key indicators such as prover time and verification time, compared with the current mainstream ZKRP algorithms [12], and combined with the actual application requirements of supply chain scenarios. From the perspective of performance alone, the HashWires [8] algorithm is better than the Bulletproofs algorithm, but it supports compressing multiple range proofs into a single one, which is suitable for batch verification of multiple indicators in the supply chain, such as simultaneous verification of capacity, inventory, and pass rate. HashWires does not support aggregation, thus the time cost of multiple verifications would be relatively large. On the contrary, the time cost of Bulletproofs is more acceptable in the supply chain scenario. Overall, we choose the Bulletproofs algorithm to instantiate ZKRP in our framework. Table 1 tabulates the comparison of different representative range proof algorithms.

3   Scenarios Involving Range Proof in Supply Chain

Hereunder we introduce the typical scenarios that involve range proof in supply chain. We sort out typical business processes covering marketing, accessories, after-sales in the supply chain field from public data, and analyze the roles and business logic of users in each process to calculate the scale of applications that need to use the protocol to complete the proof of trusted ability. The results show that the range proof is not an edge requirement in the supply chain, but a common scenario that runs through multi-process and multi-role interaction, and this framework can effectively tackle the problems of data privacy protection and trusted verification in the supply chain, and improve the efficiency of collaboration. The typical supply chain scenarios are tabulated in Table 2.

4   Preliminaries

Hereunder we introduce the involved primitives including Elgamal additive homomorphism, non-interactive chaum-pedersen protocol, and Bulletproofs.

Table 2. Typical scenarios involving range proof in supply chain.

Category	Business Process	Interacting Parties	Verified Attribute	Need RP
Purchasing and Sales	Procurement Inspections	Suppliers → Manufacturer	Product Quality	✓
	Dealer Procurement Program	Dealers → Manufacturer	Market Demand	✓
	Order Management	*	*	*
	Outbound Shipments	*	*	*
	Storage	Manufacturer → Dealers	Product Quality	✓
	Market-based procurement	Seller → Buyer	Supply Ability	✓
	Manufacturer Shipment	*	*	*
	Sales Delivery & Receipt	Seller → Buyer	Shipment Quantity	✓
	Market Procurement Warehousing	*	*	*
	Parts Invoicing	*	*	*
	Parts Demand Forecast	*	*	*
After-sales Service	After-sales Parts Procurement	Supplier → Manufacturer	Inventory	✓
	Agent Return	Agent → Manufacturer	Product Quality	✓
	Service Station Warranty Purchase	*	*	*
	Warranty Period Return	Service Station → Manufacturer	Return Quantity	✓
	After-sales Return	Service Station → Agent	Return Compliance	✓
	After-sales Parts Return	*	*	*
	Return Inspection	*	*	*
Inventory and Logistics Mgt.	Agent Parts Outbound	*	*	*
	Internal Stock Transfer	*	*	*
	Centralized Allocation	*	*	*
	Passive Agent Allocation	Agent → Manufacturer	Inventory	✓
	Agent Parts Stocktaking	*	*	*
	Agent Parts Inventory Monitoring	*	*	*
	Shared Parts Inventory Release	Agent → Agent	Inventory	✓
	Urgent Parts Demand Release	Agent → Agent	Inventory	✓
	Shared Parts Inventory Mgt.	Agent → Agent	Inventory	✓
	Urgent Parts Mgt.	Agent → Agent	Inventory	✓

† The notation → indicates from a prover proves to a verifier.

4.1   ElGamal Additive Homomorphism

The ElGamal encryption algorithm [15], while inherently possessing multiplicative homomorphism, can be adapted to support additive homomorphism by mapping a plaintext m to its exponential form g^m. This makes it highly suitable for applications requiring privacy-preserving numerical operations, such as balance updates in supply chain asset transfers. The scheme operates over a cyclic group $\mathcal{G}$ of prime order p with generator g. A private key s corresponds to a public key $h = g^s \pmod{p}$. The encryption of a message m with randomness r yields a ciphertext $C = (g^r, g^m \cdot h^r)$. The key property is that the component-wise multiplication of two ciphertexts, C_a encrypting m_1 and C_b encrypting m_2, results in a new ciphertext C' that correctly encrypts the sum $m_1 + m_2$. The decryption of $g^{m_1 + m_2}$ from C' is possible with the private key s, and $m_1 + m_2$ can be recovered if the plaintext space is small enough to compute the discrete logarithm.

4.2   Non-interactive Chaum-Pedersen Protocol

The Chaum-Pedersen protocol [9] can be rendered non-interactive via the Fiat-Shamir heuristic to prove that two ElGamal ciphertexts encrypt the same message, even under different public keys. This is a proof of knowledge of a secret message m and randomness r_a, r_b corresponding to the ciphertexts. Specifically, given a group $\mathcal{G}$ with generator g, let $C_a = (g^{r_a}, g^m \cdot h_a^{r_a})$ and $C_b = (g^{r_b}, g^m \cdot h_b^{r_b})$ be two ciphertexts under public keys h_a and h_b, respectively. The goal is to prove that both encrypt the same m. Then a non-interactive proof π is generated as follows:

- **Commitment:** Choose random $k_a, k_b \in \mathbb{Z}_p$. Compute commitments $A = (g^{k_a}, h_a^{k_a})$ and $B = (g^{k_b}, h_b^{k_b})$.
- **Challenge:** Compute a challenge by hashing all public values and commitments: $e = H(g, h_a, h_b, C_a, C_b, A, B)$.
- **Response:** Compute responses $z_a = k_a + e \cdot r_a \pmod{p}$ and $z_b = k_b + e \cdot r_b \pmod{p}$.

The final proof is $\pi = (A, B, z_a, z_b)$. A verifier checks the validity of π by re-computing the challenge e and verifying two corresponding equations. A valid proof confirms the equality of the plaintexts.

4.3   Bulletproofs

Bulletproofs [7] is an efficient non-interactive zero-knowledge proof system for verifying that a committed value v lies within an interval, typically $[0, 2^n - 1]$. Its key advantages are a proof size that scales logarithmically with the range's bit-length ($O(\log n)$) and its reliance on a transparent setup, which does not require trust. Furthermore, proofs for an arbitrary range $[a, b]$ are constructed via a problem reduction. The protocol operates in a cyclic group $\mathcal{G}$ with generators g, h. Given a Pedersen commitment $V = g^v h^\gamma$ to a value v with blinding factor γ, the protocol proves that a binary vector $\mathbf{a}_L \in \{0, 1\}^n$ exists satisfying two core conditions:

- **Value Representation:** $\langle \mathbf{a}_L, \mathbf{2}^n \rangle = v$, where $\mathbf{2}^n = (1, 2, 4, \ldots, 2^{n-1})$. This confirms the binary vector correctly represents the value v.
- **Bit Validation:** $\mathbf{a}_L \circ (\mathbf{a}_L - \mathbf{1}^n) = \mathbf{0}^n$. This clever construction confirms that every element of $\mathbf{a}_L$ is either 0 or 1.

Bulletproofs compresses the proof of these vector relations into a very small size using an inner product argument. The non-interactive proof is generated via the Fiat-Shamir heuristic. The prover first encodes the vector constraints into polynomial representations and then, through a series of commitments and hash-based challenges, creates a compact proof π. Verification is highly efficient, as it requires the verifier to perform only a single, final verification check. A successful check holistically validates all the underlying relations, confirming that the committed value v lies within the specified range.

5 Problem Formulation

In this section, we formulate the ability proof in supply chain by elaborating the system model, syntax of the Π_{SCAP} protocol and design goals.

5.1 System Model

There are two parties involved in the supply chain ability proof protocol.

- **Prover ($\mathcal{P}$):** An entity with a private attributes value $v \in \mathcal{N}$ and would like to prove to a verifier about its ability for completing a business task.
- **Verifier ($\mathcal{V}$):** An entity who takes as input the proof from a prover and validates if the prover possesses the ability to complete a given business task.

5.2 Syntax of Π_{SCAP} Protocol

The proposed ability proof protocol Π_{SCAP} follows the following syntax.

- $(sk, pk) \leftarrow \mathsf{KGen}(1^\lambda)$. A trusted certificate authority runs its key generation algorithm, which takes as input the security parameter λ and outputs a pair of keys for the user, i.e., a private key sk and a public key pk.
- $\pi \leftarrow \mathsf{GenProof}(v, \lambda, L, U)$. The prover can invoke an interface $\mathsf{GenProof}(\cdot)$ with inputting the value v of the to-be-proved attribute, the range of the attribute denoted by $[L, U]$ and the security parameter λ. A proof π is generated, indicating the valid range of v.
- $b \leftarrow \mathsf{Verify}(\pi, \lambda)$. The verifier $\mathcal{V}$ takes as input the proof π generated by $\mathsf{GenProof}()$, the cryptographic security parameter λ, and output the range verification result $b = 0/1$ indicating invalid or valid.
- $b' \leftarrow \mathsf{FairExchange}(\lambda, m, h, pay)$. The prover and the verifier execute the fair exchange process to exchange their assets, where m is the digital goods, h represents the globally known identifier of m, pay is the monetary payment for m. At the end, either each party obtains the other one's input, i.e., $b' = 1$ or neither does by outputting $b' = 0$.

5.3 Design Goals

The proposed supply chain ability proof protocol Π_{SCAP} should satisfy the following security properties:

- **Completeness**: A prover $\mathcal{P}$ in the supply chain field can always convince a verifier $\mathcal{V}$ about her ability in term of a valid quantitative range.
- **Soundness**: If the statement about the prover $\mathcal{P}$'s ability in terms of quantitative range is false, then no cheating $\mathcal{P}$ can convince the verifier $\mathcal{V}$ to accept the proof π.
- **Zero-Knowledge**: The verifier $\mathcal{V}$ learns only the statement, i.e., the validity of the input in terms of its quantitative range, is true, and nothing else about the input.

Since blockchain is introduced to coordinate the business activities in supply chain field, the following properties regarding efficiency should be ensured.

- **Small proof size.** The generated proof π is sent to the verifier for recording, the proof size should be as minimum as possible due to limited storage capability in smart contract.
- **Efficient verification.** The verifier can efficiently verify the proof in $O(\log n)$, where n represents the bit length of the secret value. Besides, multiple proofs can be aggregated and verified together in a batch, achieving significant amortized efficiency, thus facilitating highly frequent business activities.
- **Non-interactive.** The prover only needs to send the proof once instead of interacting with the verifier multiple rounds.

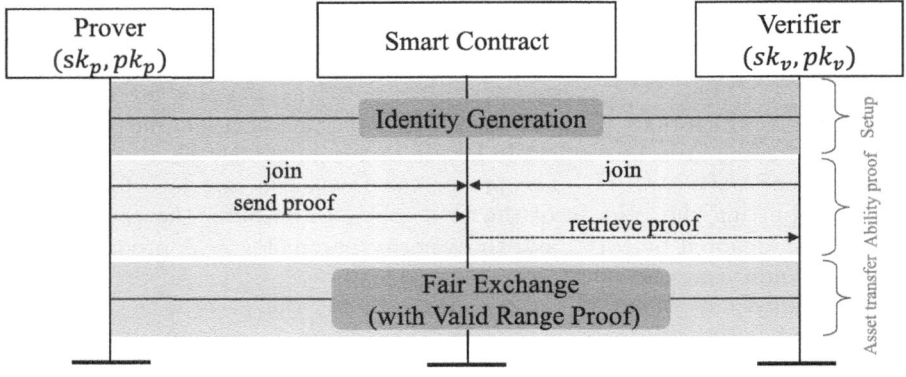

Fig. 2. The message flow of blockchain-based range proof and asset transfer.

6   Designs

This section elaborates on the implementation of the blockchain-based non-interactive range proof protocol, which operates by a prover ($\mathcal{P}$), a verifier ($\mathcal{V}$) and the smart contract (denoted by $\mathcal{C}$) deployed in a blockchain network.

6.1   Protocol Details

As illustrated in Fig. 2, the protocol consists of three phases, *setup, range proof* and *asset transfer*. The setup phase aims to realize identity generation (and identity management in a holistic system). The range proof phase allows the prover to prove its business ability in terms of a valid range, and the verifier can be convinced by a correct proof. The asset transfer phase allows the prover and the verifier to fairly exchange their inputs, i.e., digital goods and payment. Blockchain acts as a TTP to record immutable transactions and coordinate the exchange and business processes.

Phase I for Setup: This phase aims to set up identities for participants in supply chain. Blockchain acts as a trusted entity for issuing unique identifier and credentials for them [22], e.g., for an entity, its private key and public key can be realized via $(sk, pk) \leftarrow \mathsf{KGen}(1^\lambda)$ where λ is the security parameter. After the corresponding identity information of the participant is generated, it can enter the proof of ability phase.

Phase II for Ability Proof: The Prover $\mathcal{P}$ and the verifier $\mathcal{V}$ starts by sending join message to the contract with input parameters $(pk, AIC, metadata[L, U, \Delta_{max}])$, where pk uniquely identifies the participant, $metadata$ indicates the auxiliary information such as maximum payment amount Δ_{max} during the asset transfer phase, AIC indicates the attribute index that can be indexed to the target value, and $[L, U]$ defines the required value range for ability verification. Once both parties joined, $\mathcal{P}$ calls the $\mathsf{GenProof}(v, [L, U], g, h, r)$ locally while passing the current value v (retrieved from AIC) and execute the BulletProof algorithm to generate the zero-knowledge proof (π, C, op_i). Here $(g, h) \in \mathcal{G}$ represent elliptic curve base points, $r \leftarrow \mathbb{Z}p$ is a random blinding factor, $C = v \cdot G + r \cdot H$ constitutes the Pedersen commitment, and op_i contains business context data including order IDs and timestamps along with their digital signatures. Subsequently, $\mathcal{P}$ submits the encrypted proof package $c_\pi \leftarrow \mathsf{Enc}(\pi, C, op_i, pk_v)$ to the smart contract. After obtaining c_π, $\mathcal{V}$ first decrypts the data, then invokes verification algorithm $\{0, 1\} \leftarrow \mathsf{Verify}(\pi, \lambda)$. Upon successful validation, the subsequent asset transfer phase is triggered.

Phase III for Asset Transfer: To achieve a secure asset transfer, the entire process is driven by a series of interface calls, and its core exchange security is guaranteed by an instantiated fair exchange protocol such as FairSwap [14] or zkPoD [23], Once $\mathcal{P}$ have passed the ability proof phase, $\mathcal{P}$ and $\mathcal{V}$ enable fair assets transfer through $b \leftarrow \mathsf{FairExchange}(\lambda, m, h, pay)$. Both parties will determine the execution of the transaction through the execution result b, and would record it on the chain for storage, so that for later traceability and accountability.

6.2 Property Analysis

Π_{SCAP} combines blockchain with the Bulletproofs algorithm to provide private verification of supply chain ability proof. The properties are analyzed as follows.

- Completeness: Any ability data that really exists within the agreed range, an honest $\mathcal{P}$ can always use Bulletproofs to generate a valid proof that will inevitably pass the verification algorithm.
- Soundness: The discrete logarithmic puzzle on which the Bulletproofs algorithm depends, which means that any malicious party trying to forge proofs for data that does not meet the conditions is computationally unfeasible.
- Zero-Knowledge: The range proof generated by Bulletproofs only reveals the fact that the promised value is within the specified range, and does not disclose specific information about that value.
- Small proof size: Bulletproofs implement small proof sizes that only increase with the logarithm of bits in the verified numerical range ($O(\log n)$), significantly reducing the cost of on-chain storage and network transfers.
- Efficient verification: The verification time is also logarithmic relation to the number of digits in the numerical range ($O(\log n)$), making the verification process fast and the computational overhead extremely low.
- Non-interactive: With the Fiat-Shamir transform, Bulletproofs can generate proofs independently, and $\mathcal{V}$ can complete verification independently without any communication with the $\mathcal{P}$. So the protocol is non-interactive.

Remark. We also have the following remark: in the proposed framework, the range proof step and the asset transfer is loosely coupled, the advantage lies in modularity where both steps can be instantiated by different concrete protocols. However, another design thinking is that these two steps can be integrated such that the range proof is embedded into the asset transfer process. For instance, in FairSwap, the range proof can be sent in the first round together with its original message. Designing such an protocol with provable security naturally forms an interesting extension.

7   Experiment and Analysis

In this section, we conduct experiments and perform analysis to demonstrate the efficacy and effectiveness of the proposed protocol.

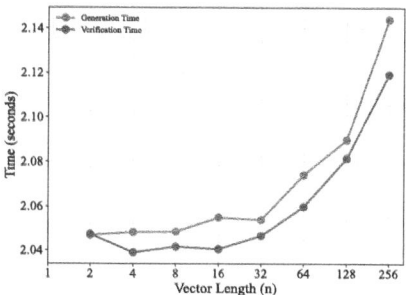

Fig. 3. Time cost of Bulletproofs

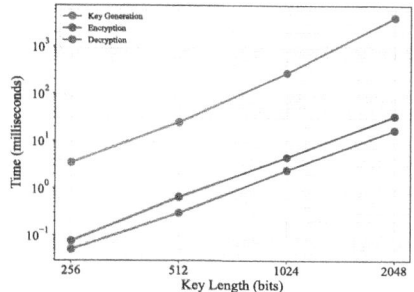

Fig. 4. Time cost of ElGamal operations

Experimental Environment. We deploy a four-node Hyperledger Fabric [24] network through docker on a cloud server to run experiments. Each node is allocated with 2 vCPU, 4 GB of memory. The host environment is a PC with Windows 10, Core(TM) i5-12400F CPU 2.50 GHz and 16 GB RAM. The chaincode code is implemented with Golang 1.19.11.

Experiment and Analysis. First, we test two performance metrics for different secret value bit vector lengths n, i.e., the time taken to generate off-chain proofs and pass them to on-chain storage, and the time to complete verification after obtaining proofs from on-chain. As depicted in Fig. 3, after excluding the basic communication time between nodes, the proof generation time shows a linear growth trend as n continues to increase, while the verification time shows a logarithmic growth. This asymmetric complexity highlights the excellent scalability of the protocol in the verification process, making it an efficient adaptation to blockchain application scenarios that require fast verification of large-scale data. Second, we simulate the performance of different key lengths of the ElGamal algorithm in the core link of the asset transfer phase, as shown in Fig. 4, increasing the key length would significantly increase the time consumption of the asset transfer process, and would also increase the system security level, which can balance efficiency and security requirements according to the actual supply chain scenario.

8   Conclusion

This paper proposes a solution to a critical challenge in the supply chain, i.e., achieving verifiability of promises without sacrificing business privacy. The proposed blockchain-based non-interactive zero-knowledge range proof protocol enables enterprises to prove their ability to meet transaction requirements while avoiding the exposure of sensitive data. It provides a concrete technical path to a more credible and efficient supply chain in the real world. Blockchain, acting as the underlying infrastructure, supports recording the proving activities, thus realizing traceability and accountability. Future research would focus on further optimized performance and expanding the coverage of verifiable attributes.

Acknowledgement. This work is supported by NSFC (No. 62302403).

References

1. Aceto, G., Persico, V., Pescapé, A.: A survey on information and communication technologies for industry 4.0: state-of-the-art, taxonomies, perspectives, and challenges. IEEE Commun. Surv. Tutor. **21**(4), 3467–3501 (2019)
2. Ajaero, T.K.: 30 Supply Chain Statistics to Keep in Mind in 2024. Procurement Tactics (2024)
3. Alikhani, P., Brunner, N., Crépeau, C., et al.: Experimental relativistic zero-knowledge proofs. Nature **599**, 47–50 (2021)
4. Alizadeh, R., Jokar, M.: Mathematical models and concepts for blockchain network design in supply chain. Comput. Ind. Eng. **204**, 111118 (2025)
5. Attema, T., Lyubashevsky, V., Seiler, G.: Practical product proofs for lattice commitments. In: Micciancio, D., Ristenpart, T. (eds.) CRYPTO 2020. LNCS, vol. 12171, pp. 470–499. Springer, Cham (2020). https://doi.org/10.1007/978-3-030-56880-1_17
6. Boneh, D., Fisch, B., Gabizon, A., Williamson, Z.: A simple range proof from polynomial commitments. Cryptology ePrint Archive, Report 2020/152 (2020)
7. Bünz, B., Bootle, J., Boneh, D., Poelstra, A., Wuille, P., Maxwell, G.: Bulletproofs: short proofs for confidential transactions and more. In: 2018 IEEE Symposium on Security and Privacy (SP), pp. 315–334. IEEE (2018)
8. Chalkias, K., Cohen, S., Lewi, K., Moezinia, F., Romailler, Y.: Hashwires: hyper-efficient credential-based range proofs. Proc. Priv. Enhancing Technol. **2021**(4), 76–95 (2021)
9. Chaum, D., Pedersen, T.P.: Wallet databases with observers. In: Brickell, E.F. (ed.) CRYPTO 1992. LNCS, vol. 740, pp. 89–105. Springer, Heidelberg (1993). https://doi.org/10.1007/3-540-48071-4_7
10. Chen, X., He, S., Sun, L., Zheng, Y., Wu, C.Q.: A survey of consortium blockchain and its applications. Cryptography **8**(2), 12 (2024)
11. Chopra, S., Meindl, P.: Supply Chain Management: Strategy, Planning, and Operation, 7th edn. Pearson (2019)
12. Christ, M., Baldimtsi, F., Chalkias, K., Maram, D., Roy, A., Wang, J.: SoK: Zero-knowledge range proofs. Technical Report 2024/430, Cryptology ePrint Archive (2024)
13. Du, M., Chen, Q., Xiao, J., Yang, H., Ma, X.: Supply chain finance innovation using blockchain. IEEE Trans. Eng. Manage. **67**(4), 1045–1058 (2020)
14. Dziembowski, S., Eckey, L., Faust, S.: FairSwap: how to fairly exchange digital goods. In: Proceedings of the 2018 ACM SIGSAC Conference on Computer and Communications Security (CCS), pp. 967–984. ACM (2018)
15. Gamal, T.E.: A public key cryptosystem and a signature scheme based on discrete logarithms. IEEE Trans. Inf. Theory **31**(4), 469–472 (1985)
16. Groth, J.: On the size of pairing-based non-interactive arguments. In: Fischlin, M., Coron, J.-S. (eds.) EUROCRYPT 2016. LNCS, vol. 9666, pp. 305–326. Springer, Heidelberg (2016). https://doi.org/10.1007/978-3-662-49896-5_11

17. He, S., et al.: Blockchain-based automated and robust cyber security management. J. Parallel Distrib. Comput. **163**, 62–82 (2022)
18. He, S., Lu, Y., Tang, Q., Wang, G., Wu, C.Q.: Blockchain-based P2P content delivery with monetary incentivization and fairness guarantee. IEEE Trans. Parallel Distrib. Syst. **34**(2), 746–765 (2022)
19. He, S., Lyu, X., Chu, D.: Legacy compatible and sybil resistant decentralized identity management for IoTs. In: International Conference on Blockchain, pp. 33–49. Springer (2024)
20. He, S., et al.: Secure and efficient agreement signing atop blockchain and decentralized identity. In: International Conference on Blockchain and Trustworthy Systems, pp. 3–17. Springer (2022)
21. He, S., Tang, Q., Wu, C.Q., Shen, X.: Decentralizing IoT management systems using blockchain for censorship resistance. IEEE Trans. Industr. Inf. **16**(1), 715–727 (2019)
22. Henrichs, E., Boller, M., Stolz, J., Krupitzer, C.: Quantum of trust: overview of blockchain technology for product authentication in food and pharmaceutical supply chains. Trends Food Sci. Technol. **157**, 104892 (2025)
23. Hu, Y., et al.: zkPoD: a practical decentralized system for data exchange. In: IEEE Symposium on Security and Privacy (SP), pp. 893–910. IEEE (2020)
24. IBM: Private and confidential transactions with hyperledger fabric. IBM developerWorks (2018)
25. Li, L., Huang, D., Zhang, C.: An efficient DAG blockchain architecture for IoT. IEEE Internet Things J. **10**(2), 1286–1296 (2023)
26. Li, W., et al.: CoralDB: a collaborative database for data sharing based on permissioned blockchain. IEEE Trans. Mob. Comput. **23**(9), 8886–8901 (2024)
27. Ma, C., Zhao, H., Zhang, K., Zhang, L., Huang, H.: A federated supply chain finance risk control method based on personalized differential privacy. Egypt. Inform. J. **31**, 100704 (2025)
28. Natanelov, V., Cao, S., Foth, M., Dulleck, U.: Blockchain smart contracts for supply chain finance: mapping the innovation potential in Australia-China beef supply chains. J. Ind. Inf. Integr. **30**, 100389 (2022)
29. Pagnia, H., Gärtner, F.: On the impossibility of fair exchange without a trusted third party. Technical Report TUD-BS-1999-02, Darmstadt University of Technology (1999)
30. Pibernik, R., Zhang, Y., Kerschbaum, F., Schröpfer, A.: Secure collaborative supply chain planning and inverse optimization – the JELS model. Eur. J. Oper. Res. **208**(1), 75–85 (2011)
31. Pradabwong, J., Braziotis, C., Pawar, K., Tannock, J.: Business process management and supply chain collaboration: a critical comparison. Logist. Res. **8**(1), 6 (2015)
32. Precedence Research: Supply Chain Management Market (By Component: Hardware, Software, Services; By Deployment: On-premise, Cloud-based) - Global Industry Analysis, Size, Share, Growth, Trends, Regional Outlook, and Forecast 2024–2034. Technical report, Precedence Research (2024)
33. Qader, G., Junaid, M., Abbas, Q., Mubarik, M.: Industry 4.0 enables supply chain resilience and supply chain performance. Technol. Forecast. Soc. Change **185**, 122026 (2022)
34. Sarfaraz, A., Chakrabortty, R., Essam, D.: AccessChain: an access control framework to protect data access in blockchain enabled supply chain. Futur. Gener. Comput. Syst. **148**, 380–394 (2023)

35. Shakhbulatov, D., Medina, J., Dong, Z., Rojas-Cessa, R.: How blockchain enhances supply chain management: a survey. IEEE Open J. Comput. Soc. **1**, 230–249 (2020)
36. Tang, X., et al.: Federated graph neural network for privacy-preserved supply chain data sharing. Appl. Soft Comput. **168**, 112475 (2025)
37. Wang, M., Guo, Y., Zhang, C., Wang, C., Huang, H., Jia, X.: MedShare: a privacy-preserving medical data sharing system by using blockchain. IEEE Trans. Serv. Comput. **16**(1), 438–451 (2023)
38. Xu, C., Qu, Y., Xiang, Y., Luan, T., Gao, L.: An optimized privacy-protected blockchain system for supply chain on internet of things. IEEE Internet Things J. **11**(5), 9019–9030 (2024)
39. Yan, Z., He, S., Wu, C., Hou, A.: Optimized deliverer selection in blockchain-based P2P content delivery networks. In: IEEE International Performance, Computing, and Communications Conference (IPCCC), pp. 1–8. IEEE (2024)
40. Zheng, P., et al.: Aeolus: distributed execution of permissioned blockchain transactions via state sharding. IEEE Trans. Industr. Inf. **18**(12), 9227–9238 (2022)

Regulated Blockchain Enabled Market for Internet of Things

Pengyu Liu[1], Enyuan Zhou[2(✉)], Song Guo[2], Zicong Hong[2], Wuhui Chen[3], and Bin Xiao[1]

[1] Hong Kong Polytechnic University Shenzhen Research Institute, Shenzhen, China
`b.xiao@polyu.edu.hk`
[2] Hong Kong University of Science and Technology, Hong Kong SAR, China
`{eyzhou,congcong}@ust.hk, songguo@cse.ust.hk`
[3] Sun Yat-sen University, Guangzhou, China
`chenwuh@mail.sysu.edu.cn`

Abstract. Trading is an effective way to exchange resources such as energy, data, and computing services between Internet of Things (IoT) for mutual benefit. The emerging blockchain-enabled market facilitates the transparency and traceability of trading, but poses new challenges to the financial stability of the market. The existing blockchain-enabled market framework is designed as a completely free market, and due to the inherent characteristics of blockchain, it is difficult to take effective measures to maintain financial stability. To address this challenge, we propose a regulated blockchain-enabled market framework for IoT devices. Based on the heterogeneous interacting agent theory in economics, we study the price dynamics and equilibrium in the market. We establish a trading smart contract that supports trading among IoT devices, and provides the market regulator with interfaces to adjust the regulatable factors in the market to promote financial stability. A prototype system of our framework is implemented in Ethereum. The experimental results demonstrate the low execution cost of the smart contract, the correctness of our theoretical analysis for the market, and the effectiveness of the regulatory policies.

Keywords: Blockchain enabled market · Financial stability · Market regulation · Smart contract · Internet of Things

1 Introduction

By connecting the devices and users with the "smart world", the Internet of Things (IoT) has attracted tremendous attention to its competitive advantages of reshaping various industries, such as autopilot, smart grid, natural language processing, and urban search and rescue [13, 21]. The IoT devices are often heterogeneous in many aspects, so there is often trading among them to exchange resources for mutual benefit. For example, for some IoT devices with limited

R. K. Shyamasundar et al. (Eds.): ICBC 2025, LNCS 16155, pp. 59–73, 2026.
https://doi.org/10.1007/978-3-032-06176-8_4

computational resources, the latency and battery consumption of task processing can be greatly improved by buying the offloading services from the edge servers (ESs) and then paying a certain amount of money to the ESs [19]. As another example, different IoT devices may be equipped with different sensors, then to get more types of data, the IoT devices will choose to trade with others [4]. However, in these markets, the transparency and traceability of transactions cannot be guaranteed if they are under the central control of the platform.

With the dramatic development of a blockchain technology supporting Turing-complete programming language named Ethereum [18], a large variety of blockchain enabled markets for IoT devices are emerging and gaining popularity, such as OpenSea[1] and Gridplus[2]. Compared with the traditional markets, these blockchain enabled markets have a lot of impressive characteristics owing to the underlying blockchain technology. One of the most impressive characteristics is that each user can create the *smart contracts* as some autonomous agents that execute the predefined code stored in the decentralized blockchain networks without any censorship or third-party interference [3]. Therefore, using the smart contracts, a lot of fair, transparent and autonomous auctioneers and exchanges can be created easily and then the commodities can be traded among the IoT devices in the blockchain enabled markets securely and automatically. Nowadays, many kinds of digital assets are being traded in these markets, such as CryptoKitties[3]. Some theoretical blockchain enabled market frameworks for IoT devices have been proposed recently, such as the blockchain enabled computation offloading service markets [10], the blockchain enabled energy markets [20] and the blockchain enabled data markets [11].

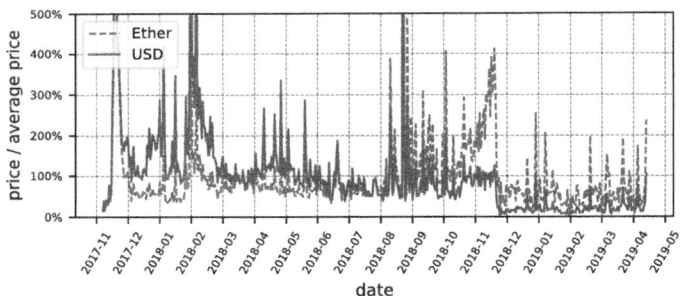

Fig. 1. Price dynamics of CryptoKitties in USD and Ether.

However, future commodity transactions using existing blockchain-enabled markets face significant price volatility risks. Figure 1 illustrates historical price dynamics of CryptoKitties, a popular blockchain commodity, showing dramatic

---

[1] https://opensea.io/.

[2] https://gridplus.io/.

[3] http://www.cryptokitties.co/.

fluctuations measured in both USD and Ether. Quantitatively, the Coefficient of Variation (CV) [1] from Nov. 2017 to May 2019 is 1.08 (USD) and 1.16 (Ether), significantly higher than that of most essential commodities (CV < 0.2) [14].

The substantial price volatility limits blockchain-enabled markets to speculative activities, deterring IoT devices due to uncertain purchasing power [8]. Conventional markets rely on government regulation and fiscal policy to maintain stability [5]; however, existing blockchain frameworks resist such interventions due to cryptocurrency issuance rules, unrestricted transaction validation, and anonymous identities hindering malicious speculator tracing. Consequently, governments are exploring technical approaches to enhance blockchain market stability [22].

To overcome the above challenges, we proposes a novel regulated blockchain-enabled market framework for IoT devices to promote financial stability. Based on the heterogeneous interacting agents theory in economics, we model the IoT buyers and IoT sellers in the market as some heterogeneous interacting agents. We study the price dynamics of the market, and then investigate the existence and uniqueness of the equilibrium of the price dynamics. The core of the proposed framework is a trading smart contract, which supports the trading among IoT devices and provides the market regulator with interfaces to adjust the regulatable factors in the market. Finally, the experimental results demonstrate the low execution cost of the trade smart contract. The simulation results show the correctness of our theoretical analysis for the market and the effectiveness of the market regulation. Our main contributions can be summarized as follows.

- We propose a regulated blockchain-enabled market framework for IoT devices. In the framework, a blockchain market adapter provides the IoT devices with an interface to connect the IoT commodities and the blockchain, and a trading smart contract provides the trading functionality for the upper IoT devices while maintaining the advantages of the underlying blockchain, i.e., non-tampering and non-repudiation.
- To analyze the dynamics and equilibrium of the market, we formulate the market as a heterogeneous interacting agent model and then transform it into a deterministic process. We analyze the existence and uniqueness of the equilibrium in the deterministic process and study the asymptotically stable condition for the equilibrium.
- We verify the feasibility of the proposed framework by implementing a prototype system in the Ethereum platform. The experimental study shows the low execution cost of the proposed smart contract. The simulation study demonstrates the correctness of our theoretical analysis, the financial stability of the market, and the effectiveness of the proposed regulation policies.

2   Related Work

There have been many works about the market for different kinds of resources among IoT devices. They mainly focus on the design of efficient resource exchang-

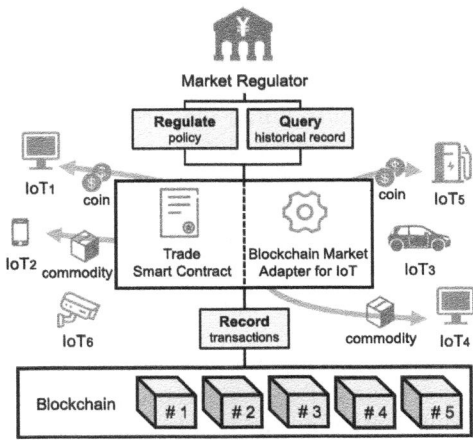

Fig. 2. Regulated blockchain enabled market model for IoT devices.

ing mechanism. For the trading of computing resource, Tan *et al.* [15] designed a computing resource coordination model that utilizes smart contracts to allocate the idle resources of full nodes to multiple services at the network edge. Zhou *et al.* [17] proposed a cooperative demand response management framework aimed at enhancing resource synergy. For the trading of data, Bi *et al.* [2] investigated the trading problem of a data market with heterogeneous roles and proposed a mechanism that employs game theory to coordinate transactions, particularly in the context of data pricing. However, these markets either do not consider the security problem for trading or assume that the trading platforms are absolutely reliable.

Blockchain [18] is a promising technique to guarantee the transparency and traceability of transactions in the market, which hastens the birth of a new market paradigm named blockchain enabled market for IoT devices. Wang *et al.* [16] proposed the implementation of a collaborative offloading CRS framework leveraging blockchain and edge computing technologies. Lorenzo *et al.* [7] design a decentralized IoT market architecture to decouple data sources, and ensure the efficient exchange of high-quality resources. In the above blockchain enabled markets, a centralized, reliable platform is no longer needed and the security problem can be solved.

But all the previous blockchain enabled markets for IoT devices are designed as completely free markets and unabled to take effective regulation measures, which make the financial stability of the market become a challenge. Many regulators and governments seek for methods to regulate the blockchain enabled market and reinforce its financial stability, such as the UK Treasury and US Financial Stability Oversight Council. Our idea is based on the heterogeneous interacting agent theory in economics proposed in [6].

3   Blockchain Enabled Market Framework for IoT Devices

3.1   System Overview

Figure 2 illustrates our blockchain enabled market framework for IoT devices. The framework runs on a smart contract enabled blockchain and consists of two major components, i.e., an off-chain *blockchain market adapter* and an on-chain *trade smart contract*. The blockchain market adapter provides the IoT devices with an interface to connect IoT commodities and the blockchain, which enables commodities be traded in the form of digital assets. For example, we consider three most common IoT commodities and sum up the usual functions of the adapter in Table 1.

Table 1. Blockchain market adapter for IoT commodities.

Commodity	Function of Blockchain Market Adapter
computing service	virtual machine interface
data	metadata
energy	smart meter

In the market, each IoT device possesses a certain amount of *coins* which are the cryptocurrency on this blockchain and can be used for trading among the IoT devices. Besides the IoT devices, there exists a *market regulator* in the framework. Its aim is to regulate the market for financial stability. Often, the government or the bank can act as the role.

All tradings in the framework are based on the trade smart contract and the detailed procedure of the trade smart contract will be described in next section. We here introduce its four characteristics as follows.

- It is created by the market regulator and its parameters can only be adjusted by the market regulator.
- In each time slot, the trade smart contract will be activated once and begin an auction among IoT devices.
- The rule of the trade smart contract is written in the blockchain thus it is non-repudiation and non-tampering.
- The operations of the trade smart contract and the policies adopted by the market regulator are open and transparent.

3.2   System Model

We define the IoT devices possessing some commodities as sellers $\mathbf{S}$ and the IoT devices intending to buy commodities as buyers $\mathbf{B}$. The number of the buyers and sellers are $|\mathbf{B}|$ and $|\mathbf{S}|$. The ratio between the sellers and buyers is $\chi = \frac{|\mathbf{S}|}{|\mathbf{B}|}$. The full set consisting of sellers and buyers is $\mathbf{F} = \mathbf{S} \cup \mathbf{B}$ and the number of it is $|\mathbf{F}|$. The coins owned by IoT buyer $i \in \mathbf{B}$ is defined as w_i. Although the wealth of each individual buyer may increase or decrease over time, our analysis focuses

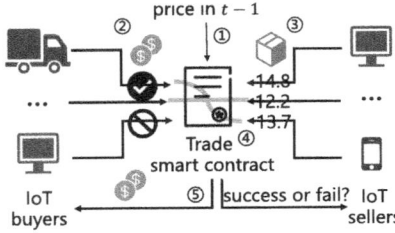

Fig. 3. Procedure of auction for trading in time slot t.

on a relatively short period (e.g. several months), thus the distribution of wealth $f_w(x)$ among the buyers can be approximately considered to stay unchanged. In other words, w_i can be seen as a positive random variable with probability density function (PDF) $f_w(x)$.

The whole time $\mathbf{T}$ of the market is divided into many equal time slots, i.e., $\mathbf{T} = \{1, 2, \cdots, t-1, t, t+1, \cdots, T\}$. Each time slot corresponds to some block intervals in the blockchain, which can be preset in the smart contract by the market regulator. In each time slot t, the set of transactions denotes $\mathbf{R}_t$ and the price of transaction $i \in \mathbf{R}_t$ denotes $\mathbf{P}_t^i$. We define the *market price* in t as $\mathbf{P}_t = \frac{1}{|\mathbf{R}_t|} \sum_{i \in \mathbf{R}_t} \mathbf{P}_t^i$.

The auction organized by the trade smart contract consists of five stages and their detailed procedures follow.

First, in time slot t, the trade smart contract will set a *front money price* based on the historical price in $t-1$ (procedure 1) as shown in Fig. 3. The rule of setting depends on the market regulator. Here we define the rule is a continuous function $r : R^+ \to R^+$ named *front money function* and $r(0) = 0$, thus the front money price in time slot t is $r(\mathbf{P}_{t-1})$.

Second, for the entrance of the auction, an IoT buyer should transmit some coins with the amount equal to the front money price to the trade smart contract (procedure 2). After entering the auction, the buyer becomes a *potential buyer*. The set of potential buyers in time slot t is defined as $\mathbf{B}_t$. Based on the distribution of wealth $f_w(x)$, given $\mathbf{P}_{t-1} = \mathbf{p}_{t-1}$, the number of potential buyers $|\mathbf{B}_t|$ follows a binomial distribution, i.e., $|\mathbf{B}_t| \sim B(|\mathbf{B}|, \mathbf{q}_t^b(\mathbf{p}_{t-1}))$, where the probability for each IoT buyer to become a potential buyer is

$$\mathbf{q}_t^b(\mathbf{p}_{t-1}) = \int_{[r(\mathbf{p}_{t-1}), +\infty)} f_w(x)dx. \tag{1}$$

Third, before the IoT sellers give their ask price, they can check the history record from the past blocks in the blockchain, such as price, participant, and so forth. Next, each seller will give its ask price to the trade smart contract (procedure 3). For the bidding behaviors of the IoT sellers, we adopt a method from the market model in [12]. The bid price of seller $i \in \mathbf{S}$ in time slot t is defined as $\mathbf{A}_t^i = u_i \mathbf{P}_{t-1} \mathbf{D}_{t-1}$. u_i, a random variable with PDF $h(x)$ and CDF $H(x)$, denotes IoT seller i's subjective judgment of the market. $\mathbf{P}_{t-1}$

is the historical price in $t-1$. $\mathbf{D}_{t-1}$ is a *demand function* in $t-1$ representing the memory of the IoT sellers for history records about the market. It is defined as $\mathbf{D}_t = (\mathbf{D}_{t-1})^w \exp(m\frac{|\mathbf{B}_t|-|\mathbf{S}_t|}{|\mathbf{F}|})$, where $w \in [0,1)$ and $m > 0$ denote memory decay parameter and demand sensitivity parameter, respectively. A larger memory decay parameter w means the sellers attach more importance to the historical demand. A larger demand sensitivity parameter m means the sellers will react sharply to the supply and demand.

Forth, only the sellers with a bid price lower than the front money price can be taken into account by the buyers. Therefore, the trade smart contract will match the buyers with these sellers randomly (procedure 4). If the bid price of seller i is less than the front money price, i.e. $\mathbf{A}_t^i < r(\mathbf{P}_{t-1})$, seller i can enter the auction and become a *potential seller*. The number of potential sellers $|\mathbf{S}_t|$ follows a binomial distribution, i.e., $|\mathbf{S}_t| \sim B(|\mathbf{S}|, \mathbf{q}_t^s(\mathbf{p}_{t-1}, \mathbf{d}_{t-1}))$, where the probability for each seller to become potential seller is

$$\mathbf{q}_t^s(\mathbf{p}_{t-1}, \mathbf{d}_{t-1}) = H(\frac{r(\mathbf{p}_{t-1})}{\mathbf{p}_{t-1}\mathbf{d}_{t-1}}). \tag{2}$$

Furthermore, there may exist some buyers that fail to be matched when demand exceeds supply or exist some sellers that fail to be matched when supply exceeds demand. When demand exceeds supply, the trade smart contract will return the change to the successful buyers and return the front money to the failed buyers (procedure 5). Meantime, the trade smart contract will also inform the sellers about the matching result (procedure 5).

For the auction process in time slot t, if a buyer can be matched successfully, we call it as a *successful buyer*. The set of successful buyers in t is denoted by $\mathbf{B}_t^{su}$. The *successful sellers* can be defined in a similar way and the set of successful sellers in t is denoted by $\mathbf{S}_t^{su}$. Because the match between potential sellers and potential buyers is one-to-one, the number of successful sellers equals to the number of successful buyers, i.e., $|\mathbf{R}_t| = |\mathbf{B}_t^{su}| = |\mathbf{S}_t^{su}| = \min\{|\mathbf{B}_t|, |\mathbf{S}_t|\}$.

4 Dynamic and Equilibrium for Market

The state of market in t can be denoted as $\mathbf{M}_t = (\mathbf{P}_t, \mathbf{D}_t)$ and the dynamic of market state for the whole time $\mathbf{T}$ can be denoted as a stochastic process $\mathbf{M} = \{\mathbf{M}_1, \mathbf{M}_2, \cdots, \mathbf{M}_T\}$ with the following properties.

Theorem 1. *In each time slot t, given the market price in time slot $t-1$ $\mathbf{p}_{t-1}$ and the demand function in time slot $t-1$ $\mathbf{d}_{t-1}$, i.e., $\mathbf{M}_{t-1} = (\mathbf{p}_{t-1}, \mathbf{d}_{t-1})$, we can get*

$$\log \mathbf{D}_t \xrightarrow[|\mathbf{F}| \to +\infty]{P} E_{t-1}(\log \mathbf{D}_t), \tag{3}$$

$$\mathbf{P}_t \xrightarrow[|\mathbf{F}| \to +\infty]{P} E_{t-1}(\mathbf{P}_t), \tag{4}$$

where $\xrightarrow[|\mathbf{F}|\to+\infty]{P}$ means convergence in probability and $E_{t-1}(\cdot)$ denotes the expected value conditional on $\mathbf{M}_{t-1} = (\mathbf{p}_{t-1}, \mathbf{d}_{t-1})$, i.e., $E_{t-1}(\cdot) = E(\cdot|\mathbf{M}_{t-1} = (\mathbf{p}_{t-1}, \mathbf{d}_{t-1}))$.

According to Theorem 1, as the number of IoT buyers and IoT sellers increases, the stochastic process of the market can be described by the following deterministic process

$$
\begin{cases}
\mathbf{p}_t = \mathbf{p}_{t-1} \int_{[0, \frac{r(\mathbf{p}_{t-1})}{\mathbf{p}_{t-1}}]} (1 - \dfrac{H(\frac{x}{\mathbf{d}_{t-1}})}{\mathbf{q}_t^s(\mathbf{p}_{t-1}, \mathbf{d}_{t-1})}) dx, \\[4mm]
\mathbf{d}_t = (\mathbf{d}_{t-1})^w \exp(\frac{m}{1+\chi}(\mathbf{q}_t^b(\mathbf{p}_{t-1}) - \chi\mathbf{q}_t^s(\mathbf{p}_{t-1}, \mathbf{d}_{t-1}))),
\end{cases}
\tag{5}
$$

which has the following properties.

Property 1. *If the ratio between IoT sellers and IoT buyers χ is kept constant, no matter how many sellers and buyers in the market, its deterministic process will be same.*

Property 2. *If the front money price in t is less than the market price in $t-1$, then the market price in t will be less than the market price in $t-1$, i.e., $r(\mathbf{p}_{t-1}) < \mathbf{p}_{t-1} \Rightarrow \mathbf{p}_t < \mathbf{p}_{t-1}$.*

Proof. Because $r(x) > 0$, $H(x)$ is CDF and $\mathbf{q}_t^s(\mathbf{p}_{t-1}, \mathbf{d}_{t-1})$ is probability, we can get that $\int_{[0, \frac{r(\mathbf{p}_{t-1})}{\mathbf{p}_{t-1}}]} \frac{H(\frac{x}{\mathbf{d}_{t-1}})}{\mathbf{q}_t^s(\mathbf{p}_{t-1}, \mathbf{d}_{t-1})} dx > 0$. Therefore, if $r(\mathbf{p}_{t-1}) < \mathbf{p}_{t-1}$, we can get that $\frac{r(\mathbf{p}_{t-1})}{\mathbf{p}_{t-1}} < 1$. The following inequations also hold

$$
\int_{[0, \frac{r(\mathbf{p}_{t-1})}{\mathbf{p}_{t-1}}]} \frac{H(\frac{x}{\mathbf{d}_{t-1}})}{\mathbf{q}_t^s(\mathbf{p}_{t-1}, \mathbf{d}_{t-1})} dx > 0 > \frac{r(\mathbf{p}_{t-1})}{\mathbf{p}_{t-1}} - 1
$$

$$
\int_{[0, \frac{r(\mathbf{p}_{t-1})}{\mathbf{p}_{t-1}}]} (1 - \frac{H(\frac{x}{\mathbf{d}_{t-1}})}{\mathbf{q}_t^s(\mathbf{p}_{t-1}, \mathbf{d}_{t-1})}) dx < 1
\tag{6}
$$

$$
\mathbf{p}_{t-1} \int_{[0, \frac{r(\mathbf{p}_{t-1})}{\mathbf{p}_{t-1}}]} (1 - \frac{H(\frac{x}{\mathbf{d}_{t-1}})}{\mathbf{q}_t^s(\mathbf{p}_{t-1}, \mathbf{d}_{t-1})}) dx < \mathbf{p}_{t-1}
$$

$$
\mathbf{p}_t < \mathbf{p}_{t-1}.
$$

To avoid price fluctuation, the market regulator aims at regulating the market into an equilibrium, i.e., $\mathbf{m}^* = (\mathbf{p}^*, \mathbf{d}^*)$, and keeps it under a stable state.

Theorem 2. *If*

- $r(x) \geq x$ *for all* $x > 0$,
- $\lim_{y \to 0} \frac{yh(y)}{H(y)} > \frac{x}{r(x)-x}$ *for all* $x > 0$ *and*
- $\frac{H(y)\int_{[0,y]} xh(x)dx - yh(y)\int_{[0,y]} H(x)dx}{(H(y))^2} > 0$ *for all* $y > 0$,

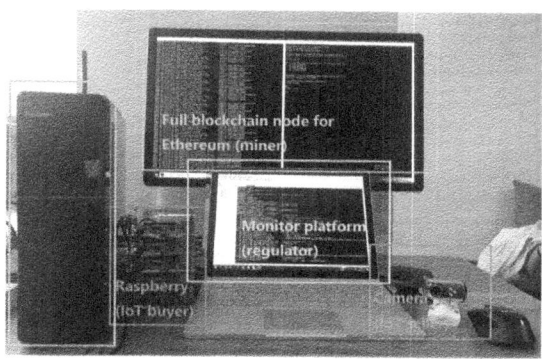

Fig. 4. Prototype system for regulated blockchain enabled market framework for IoT devices.

then there exists a unique $\mathbf{d}^*$ *such that when the demand function in* $t-1$ *equals to* $\mathbf{d}^*$, *the market price in* t *will be same as the market price in* $t-1$, *i.e.,* $\mathbf{d}_{t-1} = \mathbf{d}^* \Rightarrow \mathbf{p}_t = \mathbf{p}_{t-1} = \mathbf{p}^*$.

Next, if $\mathbf{d}^* = (\mathbf{d}^*)^w \exp(\frac{m}{\chi+1}(\mathbf{q}_t^b(\mathbf{p}^*) - \chi\mathbf{q}_t^s(\mathbf{p}^*, \mathbf{d}^*)))$ holds, the deterministic process has an equilibrium $(\mathbf{p}^*, \mathbf{d}^*)$.

Theorem 3. *The equilibrium* $(\mathbf{p}^*, \mathbf{d}^*)$ *is stable if and only if the absolute value of all the eigenvalues are less than 1, i.e.,* $|\frac{\mathcal{A}\pm\sqrt{\mathcal{A}^2-4\mathcal{B}}}{2}| < 1$, *where*

$$\mathcal{A} = 1 + \mathbf{p}^*\mathcal{P}'_{\mathbf{p}}(\mathbf{p}^*, \mathbf{d}^*) + w - \mathbf{d}^* \frac{m\chi}{\chi+1}\mathbf{q}_{t\,\mathbf{d}}^{s\prime}(\mathbf{p}^*, \mathbf{d}^*)$$

and

$$\mathcal{B} = (1 + \mathbf{p}^*\mathcal{P}'_{\mathbf{p}}(\mathbf{p}^*, \mathbf{d}^*))(w - \mathbf{d}^* \frac{m\chi}{\chi+1}\mathbf{q}_{t\,\mathbf{d}}^{s\prime}(\mathbf{p}^*, \mathbf{d}^*))$$

$$- \mathbf{p}^*\mathcal{P}'_{\mathbf{d}}(\mathbf{p}^*, \mathbf{d}^*)\mathbf{d}^*m(\frac{1}{\chi+1}(\mathbf{q}_t^b(\mathbf{p}^*))' - \frac{\chi}{\chi+1}\mathbf{q}_{t\,\mathbf{p}}^{s\prime}(\mathbf{p}^*, \mathbf{d}^*)).$$

5 Prototype Implementation and Evaluation

5.1 Prototype Implementation

According to the design of our regulated blockchain enabled market framework, we implement a prototype system on the Ethereum[4]. As shown in Fig. 4, the prototype includes a Dell Inspiron desktop computer to support the running of Ethereum, a Surface Book 2 laptop to monitor and manage the whole system and two cameras and five Raspberry Pi 3 Model B with a 1.2 GHz quard-core ARM Cortex-A53 CPU as IoT devices. On each machine, an Ethereum

---

[4] https://ethereum.org/.

Table 2. The gas cost of the interfaces in the trade smart contract when there are 20 buyers and 5 sellers.

Role	Interface	Transaction Cost (Gas)	Execution Cost (Gas)	Total Cost (Gas)	Total Cost ($)
Market Regulator	Create	2803793	2115045	4918838	22.1348
	AddBuyer	71703	49023	120726	0.5433
	AddSeller	106567	83887	190454	0.8570
	RemoveBuyer	28988	6308	35296	0.1588
	RemoveSeller	29362	6682	36044	0.1622
	AdjustFrontMoney	27466	5810	33276	0.1497
	Auction	241620	280348	521968	2.3488
Buyer	CheckFrontMoney	22481	1209	23690	0.1066
	PayFrontMoney	28859	7587	36446	0.1640
Seller	CheckMarketPrice	22448	1048	23496	0.1057
	CheckBuyerNum	22115	715	22830	0.1027
	CheckSellerNum	22335	935	23270	0.1047
	Bid	49417	27953	77370	0.3482

Go client named Geth, is installed to set up the Ethereum nodes, create Ethereum accounts, deploy smart contracts. We use Python 3.6 to implement the blockchain market adapter for IoT data, i.e., photos taken by the cameras. The adapter can extract the metadata of IoT data, such as location, time and hash of data etc., which will be recorded into the transactions of blockchain.

In the prototype, the coins are implemented based on ERC20, a cryptocurrency standard including basic functionalities (transfer and approve). There are three roles in the protocol, i.e., IoT buyers, IoT sellers and the market regulator. Each of them has a unique address for identification. Based on the address, the trade smart contract can restrict the specified role to interact the certain interfaces. The interfaces own by each role and their detailed functionality are described as follows. The interfaces are in italic type.

1) The market regulator plays a guiding role in the market. At the beginning of the market, it can create a trade smart contract via *Create(interval, initPrice)* where the parameter *interval* is the number of blocks in the blockchain for each time slot and *initPrice* is the initial price preset by the regulator. The regulator can regulate the market via two kinds of interfaces. The first kind includes *AddBuyer(addr)*, *AddSeller(addr)*, *RemoveBuyer(addr)* and *RemoveSeller(addr)* where *addr* indicates the address of a specified buyer (or seller). They can be used for the management of the number of buyers and sellers in the market. The second kind is *AdjustFrontMoney(fmFunc)* where *fmFunc* indicates the front money function to be used as a replacement. In each time slot, the market regulator can use *Auction()* to start the auction.
2) The IoT buyers need to use *CheckFrontMoney()* to check the front money price given by the trade smart contract and then transmit the equal coins via *PayFrontMoney()* to the trade smart contract for the entrance of the auction.
3) Before bidding, the IoT sellers can check the historical record about market price via *CheckMarketPrice*(ID) and number of buyers and sellers via *CheckBuyerNum(ID)* and *CheckSellerNum(ID)*, where *ID* is a unique identification

indicating an auction. Based on the record and its own judgment, an IoT seller bids its ask price via *Bid(price)*.

5.2 Experimental Study

In order to demonstrate the overhead of the trade smart contract on the blockchain, we deploy it in a test net of Ethereum. The cost of setting up and executing the trade smart contract is shown in Table 2. The gas cost is converted into the dollars by using an exchange rate of 1 Gas $\approx 2*10^{-9}$ Ether and 1 Ether $\approx \$139$ in January 2020. The execution cost is the cost of computational operations in EVM, the other cost is the cost of sending data to the blockchain, and the transaction cost is the sum of them.

According to Table 2, we can get that the cost for most interfaces is about $0.1, such as all *Check* operations and *Remove* operations. It is because they do not need additional memory space and complex computation. Although the cost of *Create* is about $22 which is high, it will only be invoked once in the whole life of the market because the trade smart contract will be created once and can be reused for many times. In addition to *Create*, the cost of *Auction* is $2.3488 higher than most other interfaces, because it needs to match the buyers and sellers and record some details of the auction such as the price and number of participants. However, if the simplest smart contract-based auction (first price auction) given by official reference of Solidity is used to accomplish the same goal (20 buyers and 5 sellers), according to our test, it will cost $0.4823 for the creation of the smart contract and $2.5265 for each auction. The cost for each auction in this smart contract and our trade smart contract are similar. In conclusion, the overhead for executing the trade smart contract on the Ethereum network is low, which demonstrates the practicality of the trade smart contract.

6 Simulation

To simulate the proposed regulated market, we first define all distributions in our model based on some common distributions in economics as follows. Note that the parameters of the following distributions are not fixed and can be easily adjusted depending on the actual market.

The log-normal distribution outperforms in the description of distribution of wealth for many countries [9], thus the distribution of wealth among the IoT buyers in our market also follows a log-normal distribution, i.e., $f_w(x) = \frac{1}{x\sigma\sqrt{2\pi}} \exp\left(-\frac{(\ln x - \mu)^2}{2\sigma^2}\right)$ where $\mu = 0.8$, $\sigma = 0.6$. We assume that the subjective judgment of IoT seller i follows a Dagum distribution, i.e., $h(x) = \frac{ap}{x}\left(\frac{(\frac{x}{b})^{ap}}{((\frac{x}{b})^a+1)^{p+1}}\right)$ and $H(x) = (1 + (\frac{x}{b})^{-a})^{-p}$ where $a = 15$, $b = 1$ and $p = 5$. Based on the library Scipy[5] in Python, we can get that $\lim_{y \to 0} \frac{yh(y)}{H(y)} = 75$ and

---

[5] https://www.scipy.org/.

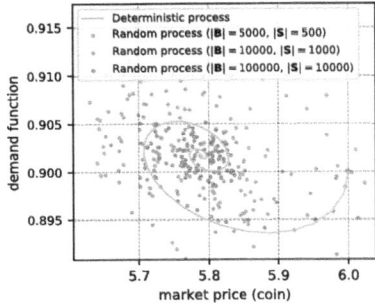

Fig. 5. Random process with different number of sellers and buyers vs deterministic process. (Color figure online)

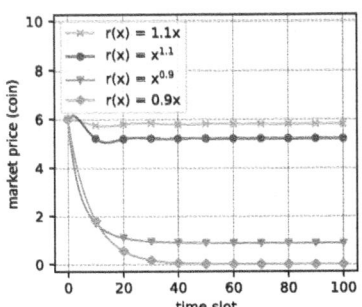

Fig. 6. Market price dynamics for different front money function $r(x)$.

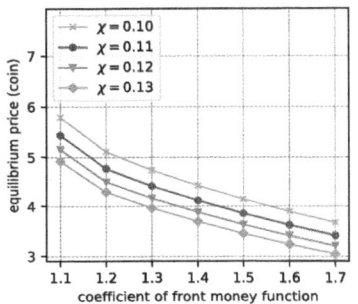

Fig. 7. Equilibrium price vs ratio of sellers and buyers & coefficient of front money function.

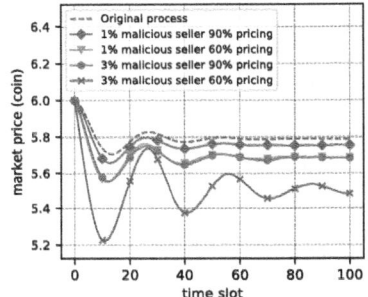

Fig. 8. Price dynamics with malicious sellers with low pricing strategy.

$\frac{\int_{[0,y]}(xh(x)-yh(y))dx}{H(y)} + \frac{yh(y)\int_{[0,y]}(H(y)-H(x))dx}{(H(y))^2} > 0$ for all $y > 0$. According to Theorem 2, there exists a unique $\mathbf{d}^*$ such that $\mathbf{d}_{t-1} = \mathbf{d}^* \Rightarrow \mathbf{p}_t = \mathbf{p}_{t-1} = \mathbf{p}^*$. For the demand function, the memory decay parameter w is set as 0.6 and the demand sensitivity parameter m is set as 0.8.

Figure 5 illustrates the price and demand function over time for the deterministic process and stochastic process with the different number of IoT buyers and IoT sellers. In the market, the front money function is defined as $r(x) = 1.1x$ and the ratio between sellers and buyers χ remains at 0.1. First, according to Property 1, if the ratio χ remains the same, no matter how many buyers and sellers in the market, its deterministic process will be also same. In Fig. 5, the orange line denotes the deterministic processes of all three random processes. Second, according to Theorem 1, as the number of buyers and sellers increases, the stochastic process of the market can be described by the deterministic process better. In Fig. 5, the points with different color denote random processes with a different number of buyers and sellers. The figure shows that the distribution of

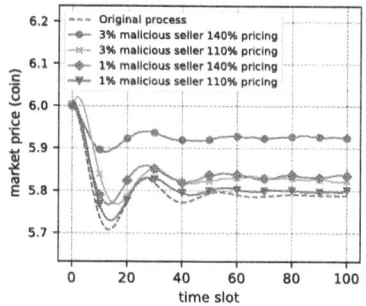

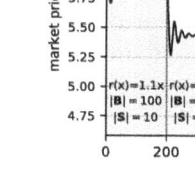

Fig. 9. Price dynamics with malicious sellers with high pricing strategy.

Fig. 10. Market regulation about front money function $r(x)$ & ratio of IoT sellers and IoT buyers χ.

random process with the most number of sellers and buyers (denoted by the blue points) is the closest to the orange lines, followed by the red points, the green points are the worst. In summary, Property 1 and Theorem 1 can be confirmed according to Fig. 5.

Figure 6 illustrates the price dynamics for four different front money function. According to Property 2, if the front money price in t is less than the market price in $t-1$, the market price in t must be less than the market price in $t-1$. Note that Property 2 is only a sufficient condition. From the figure, we can see that when $r(x) = 0.9$, the price will decrease to 0, because $0.9x < x$ holds for all $x > 0$. When $r(x) = x^{0.9}$, from 6 to 1, the price keep decreasing because $x^{0.9} < x$ holds for all $x > 1$. However, for $r(x) = 1.1x$, $r(x) > x$ holds for all $x > 0$ and for $r(x) = x^{1.1}$, $r(x) > x$ holds for all $x > 1$, thus the price in them can not only increase but also decrease. In summary, Property 2 can be confirmed based on Fig. 6.

Figure 7 illustrates the equilibrium price under different front money functions $r(x)$ and various IoT seller-buyer ratios χ. As indicated in Table 2, both factors are adjustable by the market regulator. Here, we assume a linear front money function $r(x) = kx$, where k is the front money coefficient. The figure demonstrates that as k increases, the equilibrium price decreases. This occurs because a higher k reduces the number of potential buyers while increasing the number of potential sellers, as described in (1) and (2). This shift weakens overall demand, leading to lower prices. Moreover, when χ decreases, the equilibrium price rises, as fewer sellers or a larger pool of buyers intensifies demand. In summary, a higher front money coefficient suppresses prices, whereas a lower seller-buyer ratio drives them upward.

In real-world markets, a small fraction of malicious sellers may bid significantly above or below the market price for personal gain, jeopardizing financial stability. To examine market adaptation to such behaviors, we introduce malicious sellers and design their pricing strategy. In the legends of Fig. 8 and Fig. 9, the first percentage indicates the proportion of malicious sellers, while the second represents their bid price relative to the market price. As shown in Fig. 8, low-priced bids drive the market price down, whereas in Fig. 9, high-priced bids push it up. However, when malicious sellers constitute only 1% or their pricing deviates by 10%, the market remains largely stable. Significant price disruption occurs only when 3% of sellers are malicious and their pricing deviates by 40%.

Figure 10 illustrates market regulation through adjustments to the front money function $r(x)$ and the seller-buyer ratio χ. The process unfolds in five stages:

- Initial State: The regulator sets $r(x) = 1.1x$ and $\chi = 0.1$. The market reaches equilibrium after 200 time slots.
- Supply Increase: Raising χ boosts supply, lowering the price to 5.45 coins (200–400 time slots).
- Supply Decrease: Lowering χ reduces supply, raising the price to 6.25 coins (400–600 time slots).
- Demand Suppression: Adjusting $r(x)$ to $1.3x$ discourages buyers and increases sellers, decreasing the price to 5.2 coins (600–800 time slots).
- Demand Stimulation: Adjusting $r(x)$ to $1.2x$ encourages buyers and reduces sellers, raising the price to 5.6 coins (800+ time slots).

The regulator guides market trends rather than controlling exact prices, achieving regulation through these adjustments.

7   Conclusion

In this paper, we propose a regulated blockchain-enabled market framework for IoT devices, modeled as a heterogeneous interacting agent system. We show that as the number of devices increases, the model's stochastic behavior converges to a deterministic process. We analyze equilibrium existence, uniqueness, and stability. A prototype implementation on Ethereum demonstrates low execution costs, confirming practicality. Simulation results validate our theoretical analysis and regulation effectiveness. Future work includes maximizing social profit while ensuring financial stability.

Acknowledgments. This work is partially supported by the National Key R&D Program of China (No.2023YFB2703600) and NSFC/RGC Collaborative Research (62461160332, CRS HKUST602/24).

References

1. Abdi, H.: Coefficient of variation. Encycl. Res. Des. **1**, 169–171 (2010)
2. Bi, Y., Wu, Y., Liu, J., Ren, K., Xiong, L.: When data pricing meets non-cooperative game theory. In: 2024 IEEE 40th International Conference on Data Engineering (ICDE), pp. 5548–5559. IEEE (2024)

3. Buterin, V., et al.: A next-generation smart contract and decentralized application platform. White paper (2014)
4. Cao, X., Chen, Y., Liu, K.J.R.: Data trading with multiple owners, collectors, and users: an iterative auction mechanism. IEEE Trans. Signal Inf. Process. Netw. **3**(2), 268–281 (2017)
5. Easterly, W., Rebelo, S.: Fiscal policy and economic growth. J. Monet. Econ. **32**(3), 417–458 (1993)
6. Gao, J., Zhang, W., Guan, T., Feng, Q., Mardani, A.: The effect of manufacturing agent heterogeneity on enterprise innovation performance and competitive advantage in the era of digital transformation. J. Bus. Res. **155**, 113387 (2023)
7. Gigli, L., Zyrianoff, I., Montori, F., Aguzzi, C., Roffia, L., Di Felice, M.: A decentralized oracle architecture for a blockchain-based iot global market. IEEE Commun. Mag. **61**(8), 86–92 (2023)
8. Kiviat, T.I.: Beyond bitcoin: issues in regulating blockchain tranactions. Duke LJ **65**, 569 (2015)
9. Kleiber, C., Kotz, S.: Statistical Size Distributions in Economics and Actuarial Sciences, vol. 470. John Wiley & Sons, Hoboken (2003)
10. Lin, B., Chen, X., Chen, X., Ma, Y., Xiong, N.N.: Sgcs: an intelligent stackelberg game-based computation offloading and resource pricing scheme in blockchain-enabled mec for iiot. IEEE Internet Things J. (2024)
11. Liu, K., Chen, W., Zheng, Z., Li, Z., Liang, W.: A novel debt-credit mechanism for blockchain based data-trading in internet of vehicles. IEEE Internet Things J. (2019)
12. de Oliveira Antunes, M., de Almeida Prado, F.: A housing price dynamics model using heterogeneous interacting agents. SIAM J. Appl. Math. **78**(5), 2648–2671 (2018)
13. Rivkin, D., et al.: Aiot smart home via autonomous llm agents. IEEE Internet Things J. (2024)
14. Rural and Environment Analytical Services (REAS) Scotland: risk and risk management strategies in agriculture: an overview of the evidence (2010)
15. Tan, J., Shi, J., Wan, J., Dai, H.N., Jin, J., Zhang, R.: Blockchain-based data security and sharing for resource-constrained devices in manufacturing IoT. IEEE Internet Things J. **11**(15), 25558–25567 (2024)
16. Wang, D., Du, X., Zhang, H., Wang, Q.: Blockchain enabled credible computing resource sharing: a multi-leader multi-follower stackelberg game approach. IEEE Trans. Veh. Technol. (2024)
17. Wang, K., et al.: Embedding p2p transaction into demand response exchange: a cooperative demand response management framework for ies. Appl. Energy **367**, 123319 (2024)
18. Wood, G.: Ethereum: a secure decentralised generalised transaction ledger. Ethereum Proj. Yellow Paper **151**, 1–32 (2014)
19. Wu, J., et al.: Fairness-aware budgeted edge server placement for connected autonomous vehicles. IEEE Trans. Mob. Comput. (2025)
20. Zhang, P., et al.: Toward a blockchain-based, reputation-aware secure transactive energy market. Blockchains **2**(1), 61–78 (2024)
21. Zhang, Z., et al.: Vulnerability of machine learning approaches applied in IoT-based smart grid: a review. IEEE Internet Things J. **11**(11), 18951–18975 (2024)
22. Ølnes, S., Ubacht, J., Janssen, M.: Blockchain in government: benefits and implications of distributed ledger technology for information sharing. Gov. Inf. Q. **34**(3), 355–364 (2017)

Useful Proof of Work Consensus for Efficient Route Planning as Block Mining

Yiheng Jiang[1,2], Yuwei Le[2], Rui Jiang[1,2], Xiaoyang Zhou[3], and Jiaheng Wang[1,2(✉)]

[1] National Mobile Communications Research Laboratories, Southeast University, Nanjing 210096, China
{cyluo,ruijiang,jhwang}@seu.edu.cn
[2] Purple Mountain Laboratories, Nanjing 211100, China
yueyuwei@pmlabs.com.cn
[3] China Mobile Zijin (Jiangsu) Innovation Research Institute Company Ltd., Nanjing 210023, China
zhouxiaoyang@js.chinamobile.com

Abstract. Blockchain serves as the cornerstone of decentralized trust and distributed data management in the Web3 era. Its applications have expanded from decentralized finance (DeFi) to various industrial and societal sectors. As one of the most recognized foundations behind those blockchain systems, the proof-of-work (PoW) consensus mechanism suffers from excessive computational and energy consumption. Encountering this challenge, a number of projects such as Quilibrium, Qubic, and TIG have pioneered several initiatives, including proof-of-stake (PoS) and useful proof-of-work (UPoW), to lower blockchain's reliance on hard and intensive hash trails. However, these initiatives still encounter challenges related to wasted computation resources, procedural complexity, incentive fairness, and centralization concerns. In this work, we propose a route-planning-based consensus mechanism that transforms the route-planning works into useful mining puzzles of the blockchain consensus procedure. We conduct a comprehensive analysis of the mining puzzle, design a problem-solving algorithm as the fair and efficient consensus mining process. We employ a series of experiments to evaluate the performance of the proposed mining puzzle and the problem-solving algorithm and demonstrate their effectiveness in converting the majority of computational effort into useful work.

Keywords: Blockchain · Route planning · Mining puzzle

1 Introduction

Blockchain serves as a cornerstone technology for establishing decentralized trust among untrusted parties in the upcoming Web3 era. It underpins the development of critical Web3 technologies and infrastructure [15]. Currently, blockchain-enabled Web3 applications are evolving from finance to diverse industrial and societal sectors, such as governance, healthcare, and digital identity management, among others [4,14,17]. Applications including decentralized

R. K. Shyamasundar et al. (Eds.): ICBC 2025, LNCS 16155, pp. 74–88, 2026.
https://doi.org/10.1007/978-3-032-06176-8_5

finance (DeFi) [2], decentralized physical infrastructure networks (DePIN) [13], decentralized science (DeSCI) [5] are experiencing growing adoption across user communities.

Consensus mechanisms are fundamental to blockchain systems, ensuring state consistency, immutability, and security across network nodes, even in the presence of malicious actors. Among them, the proof-of-work (PoW) protocol introduced by Bitcoin remains the most robust and widely adopted, owing to its cryptographic simplicity and long-standing resilience [16]. However, the PoW consensus mechanism also suffers from energy inefficiency due to its computational design. Using the PoW, miners have to repetitively execute hash computations to solve cryptographic puzzles, a process requiring specialized hardware with intensive resource consumption. This has created a paradox. On the one hand, soaring operational costs and energy expenses in blockchain may outweigh system benefits and contradict the global sustainability goals [11]. On the other hand, the performance benefits in terms of security and scalability improvements inherent in blockchain have to rely on intensive resource consumptions [1]. The conflicts between blockchain consensus requirements and sustainable goals have been challenging its long-term adoption.

To tackle this bottleneck, a new paradigm shift must be called. One representative example is Ethereum's 2021 transition to proof-of-stake (PoS) consensus [21]. In PoS, validator nodes compete for block proposals proportional to their staked holding tokens. Building upon this, Solana integrates delegated proof-of-stake (DPoS) with proof-of-history (PoH) [12,22], and further enhances blockchain performance by expanding blockchain's scalability. Another example focuses on useful-proof-of-work (UPoW) [3], which replaces energy-intensive hash trails with computationally difficult yet socially valuable tasks as mining puzzles. Current explorations on these mining puzzles span a diverse set of NP-hard and high-dimensional problems, including orthogonal vector detection, boolean satisfiability (3-SAT) resolution [10,20], and artificial intelligence (AI) model training. These paradigm shifts aim to transform blockchain energy expenditure into productive computational resources for scientific and industrial use.

So far, several projects have been initiated with consensus mechanisms that are more efficiency-oriented or integrated with practical tasks. The Quilibrium network constructs a peer-to-peer multi-party computation platform [9]. In this network, verifiable delay functions (VDF) are adopted for the PoW replacing hash computation. The Qubic project integrates artificial neural networks to build a UPoW network, with an eye toward the future of artificial general intelligence [19]. Likewise, the TIG project explores UPoW by integrating NP-hard challenges [18], such as vector search optimization and the resolution of quadratic knapsack problems, into its mining puzzles.

Although existing studies have proposed UPoW mechanisms to reduce the energy waste inherent in traditional PoW designs, several key challenges remain unresolved. Some approaches fail to fully utilize available CPU resources for productive computation, while others rely on centralized validation processes, which undermine the decentralization and fairness principles of blockchain systems [9,18,19]. To tackle these problems, we design a route-planning-based consensus mechanism that transforms useful route-planning works into working proofs. The main contributions of this paper are summarized as follows:

1. We design a UPoW blockchain mining puzzle by retaining the essential properties of PoW and practical route planning problems, that transform computation resources into valuable working proofs.
2. We design a corresponding problem-solving process, which includes graph generation, path finding, path generation, and hash attempts, to ensure fairness, simplicity, reproducibility, verifiability, and resistance to GPU mining of the proposed mining puzzle.
3. We conduct a comprehensive analysis of the route-planning-based UPoW mining puzzle and a series of experiments to evaluate the performance. The results demonstrate that most of the computational effort is successfully converted into useful work, improving overall system efficiency and resource utilization, while simultaneously promoting fairness and decentralization.

The remainder of this paper is organized as follows: Sect. 2 discusses the route planning problem and considerations for mining puzzle constructions. Section 3 proposes our route-planning-based mining puzzle design. Then a comprehensive analysis of the proposed mining puzzle is provided in Sect. 4. Section 5 demonstrates experimental results. Finally, Sect. 6 concludes the paper.

2   Route-Planning-Based Mining Workflow

2.1   Useful Proof of Work

Figure 1 illustrates the overview of our proposed UPoW blockchain consensus mechanism with a route-planning-based mining puzzle. Different from traditional PoW that miners engage in energy-intensive hash computations–a process always criticized for its computational redundancy and limited societal value. Our design reimagines the mining workflow by integrating route planning puzzles as the foundational "work" requirement. However, converting real-world route planning tasks into blockchain-compatible working proofs presents significant technical challenges. This transformation requires careful consideration of the route planning puzzle designs, verification efficiency, and result reproducibility while maintaining the system's security, fair and decentralized nature.

2.2   Hamiltonian Path and Route Planning

The traveling salesman problem (TSP) is a well-known problem in computer science and operations research, with broad applications in areas such as routing, path planning, and network optimization [8]. In this problem, a salesman must visit a set of cities exactly once and return to the origin city, all while minimizing the total travel distance. If we disregard the requirement for the traveling salesman to return to the starting place, the problem can be simplified to the Hamiltonian path problem [7]. The objective of the Hamiltonian path is to visit each

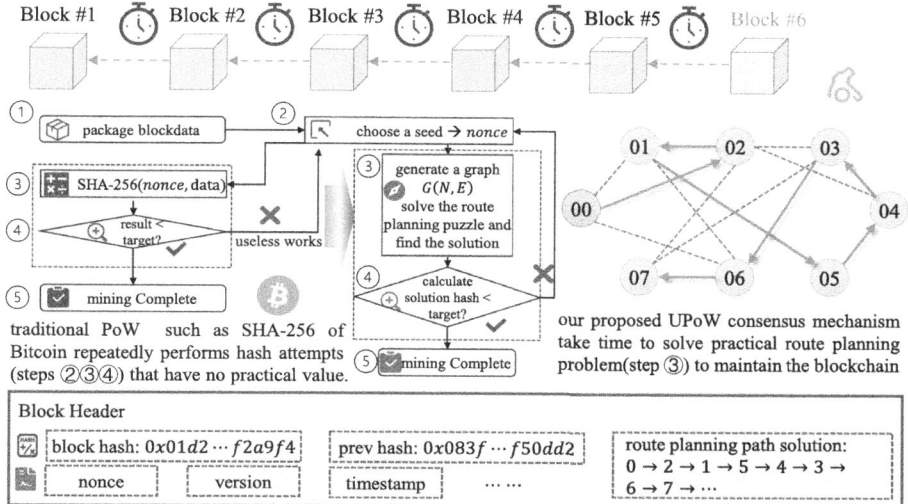

Fig. 1. An overview of the route planning based mining flow as we use route planning puzzle replacing the traditional useless hash calculations

node in a graph exactly once, starting from a given node. As shown in Fig. 1, an example Hamiltonian path is denoted by $(0 \rightarrow 2 \rightarrow 1 \rightarrow 5 \rightarrow 4 \rightarrow 3 \rightarrow 6 \rightarrow 7)$.

The Hamiltonian path problem can be regarded as a key aspect of route planning. Its applications extend to various fields such as logistics optimization, travel itinerary planning, robot navigation, and circuit layout design. Nevertheless, it has been verified to be NP-complete [6], meaning that finding an exact solution within a reasonable time frame becomes computationally infeasible as the number of nodes increases. This makes Hamiltonian path problems inherently difficult to solve but easy to verify - a critical property for designing a PoW consensus mechanism.

2.3   Mining Puzzle Requirement

The direct conversion of route planning problems into mining puzzles poses several inherent challenges. To ensure the mining puzzle maintains the essential properties of a blockchain consensus mechanism while effectively leveraging route planning computations, certain conditions must be satisfied:

– Solving difficult but easy to verify: The puzzle must be computationally intensive to solve, requiring significant effort to find a valid solution. Conversely, verifying the correctness of a proposed solution must be computationally light and straightforward. This asymmetry is fundamental for efficient and secure PoW-based consensus.

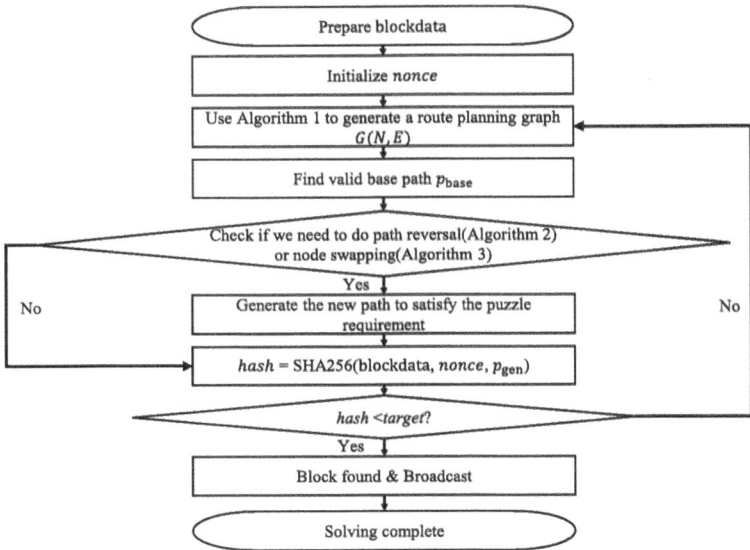

Fig. 2. Route planning puzzle solving process

- Hard to parallelize (GPU resistance): To prevent centralization and uphold the"one-CPU-one-vote" principle [16], mining puzzles should be designed to resist highly parallelized computations. In particular, they must limit the advantage of specialized hardware such as GPUs and ASICs, thereby promoting a more equitable and decentralized mining environment.

3   Route Planning Puzzle

To construct the mining puzzle based on a route planning problem, three main steps are designed: graph generation, path finding, and hash attempts. Graph generation involves creating a random graph with its edges, which serves as the problem instance for finding a valid path solution. For path finding, algorithms such as Breadth-First Search (BFS) or Depth-First Search (DFS) can be employed to identify a potential solution. Finally, hash attempts are used to verify the solution's eligibility for new block creation. Figure 2 illustrates the core solving process of the route planning puzzle presented in this paper.

Our primary objective is to reallocate computational time towards meaningful tasks, specifically graph generation and route planning, rather than traditional SHA256 computations. Consequently, within our solving process, we aim to minimize the number of SHA256 executions. This is achieved by enhancing the inherent difficulty of finding the solution route itself, thereby reducing the need for frequent hash attempts.

Algorithm 1. Graph generation algorithm

Input: N, blockdata
Output: G (adjacency matrix)
1: $nonce \leftarrow$ generateNonce()
2: $seed \leftarrow$ **SHA256**($nonce$, blockdata)
3: $r \leftarrow$ **PRNG**($seed$)
4: **for** $i = 0$ **to** $N - 1$ **do**
5:    **for** $j = 0$ **to** i **do**
6:       $E_{ij} = E_{ji} = r_{i(i+1)/2+j}$
7:    **end for**
8: **end for**
9: $G = (N, E)$

3.1 Graph Generation

Graph generation forms the foundation for solving the route planning puzzle. To define a graph $G = (N, E)$, we first determine two key parameters: N, representing the number of vertices, and E, representing the set of edges connecting them.

As detailed in Algorithm 1, the existence probability for an edge, denoted as p, is assumed to be $1/2$ for default generation.[1] Similar to Bitcoin's approach, a *nonce* is generated for each graph instance to ensure diversity. This nonce is then combined with the block data to form the seed for a pseudo-random number generator (PRNG). The PRNG function produces a sequence of numbers that appears random but is deterministically generated from this specific initial seed. This design ensures the reproducibility of the graph and its solution for verification purposes, while maintaining randomness for each new puzzle instance.

Utilizing the PRNG function, a random bitstream of $N(N + 1)/2$ bits is generated. Let r_k denote the k-th bit of this stream, which takes a value of 0 or 1. The existence of an edge between node i and node j is then deterministically established by $E_{ij} = E_{ji} = r_{i(i+1)/2+j}$ for $j \leq i$. This method efficiently constructs the graph based on the seeded PRNG.

3.2 Path Finding and Generation

After constructing the graph G, the next step involves searching for valid solution paths. Numerous algorithms, such as BFS and DFS, can be employed to traverse possible paths within the graph to locate a Hamiltonian path solution.

---

[1] While edges can theoretically be generated with any arbitrary probability, the practical application reveals that checking if a random value falls below an arbitrary threshold introduces significant time and space overhead. To mitigate this, we can select p as 2^{-k}, where $k \in \mathbb{Z}_+$. This allows for an efficient generation process: k random bits are combined using a bitwise AND operation to determine edge existence. For instance, if the probability is set to $p = 12.5\%$ (2^{-3}), the random value r in Algorithm 1 can be generated as $r = \text{PRNG}(seed)\&\text{PRNG}(seed)\&\text{PRNG}(seed)$.

Algorithm 2. Path generation (with path reversal)

Input: G, p_{base}, N
Output: p_{gen} (generated paths)
1: $p_{\text{gen}} \leftarrow$ empty list
2: **for** $i = 1$ to $N - 1$ **do**
3:    **for** $j = i + 1$ to $N - 1$ **do**
4:        $p = p_{\text{base}}.\text{copy}()$
5:        **if** $G_{p^{i-1},p^j} = 1$ **and** $G_{p^i,p^{j+1}} = 1$ **then**
6:            $p_{\text{gen}}.\text{push}(p.\text{reverse}(i,j))$
7:        **end if**
8:    **end for**
9: **end for**

Algorithm 3. Path generation (with node swapping)

Input: G, p_{base}, N
Output: p_{gen} (generated paths)
1: $p_{\text{gen}} \leftarrow$ empty list
2: **for** $i = 1$ to $N - 1$ **do**
3:    **for** $j = i + 1$ to $N - 1$ **do**
4:        $p = p_{\text{base}}.\text{copy}()$
5:        **if** $G_{p^{i-1},p^j} = 1$ **and** $G_{p^j,p^{i+1}} = 1$ **and** $G_{p^{j-1},p^i} = 1$ **and** $G_{p^i,p^{j+1}} = 1$ **then**
6:            $p_{\text{gen}}.\text{push}(p.\text{swap}(i,j))$
7:        **end if**
8:    **end for**
9: **end for**

It is important to note that within our designed mining process, a given graph may have multiple valid Hamiltonian path solutions. Assuming that an initial path-finding process can yield at least one valid Hamiltonian path, p_{base}. The role of path generation is to derive additional solutions that meet the required criteria, based on this base path. However, generating numerous paths without effective criteria can lead to inefficient computational work. Therefore, we analyze path generation algorithms to identify a suitable trade-off between solution diversity and computational efficiency. Two primary algorithms are used for path generation: path reversal and node swapping.

Figure 3 and Algorithm 2 illustrate the path reversal algorithm. As shown in Fig. 1, given $G_{2,3} = G_{1,6} = 1$, a sub-path such as $1 \rightarrow 5 \rightarrow 4 \rightarrow 3$ can be reversed to $3 \rightarrow 4 \rightarrow 5 \rightarrow 1$ and substituted into p_{base} to form a new valid solution. The success probability for a reversal between two nodes is p^2, yielding up to $\frac{N(N+1)}{2}p^2$ possible paths. In contrast, the node swapping algorithm (Algorithm 3) requires additional edge checks, resulting in a lower success probability of p^4. For example, in addition to $G_{2,3} = G_{1,6} = 1$, verifying $G_{0,6} = G_{2,7} = 1$ ensures valid node swapping, with up to $\frac{N(N+1)}{2}p^4$ paths generated. Both techniques can be applied iteratively or in combination to derive multiple similar valid paths.

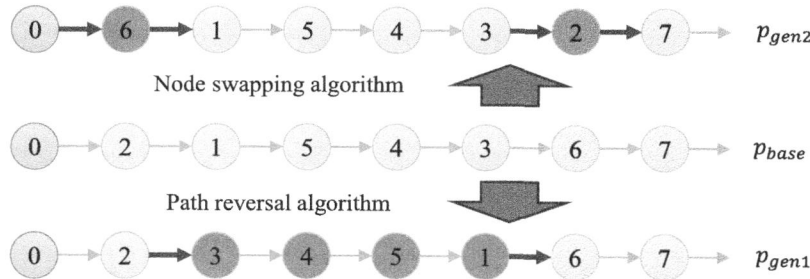

Fig. 3. Examples of path generation

In practical applications, generating an excessive number of redundant or sub-optimal paths from a single base solution can be computationally inefficient. To mitigate this, we introduce a path validation constraint rooted in practical utility. For example, when planning routes where destinations have varying importance (e.g., attractiveness), this constraint ensures that only 'meaningful' path variations are considered. Specifically, a newly generated Hamiltonian path is deemed valid only if the nodes involved in the reversal or swapping operation (e.g., the pivot nodes for reversal or the swapped nodes) adhere to a predefined priority ordering. This ordering could be based on their original position (index) in p_{base} (requiring $p_{\text{base}}^{i} < p_{\text{base}}^{j}$). This mechanism ensures that only paths aligning with predefined quality or preference criteria are utilized, thus optimizing computational resource allocation by preventing the proliferation of less effective solutions.

3.3   Hash Attempts

While the core computational work of our puzzle is deliberately shifted from brute-force hashing to meaningful route planning, hash functions remain an integral component for ensuring the cryptographic security and integrity of the blockchain. In our proposed scheme, the reliance on hash computations is significantly reduced and only for final step. A blockchain node first computes a Hamiltonian path that satisfies the puzzle's predefined constraints. Upon identifying a valid path, the node proceeds to calculate a hash value using the SHA-256 function:

$$\text{SHA256}(\text{blockdata}, nonce, \text{path}) < target,$$

where the target is dynamically adjusted based on the network's aggregate computational capacity. If the resulting hash is less than the specified target, the node is deemed to have successfully solved the puzzle and is thereby granted the right to generate a new block and receive the corresponding coinbase reward. The newly mined block is then propagated throughout the network to inform other participants of its creation.

Algorithm 4. Path validation

Input: G, p_{base}, N
Output: $if valid$ (boolean)
1: **for** $i = 0$ to $N - 1$ **do**
2:     **if** $G_{p_{\text{base}}^i, p_{\text{base}}^{i+1}} \neq 1$ **then**
3:         **return false**
4:     **end if**
5: **end for**
6: **for** $i = 1$ to $N - 1$ **do**
7:     **for** $j = i + 1$ to $N - 1$ **do**
8:         **if** $G_{p_{\text{base}}^{i-1}, p_{\text{base}}^j} = 1$ **and** $G_{p_{\text{base}}^i, p_{\text{base}}^{j+1}} = 1$ **and** $p_{\text{base}}^i > p_{\text{base}}^j$ **then**
9:             **return false**
10:         **end if**
11:     **end for**
12: **end for**
13: **return true**

3.4 Path Validation

Algorithm 4 details the validation process for submitted solutions to the route planning puzzle. For any submitted path, the following verifications are critically conducted by network nodes: 1) Hamiltonian path verification: It is confirmed whether the submitted path is indeed a Hamiltonian path, meaning it visits every vertex in the graph and exactly once. 2) Priority requirements check: It is verified whether the path satisfies the predefined priority criteria (as discussed in Sect. 3.2). Its purpose is to prevent the generation of redundant or less effective solutions by enforcing a strict ordering rule on potential path modifications.

This mechanism ensures that only paths aligning with predefined quality or preference criteria are utilized, thereby optimizing computational resource allocation and ensuring more efficient and relevant solution exploration within the network.

4   Solving Process Analysis

This chapter presents a comprehensive analysis of the proposed route-planning mining puzzle. The goal is to address fairness vulnerabilities in decentralized consensus, particularly those introduced by specialized optimizations-commonly referred to as "scientists" in the community[2]. Unlike traditional PoW schemes based on uniform cryptographic operations, our puzzle is modularly structured into five stages: graph generation, path finding, path generation, hash attempt, and solution validation. By tuning key parameters including node count N, edge probability p, and time threshold $timeout$—we achieve a trade off between computational efficiency and fair participation of miners.

---

[2] These optimizations, whether algorithmic or hardware-based, may compromise fairness and security due to their opacity and lack of peer review.

To rigorously evaluate the puzzle's performance characteristics and ensure its integrity, we delineate the computational capacities of the solving process into several key phases: f_{sol} represents valid solutions can be discovered per unit time, f_{gen} accounts for the performance of deriving new solutions from base solution p_{base}, f_{hash} stands for SHA-256 capability for proof generation and f_{check} represents the performance of verifying a solution's validity according to Algorithm 4.

A fundamental design principle is to allocate the majority of solving time to meaningful computation, while ensuring that the verification cost remains significantly lower than the solution discovery cost. Therefore, for the system to be robust and efficient, it is critical that f_{check} and f_{hash} are substantially greater than f_{sol} ($f_{check}, f_{hash} \gg f_{sol}$).

4.1 Path Finding Timeout

To ensure the efficient discovery of valid solutions for the route-planning puzzle and maintain blockchain stability, we introduce a *timeout* parameter that defines the maximum allowable duration for path finding within a single graph. Modern blockchain systems demand rapid transaction confirmation, far exceeding the prolonged block times of early systems. Consequently, our design expects that the time for finding a single path does not exceed 1 s. This can help reduce the instability of block generation. Should a path not be discovered within this allocated time, the system is designed to promptly switch the random number (*nonce*) to generate a new graph, thereby initiating a fresh puzzle search. Our experiments, detailed in Sect. 5, confirm that with properly designed parameters, the path-finding algorithm consistently achieves effective solutions within several milliseconds, thereby validating the feasibility of this stringent timeout.

4.2 Path Generation Restriction

In the route-planning puzzle, path generation algorithms can produce a large number of similar solutions based on the base path p_{base}. However, since only one valid solution is required, it is necessary to impose puzzle constraints to prevent redundant computations. This constraint stipulates that for any nodes p_{base}^i and p_{base}^j eligible for path reversal or node swapping, the condition $p_{base}^i < p_{base}^j$ must be strictly enforced. By requiring an ordered relationship between the selected nodes, this mechanism effectively limits the search space for derived solutions, thereby mitigating the risk of generating an overwhelming number of predictable proofs and promoting a more equitable mining environment.

4.3 SHA-256 Computation Capability

While SHA-256 hashing is utilized for the final proof generation to align with standard blockchain practices, it is crucial to emphasize that SHA-256 computation is not designed to be the primary computational bottleneck of our

Table 1. SHA-256 computation capability

number of blocks	N range	f_{hash} per second per core
2	$[1, 20]$	1, 584, 794
3	$[21, 84]$	1, 523, 937
4	$[85, 148]$	1, 457, 865
5	$[149, 212]$	1, 411, 247
6	$[213, 276]$	1, 363, 120
7	$[377, 340]$	1, 289, 057
$\vdots$	$\vdots$	$\vdots$

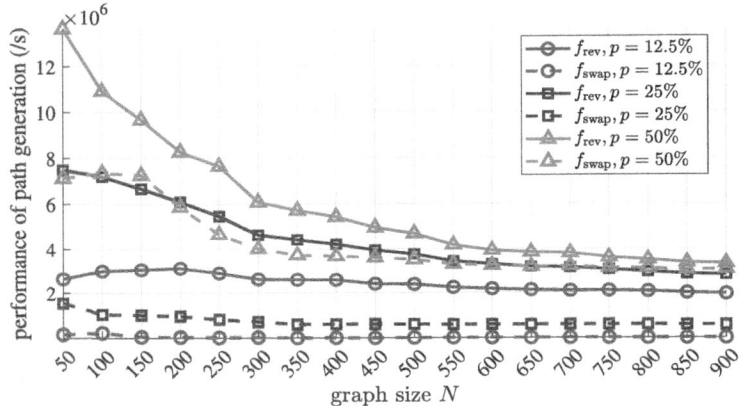

Fig. 4. The performance of the path generation algorithm

route-planning puzzle. The true "work" and computational burden are intentionally allocated to the complex route planning process. This means we require the hash performance (f_{hash}) to be significantly faster than the puzzle's solution generation rate (f_{sol}), confirming its non-dominant role in overall difficulty.

5   Experiment Results

We conduct experiments to evaluate the parameter configurations of our proposed route-planning-based mining puzzle. All simulations were conducted on a platform powered by an AMD Ryzen 7950X processor, featuring 32 logical CPU cores and the time unit is set to 1 s. We evaluated the CPU SHA-256 computation capability, the performance of the path generation algorithm, the efficiency of the verification algorithm, and the overall solution rate of the proposed UPoW consensus mechanism under various parameter settings.

Initially, we measured the SHA-256 computational capability of the CPU. Based on the data presented in Table 1, it can be inferred that for smaller values of N, the CPU's SHA-256 performance is approximately 1 million hashes per second per core.

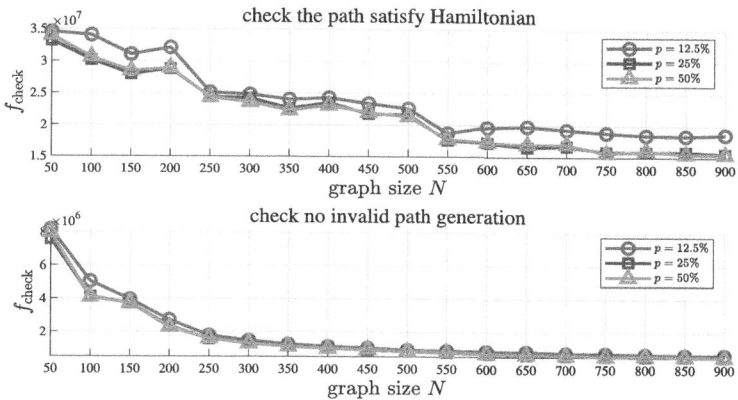

Fig. 5. The performance of checking the solution of route planning puzzle

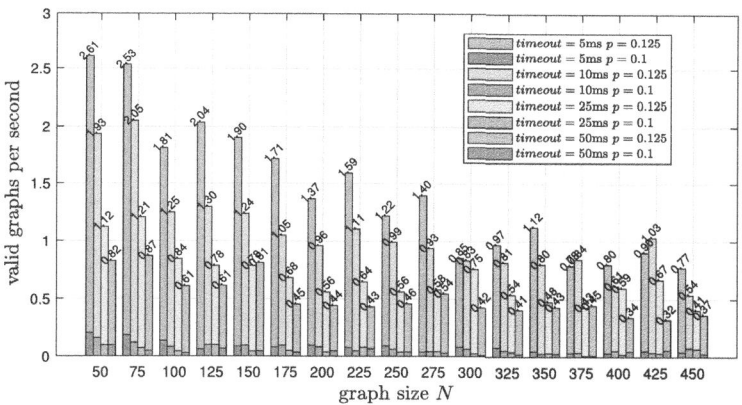

Fig. 6. Valid graph generated within *timeout* per second

Figure 4 illustrates the computational capability of Algorithm 2 and 3(f_{rev} and f_{swap}) in terms of operations per second per core, under varying graph sizes N and edge presence probabilities p. As shown, the performance for both algorithms stabilizes as N increases. Notably, the path reversal algorithm consistently outperforms the node swapping algorithm, particularly as p decreases due to the stricter conditions and additional validation steps required for node swapping. Specifically, when $p \leq 0.5$, since $f_{\mathrm{rev}} > f_{\mathrm{swap}}$, it holds that $f_{\mathrm{gen}} = max\{f_{\mathrm{rev}}, f_{\mathrm{swap}}\} \approx f_{\mathrm{rev}}$.

Since the simulations reveal that f_{gen} generally outperforms f_{hash}, to prevent the computational bottleneck from shifting to hash computation and avoid inefficient resource utilization, we introduce the priority check to avoid arbitrary generations. This strategy needs additional verification checks, which introduce overhead, as illustrated in Fig. 5. These checks include non-Hamiltonian path detection, exhibiting linear time complexity and achieving over 10 million oper-

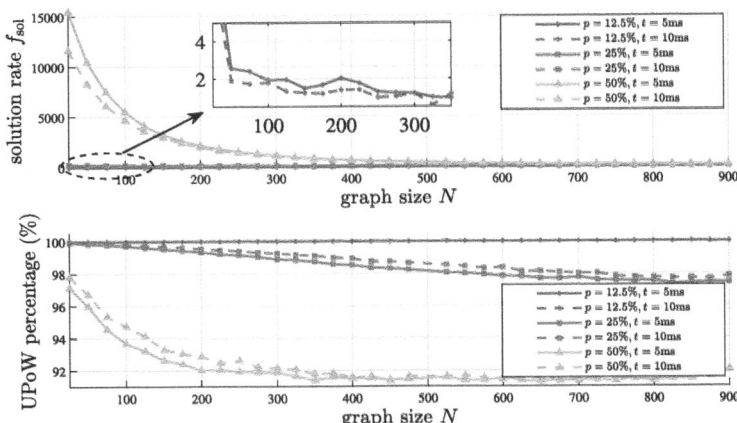

Fig. 7. Solution rate performance f_{sol} and the UPoW time consumption percentage of the mining process

ations per second, and illegal reversal detection, which has an $O(N^2)$ complexity that significantly degrades with increasing graph size. Consequently, while the validation rate f_{check} can reach millions of operations per second for N less than 250, smaller graph sizes are advisable to mitigate the risk of node overload from malicious validation requests.

Figure 6 illustrates the number of valid graphs containing feasible paths generated per second for different graph sizes and path-finding timeout settings, specifically for $p = 0.125$ and $p = 0.1$. The darker shaded region at the bottom indicates that at $p = 0.1$, the valid graph generation rate is less than 0.2 graphs/s. Conversely, for higher p values, an excessive number of graphs can be generated. For instance, when $p = 0.25, N = 50$, and with a timeout of 5 ms, 233 valid graphs can be generated per second. Through simulations, we identified that $p = 0.125$ strikes a good balance, maintaining the graph generation rate within a reasonable range.

Finally, we simulated the overall performance of the proposed mining puzzle. Figure 7 depicts the solution rate under diverse parameter settings. Specifically, when the parameter N falls within the range $[50, 150]$ and $p = 12.5\%$, the overall solution rate f_{sol} is found to be approximately 1 to 2. In this scenario, the time dedicated to UPoW, which encompasses graph generation and path finding, constitutes nearly 100% of the total time. It is worth noting that the parameter p plays a pivotal role in significantly influencing the proportion of time allocated to UPoW. An increase in the value of p would result in an excessive number of hash computations, thereby leading to inefficient resource utilization.

Consequently, to attain a more balanced mining process where useful work dominates, aiming for an overall solution rate of approximately 1 solution per second proves to be a rational choice. This approach, by favoring smaller graph sizes to maintain a high proportion of useful work, effectively reduces storage overhead and contributes to improved overall system efficiency and resource utilization.

6   Conclusion

In this paper, we proposed a route-planning-based UPoW consensus mechanism that replaces energy-intensive hash computations with NP-hard route-planning tasks. By embedding meaningful problem-solving into the mining process, the proposed approach improves the utility of computational resources and enhances the overall sustainability of blockchain systems. We designed a fair and efficient mining flow, incorporating generation restrictions to mitigate the inherent unfairness risks of UPoW, improve GPU resistance, and promote decentralization. A series of experiments were conducted to evaluate the feasibility and performance of the proposed mechanism. The results demonstrate that it effectively transforms computational effort into useful work, enhances fairness, and mitigates centralization risks, thereby overcoming key limitations of existing UPoW approaches that rely on inefficient computation or centralized validation.

Acknowledgments. This work was supported in part by the Key Technologies R&D Program of Jiangsu (Prospective and Key Technologies for Industry) under Grants BE2022068 and BE2022068-3, the National Natural Science Foundation of China under Grants U22B2006 and 62331024, the National Science and Technology Major Project of China under Grant 2025ZD1303100, the Natural Science Foundation on Frontier Leading Technology Basic Research Project of Jiangsu under Grants BK20222001 and BK20212001, the Science and Technology Major Project of Nanjing under Grant 202405020, the Taihu Lake Innovation Fund for the School of Future Technology of Southeast University, the Fundamental Research Funds for the Central Universities under Grant 2242022K60002, and the Huawei Cooperation Project under FA2019051081-2021-01.

References

1. Aponte-Novoa, F.A., Orozco, A.L.S., Villanueva-Polanco, R., Wightman, P.: The 51% attack on blockchains: a mining behavior study. IEEE Access **9**, 140549–140564 (2021). https://doi.org/10.1109/ACCESS.2021.3119291
2. Aramonte, S., Huang, W., Schrimpf, A.: DeFi risks and the decentralisation illusion. BIS Q. Rev. **6** (2021). https://www.bis.org/publ/qtrpdf/r_qt2112b.htm
3. Ball, M., Rosen, A., Sabin, M., Vasudevan, P.N.: Proofs of useful work. Cryptol. ePrint Arch. (2017). https://eprint.iacr.org/2017/203
4. Calzada, I.: Decentralized Web3 reshaping internet governance: towards the emergence of new forms of nation-statehood? Future Internet **16**(10) (2024). https://doi.org/10.3390/fi16100361
5. Ding, W., et al.: DeSci based on Web3 and DAO: a comprehensive overview and reference model. IEEE Trans. Comput. Social Syst. **9**(5), 1563–1573 (2022). https://ieeexplore.ieee.org/abstract/document/9906878/

6. Garey, M.R., Johnson, D.S., Stockmeyer, L.: Some simplified NP-complete problems. In: Proceedings of 6th Annual ACM Symposium Theory Computing (STOC'74), pp. 47–63. ACM Press, Seattle (1974). https://doi.org/10.1145/800119.803884. http://portal.acm.org/citation.cfm?doid=800119.803884

7. Garrod, C.: Hamiltonian path-integral methods. Rev. Mod. Phys. **38**(3), 483 (1966). https://journals.aps.org/rmp/abstract/10.1103/RevModPhys.38.483

8. Gutin, G., Punnen, A.P.: The Traveling Salesman Problem and its Variations, vol. 12. Springer, Heidelberg (2006). https://link.springer.com/book/10.1007/b101971

9. Heart, C.A.: Quilibrium: a peer-to-peer MPC platform as a service. Technical Report (2022). https://quilibrium.com/quilibrium.pdf

10. Karp, R.M.: Reducibility Among Combinatorial Problems, pp. 219–241. Springer, Heidelberg (2010). https://doi.org/10.1007/978-3-540-68279-0_8

11. Krause, M.J., Tolaymat, T.: Quantification of energy and carbon costs for mining cryptocurrencies. Nat. Sustainabil. **1**(11), 711–718 (2018). https://doi.org/10.1038/s41893-018-0152-7

12. Larimer, D.: Delegated proof-of-stake: DPoS. Bitshare whitepaper (2014)

13. Lin, Z., Wang, T., Shi, L., Zhang, S., Cao, B.: Decentralized physical infrastructure network (DePIN): challenges and opportunities (2024). https://doi.org/10.48550/arXiv.2406.02239. http://arxiv.org/abs/2406.02239

14. Liu, Y., Zhao, B., Zhao, Z., Liu, J., Lin, X., Wu, Q., Susilo, W.: SS-DID: a secure and scalable Web3 decentralized identity utilizing multilayer sharding blockchain. IEEE Internet Things J. **11**(15), 25694–25705 (2024). https://doi.org/10.1109/JIOT.2024.3380068

15. Liu, Z., et al.: Make Web3.0 connected. IEEE Trans. Depend. Sec. Comput. **19**(5), 2965–2981 (2021). https://ieeexplore.ieee.org/abstract/document/9428608/

16. Nakamoto, S.: Bitcoin: a peer-to-peer electronic cash system. Technical Report (2008). https://bitcoin.org/bitcoin.pdf

17. Narayan, A., Weng, K., Shah, N.: Decentralizing health care: history and opportunities of Web3. JMIR Form Res. **8**, e52740 (2024). https://doi.org/10.2196/52740

18. TIG: The Innovation Game (2024). https://www.tig.foundation/home

19. Vivancos, D., García, J.: Qubic AGI journey human and artificial intelligence: toward an AGI with aigarth (2024). https://doi.org/10.13140/RG.2.2.19891.13608

20. Williams, R., Yu, H.: Finding orthogonal vectors in discrete structures, pp. 1867–1877. Society for Industrial and Applied Mathematics (2014). https://doi.org/10.1137/1.9781611973402.135

21. Wood, D.G.: Ethereum: a secure decentralised generalised transaction ledger. Technical Report (2025). https://ethereum.github.io/yellowpaper/paper.pdf

22. Yakovenko, A.: Solana: a new architecture for a high performance blockchain. Technical Report (2018). https://github.com/solana-labs/whitepaper/blob/master/solana-whitepaper-en.pdf

Trusted Department Recommendation Based on Blockchain for Industrial Chain Collaboration

Zhenchao Yan[1,2], Songlin He[1,2(✉)], Chase Wu[3], and Haohui Cai[1,2]

[1] Southwest Jiaotong University, Chengdu 610031, Sichuan, China
{yanzhenchao,1040554989}@my.swjtu.edu.cn, sohe@swjtu.edu.cn
[2] Manufacturing Industry Chain Collaboration Industrial Software Key Laboratory of Sichuan Province, Chengdu 610031, Sichuan, China
[3] Department of Data Science, NJIT, Newark, NJ 07102, USA
chase.wu@njit.edu

Abstract. Business process management is a vital technology for managing and analyzing business processes in industrial chain. Blockchain, as a decentralized and tamper-proof distributed ledger technology, emerges as a promising infrastructure to support business process management and collaboration. In industrial chain collaboration, finding the most suitable business department to complete the business task can significantly increase the business execution efficiency. However, one of the critical challenges lies in reliably evaluating a department of its capability of completing the task. Existing related works either rely on subjective selection or the evaluation lacks of verifiability and trustworthiness. To this end, we propose a blockchain-based trusted business department recommendation protocol. Firstly, several dimensions are designed for evaluating local business departments and cross-enterprise collaborated departments. Secondly, a blockchain-based protocol is proposed to accumulatively generate verifiable values of these dimensions. Thirdly, we propose the fuzzy information entropy-enabled weighted fusion of these dimensions and produce comprehensive evaluation results for departments. Finally, the designed smart contracts are implemented and deployed on the Ethereum Sepolia test network, and the experimental results demonstrate efficient on-chain gas cost.

Keywords: Business process management · Blockchain application · Industrial collaboration · Department recommendation

1 Introduction

In the context of industrial chains, diverse business scenarios have emerged across various sectors [6], and years of practical experience have led to the evolution of increasingly optimized business processes. A business process (BP) is a logical structure or execution framework consisting of a set of activities or tasks that need to be coordinated. Business Process Management (BPM) is used to manage and analyze business processes (BPs) [23], including the combination, coordination, analysis and diagnosis of business processes. BPM helps enterprises improve operational efficiency and product quality, and is widely used in various industries such as manufacturing, finance [21]. However, traditional BPM is based on centralized information systems for process control, such as ERP system [17], workflow engines [14,24] and so forth, which are insufficient to cope with complex business scenarios especially involving collaborative participation of multiple heterogeneous enterprises and departments. To meet this challenge, blockchain technology exposes promising potential to act as an infrastructure. As a trusted entity in a trustless environment, its distributed ledger technology brings non-repudiation and tamper-proof features that can ensure collaborative trust between multiple collaborative enterprises or departments [23]. Meanwhile, its turing-complete smart contract execution guarantee function [4] can ensure that all parties involved in the business process fulfill their obligations and ensure fairness and many other important security features [5,9,11,25].

Although the application of blockchain technology [3,10] has eliminated the dependence on expensive trusted third parties in cross-organizational collaboration to a certain extent [22], and ensured the safe execution of business processes [13], the problem of business process execution efficiency still exposes improvement room. In this study, we target the scenario where multiple departments in a specific enterprise or different departments are available to complete a same business task. In such a setting, the selection of proper departments may greatly influence the business execution efficiency [7,12]. For instance, in the aftermarket service sector, the approval process for parts transfer business may be conducted by either the after-sales service department or the financial management department. However, disparities in procedural complexity and response time between these two entities directly impact the transfer lead time and customer satisfaction. Indeed, with the advancement of supply chain globalization and industrial Internet technology, the number of available execution entities in each business node who is responsible for a concrete task in the business process is becoming more flexible. Personalized recommendation of a group of suitable business departments can undoubtedly accelerate the entire business processes, yielding a more efficient commerce ecosystem.

However, finding the most suitable and relevant business department presents challenges. One of the most critical ones lies in ensuring the trustworthiness of relevance computation of a department to a specific business node. The available departments for a same business node definitely share the same business capability. However, how to ensure the relevance of a department so that all participants in a collaboration instance or all participants in cross industrial chain cooperation can publicly verify and trust the evaluation result, is a challenging task. In existing work, the initiator of a business process often defaults to selecting a collaborative enterprise that has cooperated or is familiar with to execute the business node, ignoring the potential collaborative enterprises with strong execution capabilities, or sometimes selects at its discretion.

To this end, we design a blockchain-based industrial chain collaboration framework, which allows reliable computation of a department's relevance to a specific business node, i.e., a holistic business piece during an end-to-end business process. Each department is evaluation through multiple dimensions and each dimension result is automatically computed by smart contract. All the dimensional results are also weighted aggregated, leading to a comprehensive relevance computation and more convincing recommendation.

Contributions. In summary, our contributions are summarized as follows.

- Dimensions for evaluating a business department's relevance to business nodes are designed. Then a blockchain-based department collaboration and recommendation protocol Π_{B3DR} is proposed to generate verifiable and trustworthy evaluation results.
- Weighted fusion of the verifiable relevance evaluation results is performed based on the fuzzy information entropy method to recommend the business department with the highest relevance.
- Experiments are conducted in the blockchain network, and the on-chain costs are measured to the on-chain cost of contracts to demonstrate the effectiveness of our proposed method.

2 Background

2.1 Business Process Management Based on Blockchain

As a decentralized distributed ledger technology, blockchain technology has shown great potential in managing complex business processes because it can record and manage data in business processes securely and tamper-proof. According to its functional characteristics, existing related work can be divided into: (i) Ensure data security and immutability in business processes [22], For example, through the distributed ledger technology of blockchain, the authenticity and reliability of key information such as process execution order and business process ownership can be ensured. (ii) As a decentralized trusted third party, it ensures fairness among all parties involved in the business process [2,13,22], Smart contracts ensure the trustworthiness of process execution. (iii) Through the incentive mechanism, the development of the node network can be promoted [16,19,20], The cryptocurrency mechanism in the blockchain can effectively motivate executors to correctly and efficiently execute business nodes in order to obtain rewards while ensuring the safety of the funds of the participants. However, the above studies assume that appropriate execution departments have been selected for business nodes in business processes. In practical applications, the realization of this assumption is full of challenges. Due to the large number of execution departments, the reliable execution of business processes can be guaranteed by recommending the optimal execution department.

2.2 Department Recommendation for Business Process Execution

Business process management optimizes the business process execution process. However, to achieve a more fundamental efficiency improvement, it is necessary to select the optimal execution department for the business nodes in the business

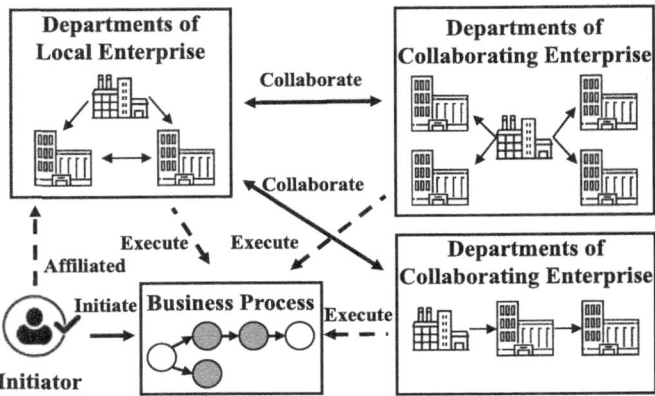

Fig. 1. The system model of ICCS.

process. Existing related work includes: (i) business process engineers subjectively recommend a series of responsive candidate executors [1,8,12]. (ii) combining social computing with business processes to quantify the social attributes of executors by simulating social relationships to complete the recommendation of executors [7,15,18]. In essence, it is to comprehensively assess the performers through a single or multiple evaluation dimensions. However, the above research cannot ensure the authenticity of the recommended dimensions. Moreover, the lack of dynamic mechanisms for continuously adjusting the evaluation dimensions leads to limited adaptability of these methods when facing with environmental changes or multi-party collaboration scenarios. Therefore, ensuring the authenticity, effectiveness, and evolvability of evaluation dimensions remains a key challenge to improve the credibility and applicability of evaluation methods.

3   System Model and Design Goals

In this section, we formulate the trusted department recommendation problem in an industrial chain collaboration system (ICCS) by introducing the system model, problem description and design goals.

3.1   System Model

Parties. As depicted in Fig. 1, the industrial chain collaboration system (ICCS) consists of three types of parties.

– *Initiator* (denoted by $\mathcal{I}$) is the primary entity responsible for assembling the business process $B = \{b_1, b_2, ...\}$, where $b_i \in B$ represents a business node. An initiator hopes to assign a business department to a business node to execute and complete the entire business process. The initiator can be a business personnel or a manager in the local enterprise.

- *Local Department* (denoted by $\mathcal{LD}$) refers to an internal business unit within the enterprise that processes concrete operational capabilities. For a business task, there may exist multiple departments being capable of completing it. Meanwhile, $\forall d_l \in \mathcal{LD}$ and the initiator belong to the same enterprise.
- *Collaboration Department* (denoted by $\mathcal{CD}$) refers to an external business unit belonging to collaborated enterprises. When the local department $\mathcal{LD}$ cannot handle for a certain business node, the collaborated department $d_c \in \mathcal{CD}$ of other enterprises sharing the same capability can be candidate.

In an ICCS, we consider that a department d (namely a local department $d_l \in \mathcal{LD}$ or a collaborated department $d_c \in \mathcal{CD}$) is identified by a public-private key pair (pk_d, sk_d) and a set of key-value pairs $\{\{bid_1 : \mathcal{F}(Q)\}, \{bid_2 : \mathcal{F}(Q)\}, ...\}$ where bid is the unique business node identifier, $\mathcal{F}(\cdot)$ is an evaluation function that evaluates the relevance of a department d to a business node bid, and the set $Q = \{q_1, q_2, ... \}$ contains a set of practical dimensions $\{q_i\}$ for evaluating a department. An initiator i is identified by a public-private key pairs (pk_i, sk_i). Furthermore, the participants have released public keys that are bound to their private keys.

3.2   Problem Description

A business process consists of a set of logically related tasks (business nodes) that need to be executed by appropriate departments (from local enterprise or collaborated enterprises) to achieve specific business goals. The selection of execution department greatly affects the efficiency of business process flow and the achievement of business goals. Though most typical business processes have default department, not every company owns the corresponding standard departments. Therefore, it is needed to trustfully recommend highly relevant execution departments for business nodes in different business processes, and we give the following definition for optimized department recommendation problem.

Definition 1 Optimized Department Recommendation (ODR). *Given an industrial chain collaboration system ICCS consisting of an initiator $\mathcal{I}$ who needs to build a business process B with n business nodes, a set of departments $\mathcal{LD} \cup \mathcal{CD}$ are candidates to recommend as execution business nodes and these candidates are evaluated by relevance Δ_d^{bid} for each business node bid, we wish to find a recommendation department set Γ containing n departments from $\mathcal{LD} \cup \mathcal{CD}$ such that the total relevance is maximized, defined as*

$$\max \sum_{i=1}^{n} \Delta_{d_i}^{bid}, d_i \in \Gamma, |\Gamma| = n, \tag{1}$$

where $\Delta_d^{bid} = \sum_{i=1}^{|Q|} \alpha_i \cdot V(d, q_i)$ is the relevance of department d related to business node bid, $V(d, q_i)$ is the dimension value of department d under dimension q_i. Essentially, the value of Δ_d^{bid} is the weighted sum of $|Q|$ evaluation dimensions.

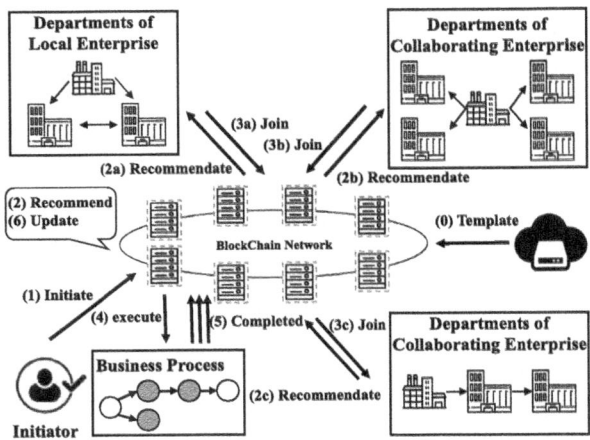

Fig. 2. An overview of blockchain-based business department recommendation.

3.3 Design Goals

The framework aims to meet the following design goals.

- **Effectiveness.** Conditioned that the departments are sufficient and honestly execute according to the framework, it ensures that department recommendations are completed for all business nodes of the business process.
- **Fairness.** The honest department should receive its well-deserved evaluation in the recommendation process.
- **Verifiability.** Each dimension used to evaluate the department is verifiable and therefore trusted.

4   Design

In this section, we introduce the blockchain-based business department recommendation protocol Π_{B3DR}. It can generates verifiable dimensional values for evaluating the relevance between departments and business nodes. A weighted fusion method based on fuzzy information entropy can obtain the final relevance. As shown in Fig. 2, the business process information and template departments (namely by default a business node should be handled by a department) are uploaded to the blockchain. The template departments are used for cold start when the system has no execution experience at the beginning. Once the initiator initiates a business process, the blockchain smart contract recommends departments based on the relevance updated by means of fixed-interval. After confirming the execution departments, all business nodes are executed and subjected to completeness verification through interdepartmental collaboration, ultimately completing the entire business process.

Table 1. An overview of evaluation dimensions.

Evaluation Object	Dimensions	Description
Local_ department	execute_nums	the number of participated execution
	avg_time	the average execution time
	complete_nums	the number of completed execution
	uncomplete_nums	the number of uncompleted execution
Collaborated_ department	execute_nums	the number of participated execution
	avg_time	the average execution time
	complete_nums	the number of completed execution
	uncomplete_nums	the number of uncompleted execution

4.1 Protocol Details

The Π_{B3DR} protocol aims to recommend the optimal department for the business node in a business process to achieve efficient execution. It supports participant collaborations and continuously generates verifiable dimensional values for evaluating the involved departments. Hereunder we first introduce some preliminaries.

- **Arbiter Contract** $\mathcal{G}_{\mathsf{B3DR}}$. The arbitration contract $\mathcal{G}_{\mathsf{B3DR}}$ inherits the core properties of smart contracts, i.e., the ability to transparently execute predefined logic once specific conditions are met, as described in Figs. 4 and 5.
- **Auxiliary Contracts**. We consider the protocol involves a global contract initiator $= \{pk_i : \{enterp, bp = [\{bid : predecessor\_id, local\_execution\}, ...]\}\}$ for retaining initiator information where $enterp$ indicates the enterprise information to which the initiator belongs and bp is the business process information which consists of a group of business nodes. Each business node consists of an business node ID, a list of preceding business node ID for this bid, and a local department execution label. And a global contract Local_department $= \{pk_{ld} : \{enterp, bid, relev, eval = \{execute\_nums, avg\_time, complete\_nums, uncomplete\_nums\}\}\}$ for retaining local department information where $relev$ is the relevance of the local_department related to the business node bid and $eval$ is the evaluation dimension information used to generate $relev$. A global contract Collaborated_department $= \{pk_{cd} : \{enterp, bid, recom, eval = \{execute\_nums, avg\_time, complete\_nums, uncomplete\_nums\}\}\}$ for retaining collaborated department. The detailed evaluation dimensions are explained in Table 1.
- **Adversarial and Communication Models**. We consider protocol Π_{B3DR} design under synchronous network model, and assuming probabilistic polytime (P.P.T.) static adversary.

As illustrated in Fig. 3, the Π_{B3DR} protocol operates in the following phases.

Phase I for Prepare: In this phase, the local departments and the collaborated departments negotiate offline and reach an agreement with *business policy*, such as the maximum execution time of each business node in a business process, the confirmation requirement for the completion of the business node execution, and interact with the contract $\mathcal{G}_{\mathsf{B3DR}}$.

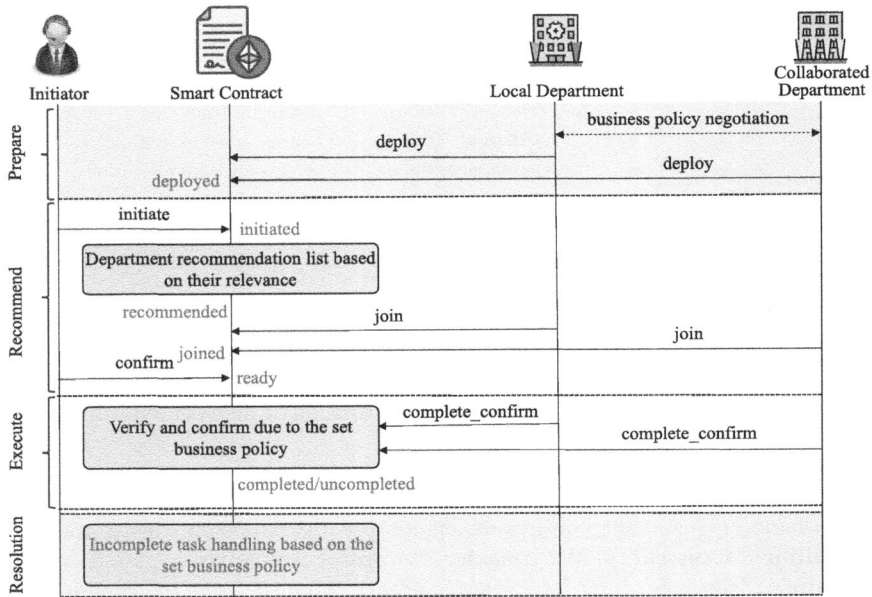

Fig. 3. The message flow of the Π_{B3DR} protocol.

- The local department performs the following operations in this phase:
  - After reaching an agreement through offline negotiations among multiple departments, sends the message (deploy, pk_{ld}) to $\mathcal{G}_{\mathsf{B3DR}}$ to complete the contract deployment.
  - Wait for (recommended) from $\mathcal{G}_{\mathsf{B3DR}}$ to enter the next phase.
- The collaborative department performs the following operations in this phase:
  - After reaching an agreement through offline negotiations among multiple departments, sends the message (deploy, pk_{cd}) to $\mathcal{G}_{\mathsf{B3DR}}$ to complete the contract deployment.
  - Wait for (recommended) from $\mathcal{G}_{\mathsf{B3DR}}$ to enter the next phase.

Phase II for Recommend: In this phase, the enterprise departments including local departments and collaborated departments that are recommended and interested to execute the business node will interact with the initiator i and the $\mathcal{G}_{\mathsf{B3DR}}$ to complete the business department recommendation as follows.

- The initiator performs the following operations in this phase:
  - Assert $\Sigma \equiv$ deployed, sends the message (initiate, pid, n) to $\mathcal{G}_{\mathsf{B3DR}}$. pid is the business process ID that the initiator needs to complete. The n-nodes is the number of business nodes in the business process.

- Upon receiving (joined, $\mathcal{L}_{\mathcal{D}}$) from $\mathcal{G}_{\mathsf{B3DR}}$, sends the message (confirm, $\mathcal{L}'_{\mathcal{D}}$) to $\mathcal{G}_{\mathsf{B3DR}}$. $\mathcal{L}_{\mathcal{D}}$ is the list of candidate executive departments that actively respond to join and $\mathcal{L}'_{\mathcal{D}}$ is the list of executive departments confirmed by the initiator.
  - Wait for (completed) from $\mathcal{G}_{\mathsf{B3DR}}$ to halt.
- The local department performs the following operations in this phase:
  - Upon receiving (Recommended, $\mathcal{L}_{\mathcal{D}}, ch$) from $\mathcal{G}_{\mathsf{B3DR}}$, if it agrees to execute, the private key sk_{ld} is used to generate a signature σ for ch to authenticate, which can be verified using the corresponding public key pk_{ld}, and sends the message (join, pk_{ld}, σ) to $\mathcal{G}_{\mathsf{B3DR}}$.
  - Wait for (ready) from $\mathcal{G}_{\mathsf{B3DR}}$ to enter the next phase.
- The Cooperative department performs the following operations in this phase:
  - Upon receiving (Recommended, $\mathcal{L}_{\mathcal{D}}, ch$) from $\mathcal{G}_{\mathsf{B3DR}}$, if it agrees to execute, the private key sk_{cd} is used to generate a signature σ for ch to authenticate, which can be verified using the corresponding public key pk_{cd}, and sends the message (join, pk_{cd}, σ) to $\mathcal{G}_{\mathsf{B3DR}}$.
  - Wait for (ready) from $\mathcal{G}_{\mathsf{B3DR}}$ to enter the next phase.

Phase III for Execute: In this phase, the executive departments complete and confirm the policies agreed upon in the prepare phase and interact with the $\mathcal{G}_{\mathsf{B3DR}}$ to complete the trusted execution of the business process as follows.

- The local department performs the following operations in this phase:
  - Upon receiving [(completed, i), ...] from $\mathcal{G}_{\mathsf{B3DR}}$, where i is the ID number of predecessor, namely, when the previous business node has been completed, the local department starts to execute the current business node. Then sends message (complete_confirm, pk_{ld}) to $\mathcal{G}_{\mathsf{B3DR}}$ after execution is completed, sends the necessary data to the collaborative department.
  - Upon receiving (completed, j) from $\mathcal{G}_{\mathsf{B3DR}}$, where j is the business node ID that needs to be confirmed whether the execution is completed. If the execution is confirmed to be completed, sends message (confirm, j, pk_{ld}) to $\mathcal{G}_{\mathsf{B3DR}}$.
  - Wait for (completed) from $\mathcal{G}_{\mathsf{B3DR}}$ to halt.
- The collaborated department performs the following operations in this phase:
  - Upon receiving [(completed, i), ...] from $\mathcal{G}_{\mathsf{B3DR}}$, where i is the ID number of predecessor, namely, when the previous business node has been completed, the collaborated department starts to execute the current business node. Then sends message (complete_confirm, pk_{cd}) to $\mathcal{G}_{\mathsf{B3DR}}$ after execution is completed.
  - Upon receiving (completed, j) from $\mathcal{G}_{\mathsf{B3DR}}$, where j is the business node ID that needs to be confirmed whether the execution is completed. If the execution is confirmed to be completed, sends message (confirm, j, pk_{cd}) to $\mathcal{G}_{\mathsf{B3DR}}$.
  - Wait for (completed) from $\mathcal{G}_{\mathsf{B3DR}}$ to halt.

Remarks. We also remark that: (i) the state of the $\mathcal{G}_{\text{B3DR}}$ changes to deployed when time $\mathcal{T}_{round}$ ends or all departments in the chain complete deployment during the prepare phase. (ii) the state of the $\mathcal{G}_{\text{B3DR}}$ changes to joined when more than n departments send messages to the $\mathcal{G}_{\text{B3DR}}$, where n is the number of business nodes in the current business process, during the recommend phase. (iii) the recommendation information for the departments is updated in smart contract during the recommend phase.

The Contract Functionality $\mathcal{G}_{\text{B3DR}}$

The contract $\mathcal{G}_{\text{B3DR}}$ has access to the global contracts initiator, local_department and collaborated_department. It interacts with the initiator i, the local department ld, the collaborated department cd and the adversary $\mathcal{A}$. It locally stores the business process information, the correlation between different departments and business nodes, the public addresses pk_i, pk_{cd}, pk_{ld}, the business department recommendation list $\mathcal{L}_{\mathcal{D}}$, the execution department confirmation list $\mathcal{L}'_{\mathcal{D}}$, the state Σ and the timers $\mathcal{T}_{round}$.

──────────────── **Phase 1: Prepare** ────────────────

— On firstly receive (deploy, pk_{cd}) from cd or receive (deploy, pk_{ld}) from ld:
  • let $Deployed\_Set = \oslash$ and start a timer $\mathcal{T}_{round}$
  • store pk_{cd} or pk_{ld} to $Deployed\_Set$
— On receive (deploy, pk_{cd}) from cd or receive (deploy, pk_{ld}) from ld:
  • assert $pk_{cd}, pk_{ld} \notin Deployed\_Set$
  • store pk_{cd} or pk_{ld} to $Deployed\_Set$
— Upon $\mathcal{T}_{round}$ times out:
  • assert $|Deployed\_Set| > 0$
  • let $\Sigma := $ deployed
  • send (deployed) to all entities in $Deployed\_Set$

──────────────── **Phase 2: Recommend** ────────────────

— On receive (initiate, pid, n) from i:
  • assert $\Sigma \equiv$ deployed
  • let $\Sigma := $ initiated
  • generate a recommendation list $\mathcal{L}_{\mathcal{D}}$ based on department relevance
  • let $\Sigma := $ recommended
  • send (recommended) to all entities in $\mathcal{L}_{\mathcal{D}}$
— On firstly receive (join, pk_{cd}) from cd or (join, pk_{ld}) from ld:
  • assert $\Sigma \equiv$ recommended
  • let $Joined\_Set = \oslash$ and start a timer $\mathcal{T}_{round}$
  • store pk_{cd} or pk_{ld} to $Joined\_Set$
— On receive (join, pk_{cd}) from cd or (join, pk_{ld}) from ld:
  • assert $pk_{cd}, pk_{ld} \notin Joined\_Set$
  • store pk_{cd} or pk_{ld} to $Joined\_Set$
— Upon $\mathcal{T}_{rount}$ times out:
  • assert $|Joined\_Set| > n$
  • let $\Sigma := $ joined
  • send ($joined$) to all entities in $Joined\_Set$
— On receive (confirm, $\mathcal{L}'_{\mathcal{D}}$) from i:
  • assert $\Sigma \equiv$ joined
  • let $\Sigma := $ ready
  • send (ready) to all entities in $\mathcal{L}'_{\mathcal{D}}$
  • invoke $\mathcal{O}^{time}$ to obtain the real-time timestamp start_execute_time
  • for any department d in $\mathcal{L}'_{\mathcal{D}}$, let execute_nums $+ +$

Fig. 4. The contract functionality $\mathcal{G}_{\text{B3DR}}$.

The Contract Functionality $\mathcal{G}_{\text{B3DR}}$

──────────────────── **Phase 3: Execute** ────────────────────

- On firstly receive (complete_confirm,pk_{cd},$num = 1$) from cd or (complete_confirm,pk_{ld},$num = 1$) from ld:
  - assert $\Sigma \equiv$ ready
  - invoke $\mathcal{O}^{time}$ to obtain the real-time timestamp end_execute_time
  - send (complete, $num = 1$) to all entities in $\mathcal{L}'_{\mathcal{D}}$
  - start a timer $\mathcal{T}_{round}$
  - generate a confirmed list $\mathcal{C}_{\mathcal{D}}$ based on the set business policy
  - send (confirm) to all entities in $\mathcal{C}_{\mathcal{D}}$
  - upon receive all response (complete, $confirm$, pk), for pk_{cd}, let complete_nums $++$ and avg_times = (avg_times + end_execute_time − start_execute_time)/2)
- On receive (complete_confirm, pk_{cd}, num) from cd or (complete_confirm, pk_{ld}, num) from ld:
  - invoke $\mathcal{O}^{time}$ to obtain the real-time timestamp end_execute_time, let start_execute_time is the latest end_execute_time among the predecessor nodes based on the set business policy
  - send (complete, num) to all entities in $\mathcal{L}'_{\mathcal{D}}$
  - start a timer $\mathcal{T}_{round}$
  - generate a confirmed list $\mathcal{C}_{\mathcal{D}}$ based on the set business policy
  - send (confirm) to all entities in $\mathcal{C}_{\mathcal{D}}$
  - upon receive all response (complete, $confirm$, pk), for pk_{cd}, let complete_nums $++$ and avg_times = (avg_times + end_execute_time − start_execute_time)/2)
- On receive (complete_confirm, pk$_{cd}$, $num = n$) from cd or (complete_confirm, pk$_{ld}$, $num = n$) from ld:
  - send (completed) to all entities

▷ Resolution

- Upon $\mathcal{T}_{round}$ times out:
  - if the verification of uncompleted task is successful:
    * for ld or cd, let uncomplete_nums $++$

Fig. 5. The contract functionality $\mathcal{G}_{\text{B3DR}}$ (cont.).

4.2 Weight Decision

Hereunder we introduce the computation of weights for dimensional values when evaluating the final relevance between departments and business nodes. Specifically, we propose to leverage fuzzy information entropy-based method, which is an effective information theory method that can mine potentially useful information only by relying on the data itself. The fuzzy information entropy FIG(q) is calculated as

$$\mathsf{FIG}(q) = -\frac{1}{|\mathcal{D}|}\sum_{d\in\mathcal{D}}log\frac{|[x_d]_{\mathcal{R}_q}|}{|\mathcal{D}|}, \tag{2}$$

$$[x_d]_{\mathcal{R}_q} = \frac{\mathcal{R}_q(x_d, x_1)}{x_1} + \frac{\mathcal{R}_q(x_d, x_2)}{x_2} + ... + \frac{\mathcal{R}_q(x_d, x_{|\mathcal{D}|})}{x_{|\mathcal{D}|}}, \tag{3}$$

where $\mathcal{R}_q(x_d, x_i) = \begin{cases} 0, & q \in Q_s \wedge f(x_d,q) \neq f(x_i,q) \\ 1, & q \in Q_s \wedge f(x_d,q) = f(x_i,q) \\ \sqrt{|f(x_d,q) - f(x_i,q)|^2}, & q \in Q_n \end{cases}$ is the

fuzzy similarity relation of feature dimension q. $[x_d]_{\mathcal{R}_q}$ is the fuzzy set which generated by fuzzy similarity relation and $|[x_d]_{\mathcal{R}_q}| = \sum_{i=1}^{|\mathcal{D}|}\mathcal{R}_q(x_d, x_i)$. Fuzzy information entropy can be used to measure the uncertainty of different dimensional features in the fuzzy division of samples. The larger the value, the weaker the fuzzy distinction between different objects, i.e., it is difficult to effectively distinguish objects in this dimension. Based on $\mathsf{FIG}(q)$, the weight of dimension q can be set by

$$\alpha = \frac{\mathsf{FIG}(q)}{\sum_{i=1}^{|Q|} \mathsf{FIG}(q_i)}, \tag{4}$$

According to Eq. (4), different weight values are set for different dimensions, i.e., $\{q_1 : \mathsf{execute\_nums}, q_2 : \mathsf{avg\_times}, q_3 : \mathsf{complete\_nums}, q_4 : \mathsf{uncomplete\_nums}\}$ and the recommendation degree of department d under business node bid is defined as

$$\Delta_d^{bid} = \sum_{i=1}^{|Q|} \alpha_i \cdot |\mathcal{N}(d, q_i)|, \tag{5}$$

where $\mathcal{N}(d, q_i)$ is the normalization function. Then in the business process, recommending the department with the highest relevance, i.e., ranking by Δ_d^{bid}, for each business node, thus facilitating more efficient business cooperation.

4.3   Properties Analysis

Theorem 1 characterizes the properties of the Π_{B3DR} protocol.

Theorem 1. Π_{B3DR} *satisfies effectiveness, fairness, verifiability under the conditions of authenticated, synchronous network, and assumptions that the underlying related primitives including blockchain and digital signature are secure.*

Proof. For effectiveness, in the prepare phase of the protocol, all enterprises need to negotiate and actively initiate deployment. In the recommend phase, more than n execution departments need to respond before entering the execute phase, thus ensuring the reliable completion of the business process. For fairness, since the collaborative execution between departments is automatically completed by smart contracts based on its state, the departments that perform honestly would receive a corresponding increased recommendation with higher dimensional values, while the departments that fail to complete the execution would have their recommendation reduced accordingly. For verifiability, since the dimensions for evaluating the relevance of business department execution are automatically and cumulatively calculated by smart contracts based on their behaviors, these dimension values are verifiable and can be trusted. Therefore, the verifiability of the dimensions is guaranteed.

5   Experiment and Evaluation

We implement the related smart contracts by Solidity programming language, and deploy as well as evaluate the cost in the Ethereum Sepolia testing network. Table 2 presents the gas costs of all functions in the contract $\mathcal{G}_{\mathsf{B3DR}}$ and Fig. 6 provides a more intuitive display of gas costs. Fig. 7 illustrates gas costs of all participants. Experimental results demonstrate that the gas costs are low and the protocol is efficient.

Table 2. The on-chain gas costs of functions in $\mathcal{G}_{B3DR}$.

Phase	Contract/Function	Caller	Gas Costs
Prepare	deploy	$\mathcal{LD}/\mathcal{CD}$	130,472
Recommend	initiate	$\mathcal{I}$	30,153
	recommend	$\mathcal{G}_{B3DR}$	330,817
	join	$\mathcal{LD}/\mathcal{CD}$	85,616
	confirm	$\mathcal{I}$	44,965
Execute	complete_confirm	$\mathcal{LD}/\mathcal{CD}$	84,835
Resolution	uncomplete	$\mathcal{LD}/\mathcal{CD}$	44,095

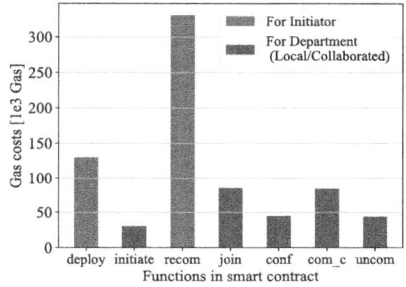

Fig. 6. The on-chain gas costs of functions in the contract $\mathcal{G}_{B3DR}$.

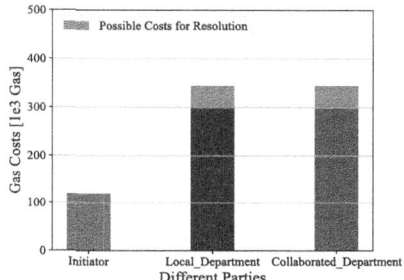

Fig. 7. The on-chain gas costs of all participants in the contract $\mathcal{G}_{B3DR}$.

6   Conclusion

We propose a blockchain-based business department recommendation protocol to solve the problem of reliable recommendation and execution of trusted departments in the collaborative execution of business processes. Several verifiable evaluation dimensions are designed and with the blockchain as an infrastructure of coordination, these dimensional values are iteratively and accumulatively updated. A weighted fusion method based on fuzzy information entropy is leveraged to obtain the final relevance between the execution department and the business node. Experiment conducted in Ethereum testing network shows the protocol's effectiveness in terms of on-chain gas costs.

Acknowledgments. This work was supported in part by National Key R&D Project of China (No. 2023YFB3308500). Songlin He is also supported in part by NSFC (No. 62302403).

References

1. Brahem, A., et al.: Towards a trustworthy and adaptive execution of business process choreographies. IEEE Trans. Serv. Comput. (2024)

2. Brahem, A., Messai, N., Sam, Y., Bhiri, S., Devogele, T., Gaaloul, W.: Running transactional business processes with blockchain's smart contracts. In: 2020 IEEE International Conference on Web Services (ICWS), pp. 89–93. IEEE (2020)
3. Chen, X., He, S., Sun, L., Zheng, Y., Wu, C.Q.: A survey of consortium blockchain and its applications. Cryptography **8**(2), 12 (2024)
4. Corradini, F., Marcelletti, A., Morichetta, A., Polini, A., Re, B., Tiezzi, F.: Engineering trustable and auditable choreography-based systems using blockchain. ACM Trans. Manag. Inf. Syst. (TMIS) **13**(3), 1–53 (2022)
5. Gu, T., Han, M., He, S., Chen, X.: Trap contract detection in blockchain with improved transformer. In: IEEE Global Communications Conference, pp. 5141–5146. IEEE (2023)
6. Guo, J., et al.: Industrial metaverse towards industry 5.0: Connotation, architecture, enablers, and challenges. J. Manuf. Syst. **76**, 25–42 (2024)
7. Hacid, H., Ugljanin, E., Sellami, M., Maamar, Z.: Adapting selection strategies of executors of business processes based on profit and social qualities. Comput. Electr. Eng. **63**, 320–331 (2017)
8. Havur, G., Cabanillas, C., Polleres, A.: Benchmarking answer set programming systems for resource allocation in business processes. Expert Syst. Appl. **205**, 117599 (2022)
9. He, S.: Blockchain-based automated and robust cyber security management. J. Parallel Distrib. Comput. **163**, 62–82 (2022)
10. He, S., Lu, Y., Tang, Q., Wang, G., Wu, C.Q.: Blockchain-based p2p content delivery with monetary incentivization and fairness guarantee. IEEE Trans. Parallel Distrib. Syst. **34**(2), 746–765 (2022)
11. He, S., Lyu, X., Chu, D.: Legacy compatible and sybil resistant decentralized identity management for iots. In: International Conference on Blockchain, pp. 33–49. Springer, Heidelberg (2024). https://doi.org/10.1007/978-3-031-77095-1_3
12. Kajan, E., Faci, N., Maamar, Z., Loo, A., Pljaskovic, A., Sheng, Q.Z., Dustdar, S.: The network-based business process. IEEE Internet Comput. **18**(2), 63–69 (2014)
13. Köpke, J., Meroni, G., Salnitri, M.: Designing secure business processes for blockchains with secbpmn2bc. Futur. Gener. Comput. Syst. **141**, 382–398 (2023)
14. Li, G., Muthusamy, V., Jacobsen, H.A.: A distributed service-oriented architecture for business process execution. ACM Trans. Web (TWEB) **4**(1), 1–33 (2010)
15. López-Pintado, O., Dumas, M., García-Bañuelos, L., Weber, I.: Controlled flexibility in blockchain-based collaborative business processes. Inf. Syst. **104**, 101622 (2022)
16. López-Pintado, O., García-Bañuelos, L., Dumas, M., Weber, I., Ponomarev, A.: Caterpillar: a business process execution engine on the ethereum blockchain. Softw. Pract. Exp. **49**(7), 1162–1193 (2019)
17. Lu, X., Nagelkerke, M., Van De Wiel, D., Fahland, D.: Discovering interacting artifacts from erp systems. IEEE Trans. Serv. Comput. **8**(6), 861–873 (2015)
18. Maamar, Z., Faci, N., Sakr, S., Boukhebouze, M., Barnawi, A.: Network-based social coordination of business processes. Inf. Syst. **58**, 56–74 (2016)
19. Mendling, J., et al.: Blockchains for business process management-challenges and opportunities. ACM Trans. Manag. Inf. Syst. (TMIS) **9**(1), 1–16 (2018)
20. Prybila, C., Schulte, S., Hochreiner, C., Weber, I.: Runtime verification for business processes utilizing the bitcoin blockchain. Futur. Gener. Comput. Syst. **107**, 816–831 (2020)
21. Pyon, C.U., Woo, J.Y., Park, S.C.: Service improvement by business process management using customer complaints in financial service industry. Expert Syst. Appl. **38**(4), 3267–3279 (2011)

22. Sturm, C., Scalanczi, J., Schönig, S., Jablonski, S.: A blockchain-based and resource-aware process execution engine. Futur. Gener. Comput. Syst. **100**, 19–34 (2019)
23. Viriyasitavat, W., Xu, L., Dhiman, G., Bi, Z.: Blockchain-as-a-service for business process management: survey and challenges. IEEE Trans. Serv. Comput. **16**(3), 2299–2314 (2022)
24. Wang, P., Sun, Z., Li, R., Chen, J., Gong, P., Du, X.: An efficient customized blockchain system for inter-organizational processes. In: 2023 IEEE International Conference on Web Services (ICWS), pp. 615–625. IEEE (2023)
25. Yan, Z., He, S., Wu, C., Hou, A.: Optimized deliverer selection in blockchain-based p2p content delivery networks. In: 2024 IEEE International Performance, Computing, and Communications Conference (IPCCC), pp. 1–8. IEEE (2024)

MEVShield: A DeFi-Friendly Blockchain Scheme Based on Order Protection

Ganwen Zheng, Wenjun Zhu, Shiyao Wang, and Jianan Hong[✉]

Shanghai Jiao Tong University, No. 800 Dongchuan Road, Minhang District,
Shanghai 200240, China
hongjn@sjtu.edu.cn

Abstract. As the value of decentralized finance (DeFi) continues to increase, it has become an increasingly sought-after area within blockchain technology. However, the accompanying Maximum-Extractable Value (MEV) issue has begun to raise concerns. MEV is closely related to transaction ordering, which makes sequencers with ordering power the primary target for participants seeking to manipulate transaction ordering for profit. This undermines market fairness and causes losses for other users. To address this issue, this paper introduces MEVShield-an anti-sequencer manipulation framework that uses a secret election mechanism to protect sequencers from malicious threats. MEVShield employs a secret election mechanism to keep sequencer identities confidential, ensuring the security of sequencers and the fairness of transaction sequencing. We conducted a comprehensive security analysis and implemented MEVShield to evaluate its performance. The experimental results demonstrate that the proposed scheme achieves a high level of security while maintaining acceptable computational and communication costs.

Keywords: Maximum Extractable Value · Decentralized Finance · Single Secret Leader Election · Transaction Arrangement · Proposer Builder Separation

1 Introduction

Decentralized finance [1, 2] is a new form of finance that differs from traditional centralized finance [1]. Unlike traditional financial services, it does not rely on trusted third-party organizations. Decentralized finance relies on blockchain technology and represents a new financial ecosystem. This ecosystem is built on blockchain platforms such as Ethereum [3], offering a variety of financial services.

Decentralized finance is one of the hottest topics in the blockchain space. It has attracted a large number of investors and developers, fostering the flourishing of the financial ecosystem. The Total Value Locked (TVL)-the total value of assets locked in all liquidity pools within the decentralized finance market-reached a record \$180 billion in November 2021 [4]. Despite massive losses in decentralized financial markets due to security incidents, the TVL remained

R. K. Shyamasundar et al. (Eds.): ICBC 2025, LNCS 16155, pp. 104–116, 2026.
https://doi.org/10.1007/978-3-032-06176-8_7

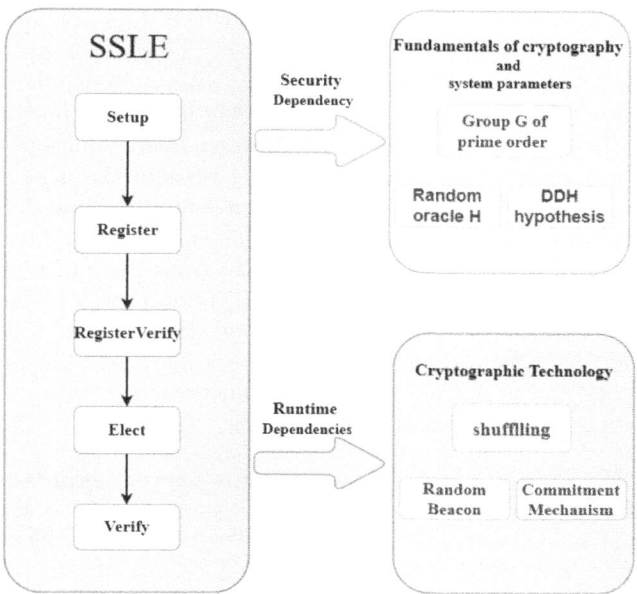

Fig. 1. Construction of SSLE framework

at \$130 billion in 2024 [4]. Such a large market scale implies that countless transactions occur in the market every minute. The ordering of these transactions harbors numerous opportunities to extract Maximum Extractable Value [5], which intrigues many DeFi participants. There are even dedicated arbitrage bots for value extraction. However, most opportunities are tied to the order in which transactions are included in blocks. In blockchains with high transaction-ordering freedom, sequencers (who possess the power to order transactions) become the primary targets for MEV hunters. To capture substantial extractable value, some attackers may bribe sequencers [6] or threaten them with DDoS or eclipse attacks. Forcing sequencers to prioritize transactions according to attackers' interests not only undermines market fairness but also inflicts losses on other market participants.

As the pursuit of extractable value opportunities by DeFi participants can harm the market and users, industry advocates are calling for extractable value to be structured such that its benefits are shared as widely as possible [7]. This approach aims to prevent certain individuals or groups from monopolizing extractable value benefits, which could otherwise undermine market fairness and decentralization. For instance, following its transition from the Proof-of-Work (PoW) to Proof-of-Stake (PoS) consensus protocol, Ethereum [3] introduced the Proposer-Builder Separation (PBS) scheme [8]. Under this framework, extractable value benefits are distributed through an auction-like bidding process. However, the PBS scheme relies on third-party plugins for implementation, introducing single-point-of-failure risks.

Academics, alternatively, advocate for explicit transaction ordering rules, such as first-come-first-served [9] or transaction-ordering agnostic mechanisms [7]. These rules limit miners' freedom to order transactions, thereby curbing extractable value hunters from bribing or coercing miners for personal gain.

By integrating insights from industry and academic solutions to mitigate MEV risks, we observe the power division in PBS and the academic concept of restricting miners' ordering autonomy. Our proposed method decouples miners' transaction sorting power and employs the Single Secret Leader Election (SSLE) method [10] to secretly elect a sequencer from the miner pool. Figure 1 illustrates the basic architecture of this secret election process. The sequencer's identity remains confidential to thwart malicious attacks, after which they sort transactions and send the ordered block to a block packager. The packager then receives the block and performs necessary verifications.

Our contributions are summarized as follows.

– **Utilizing the secret election method for secret sequencer election to thwart malicious attacks.** We employ the secret election algorithm to secretly elect a sequencer for each round. The sequencer's identity remains confidential, known only to the node itself. This mechanism prevents malicious actors from bribing or coercing the sequencer to manipulate transaction ordering, thereby safeguarding market fairness and user interests. By eliminating malicious MEV extraction, this feature enhances DeFi compatibility.
– **Introducing a sequencer role and establishing transaction ordering rules to restrict sequencing autonomy.** Inspired by the PBS framework, our scheme formally defines a sequencer role to decouple transaction sorting power from miners, limiting their freedom to order transactions. The sequencer adheres to predefined rules when sequencing transactions.
– **Implementing integrity scores for variable-weighted sequencer elections.** We introduce integrity scores for all election participants, where higher scores correspond to higher election probabilities. This mechanism maximizes the likelihood that the elected sequencer is an honest and trustworthy node.

2   Related Work

The MEV problem emerged alongside the development of Ethereum, particularly during its upgrade to Ethereum 2.0. To mitigate MEV's negative impacts, the concept of Proposer-Builder Separation (PBS) [8] was introduced. In PBS, blockchain miners' responsibilities are split into two distinct roles: proposers and builders. Builders collect, verify, and assemble transactions into blocks, while also sequencing transactions to optimize gas efficiency. The constructed block is then submitted to proposers, who select a block from those provided by builders and add necessary metadata to form a complete block.

Currently, Ethereum implements PBS primarily through MEV-Boost [11] as an intermediary. Through this intermediary, builders can bid on the blocks they construct, and proposers select blocks based on their own interests, receiving the associated block rewards.

However, PBS based on third-party plugins causes the system to shift from peer-to-peer trust (P2P trust) to centralized intermediary dependence, introducing new security risks of plugins being attacked or bribed. Therefore, researchers are increasingly focused on enshrining Proposer-Builder Separation (ePBS) [12]—a protocol-native approach to implementing PBS without relying on third-party components.

Thus, researchers began to explore implementing transaction ordering at the consensus layer to mitigate MEV-related harms. Mahimna Kelkar et al. [13] proposed a consensus protocol that enforces strong transaction fairness in ordering while demonstrating efficiency comparable to state-of-the-art consensus protocols (without fairness guarantees). However, the protocol faces challenges from high communication complexity and parameter tuning overhead, which may hinder practical deployment. Jan Droll et al. [14] proposed a simple yet unpredictable transaction ordering scheme to address the MEV issue arising from transaction reordering in Ethereum [3]. The scheme utilizes non-malleable signature schemes and a responsibility separation framework, building upon the proposer-builder separation paradigm. While this approach enables easy implementation and rapid verification, it remains susceptible to collusive manipulation by block builders or proposers.

In addition to resisting MEV by restricting transaction reordering freedom, as prior works do, researchers have proposed an alternative approach: content-agnostic ordering (i.e., orderings independent of transaction content) [7]. Mustafa Ibrahim Alnajjar et al. [15] proposed a two-layer architecture based on verifiable encryption to enhance the PBS protocol. By introducing a verifiable encryption mechanism, they ensured transparency and non-repudiation in transaction processing-preventing malicious builders/proposers from reordering transactions or censoring specific transactions. However, the scheme encounters challenges from high computational overhead and intricate key management. Julien Piet et al. [16] proposed two practical solutions for blockchain systems under Proof-of-Work and Proof-of-Stake consensus models. These approaches effectively mitigate MEV exploitation by blindly encrypting transactions and enforcing random execution ordering.

3 Preliminaries

The security properties of this paper is preserved based on the SSLE framework [10]. This section will briefly necessary cryptographic tools for this framework, such as the Diffie-Hellman problems.

3.1 Diffie-Hellman Assumption

The Diffie-Hellman assumption is the core security foundation of the scheme. This assumption is defined as follows: let $\mathbb{G}$ be a cyclic group of prime order q, with generator g. For random exponents $a, b, c \in \mathbb{Z}_q$, the DH assumption states that it is computationally difficult to distinguish between a true DH triplet (g^a, g^b, g^{ab}) and a random triplet (g^a, g^b, g^c). A more formal statement is that the distinguishing advantage of any probabilistic polynomial-time algorithm $\mathcal{A}$ can be expressed as follows:

$$\left| \Pr[\mathcal{A}(g^a, g^b, g^{ab}) = 1] - \Pr[\mathcal{A}(g^a, g^b, g^c) = 1] \right| < \mathrm{negl}(\lambda)$$

where λ is a security parameter and *negl* denotes a negligible function.

3.2   Diffie-Hellman Commitment

Using the DH assumption, construct a commitment scheme that ensures indistinguishability and attack resistance. The form of the commitment scheme based on the DH assumption is as follows:

$$\mathrm{com}(k_i, r) = (u, v) = (g^r, g^{k_i \cdot r}) \in \mathbb{G} \times \mathbb{G}$$

where k_i is the secret in the commitment and r is a randomly selected number.

If verification of the commitment is required, the verifier only needs to provide the secret value, k_i, and check if it satisfies the verification formula $v = u^{k_i}$. Furthermore, the DH assumption provides assurance that makes it difficult for others to infer the secret value k_i from (u, v).

Then, the commitment scheme enables re-randomization of commitments. Selecting a new random number r' and re-randomizing the commitment $(u, v) \rightarrow (u^{r'}, v^{r'})$, ensures that the old and new commitments are unlinkable, thus enhancing privacy. However, both the new and old commitments are verified using the same secret value k_i.

3.3   Random Beacon

In the scheme, we use a random beacon to generate a random number R, which is used to elect a secret leader during the election phase. The generation of random numbers by the random beacon is both unpredictable and unbiased. Unpredictability means no one can predict the random number in advance. Unbiasedness means the generated random numbers are independently and uniformly distributed. Since the method of sampling random numbers is unrelated to the research content in our scheme, we do not provide the specific method for generating random numbers. A series of studies on random beacons is available for reference [17,18].

4   System and Security Model

4.1   System Model

As shown in Fig. 2. Our proposed scheme consists of three primary entities: candidate $\mathcal{C}$, sequencer $\mathcal{S}$, and proposer $\mathcal{P}$. $\mathcal{C}$ and $\mathcal{S}$ have a secret key sk_i used

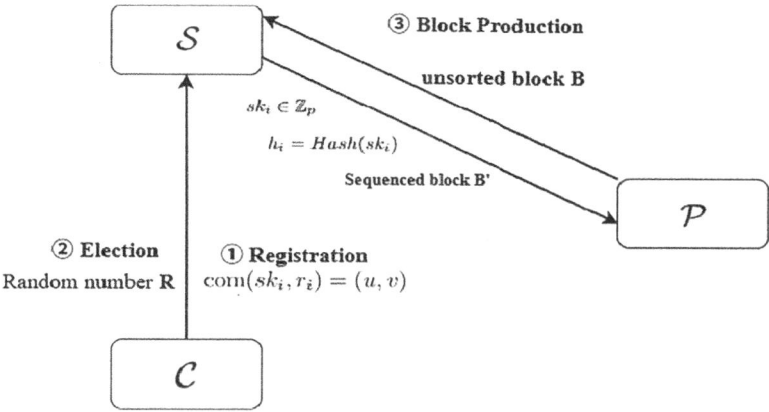

Fig. 2. System Model

for registration, and $\mathcal{P}$ has the authority to package transactions into blocks and verify which blocks are added to the chain. The specific interaction process is described as follows:

In order to secretly elect $\mathcal{S}$, $\mathcal{C}$ who wish to participate in the election need to construct a commitment using their secret key sk_i and place it in a candidate pool. To ensure the unpredictability and secrecy of the election result, the candidate pool must be blinded before $\mathcal{S}$ is elected. Finally, $\mathcal{S}$ is secretly elected using the generated random number $\mathcal{R}$.

Subsequently, $\mathcal{P}$ packages transactions from the transaction pool according to the rules and submits them to $\mathcal{S}$. $\mathcal{S}$ processes the block and sequences the transactions according to the rules. The sequenced block and related verification data are then handed over to $\mathcal{P}$. $\mathcal{P}$ verifies the sequenced block, and if the verification is correct, the block is added to the chain.

4.2 Threat Model and Security Requirement

Adversaries can only access public information about $\mathcal{C}$ and $\mathcal{P}$, as well as public information in the candidate pool.

For entities in the system, we assume that $\mathcal{S}$ is trustworthy, while $\mathcal{C}$ and $\mathcal{P}$ are not necessarily trustworthy. Specifically, $\mathcal{S}$ will honestly sequence transactions according to the rules, while malicious nodes exist in the group of $\mathcal{C}$ and $\mathcal{P}$, attempting to manipulate the transaction order to gain benefits.

The detailed security requirements are outlined below based on the established security assumptions:

- **Uniqueness:** After each round of secret elections, at most one $\mathcal{C}$ can be secretly elected as $\mathcal{S}$.
- **Unpredictability:** Before the secret election is over, no one can guess who will be secretly elected as $\mathcal{S}$ based on public information.

- **Anonymity:** Unless $\mathcal{S}$ voluntarily reveals his identity information, adversaries will not be able to know the identity information of $\mathcal{S}$ or bribe/attack $\mathcal{S}$.
- **Anti-sequential manipulation:** This property ensures that adversaries cannot manipulate the transaction order for profit or attack purposes.

5 Construction of MEVShield

In this section, we propose the specific construction of the scheme. The general process of the scheme is shown in Fig. 3. Then, we describe in detail the process from initialization, registration, election to block production. As is shown in the following subsections, the proposed scheme effectively addresses all of the challenges outlined in the overview.

5.1 Initialization

The scheme emphasizes the interactive relationship between $\mathcal{C}$, $\mathcal{S}$, and $\mathcal{P}$, and we must perform related initialization settings that are crucial for instantiating and constructing the system. First, $\mathcal{C}$ must create a secret key sk_i, then initialize the public parameter pp and the system state set st. These operations form the basis for subsequent processes.

Select a group $\mathbb{G}$ of prime order q where DDH is hard. Randomly select an element g from the group $\mathbb{G}$ and create empty vectors $\boldsymbol{H} = \emptyset$ and $\boldsymbol{L} = \emptyset$. After the vectors are initialized, public parameters pp are generated. The specific public parameters are as follows:

$$pp = (q, g, \mathbb{G}, \boldsymbol{H}, \boldsymbol{L})$$

$\mathcal{C}$ needs to generate a secret key sk_i, which is used for subsequent commitment generation. sk_i is a random element in $\mathbb{Z}_q$. After sk_i is set, the initialization of the system state set st is completed. The specific system state set is as follows:

$$st = (pp, sk_1, ..., sk_n)$$

Finally, the public parameter pp will be published to the blockchain, and anyone can access the information in pp.

5.2 Registration

After the system initialization phase is complete, $\mathcal{C}$ begins registering its identifier on the blockchain. A key part of the registration process is generating a commitment. The detailed process is as follows.

In our construction, $\mathcal{C}$ randomly selects an element from $\mathbb{Z}_q$ as its secret key sk_i. Then, sk_i is hashed using $H(\cdot)$ to obtain the corresponding hash value h_i, which is stored in the candidate identity proof vector $\boldsymbol{H}$ as the identity proof of $\mathcal{C}$. This identity proof is unique.

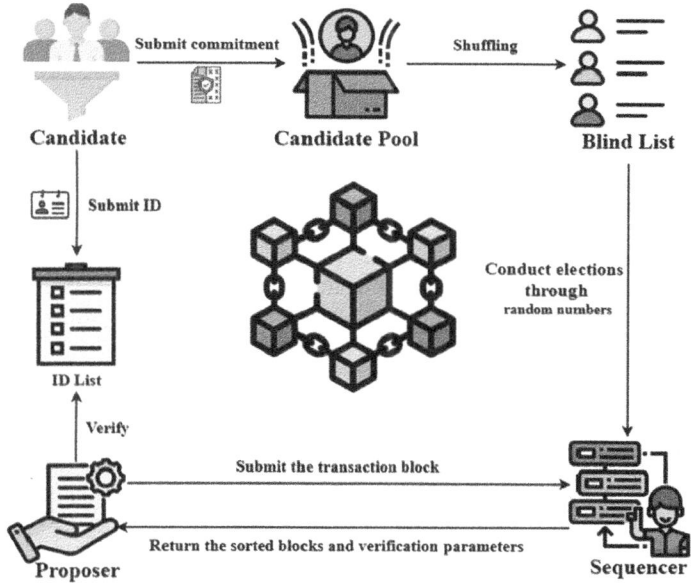

Fig. 3. Visualization of MEVShield

Then, $\mathcal{C}$ samples a number r_i from $\mathbb{Z}_q$ and constructs a commitment.As follows:

$$\text{com}(sk_i, r_i) = (u, v) = (g^{r_i}, g^{r_i \cdot sk_i})$$

Finally, the commitment is added to the candidate pool vector L to complete the registration. In the system architecture, each node is assigned a reputation score. If a node participating in the election has a high score, it can sample multiple random numbers. Based on the current number of candidates, the number of commitments added to the candidate pool is increased proportionally.

Additionally, candidate $\mathcal{C}$ will compare the identity proof and constructed commitment of a newly registered candidate $\mathcal{C}_j$ with the existing elements in the vectors H and L to ensure that the new elements are not duplicates of the existing elements. If there is a duplicate, registration will fail.

5.3 Election

After registration is complete, the election phase begins. The most important step is to blind the entries in L. Randomly sample a random number r_i' from $\mathbb{Z}_q$. Re-randomize the commitments in L as follows:

$$(g^{r_i}, g^{sk_i r_i}) \rightarrow (g^{r_i r_i'}, g^{sk_i r_i r_i'})$$

Finally, shuffle and permute the candidate pool L to complete the blinding operation. As follows:

$$L = [c_1, c_2, ..., c_n] \rightarrow L' = [c_1', c_2', ..., c_n']$$

where L is the input list, L' is the output list,each c_i is an encrypted commitment and Each c'_i is a re-randomized commitment.

Furthermore, the output list L' and the input list L satisfy several conditions. First, L' is an arrangement of L, meaning the elements are exactly the same, but their sequence is distinct. Secondly, Each c'_j is a re-randomized version of c_i, such as

$$c_i = (g^r, g^{kr}) \rightarrow c'_j = (g^{rs}, g^{krr'})$$

where r' is a new random number.

Once blinding is complete, a random number R is obtained via random beacon. Then, the selected commitment position is calculated as follows:

$$l = R \bmod N$$

where l is the selected position and $N = |L|$ is the total number of commitments in the candidate pool. The owner of the commitment at this position is the selected sequencer S.

5.4 Block Production

After the secret election is over, P packages transactions from the transaction pool according to relevant rules, such as prioritizing transactions by their fees. Then, the packaged transactions are submitted to the group of C.

After the group of C receives the block B, S, who is elected by secret ballot within the group, selects B from those submitted by P and then sorts B by computing the XOR distance between the hash value of each transaction in the block and its own identity proof h_i.

After completing the sorting, S hands over the sorted block B' to P, the submitter of B, and simultaneously submits its secret key sk_i and identification proof h_i. After receiving B' and related parameters, P verifies whether h_i is equal to $H(sk_i)$ and whether the selected commitment (u, v) satisfies the equation $u^{\mathrm{sk}_i} = v$. If both conditions hold, the commitment is valid and generated by S. If all verifications succeed, the block is formally proposed.

After the block is successfully added to the chain, S will receive more rewards than P does, while P will receive a portion of the rewards and an increase in reputation points.If S wants to continue participating in the next round of elections, it must regenerate the new sk_i and then re-register.

6 Security Analysis

This section provides a brief security analysis. We will prove that the election process is *unpredictable* and that the election results satisfy *Uniqueness* and *Anonymity*. At the same time, the scheme can achieve *anti-sequence manipulation* (Table 1).

Table 1. Notion

SYMBOL	DESCRIPTION
$\mathcal{C}, \mathcal{S}, \mathcal{P}$	Candidate, Sequencer, Proposer
h_i	Identity proof of candidate, stored in $\boldsymbol{H}$, $h_i = Hash(sk_i)$
sk_i	Secret key of Candidate, $sk_i \in \mathbb{Z}_q$
$\boldsymbol{H}, \boldsymbol{L}$	Two vectors are used to store identity proof and registration commitments, respectively.
l	The selected position is represented by it.
pp, st	Public parameters and global system parameters
r_i, r_i'	Random numbers are used to generate commitments. $r_i, r_i' \in \mathbb{Z}_q$
B, B'	Blocks and sorted Blocks
R	Unbiased random numbers generated by random beacons
N	Number of people participating in the secret election

Table 2. Comparison with related work

Scheme	Uniqueness	Unpredictability	Anti-sequence manipulation	Anonymity	Overhead
ONE-TO-THREE [14]	✓	✓	✗	✗	High
Themis [19]	-	✗	✓	✗	Low
MEVShield	✓	✓	✓	✓	Low

1. *Unpredictability:* During the election process, no one can predict the election results. This is because the results are determined by the random number R generated by the random beacon, and the numbers generated by the random beacon are uniformly and unbiasedly distributed. No one can predict what numbers the random beacon will generate.

2. *Uniqueness:* The election results ensure uniqueness (at most one winner). During registration, each candidate must generate their own unique identity certificate by hashing their secret key. The certificates are then verified by the system during registration to ensure the candidates' identities are unique, thereby ensuring that no multiple candidates can claim the election result.

3. *Anonymity:* The election results ensure anonymity of the selected nodes. During the election process, the unlinkability between pre-election and post-election candidate pools is ensured through cryptographic re-randomization and shuffling, thereby blinding the election entries. When the election results are produced, except for the selected nodes themselves, other nodes cannot determine the identities of the selected nodes.

4. *Anti-sequence manipulation:* The sorting results are unmanipulable by adversaries. Sorting results are generated based on the identity proof of the secretly elected nodes. The election results are unpredictable, and the identity verification process is unique with its rules determined prior to the election. At the same time, the identity of the secretly elected nodes is confidential. Therefore, adversaries cannot manipulate the sorting results.

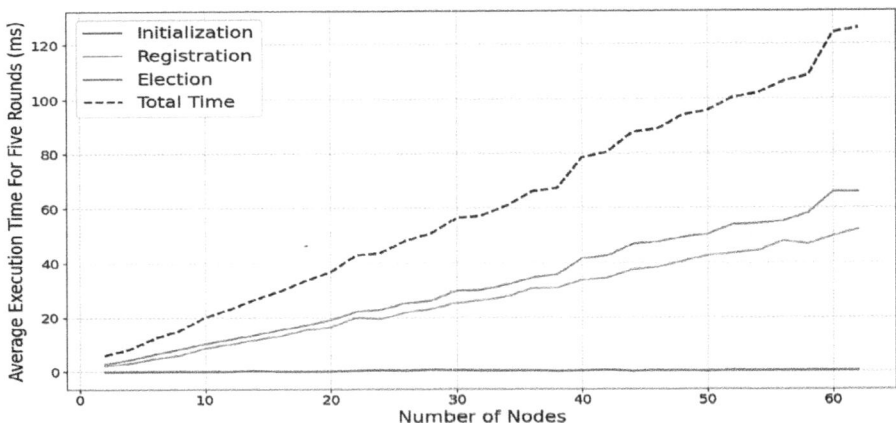

Fig. 4. Relationship between the number of nodes and time cost

7   Evaluation

We evaluated the MEVShield implementation on an Ubuntu 22.04 instance running on the Windows Subsystem for Linux (WSL2). The test device had an Intel Core i7-10750H CPU and 16GB of RAM.

We implemented MEVShield in Python and used the cryptographic library `Charm-Crypto` to provide basic cryptographic methods.

The primary emphasis and cost of our proposal is allocated to the implementation of secret elections. The subsequent consensus process is outside the scope of our concern. Thus, the experiment primarily considers the computational and communication costs associated with the secret election process. As shown in Fig. 4, MEVShield is operationally efficient. As the number of participating nodes increases, the time required generally increases linearly (Table 4).

Additionally, we evaluated communication costs by serializing identity verification and commitments in the MEVShield scheme. As shown in Table 3, the scheme requires minimal communication costs. For 50 participants, the communication costs for an election are approximately 12 KB, which is not an additional burden. A comparative analysis was conducted between MEVShield and other anti-MEV solutions in terms of attributes and temporal costs. As demonstrated in Table 3 and Table 2, our proposed solution exhibits a clear advantage in terms of time costs while offering more security attributes. This suggests that our solution can achieve anti-MEV goals more efficiently and with greater security and robustness.

In summary, our comprehensive evaluation shows that MEVShield is an efficient and practical solution for mitigating transaction order manipulation. The secrecy of secret elections protects sequencers from malicious actors. Therefore, MEVShield effectively addresses security and efficiency requirements by ensuring that transaction ordering is not easily manipulated.

Table 3. Communication cost of MEVShield

Scheme	Type	Communication Load (Byte)		
		n = 10	n = 20	n = 50
MEVShield	List of identity verification	600	1200	3000
	Candidate Pool	1848	3528	9072

Table 4. Time consumption of schemes

Scheme (N = 30)	Time (ms)
ONE-TO-THREE [14]	2100
Themis [19]	53
MEVShield	55

8   Conclusion

This paper proposes a low-cost, MEV-resistant MEVShield framework that supports low-computational-overhead resistance to order manipulation. To address the challenges posed by extractable value in decentralized finance, MEVShield defines a clear framework that outlines the interaction relationships among all roles. We provide a detailed description of MEVShield's design and have ensured that it meets all functional and security requirements. We have implemented our solution and conducted a formal security analysis. Experimental results demonstrate that our solution has significantly low computational and communication costs, making it highly feasible. For future work, we will explore additional features to further enhance the comprehensiveness and robustness of our framework.

Acknowledgments. This work is supported by the National Key Research and Development Program of China (2023YFB2704900), and National Natural Science Foundation of China (Grant Nos. 62202290).

References

1. Gogol, K., Killer, C., Schlosser, M., Bocek, T., Stiller, B., Tessone, C.: SoK: decentralized finance (DeFi)–fundamentals, taxonomy and risks. arXiv preprint arXiv:2404.11281 (2024)
2. Liu, M., et al.: I experienced more than 10 {DeFi} scams: On {DeFi} users' perception of security breaches and countermeasures. In: 33rd USENIX Security Symposium (USENIX Security 24), pp. 6039–6055 (2024)
3. Wood, G.: Ethereum: a secure decentralised generalised transaction ledger (2013)
4. DeFiLlama. Defillama dashboard (2024). https://defillama.com
5. Daian, P., et al.: 'Flash boys 2.0: frontrunning, transaction reordering, and consensus instability in decentralized exchanges. arXiv preprint arXiv:1904.05234 (2019)

6. Tsabary, I., Yechieli, M., Manuskin, A., Eyal, I.: MAD-HTLC: because HTLC is crazy-cheap to attack. arXiv Cryptography and Security (2020)

7. Yang, S., Zhang, F., Huang, K., Chen, X., Yang, Y., Zhu, F.: SoK: MEV countermeasures. In: Proceedings of the Workshop on Decentralized Finance and Security, pp. 21–30 (2024)

8. D'Amato, F., Monnot, B., Neuder, M.: Potuz, and terence tsao. eip-7732: Enshrined proposer-builder separation [draft] (2024)

9. Kelkar, M., Deb, S., Long, S., Juels, A., Kannan, S.: Themis: fast, strong order-fairness in byzantine consensus. In: Proceedings of the 2023 ACM SIGSAC Conference on Computer and Communications Security, pp. 475–489 (2023)

10. Boneh, D., Eskandarian, S., Hanzlik, L., Greco, N.: Single secret leader election. In: Proceedings of the 2nd ACM Conference on Advances in Financial Technologies, pp. 12–24 (2020)

11. Flashbots. Flashbots.2024.mev-boost (2024). https://github.com/flashbots/mev-boost

12. Neuder, M.: Why enshrine proposer-builder separation? a viable path to ePBS (2022). https://ethresear.ch/t/why-enshrine-proposer-builder-separation-a-viable-path-to-epbs/15710

13. Kelkar, M., Deb, S., Kannan, S.: Order-fair consensus in the permissionless setting. In: Proceedings of the 9th ACM on ASIA Public-Key Cryptography Workshop (2022). http://dx.doi.org/10.1145/3494105.3526239

14. Droll, J., Stengele, O., Hartenstein, H.: Short paper: unpredictable transaction arrangement for mev mitigation in ethereum. In: 2024 IEEE International Conference on Blockchain and Cryptocurrency (ICBC), pp. 625–629. IEEE (2024)

15. Alnajjar, M.I., Kiraz, M.S., Al-Bayatti, A., Kardas, S.: Mitigating MEV attacks with a two-tiered architecture utilizing verifiable decryption. EURASIP J. Wirel. Commun. Netw. **2024**(1), 62 (2024)

16. Piet, J., Nair, V., Subramanian, S.: MEVade: an MEV-resistant blockchain design. In: 2023 IEEE International Conference on Blockchain and Cryptocurrency (ICBC), pp. 1–9. IEEE (2023)

17. Das, S., Krishnan, V., Isaac, I.M., Ren, L.: SPURT: scalable distributed randomness beacon with transparent setup. In: 2022 IEEE Symposium on Security and Privacy (SP) (2022). http://dx.doi.org/10.1109/sp46214.2022.9833580

18. Choi, K., Manoj, A., Bonneau, J.: SoK: distributed randomness beacons. In: 2023 IEEE Symposium on Security and Privacy (SP) (2023). https://doi.org/10.1109/sp46215.2023.10179419

19. Kelkar, M., Deb, S., Long, S., Juels, A., Kannan, S.: Themis: fast, strong order-fairness in byzantine consensus. IACR Cryptology ePrint Archive, IACR Cryptology ePrint Archive (2021)

A Federated Blockchain-Enabled 6G Streaming Architecture: Protocol Innovation and Trusted Ecology

Zihao Zhou📧, Kaibin Wei$^{(\boxtimes)}$📧, and Tuo Song📧

School of Electronic Information and Electrical Engineering, Tianshui Normal University, Gansu, China
{20240702016,20240702030}@st.tsnu.edu.cn,
weikaibin@tsnu.edu.cn

Abstract. 6G streaming advancement intensifies challenges in content security, copyright traceability, and privacy protection. This paper proposes a novel architecture integrating federated learning and blockchain. By enhancing protocol stacks and reconstructing trust mechanisms, it delivers an end-to-end solution spanning content creation, auditing, distribution, and value allocation. Federated learning metadata and blockchain interfaces are embedded within RTP/RTCP protocols, establishing a terminal-edge-cloud three-tier auditing system for hierarchical content filtering and localized privacy processing. A smart contract framework enables digital rights confirmation and value circulation through decentralized incentives and token-driven economics. Performance analysis confirms significant improvements in auditing efficiency and copyright transparency while maintaining ultra-low latency and supporting multimodal experiences, providing a systematic paradigm for secure, trustworthy streaming ecosystems.

Keywords: 6G · streaming media · Federated learning · blockchain · three-level collaboration

1 Introduction

6G technology marks a transformative milestone in the evolution of smart cities [1]. The advent of the sixth-generation mobile communication system (6G), characterized by ubiquitous coverage and intelligent connectivity, has propelled streaming media services to the forefront of next-generation applications. However, these services face increasingly stringent requirements, including high-bandwidth, ultra-low-latency transmission and, crucially, the establishment of a secure, transparent, and trustworthy service ecosystem [2], where the core challenge lies in simultaneously optimizing content security governance, verifiable copyright traceability, and user privacy protection through novel architectural solutions.

R. K. Shyamasundar et al. (Eds.): ICBC 2025, LNCS 16155, pp. 117–133, 2026.
https://doi.org/10.1007/978-3-032-06176-8_8

Addressing 6G trust challenges, research focuses on endogenous security and blockchain integration. IMT-2030 advocates decoupling security functions into pluggable trust modules [3, 4]. Blockchain's immutability enables copyright traceability and content auditing [5,6], with native trust embedding in infrastructure nodes (e.g., base stations as blockchain nodes) via Net4BC/BCaaS [7,8], reducing cross-domain authentication latency by up to 40% [9]. However, consensus throughput bottlenecks and cross-domain orchestration complexity persist [10,11]. Federated Learning (FL) enhances privacy-preserving intelligence [12], synergizing with blockchain for "available but invisible" data principles [13], improving model accuracy (+15%) while reducing privacy risks (−30%) [14]. TEEs secure on-chain runtime logging [15]. Nevertheless, protocol-level FL-blockchain integration within 6G streaming's transport layer remains unresolved, exacerbated by space-air-ground-sea connectivity demands [16] requiring decentralized PKI/smart contracts [17,18] (service interruption <0.1%) [19]. A holistic architecture natively embedding trust, intelligence, and privacy into core protocols remains lacking.

Addressing challenges of native trust-intelligence integration in streaming protocols, privacy-constrained cross-domain collaboration, and verifiable value distribution, this paper proposes a novel federated blockchain-enabled 6G streaming architecture. Primary contributions encompass: (1) We propose a native extension of the RTP/RTCP protocol stack by embedding federated learning identifiers and blockchain metadata directly into the transport layer, enabling seamless integration across communication and trust layers; (2) We design a hierarchical three-tier content audit framework that combines differential privacy at the terminal layer, intelligent inference at the edge, and immutable blockchain logging at the cloud layer; (3) We conduct a comprehensive theoretical analysis of convergence guarantees in federated learning, the scalability of blockchain-based storage, and the stability of token-driven incentive mechanisms in a decentralized ecosystem.

2   Related Work

Research on trusted 6G architectures focuses on endogenous security frameworks integrating blockchain technology. The IMT-2030 Promotion Group proposes decoupling security capabilities from business processes through blockchain-enabled distributed trust, establishing multidimensional immunity across infrastructure and data assets [3, 21]. The EU Hexa-X project enhances this by combining TEE with distributed PKI to resolve cross-domain trust challenges [22].

Blockchain integration in 6G systems has evolved from out-of-band to embedded architectures. Service models like BC4Net and BCaaS enable deep integration between communication nodes and blockchain functions (BCRF/BCSF) for smart contract orchestration [4,23]. Complementary approaches include Devitt et al.'s human-machine trust framework [24] and CAICT's intrinsic embedding paradigm [4].

For federated learning-blockchain synergy, studies demonstrate recording model hashes on-chain ensures auditability [25]. Applications show blockchain incentives accelerate convergence (+32%) while zero-knowledge proofs preserve privacy [26]. Huawei's distributed data plane enables millisecond retrieval latency for decentralized indexing [8], and China Unicom's framework achieves 99.3% malicious node detection [14].

To address 6G streaming challenges, this work introduces protocol-level innovations: reconstructing RTP/RTCP/SIP stacks for native FL-blockchain integration, establishing multi-level content auditing, and implementing decentralized copyright management.

3   Research Methods

3.1   Architecture Design of Federated Blockchain

Protocol Stack Enhancement and Cross-Layer Coordination. Metadata embedding couples content features with transport signaling by integrating federated learning model identifiers and feature hashes into extended RTP headers. Receivers interpret these identifiers to load appropriate decoders for heterogeneous device rendering. An intelligent feedback mechanism redefines RTCP Extended Reports (XR) through federated learning parameter fields and blockchain status indicators, enabling edge nodes to dynamically adjust model aggregation strategies. This simultaneously triggers smart contracts for copyright settlement, establishing a closed-loop system that binds transport-layer features to application-layer decisions.

The NFT broadcasting interface extends the SIP REGISTER method to enable content fingerprint and ownership claim submission during session initiation. Blockchain gateways encapsulate metadata (content hashes, timestamps, copyright terms) into smart contracts, with consensus verification generating NFT certificates returned via standardized responses. The system integrates W3C-compliant Decentralized Identifiers (DIDs) for distributed authentication. During SIP negotiation, terminals embed zk-SNARKs-based Verifiable Credentials in extended authorization headers. Coupled with a blockchain-based Decentralized Key Management System (DKMS), this establishes a cross-domain authentication framework that eliminates third-party certificate authorities and achieves end-to-end trusted authentication. The workflow is shown in the figure:

Transport layer enhancements extend RTP headers to incorporate federated learning model identifiers and blockchain transaction indices, bidirectionally coupling metadata with learning tasks and blockchain storage. Concurrent RTCP extensions define specialized feedback reports for federated learning, enabling encrypted gradient transmission monitoring and QoE-driven optimization to secure real-time distributed machine learning.

Deep RTP/RTCP integration enables collaborative feature binding and federated learning through header extensions incorporating federated learning model IDs and feature hashes, establishing bidirectional coupling between transport signaling and content semantics (Fig. 1):

```
struct rtp_fl_header {
uint32_t ssrc;
```

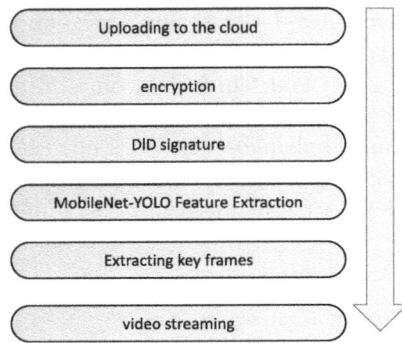

Fig. 1. Overall system workflow of the federated blockchain-enabled 6G streaming architecture.

```
uint16_t seq_num;
uint8_t payload_type;
uint8_t fl_model_id;
uint32_t feature_hash;
uint64_t block_ref;
uint16_t qoe_metric;};
```

The refactored RTCP Extended Report (XR) introduces interaction fields specific to federated learning:

$$XR_{FL} = \langle \nabla W_{local}, Sig_{DID}, H_{model} \rangle \tag{1}$$

where W_{local} denotes the local gradient updates generated at the edge device after one round of federated training. Sig_{DID} refers to the digital signature based on the Decentralized Identifier (DID), ensuring the authenticity and integrity of the local update. H_{model} is the model hash fingerprint, computed using SHA-256, used to verify model version consistency across nodes. Line.

This framework enables dynamic adjustment of model aggregation strategies at edge nodes. Receivers load model-specific decoders based on identifiers, while QoE bitmasks facilitate bidirectional optimization of transmission quality and rendering performance.

Application-layer enhancements extend the SIP REGISTER method to define an NFT foundry interface, enabling automated blockchain registration of digital fingerprints and ownership declarations. Concurrently, Decentralized Identifier (DID) integration establishes a blockchain-based distributed authentication framework, supporting trustless cross-domain security and enabling decentralized identity management with digital asset interoperability. A standardized NFT foundry interface is defined by extending the SIP REGISTER method: < SIP-blockchain message > ::= < method > SP < blockchain URI> SIP/2.0
*(< expand header >)
[< Message body >]

```
< blockchain URI > ::= "blockchain:" < address > "@" < chain id >
< extension header > ::= Copyright-ID | FL-Params | QoS-Tag
<  message body  >  : :  =  "content_hash":  <  H_content  >,
"license_terms":
<  encryption terms  >,"royalty_model": <  revenue distribution
scheme >/};
```

Encrypted metadata—including digital fingerprints and licensing terms-is encapsulated within smart contracts, generating immutable NFT-based certificates through consensus verification. The identity layer integrates W3C DID architecture with zk-SNARKs zero-knowledge proofs for cross-domain SIP session authentication, establishing a decentralized trust system via DKMS integration.

A cross-layer collaborative mechanism integrates optimization functions across protocol, computation, and storage layers:

$$\min C_{FL}(W) + \beta \cdot C_{Qos}(\theta) \tag{2}$$

where $C_{FL}(W)$ is the federated learning loss, Wis the model parameter vector, C_{Qos} is the network-level cost function reflecting Quality-of-Service, and θ denotes tunable protocol parameters. The coefficient β governs the trade-off between model accuracy and transmission efficiency. The event-driven resource scheduling strategy of blockchain dynamically allocates edge resources according to the change of the state on the chain (such as model update and storage proof), forming a global optimization closed loop covering the protocol layer, computing layer and storage layer.

Standardization efforts include IETF drafts defining the RTP-FL extension header format and SIP-blockchain gateway interface, establishing interoperability between communication protocols and distributed ledgers. Concurrent development of Federated Learning Model Exchange Format (FL-MEF) creates a unified framework for model parameters and encrypted metadata, enabling cross-platform federated model migration and joint training. This standardized ecosystem overcomes protocol, algorithmic, and operational barriers to accelerate decentralized federated learning deployment. Specific criteria are as follows:

```
< Federated Streaming standard > ::= < Protocol extensions >
< Algorithmic interfaces >< Governance specifications >
< Protocol extension > ::= RTP-FL|RTCP-XR-FL|SIP-Blockchain
< Algorithm interface > ::=
FL-Model-Exchange|Privacy-Preserving-Inference
<       Governance specification       >       ::=
DAO-Governance|Cross-Chain-Protocol
```

Multi-level Federated Review Architecture. To address the demands of distributed computing and privacy preservation, this study proposes a three-tiered review architecture comprising terminal-level preprocessing, edge-level collaborative inference, and cloud-level arbitration. At the terminal level, a lightweight MobileNet-YOLO model performs real-time detection of prohibited content. Privacy protection is achieved by injecting (ε, δ) -differential privacy into the feature extraction process, wherein Gaussian noise is added during local model updates. The formulation is as follows.

$$W_{t+1}^{local} = W_t - \eta \nabla f(x_i, y_i; W_t) + N(0, \sigma^2 I) \tag{3}$$

where $N(0, \sigma^2 I)$ is a zero-mean Gaussian noise vector ensuring (ε, δ)-differential privacy. The noise variance σ^2 is dynamically adjusted to control the privacy budget across communication rounds. This mechanism allows local model updates to remain private while preserving utility in federated aggregation (Fig. 2).

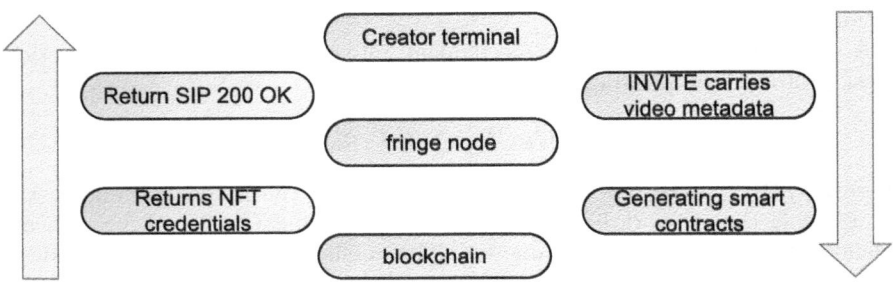

Fig. 2. Local authoring and preprocessing workflow at the terminal layer.

The privacy budget is flexibly managed by dynamically adjusting the noise variance σ. During preprocessing, key frame extraction and feature encryption are performed concurrently. The typical workflow is illustrated as follows: `def local_processing(video_stream):`

```
frames = extract_key_frames(video_stream)
features = mobile_yolo(frames)
report = sign_with_did(noisy_features)
return encrypt(report)
```

Edge nodes perform cross-device collaborative inference using multimodal federated aggregation. A content-hash-driven attention mechanism dynamically integrates visual, audio, and textual features. The aggregation weights are computed as follows:

$$W_{glabal} = \sum_{k=1}^{K} \frac{n_k}{N} W_k^{local} \otimes M_{attn}(H_{content}) \tag{4}$$

where each local model is weighted not only by data volume but also by a content-hash-driven attention mask M_{attn}, which adaptively determines the influence of different modalities. The attention weights are derived from the similarity matrix of hashed visual, audio, and text features, enhancing the model's ability to focus on semantically dominant content dimensions.Workflow of edge node: where each local model is weighted not only by data volume but also by a content-hash-driven attention mask M_{attn}, which adaptively determines the influence of different modalities. The attention weights are derived from the similarity matrix of hashed visual, audio, and text features, enhancing the model's ability to focus on semantically dominant content dimensions. Workflow of edge node (Fig. 3):

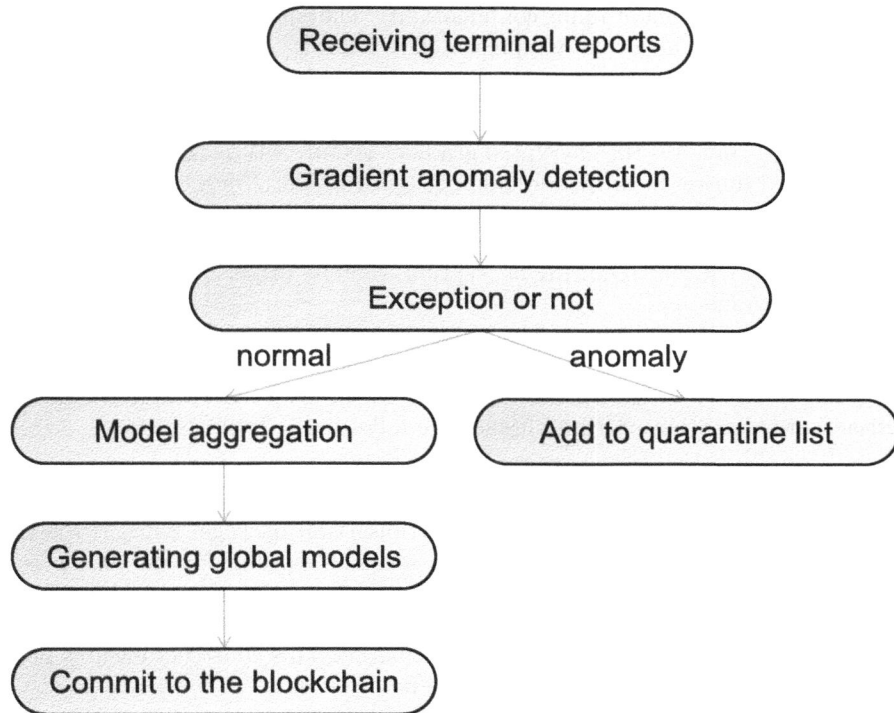

Fig. 3. Federated content review and aggregation process at edge nodes.

An arbitration module resolves low-confidence edge cases through expert review, with audit decisions and evidence immutably recorded on blockchain for full traceability. A feedback loop integrates verified manual annotations into federated learning to iteratively refine the global model and reduce false positives. This collaborative governance framework—combining automated screening, human arbitration, and continuous model optimization—ensures compliance while enhancing detection accuracy.Suspicious content determination rules:

$$ConfidenceScore = \alpha \cdot P_{visual} + \beta \cdot P_{audio} + \gamma \cdot P_{text} \qquad (5)$$

where $P_{visual}, P_{audio}, P_{text}$ are the prediction confidence scores from each modality-specific detection module. The coefficients $alpha, beta, gamma$ denote the respective weights assigned to visual, audio, and textual features, and are constrained such that *alpha+beta+gamma*=1. These weights can be statically defined or dynamically adjusted based on content context or historical model performance.

Client Privacy Protection. Homomorphic encryption enables privacy-preserving gradient aggregation in federated learning, performing computations on encrypted data while maintaining confidentiality. The encrypted transmission process of gradients can be formally represented as follows:

$$[\nabla W]_{enc} = Paillier.Enc_{pk}(\nabla W) \tag{6}$$

where $[\nabla W]_{enc}$ denotes the encrypted gradient vector; ∇W is the original gradient computed during local model training; and $Paillier.Enc_{pk}()$ represents the Paillier public-key homomorphic encryption function under the public key pkpkpk. This encryption allows aggregation operations to be performed directly on encrypted data without requiring decryption, thereby preserving privacy during federated learning.

This mechanism enables model training contributions without raw data disclosure. Integration of verifiable computation with zero-knowledge proofs generates publicly verifiable attestations for infringement detection computations.The transaction verification process satisfies the following criteria:

$$Transaction = \{Enc_{\rho k}(\nu), \pi_{ZK}\} \ s.t. \pi_{ZK} + Valid(\nu) \tag{7}$$

where $Transaction$ denotes the encrypted transaction package; $Enc_{\rho k}(\nu)$ is the encrypted transaction amount ν using the recipient's public key ρk ; π_{ZK} is a zero-knowledge proof attesting to the validity of the transaction; and $Valid(\nu)$ denotes a publicly verifiable function that checks the correctness of the transaction value ν without revealing its actual content. This construct ensures both confidentiality and verifiability of sensitive financial data.

This hybrid approach ensures simultaneous transaction value confidentiality and computational correctness through formal proofs, establishing dual-layer privacy and verifiability protection. Within the federated recommendation system, local preference modeling retains user behavior data exclusively on terminal devices during parameter updates, and model parameters are updated by optimizing the following objective function:

$$\min \sum_{i=1}^{n} f(x_i, y_i; w) + \frac{\lambda}{2}||w||^2 \tag{8}$$

where x_i represents the user behavior features for the i-th sample (e.g., click actions, view history, watch duration), and y_i denotes the corresponding target label (e.g., user rating, click-through rate). The function $f(x_i, y_i; w)$ is a loss function that measures the prediction error, typically instantiated as mean squared error (MSE) or cross-entropy loss. The vector w denotes the trainable parameters of the local recommendation model. The term $\frac{\lambda}{2}||w||^2$ is an L2 regularization term that penalizes large parameter values to prevent overfitting, where λ is a non-negative regularization coefficient. The optimization is performed over n local training samples on the terminal device. The QoE enhancement mechanism improves transmission quality via a dynamic bitrate adaptation algorithm, whose decision function is defined as:

$$Bitrate = f(ModelHash, NetworkState, UserPreference) \tag{9}$$

where $Bitrate$ is the output bitrate selected by the adaptive streaming algorithm; $ModelHash$ denotes the identifier or fingerprint of the current deep learning model in use, which reflects model capability and complexity; $NetworkState$ captures the real-time network conditions, such as bandwidth, latency, and packet loss rate; and $UserPreference$ includes both explicit preferences (e.g., resolution settings) and implicit physiological signals (e.g., eye tracking, heart rate). The function $f()$ dynamically computes the optimal bitrate to maximize perceived quality while minimizing delay and resource consumption.

This algorithm continuously adapts to network bandwidth fluctuations while integrating user physiological signals to establish a closed-loop control model. At the protocol layer, temporal labels are embedded within RTP extension headers to govern synchronization:

$$\Delta t_{sync} = \max(\Delta t_{video}, \Delta t_{audio}, \Delta t_{haptic}) \tag{10}$$

where Δt_{sync} represents the maximum allowable synchronization offset used to align multimodal data streams; Δt_{video}, Δt_{audio}, Δt_{haptic} the current temporal desynchronization values of video, audio, and haptic streams, respectively. By selecting the maximum offset as the synchronization threshold, this control equation ensures that all sensory modalities are temporally aligned, preventing perceptual dissonance in immersive applications such as virtual reality and interactive live streaming.

This synchronization mechanism ensures temporal alignment across audio, video, and haptic modalities to prevent perceptual dissonance in immersive environments. The multi-layered architecture balances data utility with privacy in decentralized systems, providing auditable privacy-preserving computation for sensitive applications while enhancing cross-modal experiences and maintaining algorithmic transparency.

3.2   Federated Blockchain Copyright Management

Smart Contract-Driven Copyright Confirmation. At the rights confirmation stage, the system employs a composite hashing algorithm that integrates video frame perceptual hashing, Mel-frequency cepstral coefficient (MFCC) hashing for audio, and semantic hashing for text. This integration constructs a robust, anti-evasion digital content fingerprint:

$$H_{content} = Blake2b(PHash(V) \parallel MHHash(A) \parallel SHA3(T)) \tag{11}$$

where $H_{content}$ represents the unified digital fingerprint of a multimedia content item, used for copyright registration and tamper detection. The function $Blake2b()$ denotes a cryptographically secure hash function that processes the concatenated modality-specific hashes. Specifically, $PHash(V)$ is the perceptual hash of video frames V, capturing visual structure and similarity; $MHHash(A)$ is the Mel-frequency cepstral coefficient (MFCC)-based hash of the audio signal A, which preserves acoustic features; and $SHA3(T)$ is the semantic hash of the textual content T, generated using a SHA-3 hashing algorithm. The operator $\|$ denotes byte-wise concatenation of the individual hashes before final hashing. This composite hash construction ensures robust identification and resistance to modality-specific evasion techniques.The copyright registration smart contract uses a hierarchical data structure to anchor content metadata, ownership relationships and transaction records on the chain:

```
struct CopyrightRecord {
bytes32 contentHash;address[] rightsHolders; uint timestamp;
mapping(uint => License) licenses; }
struct License {address licensee; uint startTime;
uint endTime; bytes usageTerms; }
```

The algorithm anchors cross-modal features via hierarchical data structures, with a CopyrightRecord storing multi-dimensional rights metadata and a License substructure encoding spatio-temporal constraints.

Time-locked smart contracts enable fine-grained authorization control through time-slicing. The blockchain-timestamped grantLicense function establishes an authorization lifecycle model, where verified rights holders trigger automated generation of time-decay streaming payment protocols. Associated duration parameters initiate network-layer QoS adjustments, while integration with cross-chain atomic swaps enables comprehensive authorization including real-time metering and heterogeneous asset interoperability. Smart contracts implement fine-grained authorization control via time-locking:

```
function grantLicense(address _to, uint _duration)
public { require(msg.sender in copyright.rightsHolders);
uint start = block.timestamp;uint end = start + _duration;
copyright.licenses[licenseCount++] =
License(_to,start, end, usageTermsHash );
emit LicenseGranted(_to, start, end);}
```

Authorization status changes trigger network-layer QoS policy adjustments that prioritize bandwidth for licensed content. A dual-value quantification model maintains ecosystem equilibrium, employing smart contracts to dynamically calculate creator revenue based on content consumption metrics and storage node contributions via duration and space parameters. This bidirectional incentive mechanism aligns token rewards with data value and resource allocation, sustaining decentralized operations.Creator revenue function:

$$R_i = \frac{\sum_j w(t) \cdot V_i(t)}{\sum_j \sum_t w(t) \cdot V_i(t)} \cdot R_{total} \tag{12}$$

where The token reward obtained by R_i creator i. $w(\ t)$ time decay weight function (such as $w(t) = e - \lambda t$ with higher weight for recent viewing).$V_i(t)$the number of views or interactions of content i in time window t. $R_{tol\ al}$: The total reward pool allocated to the creator in the current cycle.

Decentralized Storage Network Architecture. The decentralized storage architecture employs a four-dimensional coordination mechanism. At the storage model level, an enhanced LRU-K algorithm implements dynamic cache replacement, while historical access frequency optimizes hot data distribution. Cold data undergoes Reed-Solomon erasure coding with fragment storage, forming a hybrid architecture combining edge node responsiveness with distributed cluster persistence. Federated learning dynamically determines access thresholds to enable adaptive storage policy adjustment:

$$\begin{cases} \text{Hot data storage}: S_{\text{hot}} = \{c \mid \text{AccessFreq}(c) > \theta_{\text{hot}}\} \rightarrow \text{EdgeCache} \\ \text{Cold data storage}: S_{\text{cold}} = \{c \mid \text{AccessFreq}(c) \leq \theta_{\text{cold}}\} \rightarrow \text{IPFSCluster} \end{cases}$$
$$(13)$$

where S_{hot} and S_{cold} denote the sets of content classified as hot and cold data, respectively; AccessFreq(c) is the access frequency of content c, computed via federated learning based on user requests; θ_{hot} and θ_{cold} are dynamically learned frequency thresholds for hot and cold data classification. Hot content is cached on edge nodes for low-latency access (EdgeCache), while cold content is stored persistently in distributed clusters using IPFS (IPFSCluster) with redundancy via erasure coding.

The storage proof mechanism employs a spatio-temporal verification framework, enhancing the Merkle-Patricia tree for optimized proof of data possession verification. Smart contracts initiate challenge processes every 120 block cycles, requiring storage nodes to submit integrity proofs π containing timestamps. The verification algorithm is defined as follows:

$$\text{VerifyPoST}(C, \pi) = \begin{cases} 1 \text{ if } \text{Hash}(\pi) \in \text{MerkleTree}(C) \\ 0 \text{ otherwise} \end{cases}$$
$$(14)$$

where $\text{VerifyPoST}(C, \pi)$ is the verification function for Proof of Spatio-Temporal Storage (PoST); C denotes the claimed storage content, and π is the proof submitted by a storage node, which includes a timestamp. The hash of π is verified against the Merkle tree root of content C. A return value of 1 indicates valid proof of data possession; otherwise, the proof is invalid.

The storage incentive protocol quantifies node contribution values through multi-dimensional metrics including storage capacity, online time, and service stability, matching them to token rewards. A smart contract-driven repurchase strategy incorporates regular token destruction, maintaining ecosystem equilibrium via on-chain deflation. This bidirectional contribution-incentive and deflation-regulation mechanism enhances node participation while ensuring long-term economic stability. A penalty factor r constrains node behavior, with the contribution function of node k defined as follows:

$$C_k = \alpha \cdot S_k + \beta \cdot U_k - \gamma \cdot D_k \tag{15}$$

where C_k denotes the total contribution score of node k; S_k is the effective storage capacity provided by the node; U_k is the accumulated duration for which the data is continuously available; D_k is the number of service interruptions or unavailability events recorded; r is the penalty factor applied to discourage instability. The coefficients α, β, and γ are dynamically adjusted through a DAO-based governance mechanism to reflect the priorities of the decentralized network.

The governance mechanism implements an on-chain DAO-based voting framework, enabling token holders to participate in key decisions including content review revisions and economic parameter adjustments. Quadratic voting non-linearly calculates voting weights while suppressing oligopoly through increasing costs, ensuring governance fairness and broad participation. Smart contracts automatically execute passed proposals, establishing a decentralized autonomous governance paradigm that maintains ecosystem democratization and sustainability.

Infringement Detection and Dispute Resolution.   The digital content infringement detection and dispute resolution mechanism employs a blockchain-based two-level architecture. Its detection layer utilizes an enhanced Merkle Patricia Trie structure to establish a global digital fingerprint index, enabling rapid content addressing through hash key-value pairs:

$$MPT.Insert(Hcontent, \{BlockNumber, TXHash\}) \tag{16}$$

where $MPT.Insert()$ denotes the insertion operation into the Merkle Patricia Trie (MPT), a hybrid structure combining Merkle trees and radix tries for efficient and verifiable keyvalue mapping on the blockchain. Hcontent is the composite digital fingerprint hash of a content item, computed via multimodal hashing. The associated value $\{BlockNumber, TXHash\}$ records the blockchain metadata that links the content to its registration block and transaction. This structure supports logarithmic time complexity $O(logn)$ for lookup operations even at large scale.

The structure preserves O(log n) query efficiency at millions-scale data, guaranteeing real-time large-scale digital asset comparison feasibility. Upon detecting suspected infringement content Hquery, the detection engine constructs a cryptographically verifiable similarity evidence chain via zero-knowledge proof protocol, mathematically expressed as:

$$\pi = Prove(H_{query}, H_{registered})s.t.Sim(H_{query}, H_{registered}) > \delta \tag{17}$$

where π denotes a zero-knowledge proof that confirms the semantic similarity between two hashed content fingerprints H_{query} and $H_{re.g.istered}$. $Sim()$ is a similarity function applied over the hash embeddings, and δ is a predefined semantic similarity threshold. The proof is constructed such that any verifier can confirm the similarity claim without revealing the actual content, thus satisfying both privacy protection and public verifiability.

The content-obscured process enables any verifier to confirm that semantic similarity between two hash values exceeds preset threshold δ, simultaneously satisfying Digital Millennium Copyright Act privacy requirements and blockchain verifiability principles.

The dispute resolution layer employs arbitration smart contracts with a Byzantine Fault-Tolerant multi-signature arbitration pool. Dynamically randomized arbitration nodes ensure decentralized distribution. Upon voting consensus, on-chain penalties automatically execute, compressing traditional weeks-long copyright resolution cycles into blockchain confirmation intervals. Multi-signature-verified outcomes immutably record on-chain, eliminating human intervention while establishing a WTO/TRIPS-compliant digital dispute framework.Multi-signature arbitration contract execution dispute award process:

```
struct Dispute {address claimant; address defendant;
bytes evidenceHash; uint arbitratorCount;
mapping(address => bool) votes; }


function resolveDispute(bytes32 _disputeID, bool _ruling) public{
require(isArbitrator(msg.sender));
disputes[_disputeID].votes[msg_sender] = _ruling;
if (consensusReached(_disputeID)) {executePenalty(_disputeID);}}
```

4   Performance Analysis

4.1   Optimization Analysis of Communication Efficiency

According to the RTP protocol extension based on IETF RFC 3550, the enhanced header introduces additional metadata overhead as follows:

$$\Delta H = \text{sizeof}(fl_{model\_id}) + \text{sizeof}(feature\_hash) + \text{sizeof}(block\_ref) \qquad (18)$$

where ΔH denotes the additional metadata overhead introduced by the RTP header extension; fl_{model_id} is the federated learning model identifier; $feature\_hash$ refers to the hashed content features; and $block\_ref$ is the reference to the on-chain content storage block. Each field contributes a fixed byte-length, totaling 13 bytes.Compared to the standard RTP header (12 bytes), the total size after header expansion is $H_{new} = H_{s\ td} + \Delta H = 12 + 13 = 25 bytes$

The relative increase in overhead is:

$$\frac{H_{new} - H_{std}}{H_{std}} \times 100\% = \frac{25 - 12}{12} \times 100\% \approx 108.3\% \qquad (19)$$

where the expression calculates the relative increase in RTP header overhead caused by the extension. The overhead grows by approximately 108.3% compared to the original header size.Through the adaptive decoding mechanism driven by feature 6 hash, the redundant data compression ratio $\eta_{compression} \in [0.45, 0.65]$ is measured experimentally. According to the improved Shannon channel capacity model:

$$C = B \cdot \log_2(1 + \frac{S \cdot \eta_{counpression}}{N \cdot (1 + \frac{\Delta H}{H_{Std}})}) \qquad (20)$$

where C is the effective channel capacity under header expansion and data compression; B is the channel bandwidth; $\frac{S}{N}$ is the signal-to-noise ratio (dimensionless); $\frac{\Delta H}{H_{Std}}$ reflects the normalized metadata overhead. This adaptation accounts for both compression efficiency and protocol-induced transmission overhead.

In a 10 Gbps bandwidth environment ($B = 10^9 Hz, \frac{S}{N} = 30dB$), the theoretical calculation shows that when $\frac{\Delta H}{H_{Std}} = 1.083$, the system effective capacity retention rate reaches 92.7%.

4.2   Proof of Convergence of Federated Learning

Assume that the global objective function $F(\theta)$ satisfies $\mu - strong$ convexity ($\mu = 0.15$) and L-smoothness ($L = 1.8$). With a time-dependent dynamic privacy budget strategy, the upper bound of the convergence error is given by:

$$E\left[||\bar{\theta}_T - \theta^*||^2\right] \leq \frac{1}{\mu T}\left(D^2 + \frac{2\sigma^2 d}{\mu \sum_{i=1}^{T} \epsilon_i}\right) + O\left(\frac{1}{T^2}\right) \tag{21}$$

where $E\left[||\bar{\theta}_T - \theta^*||^2\right]$ denotes the expected squared distance between the aggregated model parameter $\bar{\theta}_T$ after T rounds and the optimal parameter θ^*; $D = ||\bar{\theta}_T - \theta^*||$ is the norm of the initial error; σ^2 is the variance of the Gaussian noise used for differential privacy; d is the model dimension; ϵ_i is the local privacy budget at round i; and T is the total number of federated training rounds. The $\frac{1}{T^2}$ term accounts for higher-order convergence behavior. Among them:

$$D = ||\theta_0 - \theta^*|| = 12.5 \tag{22}$$

$$d = 2.5 \times 10^7 \tag{23}$$

$$\sigma^2 = 0.05 \tag{24}$$

where D is the Euclidean norm of the initial error between the initial model parameter θ_0 and the optimal parameter θ^*; here, D is assumed based on the initialization. After 100 rounds of federated aggregation, and under a total privacy budget of, the theoretical upper bound of convergence error is 3.2%.

4.3   Blockchain Storage Scalability

With a Reed-Solomon coding scheme (i.e., 6 data blocks and 3 redundant blocks), the resulting storage redundancy is:

$$\rho = \frac{k + m}{k} = \frac{6 + 3}{6} = 1.5 \tag{25}$$

where ρ denotes the storage redundancy factor under the (k, m) Reed-Solomon coding scheme; k = 6 is the number of data blocks and m = 3 is the number of redundant (parity) blocks. Thus, for every 6 units of original data, 9 units are stored in total, resulting in a redundancy factor $\rho = 1.5$. This represents a

50% reduction in storage overhead compared to the default IPFS setting (k = 1, m = 2), where $\rho = 3.0$.

Versus default IPFS (k = 1, m = 2, $\rho = 3.0$), the proposed scheme reduces storage costs by 50% using an enhanced Merkle-Patricia tree (k = 16), with infringement detection time complexity:

$$T(n) = 0(\log_k n) = 0(\log_{16} 10^7) \approx 6 \; levels \tag{26}$$

where T(n) represents the time complexity for querying an index structure with $n = 10^7$ entries; k=16 is the branching factor of the Merkle-Patricia Trie, optimized for high-fanout traversal. Under this configuration, the worst-case search depth is approximately 6 levels, ensuring logarithmic query efficiency for large-scale digital fingerprint indexing.

4.4   Stability of Economic Model

Suppose the total amount of tokens is $N = 1 \times 10^9$, the destruction rate is $\beta = 0.5\%$ per month, the average contribution of storage nodes is $S_i = 0.82$, and the number of nodes is $M = 1000$. Then, the system inflation rate is:

$$\pi = \frac{\alpha \cdot \sum_{i=1}^{M} S_i - \beta \cdot N}{N} = \frac{0.1 \times 820 - 0.005 \times 10^9}{10^9} = -0.499\% \tag{27}$$

Given the parameters $N = 10^9$, $\alpha = 0.1$, $\beta = 0.005$, and $M = 1000$, the resulting inflation rate is:$\pi = -0.499\%$This indicates that the token economy operates under controlled deflation. Simulation results show that under parameter bounds $\alpha \in [0.05, 0.15]$, $\beta \in [0.003, 0.007]$, and $M > 1000$, the monthly token volatility remains below 1.8%, significantly outperforming Bitcoin's benchmark volatility of 7.9%. Additionally, the Kolmogorov–Smirnov test ($p > 0.05$) confirms that the reward distribution error remains statistically insignificant (less than 0.3%).

5   Conclusion and Future Outlook

6G networks enable ultra-fast streaming but intensify conflicts among privacy, copyright, and quality-of-service demands. Future research requires: lightweight learning for edge devices with dynamic compression; scalable multi-chain blockchain for decentralized copyright; green streaming via renewable-powered infrastructure; and interpretable federated learning against deepfakes. Applications must expand into vertical domains like industrial metaverse and telemedicine for use cases including haptic-enhanced surgical training.

We propose a federated blockchain-enabled 6G architecture integrating intelligent computation and data confirmation at the transport layer. Embedding federated learning metadata and blockchain identity into a modified RTP stack enables real-time distributed processing. A three-tier audit mechanism operates:

terminals perform lightweight compliance checks; edge nodes conduct joint modeling and copyright verification; cloud handles arbitration. This achieves optimal privacy-review efficiency balance while reducing communication overhead.

Beyond technical innovation, 6G streaming must address ethical-social dimensions. Our architecture employs smart contracts for automated rights verification and income distribution, shifting from traffic economy to value economy. Governance requires dual-track oversight: algorithmic ethics committees and decentralized autonomous organizations for transparent accountability. Social embedding necessitates enhanced digital inclusion and strengthened digital twin protections. Ultimately, 6G evolution should embody "technology for good", harmonizing efficiency with equity to build a resilient, inclusive digital society.

References

1. Alyami, Y.R.: Secure IoT transmission in 6g smart cities: a quantum-resilient hybrid Galois field and Reed-Solomon approach. J. Supercomput. **81**(4), 576 (2025)
2. IMT-2030(6G) Promotion Group: White Paper on Design Principles and Typical Features of 6G Wireless Systems. IMT-2030(6G) Promotion Group, Beijing (2023)
3. IMT-2030(6G) Promotion Group: 2023 Research Report on Trusted Endogenous Security Architecture for 6G. IMT-2030(6G) Promotion Group, Beijing (2023)
4. China Academy of Information and Communications Technology (CAICT): Research Report on Blockchain Infrastructure. CAICT, Beijing (2023)
5. Ding, X., Liu, Y., Ning, J., et al.: Blockchain-enhanced anonymous data sharing scheme for 6G-enabled smart healthcare with distributed key generation and policy hiding. IEEE J. Biomed. Health Inform. (2025)
6. IMT-2030(6G) Promotion Group: 2023 Research Report on Blockchain Architecture and Key Technologies for 6G. IMT-2030(6G) Promotion Group, Beijing (2023)
7. China Information and Communication Technology Group Co., Ltd.: 6G Scenarios, Capabilities and Technology Engine White Paper (V.2021). China ICT Group Co., Ltd., Wuhan (2021)
8. Huawei Technologies Co., Ltd.: White Paper on 6G Network Endogenous Intelligence Architecture and Key Technologies. Huawei Technologies Co., Ltd., Shenzhen (2023)
9. Global 6G Technology Conference: White Paper on Alliance Network Architecture for 6G. Organizing Committee of the Global 6G Technology Conference, Beijing (2024)
10. Alimi, A.I., Popoola, J.J.: 5G and 6G enhanced broadband communications. IntechOpen (2025). https://doi.org/10.5772/intechopen.100728
11. IMT-2030(6G) Promotion Group: 2023 Research Report on 6G Network Application Enabling Technologies. IMT-2030(6G) Promotion Group, Beijing (2023)
12. Driss, M.B., Sabir, E., Elbiaze, H., Saad, W.: Federated learning for 6G: paradigms, taxonomy, recent advances and insights. ArXiv [cs.LG] (2023). https://arxiv.org/abs/2312.04688v1
13. China Academy of Information and Communications Technology (CAICT): White Paper on the Integration of Blockchain and Federated Learning Technologies. CAICT, Beijing (2023)
14. China Unicom Research Institute: 6G Network Endogenous Security White Paper. China Unicom Research Institute, Beijing (2024)

15. National Industrial Information Security Development Research Center: Technical Guide on Data Security and Privacy Protection in the 6G Era. National Industrial Information Security Development Research Center, Beijing (2023)
16. International Telecommunication Union: Standard for Integrated Space-Air-Ground Network Architecture for 6G. International Telecommunication Union, Geneva (2024)
17. China Electronics Standardization Institute: Technical Specification for Cross-Domain Identity Authentication Based on Blockchain. China Electronics Standardization Institute, Beijing (2023)
18. Alliance of Industrial Internet: White Paper on Intelligent Contract Applications in the 6G Era. Alliance of Industrial Internet, Beijing (2024)
19. National Research Center for Information Science: Tsinghua University: Research Report on 6G Network Resource Scheduling Optimization. Tsinghua University, Beijing (2023)
20. IMT-2030(6G) Promotion Group: Research Report on Trusted Endogenous Security Architecture for 6G. China Academy of Information and Communications Technology, Beijing (2023)
21. China Information and Communication Technology Group Co., Ltd.: 6G Network Architecture White Paper. CICT Mobile Communication Technology Co., Ltd., Wuhan (2023)
22. Hexa-X Consortium: European Vision for the 6G Network Ecosystem. European Commission, Brussels (2021)
23. AsiaInfo Technologies, Intel: 6G OSS Technology White Paper. AsiaInfo Technologies Holdings Co., Ltd., Beijing (2023)
24. Devitt, S.K., Scholz, J., Schless, T., Lewis, L.: Developing a trusted human-AI network for humanitarian benefit. ArXiv [cs.CY] (2021). https://arxiv.org/abs/2112.11191v3
25. IMT-2030(6G) Promotion Group: Research Report on Semantic Communication and Semantic Cognitive Network Architecture. China Academy of Information and Communications Technology, Beijing (2023)
26. China Unicom: 6G Network Architecture White Paper. China Unicom Research Institute, Beijing (2023)

Blockchain and Its Applications in the Automotive Industrial Value Chain

Tong Gu[1,2], Songlin He[1,2], Han Min[1,2(✉)], Xiaotong Chen[1,2], Zhenchao Yan[1,2], Xukang Lyu[3], and Dongliang Chu[3]

[1] Southwest Jiaotong University, Chengdu 610031, Sichuan, China
{gutong,c06720,yanzhenchao}@my.swjtu.edu.cn, {sohe,hanmin}@swjtu.edu.cn
[2] Manufacturing Industry Chain Collaboration Industrial Software Key Laboratory of Sichuan Province, Chengdu 610031, Sichuan, China
[3] Zhejiang New Rise Digital Technology Co., Ltd., Hangzhou 311899, China
{clu,chudongliang}@newrisedt.com

Abstract. The automotive industrial value chain is a highly integrated network that connects multiple stakeholders, allowing seamless coordination from product design to final delivery to users. However, the industry is often constrained by challenges such as data silos and trust deficits, which impede effective collaboration in core business processes, thus affecting operational efficiency and overall profitability. To address these issues, blockchain emerges as a promising solution to facilitate value chain collaboration in the automotive industry. As a decentralized infrastructure and computing paradigm built on a peer-to-peer (P2P) network, blockchain offers a trustworthy mechanism for value transfer. In this paper, we summarize the key functionalities of blockchain and present a conceptual framework for a blockchain-enabled automotive industrial value chain. The feasibility of blockchain adoption is theoretically analyzed through an industry application. In addition, we identify potential challenges and propose countermeasures, providing insight into the practical implementation of blockchain in the automotive industry.

Keywords: Blockchain · Automotive Industry · Value Chain

1 Introduction

As a representative paradigm of the discrete manufacturing industry, the automotive sector is structured around a multi-tiered value chain characterized by vertically integrated and horizontally coordinated value creation activities [23]. From an industrial organization perspective, the automotive value chain can be systematically segmented into three key stages. The upstream is primarily oriented towards fundamental research and development, engineering design, and prototyping of core components. The midstream focuses on vehicle assembly and manufacturing, leveraging modular production platforms and intelligent manufacturing systems to achieve efficient, scalable, and flexible production capabilities. The downstream encompasses logistics and distribution networks, after-sales services, and post-market operations. In sum, the automotive industrial value chain not only fosters technological innovation, including artificial intelligence

R. K. Shyamasundar et al. (Eds.): ICBC 2025, LNCS 16155, pp. 134–148, 2026.
https://doi.org/10.1007/978-3-032-06176-8_9

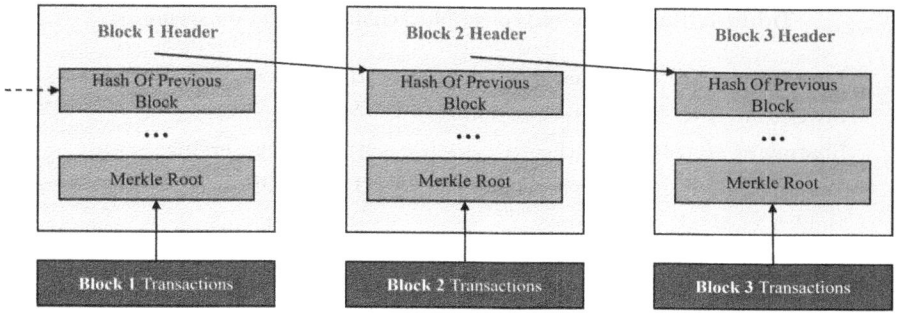

Fig. 1. A basic blockchain architecture.

(AI) [4], the Internet of Things (IoT) [14], and new energy, but also plays a pivotal role in shaping national industrial competitiveness.

However, the current automotive industrial value chain typically suffers from two fundamental challenges: **data silos** and **lack of trust**. In practical business operations, critical data, such as simulation results from research and development, equipment parameters from manufacturing processes, and user behavior data from after-sales services, are often isolated across heterogeneous system architectures [18], thus hindering interoperability and real-time data exchange. This fragmentation leads to extended product iteration cycles and delayed supply chain responses. Furthermore, upstream and downstream stakeholders face persistent issues such as high information verification costs and disputes over data ownership. Specifically, part quality traceability typically relies on manual reconciliation processes, while opaque used vehicle history records frequently cause transactional disputes. These structural inefficiencies not only inflate collaboration costs, but also impede the scalability and effectiveness of data-driven innovation models. Therefore, there is a pressing need to develop secure and efficient value chain collaboration technologies tailored for the automotive industry. Such solutions should focus on dismantling data silos and establishing trusted mechanisms among multiple stakeholders, thereby enhancing both the efficiency and resilience of cross-organizational cooperation.

Blockchain technology emerges as a decentralized ledger system grounded in cryptographic principles and consensus mechanisms [41]. As illustrated in Fig. 1, its fundamental architecture involves chronologically connected data blocks through a chain structure, supported by a P2P network that enables collaborative maintenance across multiple nodes. The system leverages asymmetric encryption to ensure secure identity authentication, hash functions and Merkle trees to guarantee data integrity, and consensus algorithms [36] such as Proof of Work (PoW) and Proof of Stake (PoS) to achieve state consistency in distributed and trustless environments. In addition, smart contracts [31] are used to automate the execution of business logic, thereby improving operational efficiency and reducing the reliance on centralized intermediaries. Importantly, the inherent properties of blockchain, such as immutability, traceability, and auditability, have facilitated its successful deployment in a variety of fields. These

Table 1. Illustration of typical blockchain application scenarios

Literature	Scenario	Highlight
Sivaselvan et al. [26]	Internet of Things	Access Control
Sharma et al. [24]	Healthcare	Privacy-Preserving
Wu et al. [34]	Supply Chain	Traceability
Baliker et al. [3]	Finance	P2P Payments
Gilman et al. [10]	Smart City	Sustainability
Gao et al. [9]	Energy Trading	Security, P2P
Nguyen et al. [21]	Metaverse	Efficiency, Sharding
Yu et al. [38]	Agriculture	Cross-chain, Efficiency
Nguyen et al. [22]	Data Sharing	Trustworthy
He et al. [12]	Cybersecurity	Cyber Security Management
Tariq et al. [27]	Education	Degree Verification
Maram et al. [20]	Identity Authentication	Decentralized Identity
Chen et al. [6]	Digital Copyright	Copyright Protection
Ibrahimy et al. [16]	E-Government	Transparency

characteristics also make blockchain a promising technological foundation for improving value chain collaboration in the automotive industry.

A bevy of literature has emerged to explore its applicability and potential impacts in various industries, as presented in Table 1. These studies span multiple domains [3,13,34], providing valuable insights into the functional characteristics and implementation pathways of blockchain technology. However, despite the fact that existing studies have to some extent uncovered the multi-dimensional value of blockchain, efforts to deeply integrate and reshape industrial value chains remain limited. This gap is particularly evident in the automotive industry, where related studies are still in its early stages due to the inherent complexity and strong cross-organizational collaboration requirements. To fill this research gap, we propose a comprehensive solution for a blockchain-enabled automotive industrial value chain. Specifically, we formulate a general description of the automotive industrial value chain by decomposing it into four critical chains and perform an in-depth analysis of the blockchain technology. We then identify the key functionalities of blockchain in the automotive industrial value chain, including robust data storage and automated business computation. On this basis, we introduce a conceptual collaboration framework based on blockchain and analyze a real-world industry case from a theoretical perspective. Finally, we outline the main technical challenges associated with blockchain adoption in this context and highlight several promising directions for future research.

Outline. The remainder of this paper is organized as follows. Section 2 introduces the essential concepts involved in this paper. Section 3 summarizes the key functionalities of blockchain and explores its applications in the automotive industrial value chain. Section 4 discusses limitations and challenges and proposes the countermeasures. Section 5 concludes this paper.

2 Preliminary

Before diving into this study, we present the context of the automotive industrial value chain and blockchain technology.

2.1 Automotive Industrial Value Chain

A value chain [25] represents a systematic sequence of interdependent and value-creating activities that an enterprise undertakes to transform inputs into final products or services. The theoretical foundation of the value chain model lies in its ability to deconstruct an enterprise's operations into two distinct yet interconnected categories: primary activities and support activities. Primary activities include inbound logistics, production operations, outbound logistics, marketing and sales, and after-sales service; while support activities include procurement, technological development, human resource management, and enterprise infrastructure. These activities do not exist in isolation, but interact synergistically to shape the operational efficiency and strategic positioning of the enterprise. Competitive advantage arises from the effective integration and coordination of these activities, enabling an enterprise to deliver superior value to customers at a lower cost or through differentiation. As a practical analytical tool, the value chain facilitates the identification of sources of value creation and inefficiencies, guiding enterprises to effectively allocate internal resources to achieve sustainable competitive advantages.

An industrial chain refers to the comprehensive vertical system of collaborative relationships and interdependencies that span the entire lifecycle of a product or service within a specific industry, from raw material extraction to final consumption. It reflects the functional division of labor and supply-demand connections among enterprises at different levels of production and distribution. Structurally, the industrial chain is typically divided into three principal tiers: (1) upstream, responsible for the supply of raw materials and foundational components; (2) midstream, encompassing core manufacturing processes and system integration; (3) downstream, focused on product distribution and value-added service provision. This tiered structure reveals the technical synergies and economic interdependence among the various segments of the industry.

The industrial value chain serves as a macro-level analytical framework that synthesizes the concepts of the industrial chain and the enterprise-level value chain. It maps the processes of value creation, transmission, enhancement, and distribution throughout the entire lifecycle of a product or service at the industry level. The central objective of this framework is to identify key value-adding nodes along the industrial chain, such as research and development, design, core component manufacturing, and after-sales services, and to examine the value-appropriation capabilities of various stakeholders within the system. By offering

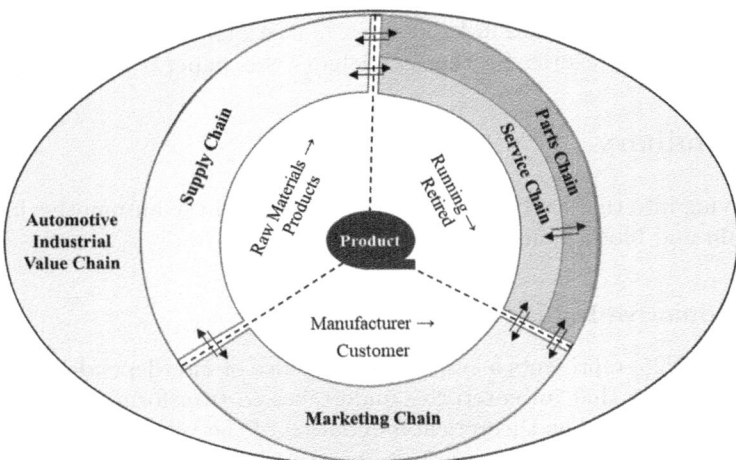

Fig. 2. A schematic diagram of the automotive industrial value chain, including supply chain, marketing chain, service chain, and parts chain.

a holistic view of the industry's value architecture, the industrial value chain concept helps uncover competitive advantages, thus providing a basis for decision-making in corporate strategy and industrial policy. In the automotive industry, the industrial value chain can be effectively conceptualized through four core sub-chains: the supply chain, the marketing chain, the service chain, and the parts chain, as presented in Fig. 2. The supply chain encompasses the value-creation process from raw material procurement to component manufacturing and final product assembly. The marketing chain represents the distribution pathway through which finished vehicles are delivered from manufacturers to end consumers, capturing the flow of value in market transactions. Both the service chain and the parts chain relate to the post-sale phase of the product lifecycle, extending from vehicle operation to its eventual retirement. However, they differ in scope and function. The service chain focuses on the structured sequence of activities involved in delivering services, from service providers to end users, such as maintenance, repair, and customer support; whereas the parts chain specifically delineates the value-added processes associated with the distribution and logistics of after-sales parts. These four chains provide a comprehensive framework for analyzing value creation, coordination, and transformation throughout the lifecycle of automotive products.

2.2   Blockchain Technology

Blockchain is a digital, decentralized and distributed ledger technology that enables the secure and verifiable recording of transactions among multiple parties in a transparent and immutable manner [7]. The blockchain architecture adopts a layered design, with each layer performing specific functions. As illustrated in Fig. 3, the following are the details of each layer.

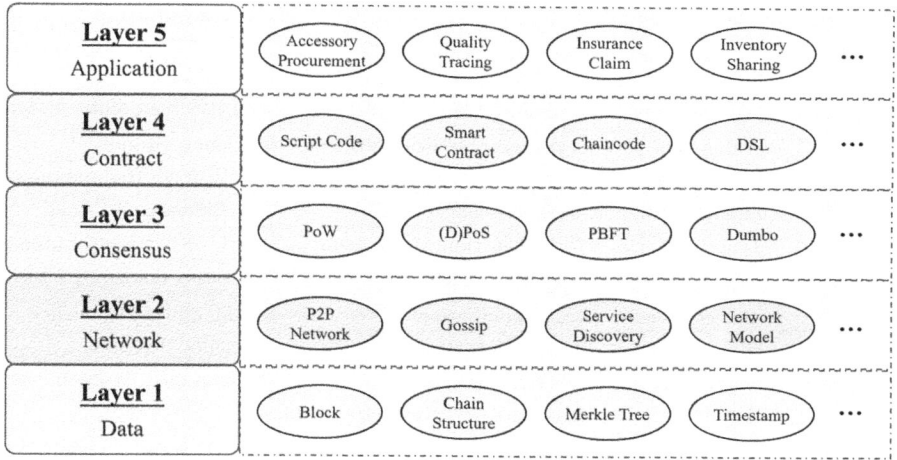

Fig. 3. The layers related to blockchain, including data layer, network layer, consensus layer, contract layer, and application layer.

The data layer serves as the foundational infrastructure of blockchain, responsible for storing and managing all transaction and block data. It ensures data immutability and verifiability through technologies such as chained structures, cryptographic algorithms (e.g., hash functions and asymmetric encryption), and Merkle trees. Each block contains the hash value of the previous block, forming a continuous chain. Any modification of the data would invalidate the subsequent hashes, thereby ensuring system security. The network layer establishes the distributed communication mechanism of the blockchain, utilizing P2P networks and protocols such as Gossip to achieve efficient data propagation and synchronization among nodes. Nodes broadcast transactions and block information across the network, ensuring global consistency while employing data validation mechanisms (e.g., verifying digital signatures and timestamps) to filter out invalid data, thus supporting the decentralized nature of the blockchain. The consensus layer addresses trust issues among distributed nodes through consensus algorithms such as PoW, PoS, and Delegated Proof of Stake (DPoS). Its primary objective is to ensure agreement among all participants on the validity of data, prevent double-spending attacks, resist malicious activities, and maintain the reliability and security of the blockchain. This layer constitutes the core technology that enables decentralized ledger functionality. The contract layer introduces programmability to the blockchain by implementing smart contracts, allowing for automated execution of logical operations. Developers can write code to define rules that automatically trigger actions when predefined conditions are met, eliminating the need for intermediaries and enhancing efficiency and transparency. The application layer acts as the interface between blockchain technology and real-world scenarios. By leveraging the decentralized and immutable nature of blockchain, it has the potential to address trust deficits and inefficiency in traditional industries.

Table 2. Key capabilities of blockchain in storage and computation.

Functionality	Literature	Technique	Highlight
Robust Data Storage	Wu *et al.* [35]	Distributed Hash Table	Security, Scalability
	Wang *et al.* [30]	Cryptographic Commitment	Efficiency, Stability
	Li *et al.* [19]	Community Detection	Low Storage Redundancy
	Zhang *et al.* [40]	Proxy Re-encryption	Low Latency and Cost
	Teng *et al.* [28]	Node Selection Mechanism	Low Overhead and Latency
Automated Business Computation	Dutta *et al.* [8]	Insurance Digitization	Trustless, Transparency
	Zhu *et al.* [42]	Resource Sharing	Sustainability, Efficiency
	Hu *et al.* [15]	Differential Attack	Efficiency, Privacy
	Ismail *et al.* [17]	Ethereum Platform	Authenticity, Traceability
	Wei *et al.* [33]	Authenticated Key Agreement	Security, Privacy

3 Blockchain Key Functionalities and Applications in Automotive Industrial Value Chain

In this section, we detail the key functionalities of blockchain and its applications in the automotive industrial value chain.

3.1 Key Functionalities of Blockchain

As blockchain technology continues to evolve and find applications in diverse industries, its transformative potential lies in the unique set of functionalities it offers. In the context of the automotive industrial value chain, where data integrity, process efficiency, and cross-organizational trust are of paramount importance, the key functionalities of blockchain can be distilled into two fundamental dimensions: **robust data storage** and **automated business computation**. We summarize the relevant literature, as presented in Table 2. These functionalities not only address critical challenges such as information asymmetry, operational inefficiency, and trust deficits, but also lay the groundwork for a more transparent, reliable, and intelligent value creation ecosystem.

Robust Data Storage. The distributed ledger properties of blockchain technology enable the secure recording and storage of all relevant data throughout a vehicle's lifecycle, including manufacturing details, maintenance records, and component provenance. Due to the immutability of blockchain data once recorded, this capability provides a highly reliable and transparent foundation to verify the authenticity and integrity of vehicle historical information. A substantial body of research has been devoted to robust data storage. Wu *et al.* [35] proposed a dual-blockchain framework for secure and scalable distributed data management in large industrial Internet of Things (IIoT) networks. Wang *et al.* [30] combined sharding to construct a blockchain-based IoT data storage solution that significantly improves the security and efficiency of the IoT system. Li *et al.* [19] proposed a layered and sharded blockchain storage model for edge computing. This model uses a master-slave structure for hierarchical blockchain deployment, with each sharded subchain responsible for storing data. Zhang *et al.* [40] proposed a data storage and circulation framework based on jointcloud computing and blockchain, aiming to ensure secure data storage and trustworthy transactions. Teng *et al.* [28] proposed an efficient off-chain blockchain storage system for IoT time series data, storing only the hash values of each batch on-chain and keeping the complete data off-chain. These advancements lay a solid foundation for building next-generation automotive industrial value chains that are not only more transparent and auditable, but also better equipped to support emerging requirements in data-driven intelligent manufacturing and services.

Automated Business Computation. Smart contracts are capable of automatically executing predefined actions or transactions upon the fulfillment of specified conditions. This functionality not only significantly reduces administrative overhead and mitigates the risk of human error, but also enhances operational efficiency by accelerating process flows across multiple stakeholders, including manufacturers, suppliers, service providers, and customers. There has been considerable research interest in automated business execution. Dutta *et al.* [8] proposed logistics insurance based on smart contracts. When a specific event occurs, the claims can be automatically returned. Zhu *et al.* [42] proposed a smart contract to address the complexity of facility location and route optimization problems while balancing resource sharing and product freshness requirements. Hu *et al.* [15] proposed an efficient and privacy-preserving data aggregation and trust management scheme for an IoT-enabled smart grid based on smart contract. Ismail *et al.* [17] used blockchain technology and smart contracts to improve supply chain traceability while improving system efficiency and transparency. Wei *et al.* [33] designed a revocation mechanism that targets expired or malicious vehicles using smart contracts to enhance system security. The aforementioned studies emphasize the potential of smart contracts in enabling automated, rule-driven business execution across complex, multi-stakeholder environments. These developments pave the way for building more agile and trustworthy business processes.

3.2 Conceptual Framework

Based on the key functionalities of blockchain, we present a conceptual collaboration framework for the automotive industrial value chain, as illustrated in Fig. 4. The framework encompasses key operational stages, including supply, manufacturing, sales, and after-sales services. Smart contracts are implemented to automate the enforcement of business rules, such as order processing, payment settlements, and quality claim adjudication, thus facilitating trusted and intermediary-free collaboration between heterogeneous stakeholders. Critical data from various nodes, such as component specifications, logistics tracking information, and warranty records, are securely stored in an encrypted

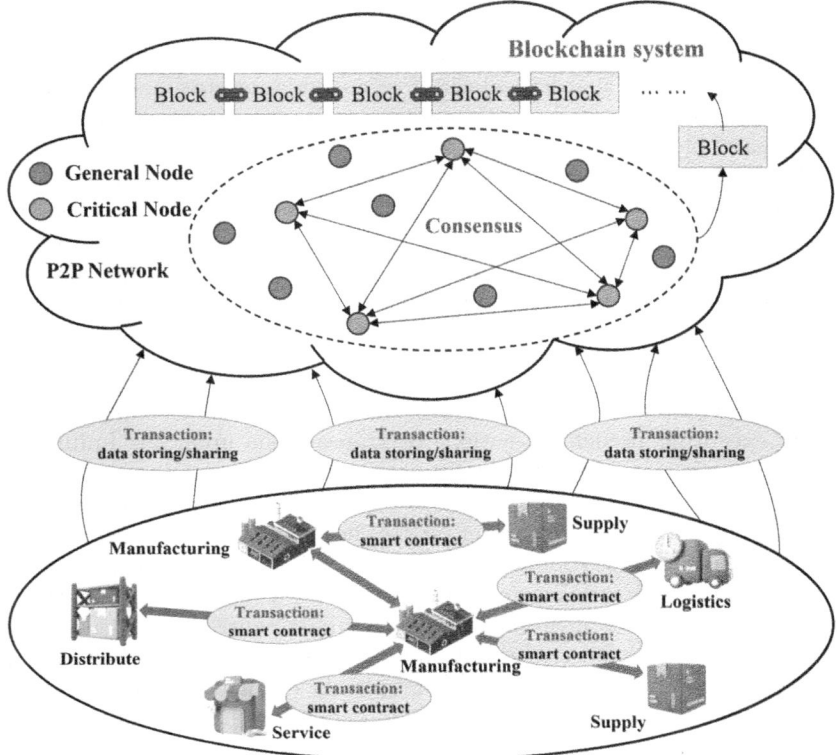

Fig. 4. A blockchain-enabled framework for the automotive industrial value chain.

and distributed manner, ensuring data integrity, confidentiality, and long-term immutability. These data management mechanisms are integrated with consensus protocols to ensure transaction consistency, regulatory compliance, and end-to-end auditability throughout the business workflow. These capabilities enable the formation of a transparent and trustworthy value network, significantly reducing coordination costs while enhancing the operational agility, accountability, and resilience of the automotive industrial value chain.

3.3   A Potential Application in the Conceptual Framework

We emphasize the importance of blockchain through the typical application of agent parts procurement. The primary workflow includes: ① submission of purchase orders by the agent; ② generation of sales orders by the manufacturer; ③ shipment from the manufacturer; ④ receipt by the agent. The detailed procedure is illustrated in Fig. 5. Specifically, the agent generates purchase orders based on the urgently needed parts, historical orders, and inventory levels, and sends the pur-

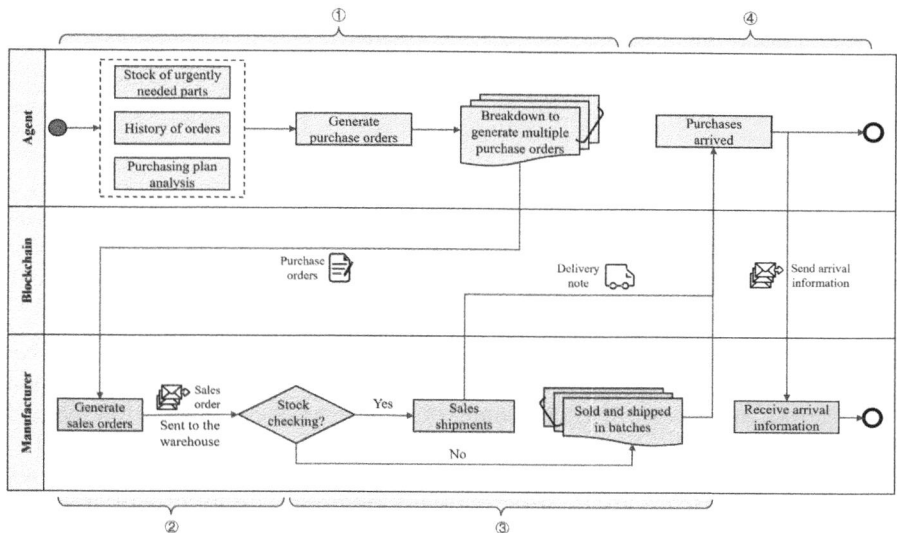

Fig. 5. The business processes of parts procurement for agents.

chase orders to each manufacturer based on actual demand to generate the manufacturer's sales orders. The manufacturer sends the sales order to the warehouse, which determines whether the number of parts in the order is satisfied according to the real-time inventory. If the inventory is satisfied, then sales are shipped; if the inventory is not satisfied, then sales are shipped in batches. The manufacturer sends the delivery order to the agent, who receives it and completes the purchase. The agent sends the arrival information to the manufacturer, who completes the purchase after receiving the arrival information.

Although the process seems clear, there are still some problems, such as information asymmetry, inefficiency, and disputes. Specifically, there may be delays in information transfer between agents and manufacturers, resulting in untimely processing of purchase orders and sales orders. Inventory status and changes in demand are not shared in real time, which may result in over-purchasing or stockouts. The manual generation and processing of orders, delivery notes, and arrival information is prone to errors and time waste. Lack of transparency between different links makes it difficult to trace the root cause of issues. To this end, we can adopt blockchain technology to optimize the conventional parts procurement process. The entire workflow achieves transparency, data sharing, and immutability, thereby enhancing collaboration efficiency among agents, manufacturers, and warehouses. Smart contracts automate key operations such as order processing, inventory checks, and shipment execution, reducing manual intervention and improving automation levels. Furthermore, all transactions and activities are recorded on-chain, ensuring traceability and auditability, which strengthens accountability and trust while effectively lowering transaction costs and business risks.

4   Discussion

Here, we highlight the challenges and countermeasures of the blockchain-enabled automotive industrial value chain.

4.1   Challenges

As mentioned earlier, blockchain essentially provides two critical functionalities, i.e., robust data storage and automated business computation. However, every coin has two sides. Although blockchain offers these advantages, it also presents several additional challenges.

- **Data source heterogeneity.** The automotive industrial value chain involves multi-tiered and geographically dispersed participants (e.g., suppliers, manufacturers and dealers), each reliant on heterogeneous information systems (e.g., ERP and WMS) and data standards (e.g., XML and JSON). This heterogeneity results in significant disparities in the format, protocol, and semantics of critical data, such as order status, logistics trajectories, and quality inspection reports. The persistence of manual data entry and offline documentation among small and medium-sized enterprises further compounds data fragmentation. Heterogeneous data not only impede automated data acquisition and real-time synchronization throughout the blockchain, but also introduce erroneous records, thereby undermining the credibility of blockchain implementations.
- **Data privacy preserving.** The robust data storage capacity offered by the blockchain paradoxically constitutes the primary challenge to protect data privacy in the automotive industrial value chain. Sensitive data (e.g., owner identities, maintenance records, and transaction information) stored in public or consortium ledgers may be exposed to unauthorized access and inference through data correlation. The permanent irreversibility of recorded data directly conflicts with privacy regulations (e.g., the "right to be forgotten" under GDPR). Additionally, vulnerabilities in private key management, such as loss and theft, represent critical single points of failure. Even when raw data are encrypted and stored off-chain, exposure of the off-chain repository could still trigger large-scale privacy breaches through metadata correlation with on-chain records.
- **Smart contract security.** Although smart contracts can automatically execute business logic, they face significant security threats. Post-deployment immutability means that any code vulnerability (e.g., logic errors, reentrancy attacks, and access control flaws) may be maliciously exploited, leading to fund theft, manipulated business operations (such as illicit ownership transfers), and system paralysis. External data introduced through oracles also poses serious risks. Compromised or erroneous oracle inputs trigger incorrect executions. Intricate cross-contract interactions may propagate unforeseen combinatorial risks, while upgradeability limitations and ambiguous legal liability frameworks exacerbate vulnerability remediation and dispute resolution, undermining trust in automated processes.

4.2 Countermeasures

The above challenges, including data source heterogeneity, data privacy preserving, and smart contract security, pose substantial obstacles to the widespread application of blockchain in the automotive industrial value chain. In the following, we propose targeted countermeasures for each challenge to provide practical solutions that align with industrial requirements.

- Establishing unified standards across the industry and implementing collaborative governance is imperative. On the one hand, middleware and universal data models should be adopted to deploy blockchain adapters that convert unstructured data into standardized formats, thereby ensuring cross-system consistency of critical data. On the other hand, a consortium-based coordination mechanism must be instituted under the leadership of core enterprises or industry associations, which enforces mandatory data interface specifications requiring participants to comply with unified data collection protocols. Simultaneously, on-chain data validation rules (such as smart contract verification logic) should be designed to trigger manual verification procedures for anomalously formatted data. Furthermore, Distributed Digital Identity (DID) [37] must be employed to uniquely identify participating entities, enabling accountability tracking through data provenance.
- Multi-layered cryptographic frameworks should be implemented to reconcile blockchain's transparency with privacy requirements. Sensitive data can be encrypted using zero-knowledge proof (ZKP) [32] or homomorphic encryption [1] to allow verification without exposing raw information. For regulatory compliance with data erasure mandates, off-chain storage architectures should be adopted, where only hashed metadata is anchored on-chain while original data resides in permissioned repositories with automated deletion mechanisms. In addition, hierarchical key management systems must be enforced, incorporating multi-signature authentication and hardware security modules (HSMs) to prevent private key compromise. Federated learning [2] can further mitigate risks by processing data locally at edge nodes and selectively integrating key information into the blockchain.
- Formal verification methods must be applied during smart contract development to eliminate code vulnerabilities prior to deployment. Runtime protection can be enhanced through automated auditing tools (e.g., Securify [29]) that detect some attacks. Moreover, the use of deep learning technology to detect contract anomalies is a promising direction [11]. Oracle-related risks require decentralized oracle networks with multi-source data aggregation and cryptographic authentication (e.g., Town Crier [39]) to ensure tamper-proof external inputs. For upgradeability, proxy-based contract patterns [5] with clearly defined governance protocols should be utilized to enable secure patch deployment without disrupting operational continuity. Finally, sandbox environments could isolate contract interactions to contain combinatorial failures, while legally binding code liability frameworks need to be established to assign accountability for autonomous transaction errors.

5   Conclusion

To address systemic challenges inherent in the conventional automotive industrial value chain, such as pervasive data silos and lack of trust mechanisms, we introduce blockchain technology to facilitate efficient, secure, and trustworthy interactions within the value chain. Through a comprehensive review of existing literature, we summarize the two key functionalities of blockchain and present a blockchain-based automotive industrial value chain collaboration framework. We also analyze practical scenarios where blockchain can generate substantial value. Additionally, we conduct a thorough discussion of the technical challenges encountered during blockchain adoption and propose potential directions for future research to support its integration into the automotive industry.

Acknowledgments. This work is supported in part by National Key R&D Project of China (No. 2023YFB3308600). Songlin He is also supported in part by NSFC (No. 62302403).

References

1. Ali, A., et al.: A novel homomorphic encryption and consortium blockchain-based hybrid deep learning model for industrial internet of medical things. IEEE Trans. Netw. Sci. Eng. **10**(5), 2402–2418 (2023)
2. Ali, W., Zhou, X., Shao, J.: Privacy-preserved and responsible recommenders: from conventional defense to federated learning and blockchain. ACM Comput. Surv. **57**(5), 1–35 (2025)
3. Baliker, C., Baza, M., Alourani, A., Alshehri, A., Alshahrani, H., Choo, K.K.R.: On the applications of blockchain in fintech: advancements and opportunities. IEEE Trans. Eng. Manage. **71**, 6338–6355 (2024)
4. Bassiouni, M.M., Chakrabortty, R.K., Hussain, O.K., Rahman, H.F.: Advanced deep learning approaches to predict supply chain risks under Covid-19 restrictions. Expert Syst. Appl. **211**, 118604 (2023)
5. Bodell III, W.E., Meisami, S., Duan, Y.: Proxy hunting: understanding and characterizing proxy-based upgradeable smart contracts in blockchains. In: Proceedings of the 32nd USENIX Security Symposium, pp. 1829–1846 (2023)
6. Chen, X., Yang, A., Weng, J., Tong, Y., Huang, C., Li, T.: A blockchain-based copyright protection scheme with proactive defense. IEEE Trans. Serv. Comput. **16**(4), 2316–2329 (2023)
7. Chen, X., He, S., Sun, L., Zheng, Y., Wu, C.Q.: A survey of consortium blockchain and its applications. Cryptography **8**(2), 12 (2024)
8. Dutta, H., Nagesh, S., Talluri, J., Bhaumik, P.: A solution to blockchain smart contract based parametric transport and logistics insurance. IEEE Trans. Serv. Comput. **16**(5), 3155–3167 (2023)
9. Gao, J., Asamoah, K.O., Xia, Q., Sifah, E.B., Amankona, O.I., Xia, H.: A blockchain peer-to-peer energy trading system for microgrids. IEEE Trans. Smart Grid **14**(5), 3944–3960 (2023)
10. Gilman, E., et al.: Addressing data challenges to drive the transformation of smart cities. ACM Trans. Intell. Syst. Technol. **15**(5), 1–65 (2024)

11. Gu, T., Han, M., He, S., Chen, X.: Trap contract detection in blockchain with improved transformer. In: Proceedings of the IEEE Global Communications Conference, pp. 5141–5146 (2023)

12. He, S., et al.: Blockchain-based automated and robust cyber security management. J. Parallel Distrib. Comput. **163**, 62–82 (2022)

13. He, S., Lu, Y., Tang, Q., Wang, G., Wu, C.Q.: Blockchain-based P2P content delivery with monetary incentivization and fairness guarantee. IEEE Trans. Parallel Distrib. Syst. **34**(2), 746–765 (2022)

14. He, S., Tang, Q., Wu, C.Q., Shen, X.: Decentralizing IoT management systems using blockchain for censorship resistance. IEEE Trans. Industr. Inf. **16**(1), 715–727 (2019)

15. Hu, C., Liu, Z., Li, R., Hu, P., Xiang, T., Han, M.: Smart contract assisted privacy-preserving data aggregation and management scheme for smart grid. IEEE Trans. Dependable Secure Comput. **21**(4), 2145–2161 (2024)

16. Ibrahimy, M.M., Norta, A., Normak, P., Nowandish, H.: Transforming e-participatory budgeting with blockchain: boosting transparency and citizen engagement. IEEE Trans. Eng. Manage. **72**, 1376–1403 (2025)

17. Ismail, S., Nouman, M., Reza, H., Vasefi, F., Zadeh, H.K.: A blockchain-based fish supply chain framework for maintaining fish quality and authenticity. IEEE Trans. Serv. Comput. **17**(5), 1877–1886 (2024)

18. Lahlou, I., Motaki, N.: Integrating blockchain with ERP systems for better supply chain performance. In: Proceedings of the 14th International Colloquium of Logistics and Supply Chain Management (LOGISTIQUA), pp. 1–6 (2022)

19. Li, C., et al.: Hierarchical sharding blockchain storage solution for edge computing. Futur. Gener. Comput. Syst. **161**, 162–173 (2024)

20. Maram, D., et al.: CanDID: can-do decentralized identity with legacy compatibility, sybil-resistance, and accountability. In: Proceedings of the IEEE Symposium on Security and Privacy (SP), pp. 1348–1366 (2021)

21. Nguyen, C.T., Hoang, D.T., Nguyen, D.N., Xiao, Y., Niyato, D., Dutkiewicz, E.: MetaShard: a novel sharding blockchain platform for metaverse applications. IEEE Trans. Mob. Comput. **23**(5), 4348–4361 (2024)

22. Nguyen, T.L., et al.: Blockchain-empowered trustworthy data sharing: fundamentals, applications, and challenges. ACM Comput. Surv. **57**(8), 1–36 (2025)

23. Reddy, K.R.K., Gunasekaran, A., Kalpana, P., Sreedharan, V.R., Kumar, S.A.: Developing a blockchain framework for the automotive supply chain: a systematic review. Comput. Industr. Eng. **157**, 107334 (2021)

24. Sharma, P., Namasudra, S., Chilamkurti, N., Kim, B.G., Gonzalez Crespo, R.: Blockchain-based privacy preservation for IoT-enabled healthcare system. ACM Trans. Sens. Netw. **19**(3), 1–17 (2023)

25. Shen, Y., Qin, C., Zhao, Y.: Research on collaboration between automotive industry value chain and blockchain technology. In: Proceedings of the 2nd International Conference on Computer Science and Management Technology (ICCSMT), pp. 477–480 (2021)

26. Sivaselvan, N., Bhat, K.V., Rajarajan, M., Das, A.K.: A new scalable and secure access control scheme using blockchain technology for IoT. IEEE Trans. Netw. Serv. Manage. **20**(3), 2957–2974 (2023)

27. Tariq, A., Binte Haq, H., Ali, S.T.: Cerberus: a blockchain-based accreditation and degree verification system. IEEE Trans. Comput. Soc. Syst. **10**(4), 1503–1514 (2023)

28. Teng, Y., Lv, J., Wang, Z., Gao, Y., Dong, W.: TimeChain: a secure and decentralized off-chain storage system for IoT time series data. In: Proceedings of the ACM on Web Conference 2025, pp. 3651–3659 (2025)
29. Tsankov, P., Dan, A., Drachsler-Cohen, D., Gervais, A., Bünzli, F., Vechev, M.: Securify: practical security analysis of smart contracts. In: Proceedings of the ACM SIGSAC Conference on Computer and Communications Security, pp. 67–82 (2018)
30. Wang, J., Chen, J., Xiong, N., Alfarraj, O., Tolba, A., Ren, Y.: S-BDS: an effective blockchain-based data storage scheme in zero-trust IoT. ACM Trans. Internet Technol. **23**(3), 1–23 (2023)
31. Wang, S., Ouyang, L., Yuan, Y., Ni, X., Han, X., Wang, F.Y.: Blockchain-enabled smart contracts: architecture, applications, and future trends. IEEE Trans. Syst. Man Cybern.: Syst. **49**(11), 2266–2277 (2019)
32. Wang, Z., et al.: On how zero-knowledge proof blockchain mixers improve, and worsen user privacy. In: Proceedings of the ACM Web Conference, pp. 2022–2032 (2023)
33. Wei, L., Cui, J., Zhong, H., Bolodurina, I., Gu, C., He, D.: A decentralized authenticated key agreement scheme based on smart contract for securing vehicular ad-hoc networks. IEEE Trans. Mob. Comput. **23**(5), 4318–4333 (2024)
34. Wu, H., Jiang, S., Cao, J.: High-efficiency blockchain-based supply chain traceability. IEEE Trans. Intell. Transp. Syst. **24**(4), 3748–3758 (2023)
35. Wu, T., Jourjon, G., Thilakarathna, K., Yeoh, P.L.: MapChain-D: a distributed blockchain for IIoT data storage and communications. IEEE Trans. Industr. Inf. **19**(9), 9766–9776 (2023)
36. Xu, J., Wang, C., Jia, X.: A survey of blockchain consensus protocols. ACM Comput. Surv. **55**(13s), 1–35 (2023)
37. Yin, J., et al.: DP-DID: a dynamic and proactive decentralized identity system. IEEE Trans. Inf. Forensics Secur. **20**, 4999–5014 (2025)
38. Yu, H.F., Mu, W.Z.: ABE-Based postquantum cross-blockchain data exchange approach for smart agriculture. IEEE Trans. Industr. Inform. **20**(10), 12083–12091 (2024)
39. Zhang, F., Cecchetti, E., Croman, K., Juels, A., Shi, E.: Town crier: an authenticated data feed for smart contracts. In: Proceedings of the ACM SIGSAC Conference on Computer and Communications Security, pp. 270–282 (2016)
40. Zhang, K., Wang, X., Qiu, L., Lv, E., Guo, J., Yi, B.: JCDC: a blockchain-based framework for secure data storage and circulation in jointcloud. Futur. Gener. Comput. Syst. **162**, 107486 (2025)
41. Zheng, Z., Xie, S., Dai, H.N., Chen, X., Wang, H.: Blockchain challenges and opportunities: a survey. Int. J. Web Grid Serv. **14**(4), 352–375 (2018)
42. Zhu, Q., Sun, Y., Mangla, S.K., Arisian, S., Song, M.: On the value of smart contract and blockchain in designing fresh product supply chains. IEEE Trans. Eng. Manage. **71**, 10557–10570 (2024)

Why is it Challenging to Overcome, Minimize or Regulate MEV?

R. K. Shyamasundar[✉]

Department of Computer Science and Engineering, Indian Institute of Technology, Bombay, Mumbai 400076, India
`rkss@cse.iitb.ac.in`

Abstract. With the increasing popularity of high-frequency trading and decentralized finance (DeFi) applications, it has become essential to implement protections for regular users of DeFi platforms against large parties with massive amounts of resources, allowing them to engage in market manipulation strategies like the maximum extractable value (MEV). MEV can be extracted using the Bellman-Ford flow algorithm, making it easy for bots to realize MEV in DeFi. In classical trading, front-running is illegal and is classified under the umbrella of insider trading. However, the classical approaches to the mitigation of MEV do not apply to DeFi applications, as the mitigation of classic insider trading is based on central enforcement through legal laws. DeFi has in it both blockchain platforms and automated market makers (AMM) on decentralized exchanges (DEX), which introduces additional stakeholders that are virtual/anonymous for which the fear of legal laws/suits do not apply. Hence, a variety of approaches have been proposed in the literature to overcome or minimize MEV. In this paper, first, we illustrate various MEV attacks in classical trading, show how MEV can be exploited algorithmically, and discuss mitigation techniques to overcome MEV in classical trading. Secondly, we show that the same mitigation techniques for overcoming MEV in DeFi do not apply as additional stakeholders are introduced. Thirdly, we describe the design of a robust AMM on XRPL blockchain ledger that overcomes MEV. From such a design on XRPL which is one of the widely used blockchain platforms that has several constraints as compared to the general permissionless or permissioned blockchain platforms, we discuss issues of overcoming MEV in general DeFi applications. It is argued that such limitations necessitate a practical regulatory approach supported by a good forensic methodology with tools to instill confidence in the use of DeFi.

Keywords: MEV · Front-Running Attacks · Ethereum · Ripple · Regulations

1 Introduction

With the surge in new technologies such as electronic networks and artificial intelligence, markets face a new and daunting mode of manipulation compared

© The Author(s), under exclusive license to Springer Nature Switzerland AG 2026
R. K. Shyamasundar et al. (Eds.): ICBC 2025, LNCS 16155, pp. 149–169, 2026.
https://doi.org/10.1007/978-3-032-06176-8_10

to traditional markets. Tom Lin [15] examines the impact of "The Flash Crash of 2010" and the publication of Flash Boys by Michael Lewis, and highlights that in addition to the traditional manipulation methods like cornering, front running, etc., arise due to technological evolutions. He argues for the dire need to meet the new threats of cyberspace market manipulation by a thorough improvement of intermediary integrity, improving financial cybersecurity, and simplifying investment strategies.

AMM [4] is one of the two popular mechanisms in prediction markets (the other being continuous double auction (CDA)). It allows traders to place all orders with the AMM, and it determines the cost of each transaction and adjusts the prices of the securities. It has several advantages for a prediction market, such as trading at all hours, reacting instantly to changes in trading, and eliminating unfortunate spreads found in thinly traded markets. For an AMM to be useful, it should satisfy the following property: the underlying algorithm should not be vulnerable to becoming a money pump to a clever trader, and its potential losses should be bounded ahead of time having tunable properties.

The recent surge in crypto-trading activity has accelerated the development of DeFi. DEXs turning out to be a major DeFi application with AMM protocols. With the increasing popularity of high-frequency trading [27], and DeFi applications, it has become essential to implement protections for regular users of DeFi platforms against large parties with massive amounts of resources that allow them to engage in market manipulation strategies like MEV[1] that has a multitude of attacks, such as front-running, sandwich, or back-running attacks.

One of the underlying rationale for unethical trading in a blockchain based platform is based on MEV [7] attacks that is a prominent family of attacks. In traditional financial markets, user transactions are sequenced by a trusted and regulated intermediary in the order in which they are received. In a blockchain, on the contrary, the updating of a block is competitive and random. For example, in a cryptocurrency based on Proof of Work (POW), such as Bitcoin, all miners use their computing power to quickly solve a puzzle that will allow only one of them to add the next block. The probability that a given miner will add the next block is equal to the miner's share of the total computing power used. This process can be considered "decentralized" and equitable in the sense that there are many different miners, and no single miner can censor a specific transaction forever. This is because if the fee that a transaction pays is high enough, some other miner will eventually include it in the block. Similar arguments hold for a Proof of Stake (POS) based network, into which the Ethereum network has transitioned. When a miner can add a new block, they are free to assemble this block in any way they want. This lets them extract value from other users. In addition to legitimate transaction fees (such as gas fees in Ethereum), they can assemble their block from all pending transactions, contained in a memory pool, called the "mempool", in such a way as to maximize MEV. The latter are profits that are made by manipulating market prices via a specific ordering. As

---

[1] also referred to as "miner extractable value" as it reflects the maximal theoretical value that can be extracted from transaction ordering in permissionless blockchains.

the ledger is public, these forms of market manipulation can be seen, even if the underlying identity of the miners or other parties in question is unknown.

The main contributions of the paper are:

1. First, we illustrate prominent attacks under MEV like front-running, sandwich and back-running attacks, etc., and discuss traditional approaches of overcoming them.
2. Overcoming MEV in blockchains that provides a basis for various DeFi applications corresponds to achieving properties like privacy of mempool transactions, forbidding ordering of transactions by the miner as well as forbidding addition of new transactions, or enforcing fairness issues while constructing a new block by a miner.
3. We show that the Bellman-Ford algorithm can be used for the exploitation of MEV or arbitrage in classical and DeFi applications.
4. We describe the design of a robust AMM[2] in XRPL Ledger [19] using batched threshold encryption [6] using our result [20] that establishes the absence of forks under enforced consensus conditions in XRPL.
5. From the robust design of AMM on XRPL, we shall discuss the issues of overcoming MEV in general DeFi applications, relating it with various approaches in the literature that have been proposed to overcome MEV.

The remainder of the paper is organized as follows. After the introduction in Sect. 1, we provide a glimpse of classic traditional trading and relate the problem with privacy and information disclosure in Sect. 2. Section 3 provides a discussion of DeFi on blockchain platforms and illustrates various primary MEV attacks followed by an algorithmic approach to exploit MEV from which we derive the challenges of mitigation of MEV in Sect. 4. Sections 5 and 6, respectively, discuss mitigations of MEV in classical platforms and discuss issues of overcoming MEV in blockchain-based platforms. Section 7 describes the design of a robust AMM on XRPL. In Sect. 8, we discuss issues of other approaches in the literature in overcoming MEV in DeFi applications followed by discussions in Sect. 9.

2   Classic Trading: A Glimpse

With a long history of asset trading on traditional exchanges, there is a spectrum of ways a trader can exploit information that is not yet public, to his gain, which is both illegal and unethical.

Front-running is a technique where a trader exploits an early access to market information about upcoming transactions and trades, obtained either due to one's privileged position or information obtained from some private sources. For example, floor traders might have become aware of a broker's negotiation with his/her client over a large purchase that made him to buy first the asset with the expectation that he will profit when the large purchase temporarily

---

[2] Assuming AMM satisfies the required conditions to avoid from becoming a money pump for a clever trader.

reduces the supply of the stock. Alternatively, a malicious broker might front-run their client's orders by purchasing the stock for themselves between receiving the instruction to purchase from the client and actually executing the purchase (similarly, the process follows for large sell orders). Front-running is *illegal* in jurisdictions with established security regulations. Front-running cases are quite often difficult to distinguish from insider trading or arbitrage. Front-running is illegal and unethical when a trader acts on insider information. Of course, there are gray areas, such as cases in which an investor may buy or sell a stock and then disclose the reasoning behind it. Some of the subtleties of such trading are given below:

1. In front-running, a trader sees a concrete transaction that is set to execute and reacts to it before it actually gets executed.
2. If, instead, the person has access to more general privileged information that could predict future transactions but does not react to it at the actual pending trade, the activity is classified as *insider trading*. Insider trading involves buying or selling a publicly traded company's stock based on nonpublic material information about that company.
3. If the person reacts after the trade is executed, or the information is made public and profits from being the fastest to react, it is considered *arbitrage* and is legal and encouraged because it helps the markets integrate new information into prices quickly.

Non-public material information is information that has not been disseminated to the general public and is not readily available through ordinary research. It is confidential or restricted to a select group of individuals within a company or those with a special relationship with the company, that is, it is *private* information. Privacy is about responsible maintenance of private information. This responsibility is hard to define, which is why laws are necessary. Insider trading is illegal and carries severe penalties, including potential fines, prison time, and other penalties. Insider transactions occur all the time and are legal when they comply with the rules set forth by respective regulatory bodies. The regulatory boards require insiders to file reports of their trades, which are publicly available. In other words, the notion of fair-trade is preserved through legal laws (through well established forensics).

3   DeFi on Blockchain Platforms

Many of the classic trading exploits highlighted above have found momentum with increased automation and technology by getting information quickly, such as in high-frequency trading [27] or the use of DEX. In the context of cryptocurrencies, research to date indicates that the ecosystem requires a greater understanding of malpractices prevalent in classical asset trading on centralized exchanges, and also demands a robust decentralized exchange design to prevent exploitation/malpractices. It must be noted that most existing legislation does not regulate crypto-exchanges to the same degree as traditional exchanges, leaving ignorant traders open to exploitation. The flexibility introduced by blockchain platforms leads to additional stakeholders, which in turn introduces additional vulnerable points of exploitation.

3.1 Additional Stakeholders in Blockchain-Based Trades

Blockchain platforms showed an attraction for asset trading, as there was no need for trusted parties and their characteristics, like immutability and distributed data, lead to a robust provenance of transactions. Although blockchain technology does not have any centralized party involved in any transaction, it introduces new participants in the process of relaying and finalizing transactions in the following way:

1. Miners are in the best position to conduct these attacks as they hold control over the exact set of transactions that will execute and in what order, and can mix it with their own transactions without broadcasting them.
2. Note that miners need to commit to what their own transactions will be before beginning to solve the POW puzzle.
3. A user who monitors network transactions can see unconfirmed transactions.
4. Furthermore, in the context of the Ethereum blockchain, users pay for computations, known as "gas price" through small amounts of Ether. The price that users pay for transactions/computations can increase or decrease based on how miners will execute them and include them within the blocks they mine. A profit-motivated miner who sees identical transactions with different transaction fees will prioritize the transaction that pays a higher gas price due to limited space in the blocks. This is referred to as *gas auction*.

A spectrum of trading attacks are possible using the following broad scenarios:

1. Any regular user who runs a full-node Ethereum client can front-run pending transactions by sending adaptive transactions with a higher gas price.
2. A well-positioned relaying node on the network can attempt to influence how transactions are propagated through the network, which can influence the order of transactions received by the miner.

In the next section, prominent attacks in the MEV family are described.

3.2 MEV Attacks on BlockChain Platforms: A Brief Overview

Three broad categories of attacks with the MEV principle are: front-running, back-running, and sandwich attacks. A brief overview of these is given below.

3.3 Front-Running Attacks

The mempool consists of various signed but pending transactions that are ordered. As it is public, it provides an opportunity for potential front-runners to monitor pending transactions and identify a profitable transaction; they need to act very quickly. That is, the adversary needs to create and broadcast its own transaction before the original transaction is included in a block. For this purpose, adversaries use bots to monitor the mempool and automatically create and send transactions to effect a front-running opportunity. Figure 1 depicts a spectrum of front-running attacks by a malicious/adversarial miner:

1. Reversing the order of transactions is the simplest that creates a bias or priority. Let the shares denoted in transactions T1 and T2 be limited. Then, just reversing the order of T1 and T2 in the new block, will lead the buyer in T2 to be deprived of getting his stock as there may not be any share left or sufficient shares for T1 to get executed.
2. The miner could add his own transaction, say T3, to the block to get executed before others; the profit realized will depend on the size and direction of the large-volume transaction.
3. The effect of inversion can also be reached by giving a higher gas price (reflected in parameters g1, g2, g3, g4 in the transactions) offer by the buyer/seller for the transaction. For example, if g4 is larger than the other gas price offers, then the transaction offering with g4 is executed before others.
4. In an Ethereum mempool for decentralized exchange transactions, a malicious miner could find a profitable "cancel transaction" and place his buy order prior to the cancel transaction in the block he mines. Through such an action, the miner can profit from the underlying trade and also get the gas cost included in the cancel transaction.

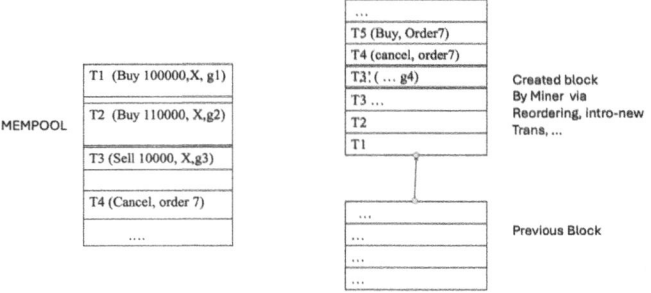

Fig. 1. Front Running Attack Schema

Front-running attacks (cf. [12]) have been broadly classified into [12] (i) *Displacement*: In this attack, it is not necessary for the victim's function to execute after the malicious trader's function executes; (ii) *Insertion*: In an insertion attack, after the adversary runs her function, the state of the contract is changed, and she needs Alice's original function to run on this modified state; (iii) Suppression of the transaction. For details, refer to [12].

3.4 Back-Running Attacks

As the name itself implies, the back-runners place their trade immediately after someone's trade. The attacker fills the block with a large number of cheap gas transactions to definitively follow the target's transaction. Compared to front-running, which only requires a single high-value transaction and is detrimental to the user being front-run, back-running is disastrous to the whole network by hindering the throughput with useless transactions. The most common back-running perpetrators are MEV bots programmed to monitor pending Ethereum transactions. These bots place strategic trades directly after existing trades to capture the *arbitrage* left over from their price impact.

3.5 Sandwich Attacks

The attack involves an adversary using a front-running strategy to push up the price and, after the execution of the user's trade, places a transaction in the opposite direction to recover its initial investment and profit from the price impact caused by the user's transaction. The aim is to exploit the maximum price that a user is willing to accept. In a financial auction transaction, users must provide a price variant called slippage to their swap to accommodate the market shifts of price (the difference between the time they broadcast their transaction and when it gets mined). Users' transactions are visible publicly while pending to be included. This provides an opportunity for an arbitrageur or miner to place a trade that shifts the price to a maximum slippage user is willing to pay, and then profit from the margin between the lower bound on that slippage and the initial market price.

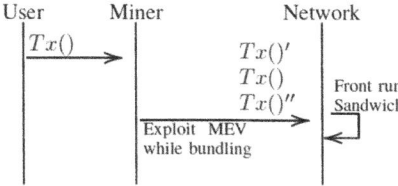

Fig. 2. Sandwich Attack

In Fig. 2, the user, say Alice, places a transaction Tx to buy a large amount of token, say T. An arbitrage trader spots Alice's transaction in the mempool and sends a competing transaction Tx with a higher gas price so that he can buy T before Alice does. The transaction of the arbitrage trader creates a shortage in the total supply of T, thus increasing the price of Alice's Tx. Immediately after Alice's Tx, the arbitrage trader sells the T he bought Tx at a higher price, thus profiting from the difference; therefore, the attack is known as sandwich attack. Note that the three transactions Tx, Tx, and Tx are all in the same block.

There are other attacks such as pump-and-dump [23], vampire attack, oracle attack, etc., that are a well-trodden ruse in conventional financial markets; the old-fashioned ploy has found a new playground to thrive in cryptocurrency exchanges.

4   Exploiting MEV Algorithmically

We can realize MEV[3] algorithmically in a spectrum of ways; we shall illustrate one of the legal techniques under MEV called "arbitrage". As already explained, it is achieved through simultaneous buying and selling of securities, currency, or commodities in different markets or in derivative forms to take advantage of differing prices for the same asset. Such algorithmic approaches can be generalized to automate different forms of MEV.

4.1   A Gentle Introduction of an Algorithm for Arbitrage

Let us consider the following Currency Exchange problem: Given the exchange rates of the currencies, *Is it possible to get the best possible conversion from X to Y going through different exchanges?* if we have a directed graph with vertices representing currencies and the edge weights representing exchange rates, the graph may have more than one distinct path from X to Y. If we find a path which would be the most profitable, then that would mean maximizing the result of the multiplication of the exchange rates in the path. During the conversion of X to Y, if we get back more than the amount given for conversion, we would have got a profit arbitrage. Let us assume that we are given a set of exchange rates among certain currencies, and we would like to determine if an "arbitrage" is possible, i.e., if there is a path by which you can start with one unit of some currency, say CUR and perform a series of barters which results in having more than one unit of CUR when you come back to the starting node. For the sake of presentation, let us assume that there are no transaction costs, exchange rates do not fluctuate, and fractional quantities of items can be sold. Consider the example of exchange rates given in Table 1.

Table 1. Sample Exchange Rate Example

	USD	EUR	GBP	CHF	CAD
USD	1	0.741	0.657	1.061	1.005
EUR	1.349	1	0.888	1.433	1.366
GBP	1.521	1.126	1	1.614	1.534
CHF	0.942	0.698	0.619	1	0.953
CAD	0.995	0.732	0.650	1.049	1

---

[3] Note that MEV is a double-edged sword with both beneficial and detrimental effects.

Suppose a person would like to covert USD 20000 using the following the sequence of barters, USD→EUR→CAD→USD, it results in USD 20142. That means it generates a profit of USD 142. As discussed above, the profit corresponds to arbitrage.

A simple algorithm to realize the above arbitrage for the USD is given below:

1. Represent the Table 1 as a directed graph with different currencies as nodes and edges as exchange rates.
2. Find paths from USD to itself passing through other nodes at most once (find cycles). Multiply the labels of the cycles and choose the largest. If the result of any cycle is greater than one, then there is a arbitrage - that is a profit; otherwise there is a loss. In the example we used, USD→EUR→CAD→USD, it corresponds to 0.741 * 1.366 * 0.995 = 1.007 > 1 reflecting a profit.

That is, we need to find a path that would maximize the result of the multiplication of the exchange rates.

Input: $G(V, E, S)$ a weighted directed graph with labels (positive or negative), where V is the list of vertices, and E is the list of edges with weight w_{uv} where u, v denoted the edge from u to v, and a source vertex $S \in V$.

Output: Vector distance2S contains distances from the vertices (in the order considered) to S, predecessor contains the predecessor vertex connected in the same order.

Table 2. Bellman Ford Algorithm For Finding Negative Cycles

1. foreach $v \in V$ do distance2[v] := ∞; predecessor[v] := null;
2. distance2S[s] := 0;
(* Iterate connecting edges repeatedly*)
3. for i:=1 to $|V| - 1$ do
4.   foreach $(u, v) \in E$ with label w do
5.   if $distance2S[u] + w < distance[v]$ then
6.   distance2S[v] := distance[u] + w
7.   predecessor[v] := u
(* Identify negative cycles*)
8   foreach $(u, v) \in E$ with label w do
9.   if $distance2S[u] + w < distance[v]$ then
10.   The graph contains a negative cycle

The above problem can be converted to an instance of the Bellman-Ford algorithm [3] by transforming the multiplicative relationship to an additive relationship. Let us indicate the exchange rate from USD to EUR by A, EUR to CAD by B, and CAD to USD by C, then check whether $A * B * C > 1$. Returning to logarithms (with the base representation e or 2), we can observe that

$log(A * B * C) = logA + logB + logC$. That is, the multiplicative relationship has been transformed into an additive relationship. Thus, we can convert the currency exchange relationship into an additive relationship, where we add the edge weights and determine if an arbitrage exists based on the sum of the edge weights of the cycle. Then, we can reformulate the condition for the existence of arbitrage as follows:

> An arbitrage exists if the sum of the weight of the edges forming the cycle is greater than a threshold. The threshold value would depend on how we convert the multiplicative relationship into an additive relationship.

In other words, if we modify the graph and make the edge weights represent the logarithm of the exchange rates, then an arbitrage will correspond to a cycle with the summation of all the edges forming the cycle being greater than zero. That is, whenever a positive weight cycle is observed, we can say that there is arbitrage. With a slight change of notation, we can transform the problem to an instance of Bellman-Ford algorithm and reduce the possibility of arbitrage to the presence of negative cycles in the network where labels can be negative. The steps for a transformation are described below.

1. Create a directed graph in which the vertices are the currencies and the weight of the edges are the negated logarithm of the exchange rate of the currencies represented by the vertices the edge connect. For example, if the exchange rate for the currency A to currency B is E, then the directed edge connecting A to B will be labeled with weight $-log\ E$.
2. Find out if there is a negative weight cycle using the algorithm described in Table 2.

It is amazing how the arbitrage problem reduces the currency conversion to the shortest-path problem, which helps us to solve (1) finding the existence of any arbitrage and (2) finding the most profitable way to convert currency X to currency Y.

Before modeling the general seller-buyer problem, let us look at the existence of uncertainty in the blockchain transactions and the mining of blocks, as that would show the possible points of attack for the adversaries.

4.2   Transaction Life Cycle and Blockchain Formation Uncertainties

Transactions and contracts are activated every day in Ethereum Network, and blocks are created at a very high rate. The Life Cycle of a Transaction [24] is given below: (1) Starts when it is constructed and signed by the initiator. Then it is submitted to the blockchain network, either directly or through a gateway. (2) Once in a miner, the miner validates the signed transaction to make sure that it is signed by the claimed account, with parameters correctly set having sufficient funds in the source account. A *nonce*, a sequence number reflects the order of transactions sought in an account and assists in detecting duplicate transactions and concurrency control mechanisms. If it is invalid, the transaction is rejected; otherwise, it is marked as validated.() If the validated transaction is already in the transaction pool, it is rejected; otherwise, it is added to the transaction pool as a pending transaction. (3) A pending transaction is also propagated to other nodes/miners using a gossip protocol. (4) Those miners also validate the transaction before further propagating it to the other miners. (5) Transactions are not treated equally: Different gas prices associated with transactions incentivize miners to sort the pending transactions based on their gas price. (6) The size of the transaction pool is limited and once reached, miners tend to drop transactions with lower gas prices. (7) If a pending transaction is resubmitted with a higher gas price but with the same source account and nonce, it is added to the transaction pool and the previous transaction is dropped. (8) A transaction that is dropped by all miners is discarded from the blockchain network.

Mining a Block: The main features of mining a block are [24]: (1) When a miner starts mining a block, it picks a set of transactions from the transaction pool, **executes them**[4], and builds a block, say $block_M$. Transactions in $block_M$ are marked as included in a mining block, (2) The number of transactions included in it is limited by the block gas limit, which is the maximum gas that all transactions within a block can consume, (3) During mining, if the miner receives a new block, say $block_N$, from the P2P network, the miner validates it. If $block_N$ is valid, the miner removes the transactions in $block_N$ from the transaction pool and marks those transactions as included in a branch, (4) If a transaction in $block_M$ is also in $block_N$ or if the miner has already completed the mining and propagated $block_M$ to the P2P network, the state of those transactions is also marked as included in a branch, (5) If the miner did not complete the mining $block_M$ before the arrival of $block_N$, the transactions that are in $block_M$ but not in $block_N$ go back to the transaction pool, and their state is set to pending, and (6) Once a transaction is included in a branch and when newly built blocks generate a sufficient number of confirmations, it is considered committed (i.e., being included in blockchain with very high probability).

4.3   Generalization of Arbitrage to the General Seller-Buyer

Let us assume that the transactions on a blockchain are buy-or-sell orders for currencies. Now, we can construct a transaction graph as follows:

1. Orders are sorted according to their retrieval, and two lists of orders are constructed for each pair of trades (in both directions).
2. Construct a graph with the "best offer" (highest bid, or lowest ask)[5] for each pair as the only edge between the two currencies.

---

[4] If the transactions are buy or sell order, one can validate the quantity of asset, say shares or currency sought and amount required for the same, and in the sell order one checks whether the account has the necessary quantity at its disposal.

[5] The bid-ask spread is the difference between the highest price that buyers are willing to pay (the bid) and the lowest price that sellers are willing to accept (the ask). While

3. While new orders are added to the order book at each new block, we keep track of whether or not we modified the position of a previous "best offer" in the sorted lists. If not, the graph remains the same with no need to re-run the cycle detection algorithm.

4. If at least one edge has been modified due to the new block, we replace all the modified edges in the smaller graph and run cycle detection again.

5. The execution of buy and sell orders can take place by choosing the execution path for MEV for the account. For instance,
   - In XRPL [19], looking at the block formation continuously, we can build a graph of transactions from which a miner can decide the transaction path according to the cycle.

6. Of course, there are a few more subtle considerations that need to be addressed depending on the blockchain platforms; as this is not of much relevance here, we shall skip them.

It should be clear from the algorithmic description that one way of preventing MEV is to ensure that the algorithm cannot extract the required information automatically; i.e., pending transactions and the transactions on the block cannot be exposed until they are committed or the ordering cannot be controlled.

5   How do we Mitigate MEV?

MEV is a double-edged sword with beneficial and detrimental effects. Positively, it encourages actors to correct market inefficiencies, thus supporting the stability and accuracy of DeFi protocols. However, it has negative ramifications at both the application and network levels, from worsening user experience through practices like sandwich attacks/back-running attacks causing network congestion and even potential blockchain reorganizations if the MEV outweighs standard block rewards.

From the discussions in the previous section and Remark 1, our intuition tells us that to overcome MEV, possible ways are

1. Make the set of Transactions Private or
2. Prevent the Miners from reordering the transactions or enforce fairness of transaction execution.

We shall discuss prominent approaches using the above strategies after looking at the way front-running attacks are handled in traditional trading.

5.1   Mitigation from Front Running Attacks in Traditional Trades

Insider trading carries severe penalties, including potential fines, jail time, and other penalties. Insider transactions occur all the time and are legal when they comply with the rules set forth by respective regulatory bodies. The regulatory

---

the spread gives you a view of market liquidity and transaction costs, the bid-ask size shows how many shares are available at each price.

boards require insiders to file reports of their trades, which are publicly available. In other words, the notion of fair trade is preserved through legal laws.

In a sense, insider trading (or front-running attacks) in a classical setting corresponds to **preserving the privacy of nonpublic information**. Suppose that we interpret privacy in the context as explored in [8], that is, *nothing about an individual should be learnable from the database that cannot be learned without access to the database.*. This notion of privacy is never achievable, as shown in [11]. The authors of [11] arrive at the general impossibility result showing that a natural formalization of Dalenius' goal along the lines of semantic security for crypto-systems cannot be achieved if the database is to be useful. Their theorem is stated informally a s follows:

Theorem 1 [11]: Given a privacy mechanism, PRIV() and distribution, D, satisfying some relevant conditions, there is always some piece of *auxiliary information*, say Z, so that Z is useless to someone trying to win, while Z in combination with access to the data through the privacy mechanism allows the adversary to win with probability close to 1.

According to their argument, the key obstacle is the side information that may be available to an adversary. The intuition behind the proof of impossibility is captured by the following parable. Suppose that the exact height of an individual is considered a sensitive piece of information and that revealing the exact height of an individual is a privacy violation. Assume that the database yields the average heights of women of different nationalities. An adversary who has access to the statistical database and the auxiliary information "Terry Gross is two inches shorter than the average Lithuanian woman" learns Terry Gross' height, while anyone learning only the auxiliary information, without access to the average heights, learns relatively little. Contrary to intuition, a variant of the result threatens privacy even if someone is not in the database. This state of affairs motivated the notion of differential privacy, a strong *ad omnia* privacy which, intuitively, captures the increased risk to privacy incurred by participating in a database. In other words, the result says: *In any "reasonable" setting, there is a piece of information that is itself innocent, yet in conjunction with even a modified (noisy) version of the data yields a privacy breach.*

Thus, traditional methods to prevent front-running attacks mainly involve investigation of transactions, and the issues, if any, are handled through legal action, essentially a postmortem of the transactions. Thus, overcoming front-running attacks needs to be handled through the following means:

1. Educating the employees is the first step taken to prevent such issues in traditional markets, however, front-running became less likely to happen mainly because of the high fine and lawsuits against firms who behaved in an unethical way.
2. Other methods such as dark pools[6] sealed bids have been explored in a variety of regulated trading systems.

---

[6] Dark pools are private exchanges for trading securities that are not accessible to the investing public. They were created to facilitate block trading by institutional investors (that is, very large volume investors) who did not wish to impact the markets with their large orders and obtain adverse prices for their trades.

Due to the complex definition of privacy, the challenges of overcoming privacy leaks in high-frequency trading are a great challenge.

6 Handling MEV on Trading Platforms Using Blockchain

The traditional methods to prevent front-running do not apply to blockchain applications, since they are mainly based on central enforcement, and further, in the case of blockchain-based platforms, the actors who are front-running could be virtual/anonymous and the fear of lawsuits would not apply.

6.1 Issues for DeFi Using Blockchain

From the attacks and their patterns discussed, it may be noted that the source of malicious behaviour can be attributed to various characteristic features of block formation and execution on blockchain platforms. Some of the prominent challenges in mitigating MEVs are:

1. As Mempool transactions are *publicly visible*[7], the life cycle of transactions on a blockchain can be misused by a malicious miner/stakeholder to his advantage, by using operations such as displacement, insertion, or suppression (cf. Remark 1 in Sect. 4).
2. Reordering or introducing transactions in a sense corresponds to *unfair* execution of transactions; that is, the transactions are not necessarily executed according to the order in the mempool or the timestamp. Thus, ensuring fair execution and prevention of collusion among miners will be a major issue.
3. Privacy-Preserving Smart Contracts: The authors of [14] describe a method to compile smart contracts with explicit public and private annotations to automatically generate an efficient cryptographic protocol for contractual parties to interact with the blockchain, using cryptographic primitives such as zero-knowledge proofs. While HAWK supports many interesting applications, it is not clear as to how smart contracts written in languages like Solidity can be transformed to such a set up.
4. In platforms using languages like Solidity, forks (leading to a plausible double spending) are plausible, and some of them could lead to data races (leading to non-deterministic behaviour). In such cases manipulations are possible by reordering of the transactions or a miner introducing additional transactions with malicious intent.
5. In fact, smart contracts can be crafted to bribe miners, or misinterpretation by the compiler may occur as smart contracts are essentially general distributed programs; some other misuses also occur due to a misunderstanding of some of the global attributes of blockchain transactions like *block.time*, *tx.origin*, sending funds to a killed contract[8] or assuming a variable to be completely local forgetting the fact that transactions are public in a public blockchain, impact of inducing exceptions using the order of execution, etc.

---

[7] A characteristic of public blockchains.

[8] One's tendency is to assume that with the killing of a contract, it may not be able to receive any funds.

7 Building a Robust AMM on an XRPL Ledger

In this section, we describe the broad steps in building[9] a robust AMM[10] on an XRPL ledger. The Ripple (XRP) network is one of the widely used platforms used in a spectrum of applications including DeFi, and it does not run with PoW used in Bitcoin or POS used in Ethereum but guarantees consistency with only a partial agreement on who participates, allowing for a decentralized open network. Thus, the XRPL protocol does not depend on mining, but uses a voting process based on validator nodes attached to each of the servers. It is through such a voting process that it achieves good scalability and performance. The main function of XRPL is to make the network agree on sets of transactions and not on the content or outcome of those transactions. That is, it provides a common global order for the transactions submitted by clients to all participating nodes inspite of faulty or malicious (Byzantine) nodes. For achieving agreement of transactions in each block, it uses a Unique Node List (UNL) for each server. Conceptually speaking, each server, say S, maintains a unique node list, which is a set of other servers that queries when determining consensus. Only the votes of the other members of the UNL of S are considered when determining the consensus. Thus, the UNL represents a subset of the network which when taken collectively, is "trusted" by S to not collude in an attempt to defraud the network. Note that this definition of "trust" does not require that each individual member of the UNL is trusted. For any node server, P_i, UNL_i denotes its UNL list, $n_i = |UNL_i|$, a parameter called quorum, q_i denotes the number of nodes in UNL_i from whom P_i should get a consensus before making a decision. For details of the protocol, the reader is referred to [19].

7.1 Realizing Robust AMM on XRPL

From Sect. 6.1, it should be clear that to overcome MEV, it is crucial to realize privacy on the mempool. Before going for the realization of privacy in the mempool of the XRPL blockchain, let us take a look at the salient features of XRPL ledger [19,20] briefly described below:

1. Initially, each server takes all valid transactions seen prior to the consensus round that have not already been applied and makes them public in the form of "candidate set". That is, it consists of new transactions initiated by end users of the server and the transactions held over from the previous consensus process.
2. Each server then amalgamates the candidate sets of all servers on its UNL, and votes on the veracity of all transactions.
3. Transactions that receive more than a minimum percentage of YES votes (i.e., the quorum) are passed on to the next round; transactions that do not

---

[9] It was presented at the APEX Ledger Conference held 10–12 June 2024 at Singapore.
[10] AMM introduces additional stakeholders similar to that discussed in Sect. 3.1 corresponding to the structure of AMM [4].

receive enough votes will either be discarded or included in the candidate set for the beginning of the consensus process on the next ledger.

4. The final round of consensus requires a minimum percentage of 80% of the UNL of the server agreeing on a transaction. All transactions that meet this requirement are applied to the ledger, closing it and becoming the new last closed ledger.

Most of the approaches used to achieve "mempool privacy" have been based on threshold encryption [5,9,18]. The broad steps of threshold public key encryption is given below:

1. It has a single public key and distributes the private key among N decryption servers so that at least a threshold number (say K) is needed for decryption.
2. For usage, a committee (corresponding to the decryption servers) is first set up so that its members have the distributed private key and all users encrypt to the public key of the committee.
3. Thus, miners can only see encrypted transactions in the mempool and create blocks containing ciphertexts.
4. With confirmation of the block, the committee jointly decrypts all transactions that are included in the block and announces them to all nodes in the network.

The authors of [6] have shown that any of the above approaches faces the following problems in the realization of mempool privacy:

1. Malleability attack: an adversary could create a related transaction ciphertext, submit that instead, and learn information about a transaction which has not been included on chain.
2. Even in the context of epoch-based threshold encryption, where clients encrypt to an epoch, with the decryption key remaining the same for all ciphertexts in that epoch, it leads to unacceptable compromises to privacy, as ciphertexts that are not included/withheld lose privacy despite not being confirmed transactions. This is called pending transaction privacy.

To overcome such issues, the authors of [6] have developed a variant of threshold encryption called batched threshold encryption (BTE) meets strict efficiency requirements in the context of blockchain environments; this method is shown to require communication proportional to $O(nB)$ to decrypt B transactions with a committee of N parties, BTE $O(n)$ communication. To decrypt an entire batch of B transactions it requires only 80 bytes per party - i.e., it is independent of the number of transactions B, making it an attractive choice. Thus, certainly, BTE would be a good choice. But one question remains: What if the blockchain forks?

As explained already, the issue of public visibility of the mempool has been overcome in the innovative work of [6]. However, under forking conditions, some of the transactions in the block in the branch during the process of merging of the blockchain, the transactions in the block that gets eliminated become available to the public. Naturally, this leads to privacy issues and the possibility of MEV. However, in the context of XRPL ledger, this does not arise as it does not fork [20], In [20], it is shown that:

1. XRPL with 80% quorum and UNLs satisfying 50% Rand Index (RI) similarity[11], is robust against 20% failures; that is, the network will not accept fraudulent transactions.
2. Furthermore, the network satisfies the consensus correctness if the UNLs of the network are greater than 50% RI, say α and α implies at least 80% quorum across all UNLs, then there will be no forks.
3. Thus, BTE enables for a robust AMM on XRPL ledger.

Thus, a robust AMM can be realized in the XRPL using BTE [6]. Robustness follows from the privacy of the mempool achieved and from the fact that XRPL does not fork [20]. Without the satisfaction of RI similarity, XRPL has the possibilities of front-running attacks as demonstrated in [21]. Furthermore, our method does not restrict the use of legal arbitrage, as shown in [16].

8   Other Approaches for Mitigating MEV in DeFi

Currently, the best solution to overcome MEV is the deployment of mempool privacy as elaborated in [6] discussed already. In the following, we shall highlight other approaches that have been explored to overcome issues of MEV:

1. *Randomizing Transaction Ordering*: is one of the strategies used in the XRPL ledger. It is shown [21] that the condition is not sufficient to overcome front-running attacks.
2. *Relative Ordering of Transaction* Enforcing a relative order requires building a dependency graph that enables partial orders on transactions adapting techniques prevalent in concurrency control [22]. Such systems have again been shown to be prone to front-running attacks [13] exploiting the lack of triangle inequality among nodes considering network latencies as the distance among nodes. The authors of [25] propose a protocol that assumes partial synchrony and that processes do not decrypt a transaction before it is committed unless it prohibits reordering transactions. Keeping in view the uncertainty of transactions (cf. Sect. 4.2), it is not clear how it can be used in the general case.
3. *Absolute Timestamping Transactions:* corresponds to providing a timestamp for each transaction. In Hedera [2] (uses ABFT consensus and never prunes a branch), a transaction is timestampped with the *median of consensus time* with an a priori bounded valid duration for being accepted by a node. Due to underlying concurrency, several transactions can have the same timestamp. The ties of concurrent transactions are broken using the identities of special nodes called *famous* nodes[12] as preferred nodes. Thus, in Hedera MEV exploitation is minimized rather than fully overcome, keeping in view front-running attacks (cf. Fig. 1), the asynchrony, and the fact that Hedera [2] does

---

[11] This is a similarity measure used in cluster analysis and used for consensus correctness in XRPL ledger in [20].
[12] Informally, this corresponds to those nodes (witnesses) that have been received by many nodes at the start of the round.

not define a notion of fairness. It is easy to observe that liveness cannot be guaranteed in such situations.

4. An Approach of Randomization of Sharding: This approach has been explored in [1] which leads to a protocol on a blockchain that reduces the profit that can be derived from sandwich attacks. The approach depends on breaking each transaction into, m smaller transactions, and randomly permuting them; scheduling such sharded transactions while using general smart contracts without locks is not possible.

5. The authors in [26] describe an approach for sharded transactions by creating a global order among the list of transactions that have been processed but have not yet been committed and a list consisting of transactions that can be committed. Keeping in view the undecidability of lineraization of distributed programs, application of such approaches using general smart contracts is not possible as the synchronization requirements will be complex [20].

8.1 PBS: An Engineering Oriented Trust Based Scheme

The proposer-builder separation (PBS) introduces a market-based mechanism where external actors, known as builders, create bundles of complete block contents, including the fee of the proposer. The proposer selects the bundle with the highest fee, introducing a more competitive and efficient system for the creation of blocks. This system aims to decentralize the power of block proposers and enhance the network's overall efficiency and security. However, the exact mechanics of who can all become block proposers under PBS is quite complex, as it needs to address the issues of fairness and prevent collusion among stakeholders.

With Ethereum having shifted to a PoS model, the dynamics of block proposing has transformed. Validators are now randomly selected to act as block proposers in each slot. These validators are responsible for creating and broadcasting new blocks while a randomly selected committee of validators confirms the blocks' validity. Note that such an approach has its own issues of one validator snatching the other validator's finding through smart contract exploitation, as highlighted earlier. The MEV-Boost approach represents a step toward decentralization; however, it does not fully resolve the centralization and censorship issues attributed to the builders and relays themselves. Thus, it is necessary to evolve the PBS scheme for Ethereum using strategies such as block withholding, trust minimization, and fair ordering.

9 Discussions

In this paper, we have illustrated prominent attacks in the MEV family and shown how MEVs can be exploited algorithmically using algorithms like Bellman-Ford flow algorithms. Reasons as to why classical mitigation techniques to overcome MEV are not amenable to DEX applications have been discussed along with the relevance of absolute information disclosure. We have described the design of a robust AMM in XRPL Ledger [19] using BTE [6] using the result of [20] that establishes the absence of forks under consensus conditions in XRPL. From such a design, we have shown the issues/challenges with various existing approaches for overcoming MEV in DEX applications. Our robust design of AMM on XRPL brings to light the limitations of techniques such as preserving the privacy of the mempool, withholding reordering of transactions or enforcing certain fairness properties; note that there cannot be a unique notion of fairness while classifying models of fairness or fairness relating to privacy [10]. One thing that is clear is that privacy of the mempool is vital to overcoming MEV. In the context of the PBS scheme for Ethereum, new strategies are required in terms of block withholding, trust minimization, and fair ordering [17] - thus making it a rich research area from both the perspective of theory and practice. The path forward involves balancing the need to harness the positive aspects of MEV for protocol efficiency with the imperative to limit its negative impacts on network security and user experience. This delicate equilibrium needs the commitment of all participants in the network to foster a sustainable, inclusive, and resilient blockchain ecosystem. As discussed already, a good fairness analysis of Hedera would allow us to have solutions to minimize/overcome MEV in various situations. Such approaches shall support the ability to respond to the new threats of cyberspace market manipulation through a thorough improvement of intermediary integrity, financial cybersecurity, and simplifying investment strategies.

References

1. Alpos, O., Amores-Sesar, I., Cachin, C., Yeo, M.: Eating sandwiches: modular and lightweight elimination of transaction reordering attacks (2023). https://arxiv.org/abs/2307.02954
2. Baird, L., Harmon, M., Madsen, P.: Hedera: a public hashgraph network & governing council. White paper, V2.1, 15 August 2020
3. Bellman, R.: On a routing problem. Qly. Appl. Math. **1**, 87–90 (1958)
4. Berg, H., Proebsting, T.A.: Hanson's automated market maker. J. Pred. Markets **3**, 45–59 (2009)
5. Boneh, D., Gennaro, R., Goldfeder, S., Jain, A., Kim, S., Rasmussen, P.M.R., Sahai, A.: Threshold cryptosystems from threshold fully homomorphic encryption. In: Shacham, H., Boldyreva, A. (eds.) CRYPTO 2018. LNCS, vol. 10991, pp. 565–596. Springer, Cham (2018). https://doi.org/10.1007/978-3-319-96884-1_19
6. Choudhuri, A.R., Garg, S., Piet, J., Policharla, G.V.: Mempool privacy via batched threshold encryption: attacks and defenses. In: Proceedings of the 33rd USENIX Security Symposium. SEC '24, USENIX Association, USA (2024)
7. Daian, P., et al.: Flash boys 2.0: frontrunning, transaction reordering, and consensus instability in decentralized exchanges. CoRR abs/1904.05234 (2019). http://arxiv.org/abs/1904.05234
8. Dalenius, T.: Towards a methodology for statistical disclosure control. Statistik Tidskrift **15**, 429–444 (1977)
9. Desmedt, Y., Frankel, Y.: Threshold cryptosystems. In: Brassard, G. (ed.) CRYPTO 1989. LNCS, vol. 435, pp. 307–315. Springer, New York (1990). https://doi.org/10.1007/0-387-34805-0_28

10. Dwork, C., Hardt, M., Pitassi, T., Reingold, O., Zemel, R.: Fairness through aware-ness. In: ACM Proceedings 3rd Innovations in TCS, pp. 214–226 (2012)
11. Dwork, C., Naor, M.: On the difficulties of disclosure prevention in statistical databases or the case for differential privacy. J. Privacy Confident. **2**(1) (2010). https://doi.org/10.29012/jpc.v2i1.585
12. Eskandari, S., Moosavi, S., Clark, J.: SOK: transparent dishonesty: front-running attacks on blockchain. In: Bracciali, A., Clark, J., Pintore, F., Rønne, P.B., Sala, M. (eds.) Financial Cryptography and Data Security. LNCS, pp. 170–189. Springer, Cham (2020). https://doi.org/10.1007/978-3-030-43725-1_13
13. Kelkar, M., Deb, S., Long, S., Juels, A., Kannan, S.: Themis: fast, strong order-fairness in byzantine consensus. Cryptology ePrint Archive, Paper 2021/1465 (2021). https://eprint.iacr.org/2021/1465
14. Kosba, A., Miller, A., Shi, E., Wen, Z., Papamanthou, C.: Hawk: the blockchain model of cryptography and privacy-preserving smart contracts. In: 2016 IEEE Symposium on Security and Privacy (SP), pp. 839–858 (2016). https://doi.org/10.1109/SP.2016.55
15. Lin, T.C.: The new market manipulation. Emory L. J. 1253 **66** (2017). https://scholarlycommons.law.emory.edu/elj/vol66/iss6/1
16. Peduzzi, G., James, J., Xu, J.: Jack the rippler: arbitrage on the decentralized exchange of the xrp ledger. In: 2021 3rd Conference on Blockchain Research Applications for Innovative Networks and Services(BRAINS). pp. 1–2 (2021). https://doi.org/10.1109/BRAINS52497.2021.9569833
17. Pillai, B.: Blockchain mev minimisation solution with price guarantee reward. TechRxiv (2022)
18. Santis, A.D., Desmedt, Y., Frankel, Y., Yung, M.: How to share a function securely. In: Leighton, F.T., Goodrich, M.T. (eds.) Proceedings of the 26th Annual ACM Symp. on Theory of Computing, 23-25 May 1994, Montréal, Québec,. pp. 522–533 (1994)
19. Schwartz, D., Youngs, N., Britto, A.: The ripple protocol consensus algorithm. In: Ripple Inc., White Paper (2014)
20. Shyamasundar, R.K.: Characterization of consensus correctness in ripple (XRP) networks. In: Proceedings of the 21st International Conference on Security and Cryptography, SECRYPT 2024, Dijon, France, July 8-10, 2024, pp. 103–113. SCITEPRESS (2024)
21. Tumas, V., Pontiveros, B.B.F., Torres, C.F., State, R.: A ripple for change: analysis of frontrunning in the XRP ledger. In: 2023 IEEE International Conference ICBC, pp. 1–9 (2023)
22. Weikum, G., Vossen, G.: Transactional Information Systems: Theory, Algorithms, and the Practice of Concurrency Control and Recovery. Morgan Kaufmann Publishers Inc., San Francisco (2001)
23. Xu, J., Livshits, B.: The anatomy of a cryptocurrency pump-and-dump scheme. In: Proceedings of the 28th USENIX Conference on Security Symposium, pp. 1609–1625. USENIX Association, USA (2019)
24. Xu, X., Bandara, H.M.N.D., Lu, Q., Zhang, D., Zhu, L.: Understanding and han-dling blockchain uncertainties. In: Chen, Z., Cui, L., Palanisamy, B., Zhang, L.-J. (eds.) ICBC 2020. LNCS, vol. 12404, pp. 108–124. Springer, Cham (2020). https://doi.org/10.1007/978-3-030-59638-5_8
25. Zarbafian, P., Gramoli, V.: Lyra: fast and scalable resilience to reordering attacks in blockchains. In: 2023 IEEE IPDPS, pp. 929–939 (2023)

26. Zhang, J., Chen, W., Luo, S., Gong, T., Hong, Z., Kate, A.: Front-running attack in sharded blockchains and fair cross-shard consensus. In: 31st NDSS San Diego (2024)
27. Zhou, L., Qin, K., Torres, C., Le, D., Gervais, A.: High-frequency trading on decentralized on-chain exchanges, pp. 428–445 (2021). https://doi.org/10.1109/SP40001.2021.00027

Design and Implementation
of a Configurable Network Benchmarking
Framework for Blockchain Systems

Huazheng Cheng, Xinwei Ning, Shengli Zhang[ID], and Taotao Wang[✉][ID]

College of Electronics and Information Engineering, Shenzhen University,
Shenzhen, China
{chenghuazheng2022,ningxinwei}@email.szu.edu.cn,
{zsl,ttwang}@szu.edu.cn

Abstract. This study proposes a blockchain benchmarking system
based on distributed architecture and network simulation techniques,
aiming to overcome the performance limitations and network edge effects
of traditional single-machine benchmarking schemes. By integrating
Docker containerization and the Linux TC tool, the system simulates
blockchain network topologies with customizable connection and latency
matrices, enabling the rapid construction of diverse network configurations. In addition, leveraging Zookeeper to coordinate multiple testing machines enables a distributed benchmarking process. This breaks
through single-machine performance bottlenecks and minimizes interference from network edge conditions. The experimental results demonstrate that the system effectively evaluates the scalability, stability,
and performance of the data layer of blockchain systems. For example,
under a high-latency network with a 132-ms delay, the TPS of PBFT-
based blockchains drops significantly. PoW-based systems show stronger
resilience. This system provides a robust and realistic testing platform for
blockchain performance evaluation and optimization, supporting practical deployment in real-world scenarios.

Keywords: Blockchain · Benchmark Framework · Configurable
Network

1 Introduction

Blockchain technology has made continuous progress in decentralized trust construction and has been widely adopted in critical domains such as the Internet
of Things (IoT), supply chain management, and financial technology. As a typical distributed system, blockchain performance is influenced by various factors,

This work is supported in part by the National Natural Science Foundation of China
under Grant 62471316, in part by the Shenzhen Science and Technology Program under
Grant JCYJ20220531101015033; and in part by the Research Center for FinTech and
Digital-Intelligent Management at Shenzhen University.

including consensus mechanisms, network topology, and transaction distribution patterns. Efficient and accurate performance evaluation under realistic network conditions has become a key technical challenge.

Existing blockchain benchmarking tools can be roughly categorized into two groups. The first includes model-based simulators, such as BlockSim [1] and DAGsim [2], which abstract and simulate key operations within blockchain systems. Although these methods offer flexibility and low deployment cost, over-simplified modeling often fails to reflect real-world behaviors, such as incentive mechanisms and dynamic network conditions. The second group relies on the real deployment of the system, including tools such as Blockbench [3] and Hyperledger Caliper [4]. These tools perform benchmarking by deploying blockchain nodes on a single machine or a small set of devices. Although capable of reflecting actual system performance to some extent, they suffer from two major limitations. First, the test load is concentrated on a single machine, so hardware constraints make it difficult to evaluate behavior under high-throughput conditions. Second, submitting requests through a single node introduces bandwidth constraints and network edge effects, and thus is less representative.

To address these limitations, this study proposes an integrated benchmarking system featuring network simulation and distributed workload generation. The solution comprises two key components: (1) a network emulation module based on Docker and the Linux Traffic Control (TC) tool, supporting customizable connection and latency matrices to replicate diverse network topologies within a single physical machine; and (2) a distributed test architecture coordinated via Zookeeper, enabling synchronized multinode workload generation across multiple machines. This architecture effectively overcomes single-machine performance bottlenecks and mitigates the influence of network edge positioning on performance metrics.

Standardized processes such as account generation, genesis configuration, and node startup are implemented to support the rapid deployment of blockchain environments with full node roles. Experimental evaluations demonstrate the proposed system's ability to simulate realistic network environments and conduct high-fidelity performance testing. In particular, the distributed architecture improves throughput by more than 3× under high-load scenarios compared to traditional single-node testing, and significantly reduces the distortion caused by edge effects.

The main contributions of this paper are:

- **Benchmarking paradigm:** We propose a new benchmarking paradigm that integrates container-based network emulation with distributed workload generation, achieving a balanced trade-off between experimental fidelity and evaluation efficiency.
- **Automated test framework:** We design and implement an automated framework that supports topology reconfiguration on the fly, substantially reducing the complexity of deploying and evaluating multi-node blockchain systems.

– **Empirical characterization:** Extensive experiments reveal a non-linear coupling between network latency and consensus performance, providing quantitative guidance for the architectural optimization of blockchain networks.

The proposed system has been successfully applied to performance testing of FISCO-BCOS and Ethereum Clique consensus networks, demonstrating its adaptability and engineering viability. It serves as a practical platform for evaluating and optimizing blockchain performance under realistic network conditions.

The remainder of this paper is organized as follows. Section 3 reviews key performance metrics and enabling technologies. Section 4 introduces the Docker-TC-based network emulation architecture. Section 5 presents the distributed benchmarking framework based on Zookeeper. Section 6 details the experimental setup and analyzes the results. Section 7 concludes the paper and describes future work.

2 Related Work

Performance benchmarking of blockchain systems is a fundamental research area for understanding system-level behaviors under diverse workloads and deployment environments. Existing efforts can be broadly classified into model-based simulation tools and empirical benchmarking frameworks, with additional work focusing on defining performance metrics and designing supporting tools for testbed orchestration.

The first group includes simulation-based approaches, such as BlockSim and DAGsim, which aim to abstract and simulate blockchain systems without full system deployment. BlockSim [1] models blockchain environments using a discrete event simulation framework, incorporating layered abstractions for network, consensus, and incentive mechanisms. It supports configurable testing for Bitcoin, Ethereum, and other protocols, enabling theoretical exploration of mining centralization and throughput. DAGsim [2], on the contrary, focuses on DAG-based protocols such as IOTA, simulating transaction approval processes and evaluating confirmation confidence and delay sensitivity. These simulators are efficient for early-stage analysis, but often oversimplify runtime characteristics such as adversarial behavior, latency jitter, and hardware-level contention.

Beyond simulation, a large body of work investigates empirical benchmarking frameworks that deploy actual blockchain implementations. Blockbench [3] introduces a modular benchmarking suite for private blockchains. Hyperledger Caliper [22] enables end-to-end testing of permissioned platforms such as Fabric and Besu, while DAGBench [6] targets DAG-based ledgers. These tools often rely on single-host or small-cluster deployments, enabling repeatable experiments but introducing artificial bottlenecks in CPU, memory, or bandwidth. To address scalability and realism, recent distributed frameworks such as DIABLO [18], DLPS [19], Gromit [20], and Hammer [21] support multihost benchmarking, workload coordination, and fault injection. Although more representative of real-world deployments, these frameworks are often complex to configure and less flexible when adapting to non-standard scenarios.

3   System Architecture and Workflow

To address the limitations of traditional testing methods, we propose an integrated platform that combines network emulation and a distributed benchmarking framework. The server hosts two core components: Blockchain Network Emulation and Distributed Benchmark Testing.

3.1   Blockchain Network Emulation Process

This process provides a large number of blockchain nodes on a single server using Docker containers. The system creates containerized nodes in parallel and connects them to a network via a generated or user-defined topology. Network constraints such as latency and bandwidth are applied using the Linux TC tool, simulating real-world distributed conditions. This yields a realistic and configurable test environment for performance evaluation.

3.2   Distributed Benchmark Testing Process

This process executes performance tests using a Master-Slave architecture. The **Master Controller** parses the test profile, distributes tasks and configurations to **Testing Clients**, and collects results. Clients invoke workloads at specified rates through a rate controller, submit transactions through a blockchain adapter, and collect metrics such as latency and success rate. The Master aggregates the results and generates a report with performance indicators such as TPS and response time.

3.3   Core Metrics and Key Technologies

Most benchmarking tools adopt a common set of performance metrics to evaluate the performance of the blockchain system. These include **Transactions Per Second (TPS)**, which reflects the system's transaction processing capacity; **Response Time (RT)**, measuring the delay between transaction creation and confirmation; and Average Response Time, representing the mean latency in all successful transactions. In addition, **Scalability** assesses the system's ability to maintain performance as the number of nodes or network load increases, while **Stability** evaluates its resilience to fluctuations in workload intensity. Together, these metrics provide a comprehensive view of both throughput and responsiveness under varying operational conditions.

Currently, our evaluation focuses on these core metrics. Future work plans to extend the framework with modules to support more fine-grained indicators such as consensus fairness, information loss rate, and block reorganization rate.

4   Configurable Emulation Method for Blockchain Networks

4.1   Containerized Deployment of Blockchain Nodes

To assess blockchain performance under realistic deployment conditions, each node in this study is instantiated as a full node. Because large-scale node deployment is resource intensive, we adopt Docker containerization to improve hardware utilization and accelerate the provisioning of numerous nodes. Docker is an open source lightweight platform that lets multiple containers share the host kernel, thus minimizing per-node overhead. Using this approach, a large-scale blockchain network can be emulated on a single physical machine.

The blockchain node generation process can be divided into four stages: image construction, account generation, creation of the genesis file, and node initialization and startup. The details are as follows:

- **Image Construction:** To deploy as many blockchain nodes as possible on a single machine with restricted resources, this study uses the lightweight base image officially provided by Ethereum as the starting point. This base image contains only the core components necessary for running an Ethereum node instance. To support network traffic control in the network simulation, additional dependencies are included by customizing a *Dockerfile* to install the *iproute2* module, enabling TC functionality.
- **Account Generation:** The account-generation phase proceeds as follows. First, the framework retrieves the target node count specified by the user. It then instantiates a hierarchical file layout: a root directory that hosts a private data folder for every node and a shared configuration folder that contains the unified password file and a global list of public key addresses. Within each node's private folder, the Ethereum client is executed in a Docker container to create a new account, after which the associated public key is appended to the shared key list.
- **Genesis File Creation:** The Ethereum network supports multiple consensus mechanisms, including Proof of Work (PoW) and Proof of Authority (PoA). Different types of consensus require different configurations in the genesis block. In this stage, a standard genesis file is generated using key parameters provided by the user—such as *consensusType*, *chainId*, *period*, *epoch*, *difficulty*, and *gasLimit*—together with the list of public keys from the account.
- **Node Initialization and Startup:** Each container initializes from its corresponding private folder using the generated genesis file and launches as an Ethereum full node. The nodes are then linked to a test network through the bootnode mechanism or static connections.

4.2   Network Topology Simulation

In their initial state, the blockchain nodes operate in isolation. To carry out meaningful performance experiments, a reproducible peer-to-peer (P2P) overlay must be constructed so that a prescribed set of nodes can communicate under controlled network conditions (for example, latency and bandwidth). We model the overlay as a graph $G = (V, E)$, where each vertex $v_i \in V$ represents a node and each edge $(v_i, v_j) \in E$ is weighted by link attributes such as one-way delay or throughput. Topology simulation therefore consists of (i) generating the graph, (ii) instantiating P2P links, and (iii) applying link parameters.

The framework offers two complementary connection schemes: **(i) Random connection Approach**, in which edges are created stochastically to mimic organic peer discovery; and **(ii) Custom connection Approach**, where users provide an adjacency or latency matrix for deterministic fine-grained control of link characteristics. Together, these schemes enable the emulation of unstructured and tightly constrained blockchain networks for rigorous performance evaluation.

Random Connection Approach. This method is based on Ethereum's native peer discovery mechanism. Designated bootnodes provide peer-to-peer (P2P) discovery services, allowing participating nodes to identify and connect to each other in a decentralized and stochastic manner. Each node generates a private key file **nodekey** which is used to derive a unique node identifier for use in connection handshakes. Upon initialization from containers, the nodes leverage this identifier to establish connections through the bootnode system, resulting in a random network topology driven by discovery logic. This setup enables the construction of dynamic and adaptive network structures, promoting both interconnectivity and resilience.

Network parameters such as latency and bandwidth can be dynamically configured. During the configuration phase, the TC tool is used to assign the link properties. Each node configures parameters only for peers it creates connections to afterward, thus preventing redundant or conflicting rule applications. A default parameter set is also provided, modeled on empirical measurements of transcontinental latency (e.g., Ohio to Tokyo).

Custom Connection Approach. In contrast, the custom topology simulation allows for precise control over node interconnections and their associated delays. Users define a connection matrix (**connMatrix**) of size $n \times n$, where each entry indicates whether there is a direct link between two nodes (1 connected, 0 not connected). The latency values between nodes are stored in a corresponding delay matrix. Static connection files are generated for each node and connections are established by invoking APIs to add peers according to the matrix specifications (Fig. 1).

Topology construction proceeds by traversing the connection matrix. Each node initiates connections only with subsequent nodes (in index order), thereby minimizing redundant operations. Similarly, the latency matrix is traversed to apply communication parameters. Using the TC tool, each node applies egress latency rules for only the necessary downstream connections, thus avoiding

	node1	node2	node3	$\cdots$	noden
node1	C_{11}	C_{12}	C_{13}	$\cdots$	C_{1n}
node2	C_{21}	C_{22}	C_{23}	$\cdots$	C_{2n}
node3	C_{31}	C_{32}	C_{33}	$\cdots$	C_{3n}
$\vdots$	$\vdots$	$\vdots$	$\vdots$	$\ddots$	$\vdots$
noden	C_{n1}	C_{n2}	C_{n3}	$\cdots$	C_{nn}

Fig. 1. Connection matrix of the nodes

double latency effects due to repeated queue settings. This static and fully controlled topology allows the reproduction of deterministic network structures and behaviors.

5   Distributed Testing Framework Using ZooKeeper

To support large-scale performance evaluation and simulate realistic blockchain workloads, this study implements a distributed testing framework using Apache ZooKeeper. ZooKeeper is used as the core coordination and communication module, enabling the design of a master-slave testing architecture with one master controller and multiple distributed testing clients.

This framework achieves two core goals:

1. **Distributed Test Control:** The testing framework is divided into a single master controller and multiple testing clients. The master controller is responsible for distributing testing tasks, collecting results, and generating the final report. The clients execute the tasks and report the results to the master.
2. **Communication via ZooKeeper:** To ensure reliable coordination and minimize communication overhead, all control signals and result data are exchanged through ZooKeeper nodes. Clients register with the ZooKeeper server and use designated input/output nodes to receive tasks and send results.

The testing process proceeds as follows: (i) The testing client registers itself on the ZooKeeper server, creates input/output communication nodes, and waits for instructions. (ii) The master controller starts by deploying testing and contract invocation logic. It fetches the registered clients and sends test instructions to their input nodes. (iii) Clients detect new instructions, execute test tasks, and write the results to their output nodes. (iv) The master controller monitors all output nodes, collects the result data, and aggregates them into the final test report (Fig. 2).

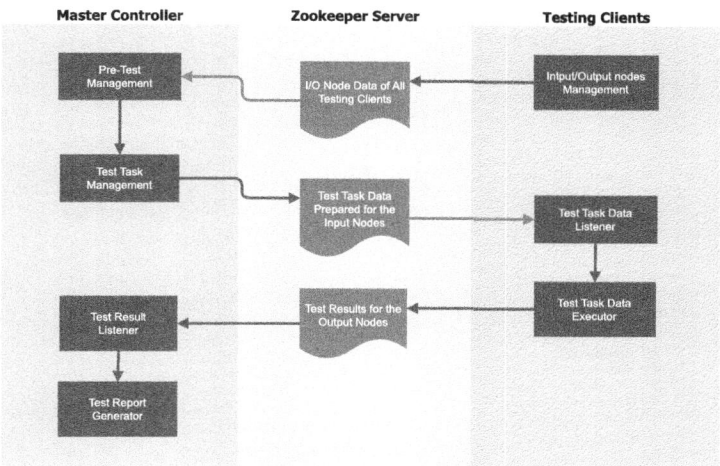

Fig. 2. Distributed Benchmark Testing Framework

5.1   ZooKeeper-Based Communication Mechanism

The ZooKeeper server provides a hierarchical namespace to facilitate efficient communication between the master controller and testing clients. The detailed interaction process is described below:

- **Client Registration:** Upon startup, each testing client creates a unique ephemeral sequential node under the `/clients` registration path (e.g. `/clients/client01`). In this node, two persistent children are created: `in` (for receiving commands) and `out` (for reporting results).
- **Master-to-Client Messaging:** The master controller sends instructions by creating persistent sequential message nodes under the `in` directory of each client. The client continuously monitors this directory to retrieve and process incoming messages.
- **Client-to-Master Reporting:** Upon completion of a testing task, the client creates a persistent sequential node under its `out` directory to store the test result. The master controller monitors these directories and retrieves the result data for further aggregation and analysis.

5.2   Master Controller and Multi-process Testing Clients

In the proposed distributed testing framework, the testing system is divided into a single master controller and multiple distributed testing clients. These components interact via Apache ZooKeeper, which acts as the coordination and communication backbone. The master controller manages the orchestration of testing tasks and result aggregation, while each client is implemented with a multi-process architecture to fully utilize computing resources on physical machines.

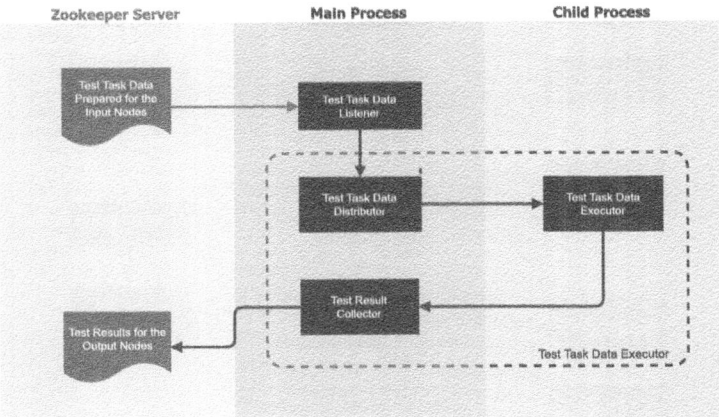

Fig. 3. Workflow of the Testing Client

Master Controller Logic: The master controller is responsible for reading configuration files, assigning testing tasks, monitoring client status, and generating the final report. At startup, it parses both the network configuration and test configuration files, deploying the smart contracts required for load testing. Retrieves information about all active testing clients from the ZooKeeper server and assigns testing tasks accordingly by writing structured task messages to the input nodes of each client.

The testing is performed in rounds, as defined by the configuration. During each round, the master controller monitors the output nodes of all clients. Once all clients return their result data, the controller aggregates the data to compute key performance metrics. After all rounds are completed, it invokes a rendering engine to embed the results into a templated HTML report, which is stored in the working directory for further analysis.

Multi-process Testing Client Design: Each testing client adopts a primary child process model to parallelize the execution of the test and efficiently consume computing resources. When a client starts, its main process registers the client on the ZooKeeper server and creates persistent input and output nodes for bidirectional communication with the master controller. The main process continuously monitors the input node for new tasks. Upon detecting new instructions, it spawns the specified number of child processes and distributes the test configuration to them (Fig. 3).

Each child process initializes its own rate control mechanism, performs the designated test workload, and reports the result back to the main process. The main process aggregates the results from all child processes and writes the final output to the ZooKeeper output node, completing one testing cycle.

After each cycle, the child processes clear their previous state and prepare for the next round. The system dynamically adapts to task complexity by adjusting the number of child processes as needed, ensuring both scalability and robustness in performance evaluation.

By combining centralized task orchestration with decentralized and parallel execution, this distributed framework enables scalable, accurate, and repeatable performance benchmarking of blockchain systems across heterogeneous environments.

6 Experimental Testing and Result Analysis

6.1 Experimental Conditions

The entire testing framework runs on three physical machines. One machine serves as the master controller, responsible for deploying the blockchain network and the Zookeeper server, while the other two act as testing clients. Although ZooKeeper is a centralized component, it is only used for client coordination during testing and does not participate in the consensus process, which simplifies deployment. Compared to Kubernetes, ZooKeeper combined with Docker enables lighter weight deployment and finer-grained latency control. The hardware specifications for all machines are detailed in Table 1.

Table 1. Hardware Specifications of Servers

Specification	Master Controller (Alibaba Cloud)	Testing Clients (Huawei Cloud)
Processor	8-core vCPU	4-core vCPU
Memory	32 GiB	8 GiB
Storage	100 GiB	70 GiB
Bandwidth	100 Mbps	5 Mbps

6.2 Workload Design

Benchmark testing executes workloads on blockchain nodes by submitting transactions. Three types of workloads were designed:

1. Data Encoding Library: Simulates computationally intensive data encoding operations, focusing on testing the performance of the blockchain execution layer.
2. Employee Information Management: Simulates a simple personnel management system with smart contracts that register and query employee information, test read-write operations, and data layer performance.
3. No-Operation (NOP): Execute a smart contract with minimal operations to isolate consensus layer performance. It also serves as a control group for comparison.

6.3 Performance Testing of Blockchain Network Simulation

This section evaluates the time and memory consumption for building blockchain networks on various node scales using a fully connected network configuration.

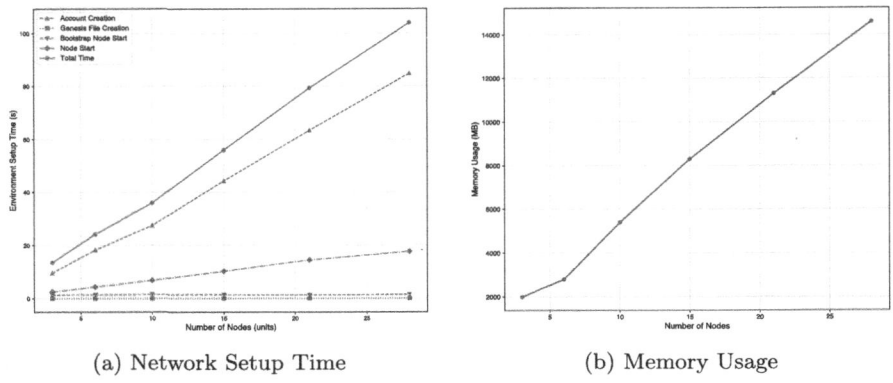

(a) Network Setup Time   (b) Memory Usage

Fig. 4. System resource consumption under different node counts.

Analysis of Network Setup Time. As shown in Fig. 4a, the time required to build the network increases rapidly with node count. Account creation, involving multiple file operations and Docker container setup, is the most time-consuming. The node startup time increases proportionally, while the creation of the genesis file and `bootnode` startup remain stable. The construction of a 28 node network took less than 2 min, demonstrating the efficiency of the scheme in accelerating the setup of the blockchain network.

Analysis of Memory Usage. Figure 4b indicates a near linear growth in memory consumption with node count, influenced by the exponential increase of TCP/IP connections in a fully connected network. Memory usage for 28 nodes remains below 16 GB, showing that typical machines can support nearly 30 nodes for effective testing.

6.4 Blockchain Performance Testing

The testing assesses blockchain system performance under various workloads, node counts, network conditions, and consensus algorithms (Ethash, Clique, PBFT). The test duration was 30 s per run with fully connected nodes.

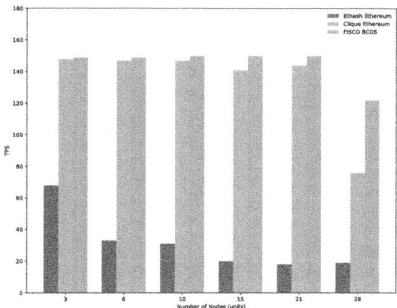
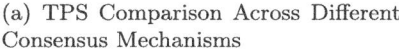
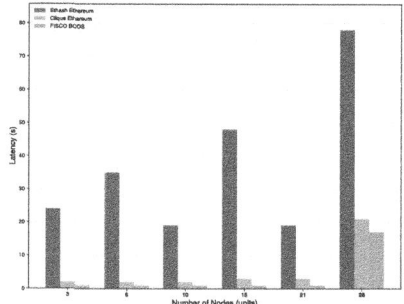

(a) TPS Comparison Across Different Consensus Mechanisms

(b) Latency Comparison Across Different Consensus Mechanisms

Fig. 5. Node Scalability Test Results

Node Scalability. Figure 5 shows that TPS generally decreases with increasing nodes for Ethash and Clique. PBFT (FISCO BCOS) latency increases steeply as node count increases, due to its high communication complexity. The latency of Ethash grows slower, consistent with PoW's node count independence. Clique shows limited scalability with higher latency growth than Ethash.

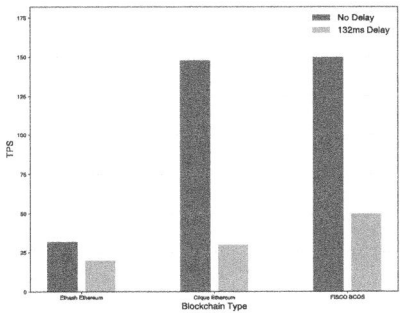
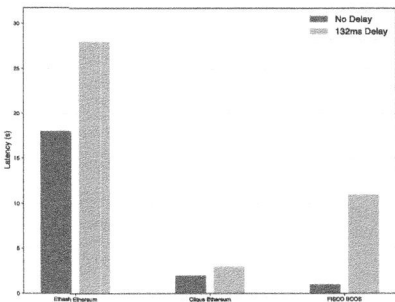

(a) TPS Comparison Under Network Delay

(b) Latency Test Result Under Network Delay

Fig. 6. Network Scalability Test Results

Network Scalability. As seen in Fig. 6, network latency (132 ms) reduces TPS and increases the latency for all blockchains tested, with PBFT most severely affected. Ethash shows relative robustness due to its reliance on computational resources over network speed.

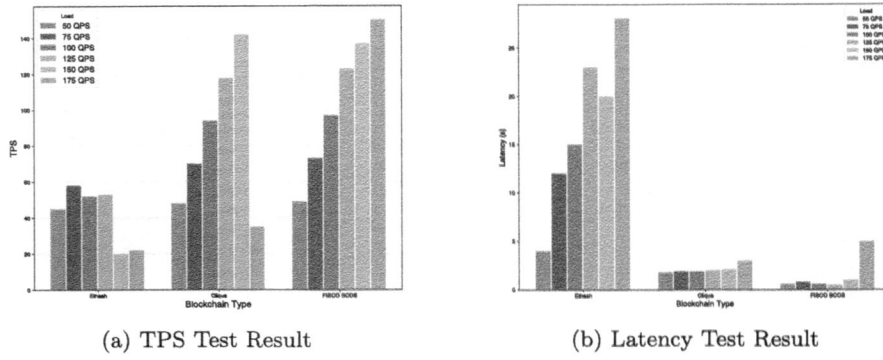

(a) TPS Test Result   (b) Latency Test Result

Fig. 7. System Stability Test Results (Left: TPS, Right: Latency)

System Stability. Figure 7 indicates that FISCO BCOS maintains a steady increase in TPS to 175 qps despite spikes in latency, showing strong stability. The TPS of Clique Ethereum drops sharply after the maximum capacity is exceeded. Ethereum's TPS decreases at high load, likely due to memory constraints affecting its PoW performance.

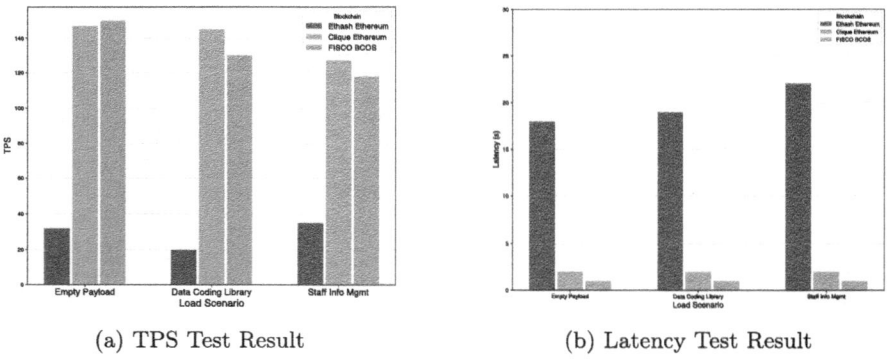

(a) TPS Test Result   (b) Latency Test Result

Fig. 8. Micro Performance Test Results

Data Layer and Execution Layer Performance. Figure 8 shows minimal latency changes for FISCO BCOS and Clique under various workloads; Ethash latency increases gradually. Clique Ethereum outperforms FISCO BCOS in TPS under data encoding and employee management workloads, indicating stronger layer-specific performance.

Ethereum with Ethash consensus demonstrates good scalability and stability, but lower absolute performance compared to FISCO BCOS and Clique

Ethereum, making it suitable for large-scale public blockchains. FISCO BCOS excels in stability and performance for smaller node counts, ideal for consortium blockchains. Clique Ethereum shows moderate scalability with better data and execution layer performance. The experiments validate the effectiveness of the distributed benchmarking framework for various blockchain evaluations.

7 Conclusion

This study proposes a configurable performance benchmarking framework that integrates network emulation and distributed architecture to overcome the limitations of traditional single-machine blockchain testing, such as resource bottlenecks and unrealistic network conditions. Using Docker and the Linux tc toolchain, the framework enables precise simulation of various network topologies and parameters, while a Zookeeper-based coordination mechanism facilitates distributed execution across multiple nodes. The framework was used to evaluate blockchain systems employing Ethash, Clique, and PBFT consensus algorithms across multiple dimensions, including node scalability, network scalability, system stability, and micro-level performance. Experimental results show that Ethereum with Ethash exhibits superior scalability and robustness for large-scale public deployments, FISCO BCOS delivers stable throughput under high concurrency making it well-suited for consortium chains, and Clique-based Ethereum offers moderate performance but is more sensitive to network latency. In general, the proposed framework enables efficient multidimensional evaluation of blockchain performance, providing practical guidance for system selection, optimization, and future consensus protocol development. Future work will explore the integration of a smart contract complexity quantification model to extend the framework to full-stack blockchain performance analysis.

Due to physical resource limitations, our current testbed includes 28 nodes; however, the framework is designed to scale to hundreds of nodes, and stress testing on larger deployments is planned. While we focus on key metrics like scalability and throughput, future work will also incorporate finer-grained metrics such as consensus convergence and chain reorganization, conduct comparisons with existing tools, and explore alternatives to ZooKeeper for improved decentralization.

References

1. Faria, C., Correia, M.: BlockSim: blockchain simulator. In: 2019 IEEE International Conference on Blockchain (Blockchain), pp. 439–446. IEEE (2019)
2. Zander, M., Waite, T., Harz, D.: DAGsim: simulation of DAG-based distributed ledger protocols. ACM SIGMETRICS Perform. Eval. Rev. **46**(3), 118–121 (2019)
3. Dinh, T.T.A., Wang, J., Chen, G., et al.: Blockbench: a framework for analyzing private blockchains. In: Proceedings of the 2017 ACM International Conference on Management of Data, pp. 1085–1100 (2017)

4. Androulaki, E., Barger, A., Bortnikov, V., et al.: Hyperledger fabric: a distributed operating system for permissioned blockchains. In: Proceedings of the Thirteenth EuroSys Conference, pp. 1–15 (2018)
5. Porcelli, F., Boucher, D., Rosenbluth, M.N.: Model for the sawtooth period and amplitude. Plasma Phys. Controlled Fusion **38**(12), 2163 (1996)
6. Dong, Z., Zheng, E., Choon, Y., et al.: DAGBench: a performance evaluation framework for DAG distributed ledgers. In: 2019 IEEE 12th International Conference on Cloud Computing (CLOUD), pp. 264–271. IEEE (2019)
7. Silvano, W.F., Marcelino, R.: Iota tangle: a cryptocurrency to communicate internet-of-things data. Futur. Gener. Comput. Syst. **112**, 307–319 (2020)
8. Zhang, C., Zhao, M., Liang, J., et al.: Nano: cryptographic enforcement of readability and editability governance in blockchain databases. IEEE Trans. Dependable Secure Comput. (2023)
9. Churyumov, A.: Byteball: a decentralized system for storage and transfer of value (2016). https://byteball.org/Byteball.pdf
10. Docker Inc. Docker (2020). https://www.docker.com/what-docker
11. Almesberger, W.: Linux network traffic control—implementation overview (1999)
12. Li, H., Lu, C., Gill, C.D.: Rt-zookeeper: taming the recovery latency of a coordination service. ACM Trans. Embedded Comput. Syst. (TECS) **20**(5s), 1–22 (2021)
13. Gheorghe, L.: Designing and Implementing Linux Firewalls with QoS using netfilter, iproute2, NAT and l7-filter. Packt Publishing Ltd. (2006)
14. Wu, K., Dai, G., Hu, X., et al.: Memory-bound proof-of-work acceleration for blockchain applications. In: Proceedings of the 56th Annual Design Automation Conference 2019, pp. 1–6 (2019)
15. Christyono, B.B.A., Widjaja, M., Wicaksana, A.: Go-ethereum for electronic voting system using clique as proof-of-authority. Telkomnika (Telecommun. Comput. Electron. Control) **19**(5), 1565–1572 (2021)
16. Buford, J., Yu, H., Lua, E.K.: P2P Networking and Applications. Morgan Kaufmann (2009)
17. Fette, I., Melnikov, A.: The WebSocket Protocol. RFC 6455 (2011)
18. Gramoli, V., Guerraoui, R., Lebedev, A., et al.: DIABLO: a benchmark suite for blockchains. In: Proceedings of the Eighteenth European Conference on Computer Systems, pp. 540–556 (2023)
19. Sedlmeir, J., Ross, P., Luckow, A., et al.: The DLPS: a new framework for benchmarking blockchains. Ledger (2021)
20. Nasrulin, B., De Vos, M., Ishmaev, G., et al.: Gromit: benchmarking the performance and scalability of blockchain systems. In: 2022 IEEE International Conference on Decentralized Applications and Infrastructures (DAPPS), pp. 56–63. IEEE (2022)
21. Zhang, R., Zhao, L., Li, K.: Hammer: a general blockchain evaluation framework. In: Proceedings of the 2023 International Conference on Blockchain and Trustworthy Systems, pp. 101–114. Springer (2023)
22. Kaushal, R.K., Kumar, N.: Exploring Hyperledger Caliper benchmarking tool to measure the performance of blockchain-based solutions. Int. J. Comput. Appl. (2020)
23. Hou, J., Huang, J., Xu, K., et al.: Blockcompass: a benchmarking platform for blockchain performance. Future Internet **14**(4), 105 (2022)
24. Guo, Y,, Huang, Y., Chen, X., et al.: BBSF: blockchain benchmarking standardized framework. Blockchain Res. Appl. 4(1): 100082 (2023)

A Novel Blockchain-Based Decentralized Drone Delivery Commercial Platform: From Concept to Practice

Shibing Xiao$^{(\boxtimes)}$, Xinxin Luo, and Burong Deng

Hong Kong University of Science and Technology, Clear Water Bay, Kowloon,
Hong Kong, China
sxiaoaj@connect.ust.hk

Abstract. In this paper, we design a decentralized drone delivery platform named CoEat. The article describes the necessity of the CoEat platform and the birth of DeFi economy, and elaborates on the three development stages of the platform in detai. Finally, the article will further discuss the innovative technologies applied in platform development and provide prospects for the platform's future growth.

Keywords: Decentralization · Delivery Service · Web3.0 ·
Low-Altitude Economy · Token Economy

1 Introduction

1.1 Industry Status Quo

The online food delivery industry in China has shown remarkable growth over the past decade [5]. In 2024, the market size of China's online food delivery industry reached 1,635.7 billion yuan, with a year-on-year growth of 7.2%, and the industry penetration rate reached 28.0% [12]. As a highly developed international metropolis, Hong Kong has unique geographical advantages for food delivery due to its dense population: over 7 million residents are concentrated in a limited urban space, which can significantly reduce delivery costs and time while improving delivery efficiency. In terms of consumption habits, the fast-paced lifestyle of Hong Kong residents has led to a growing demand for convenient living. The willingness of Hong Kong residents to order food delivery is gradually increasing with the change of their lifestyle rhythm [14]. All these indicate that the food delivery market in Hong Kong has a broad prospect and unlimited potential, and is expected to become a new growth point in the catering industry.

However, the current food delivery market in Hong Kong is relatively small, with an average of about 500,000 orders per day. The market size of food delivery in Hong Kong was approximately 6.5 billion Hong Kong dollars in 2024, and the user penetration rate is only 30%–40%, far lower than that of mainland cities.

Supported by HKUST.

High delivery fees and meal price premiums make the total price of food delivery 30% higher than dine-in, suppressing consumption demand. High labor costs (riders' monthly income is about 18,000–25,000 Hong Kong dollars), complex terrain (relying on walking/motorcycle delivery), and low order density further drive up costs, forming a vicious cycle of "high prices—low order volume" [9,10].

1.2 Advantages of Decentralized Development

Excluding brand-owned delivery platforms, the Hong Kong food delivery market has been nearly monopolized by Keeta and Foodpanda since Deliveroo's withdrawal in 2023 [9]. Issues arising from this monopoly, such as price discrimination against loyal customers and excessive commission rates, are intensifying, underscoring the need for a healthier competitive landscape.

While traditional centralized platforms offer high efficiency, they are prone to systemic risks. For instance, centralized management of orders, payments, and deliveries in conventional food delivery platforms makes them vulnerable to single-point failures and supply chain disruptions. In contrast, decentralization eliminates a single point of control, enabling nodes to operate autonomously while maintaining connectivity and collaboration, thereby enhancing system resilience. Additionally, the emergence of private domain traffic models-where merchants leverage chat groups and mini-programs to build independent customer bases and hire dedicated riders—embodies a decentralized philosophy [12]. This model inspires the development of truly decentralized platforms, where transparent smart contracts can regulate private operations and resource sharing among nodes, streamlining management and benefiting merchants.

Blockchain technology, since its inception, has attracted extensive attention and witnessed rapid growth in recent years. From the first pizza purchase using Bitcoin, efforts to integrate blockchain with the real economy have persisted. We introduce CoEat, a blockchain-based Defi platform for food delivery services, which aims to expand the application scope of blockchain technology.

2 Development Plan

Under practical constraints, we have formulated a "three-step" strategy for the CoEat platform, systematically outlining its complete development path from localized pilot projects to the integration of emerging delivery technologies and large-scale expansion. This strategy provides a feasible and constructive implementation framework.

2.1 Stage One: Pilot Phase in Start-Up Period

In the initial pilot phase, CoEat focuses on school campuses as its core testing ground, leveraging blockchain technology to introduce the innovative "Shunfeng-dai Model." This model enables customers to opt for shared delivery while placing orders, with incentive rewards automatically settled through smart contracts.

By combining blockchain's decentralized trust mechanism with user-driven collaborative delivery, CoEat redefines the participation logic of traditional food delivery services.

Although manual delivery remains the primary method at this stage, the platform's operational architecture breaks away from centralized constraints. Users assume hybrid roles as merchants, customers, and delivery personnel: blockchain's decentralized nature lowers merchant entry barriers by eliminating exorbitant commissions and control monopolies; customers benefit from transparent transaction histories and cost traceability, while gaining opportunities to earn rewards through idle capacity; delivery personnel enjoy higher compensation through a certified system, quality-based incentives, and a clear roadmap for diversifying into services like errand-running and medicine delivery.

To accelerate user adoption, CoEat implements a token-based reward system targeting active blockchain community nodes. This incentivizes early adoption and organic growth, establishing an initial ecosystem centered on school communities, blockchain technology, and the Shunfengdai Model.

2.2 Stage Two: Technology Optimization and Ecological Expansion

In the second stage, CoEat expands into densely populated areas such as Central business districts, schools, and residential complexes, introducing autonomous delivery robots to address the "last 100 m" challenge in complex urban environments. After completing trunk deliveries, human couriers hand off orders to robots, which navigate predefined routes to deliver directly to customers, significantly improving efficiency and overcoming terrain limitations.

Concurrently, CoEat constructs a dual-token economic ecosystem compliant with Hong Kong's regulatory framework. The functional token CEAT serves as the primary medium for transactions, advertising purchases, and personalized service requests, while the governance token GOVERN grants holders proportional voting rights in platform decision-making. This design fosters community engagement and long-term loyalty.

In this phase, CoEat will focus on strengthening its community attributes and further improving the dining-comment system. After users obtain community speaking rights by holding CEAT, they can not only publish food review contents, but also submit suggestions for optimizing community rules. The platform will conduct validity reviews on the contents published by users. Once approved, users will receive corresponding community governance incentives to encourage the output of more high-quality contents and the proposal of constructive opinions.

2.3 Stage Three: Drone Delivery Integration and Ecosystem Expansion

In the third development stage, the CoEat platform achieves breakthrough service expansion by introducing drone delivery. The deep application of blockchain technology enables real-time on-chain recording of end-to-end data from drone order acceptance to delivery, ensuring transparency and trustworthiness while demonstrating significant efficiency in high-density urban environments like Hong Kong. Concurrently, the platform innovatively constructs a cross-platform delivery resource integration mechanism: regardless of users' ordering channels, the system intelligently matches idle delivery capacity to merge orders with overlapping routes. This model not only addresses the resource waste of duplicate deliveries in traditional food delivery but also accurately measures carbon emissions reduced by each order through blockchain, forming tradable carbon emission reduction assets that generate additional community revenue.

In terms of business model optimization, CoEat controls drone delivery fees at a low level of HKD 5 through scaled operations, a price calculated based on daily order volumes in Hong Kong's food delivery industry reports and drone delivery case studies. Drone delivery requires supporting smart food lockers, which our market research indicates have a monthly rental cost of approximately HKD 9,000 per unit. Combined with daily order volumes, the storage cost per order is controlled within HKD 3. This design ensures lower total consumer expenditure than traditional platforms while enabling reasonable profits for restaurants, delivery parties, and the platform. Notably, the platform does not completely replace manual delivery but complements it with drones and the "Shunfengsong" model: manual delivery focuses on short-distance refined services, while the system opens order acceptance privileges to third-party drone owners, constructing a diversified delivery ecosystem. Contributions from all participants-including delivery services and carbon emission reductions-are automatically recorded via smart contracts and converted into corresponding points and token rewards, eliminating the unfair profit distribution of traditional platforms through blockchain transparency.

In Stage 3, leveraging the improved dual-token mechanism, CoEat's community operations exhibit unique Web3.0 characteristics. For example, users receive functional token rewards for inviting new members, redeemable for delivery discounts; high-frequency users unlock advanced on-chain permissions such as proposal rights or dividend eligibility. This mechanism transforms traditional "subsidy-driven user acquisition" into long-term interest binding to incentivize active promotion. The platform also collaborates with local lifestyle apps to achieve precise recommendations through data sharing-such as pushing lunch sets to office workers or holiday dinner discounts to families. This decentralized marketing approach upholds the user sovereignty concept of Web3.0 while aligning with real-world consumption scenarios, avoiding empty "on-chain gimmicks".

3   Technical Feasibility and Innovation

The design of the CoEat platform necessitates the integration of multiple cutting-edge blockchain technologies. This section will first construct the foundational smart contract framework based on the platform's functionalities, and then elaborate on the three core innovative technologies applied by the platform.

3.1   Smart Contract Framework

To build a self-operating blockchain community ecosystem, CoEat needs to construct a multi-layered smart contract system. The core contract group takes the Order Processing Contract as the hub, realizing fully automated management of the entire process from order placement to delivery. When a customer places an order, the contract not only verifies the order's validity but also triggers restaurant meal preparation notifications and drone dispatch instructions simultaneously, while linking with payment contracts to complete fund settlement. This design ensures the close connection of all transaction links, eliminating the information lag and human intervention problems common in traditional platforms.

At the same time, the platform constructs a dual trust guarantee system through smart contracts. On the one hand, the Restaurant Management Contract strictly audits merchant qualifications and monitors operational processes, automatically recording violations and executing compensation; on the other hand, the Delivery Monitoring Contract tracks device status and delivery trajectories in real time to ensure service safety and compliance. These contracts jointly maintain the benign operation of the community, not only protecting consumer rights and interests but also reducing the platform's management costs through automated supervision. It is particularly worth mentioning that all contract data is stored on the chain, providing a transparent and trustworthy foundation for community governance.

Finally, the interaction between the platform and users is completed through the Interactive Contract. This smart contract not only provides real-time order tracking functions but also constructs a complete feedback and incentive loop. Customers can submit complaints through the contract and receive automatic responses, while the platform uses interaction data to optimize service quality. In addition, the embedded referral rebate mechanism in the contract directly links user promotion behaviors with community growth, automatically calculating and distributing rewards through smart contracts, which effectively stimulates the participation enthusiasm of community members and promotes the expansion of the ecosystem.

The Fig. 1 shows the smart contract structure of the CoEat platform at different stages:

3.2   Automatic Currency Conversion Smart Contract

In the CoEat food delivery platform, to attract users from different tiers, the platform has streamlined the ordering process. CoEat has developed a smart contract system for automatic conversion between cryptocurrencies and fiat currencies, which is built upon the DAI stablecoin mechanism.

While DAI is primarily used in financial scenarios such as DeFi lending and cross-border payments [4], CoEat innovates by adapting it to daily consumer transactions. Unlike traditional DAI applications, CoEat establishes a more closed-loop ecosystem: the platform's utility token (CEAT) can only be

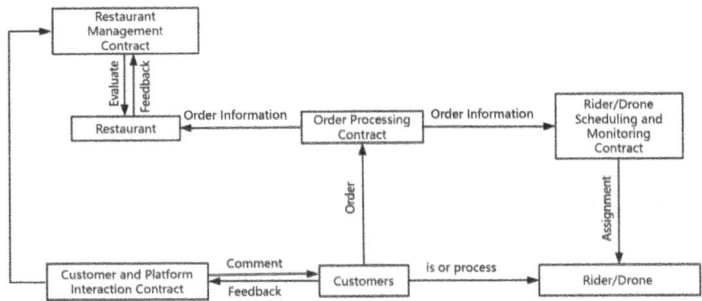

Fig. 1. Basic Smart Contract Structure

used for food orders within the platform and cannot be withdrawn for external trading, fundamentally eliminating speculative activities. Through smart contracts, CoEat achieves a "seamless blockchain" experience-when users pay with Alipay, the system automatically converts fiat currency to CEAT in the background, making the process as simple as regular mobile payments. This design retains DAI's advantages of high settlement efficiency and low fees while ensuring system stability through restricted use cases. Additionally, CoEat introduces consumption incentives, such as exclusive discounts for CEAT payments, which align better with the needs of food delivery users compared to traditional DeFi interest-based incentives.

CEAT leverages DAI to maintain a peg to the Hong Kong Dollar (HKD) and enables automatic payment conversion through the following steps. As described in the previous research of DAI, DAI's core mechanism uses smart contracts for over-collateralization and automatic adjustment to stabilize its value [8]. CoEat adapts this into a "platform-managed DAI" model tailored for commercial use. Distinct from native DAI, CoEat employs a dual-guarantee system: while using DAI for underlying cross-border USD settlements, it maintains 120% HKD reserves held by licensed institutions as an ultimate safeguard. This hybrid architecture combines DAI's mature on-chain stability mechanism for international currency conversions with HKD reserves to mitigate the volatility risks associated with cryptocurrency collateral. In practice, when users deposit HKD, the system fetches real-time HKD/USD exchange rates, converts the amount to equivalent DAI for on-chain recording, and then mints CEAT at a 1:1 ratio. For redemption, the smart contract automatically burns CEAT and initiates the conversion of DAI back to HKD, completing a closed-loop process.

To ensure the robustness of the CEAT fund pool, CoEat implements multiple safeguards. The pool uses a dynamic balancing mechanism where, during peak redemption periods, the platform uses its profits first to avoid depleting reserves directly. Daily redemption limits are set to prevent runs on the system. Smart contracts require multi-signature authorization for critical operations such as large-scale conversions or interest rate adjustments, involving the platform's management, third-party auditors, and other stakeholders. In extreme scenarios, CoEat collaborates with licensed payment institutions to establish emergency reserve funds and publishes regular audit reports to enhance transparency. Technologically, the smart contracts include a "circuit breaker" mechanism that pauses services and triggers manual reviews upon detecting suspicious transactions. These measures blend traditional financial risk management with blockchain transparency, allowing CEAT to offer a seamless payment experience while avoiding the liquidity and regulatory challenges faced by traditional DAI systems, thus perfectly fitting the requirements of food delivery payment scenarios.

Algorithm 1 in Appendix presents the pseudocode for the aforementioned exchange process between CEAT and HKD.

3.3   Carbon Measurement and Allocation Smart Contract

In Sect. 2.3, it was mentioned that blockchain technology effectively integrates delivery resources, reducing carbon emissions during the delivery process. The use of drones further accelerates this decarbonization process. Under the global trend of low-carbon economy, the saved carbon emissions can be traded in the carbon market, generating additional revenue for platform users [4, 11].

To accurately and efficiently measure tradable carbon emissions and simplify carbon management, CoEat's carbon accounting smart contract employs a novel IoT-integrated collective carbon management model. The platform first uses IoT devices to measure real-time carbon emissions from system operations, compares these with government-allocated carbon allowances to calculate surplus emissions, and then distributes profits from selling these surpluses to participating nodes.

Ensuring the authenticity of IoT-derived carbon data is a critical challenge. Drawing inspiration from the Carbon Emission Monitoring and Credit Trading System proposed by Effah, D. [1], the CoEat platform has introduced a multi-source data cross-validation mechanism and a Merkle tree-based hierarchical hash verification architecture to improve the PBFT consensus mechanism, thereby enhancing data collection accuracy and on-chain credibility. Specifically, the platform deploys redundant carbon emission sensor networks at key emission points. Each device transmits real-time data to edge computing gateways via independent links. These gateways perform local preprocessing on the received data, including outlier detection using sliding window mean and IQR (interquartile range) methods, redundant data cleaning, and timestamp standardization, generating uniquely identified data fingerprints. Subsequently, the system conducts consistency checks on data from multiple gateway nodes in the same geographic area and performs hash aggregation on data from similar time periods and identical sensor types using feature fingerprints (hashes). Each verification node independently checks the integrity and logical consistency of data packets; data is only written to the blockchain when over two-thirds of the nodes reach a consensus. In terms of storage strategy, CoEat does not directly upload raw carbon emission data to the chain. Instead, it stores the consensus-verified Merkle root as a data fingerprint on the chain, along with records of data sources, timestamps, and verification signatures. Raw emission data is stored locally at edge nodes and can only be traced and reconstructed through off-chain indexes during regulatory audits or data dispute resolution. This design ensures data auditability while preserving commercial privacy. Algorithm 2 in Appendix illustrates the processing workflow of carbon emission measurement data in the CoEat platform.

The aggregated surplus carbon data calculated through this process is publicly accessible on the platform, allowing nodes to monitor real-time metrics. Surplus emissions can be sold via traditional B2B channels to external enterprises or directly to platform nodes at market rates when additional allowances are needed. To maintain measurement accuracy and transaction integrity, CoEat establishes validator nodes elected by the community to oversee volume calculations and pricing, ensuring fairness in all transactions.

Finally, profits are distributed using a multi-dimensional contribution algorithm that considers core metrics such as node uptime, transaction validation frequency, and data quality. This design bypasses complex individual carbon quota allocation, enabling nodes to indirectly share carbon trading revenues through platform participation. By lowering entry barriers, the system streamlines distribution while ensuring equitable rewards for all participants.

In summary, CoEat's carbon accounting smart contract creates a comprehensive carbon management ecosystem through the integration of blockchain and IoT technologies. This system not only ensures credible on-chain carbon data and efficient trading but also transforms node participation into decarbonization incentives, fostering a virtuous cycle of "emission reduction - revenue generation - sustained action." This innovative model aligns with global low-carbon imperatives, offering a replicable technical framework for blockchain-enabled carbon resource management and paving the way for decentralized carbon trading and sustainable development goals.

3.4   Dual-Token Mechanism and Community Governance

As a blockchain platform connecting with the real economy, CoEat's operational mechanism is more complex than most existing DeFi platforms. Adopting a single-currency system has obvious drawbacks. First, using a single currency is more likely to attract speculative hype, leading to drastic price fluctuations that affect the stability of platform operations. Second, when both governance and transaction functions rely on one cryptocurrency, it is prone to situations such as governance power being monopolized by a few large token holders or smart contract vulnerabilities being maliciously exploited.

In contrast, CoEat's dual-token mechanism can effectively avoid these risks through functional separation: CEAT, as a stable utility token pegged to fiat currency, focuses on daily high-frequency transaction scenarios to ensure the reliability and efficiency of payment and settlement; while the governance token GOVEN focuses on community governance, endowing holders with rights such as rule voting and node election to achieve decentralized governance, avoiding functional conflicts in a single token. The dual-token mechanism will strengthen market attractiveness, enhance user stickiness and community activity, adapt to the regulatory requirements of Hong Kong's compliant cryptocurrency trading environment, and promote the improvement of the economic ecosystem. This section will specifically introduce the construction of the dual-token mechanism and the contribution of GOVEN as a governance token to community governance.

In CoEat's dual-token mechanism, we adopt the PoS (Proof of Stake) mechanism as the underlying consensus foundation, deeply binding the token economy with blockchain security through the core logic of "staking as consensus" [2,13]. Relying on the node election rules of the PoS mechanism, CoEat stakes sufficient GOVEN and CEAT through a multi-signature wallet, exclusively undertaking the responsibilities of block generation and transaction verification, and is responsible for packaging users' CEAT payments, GOVEN voting and other operations onto the chain. Under this mechanism, the PoS consensus algorithm directly grants the core team nodes the right to produce blocks, avoiding technical risks or power decentralization caused by ordinary users' participation, and ensuring the efficient support of the underlying architecture for high-frequency transaction scenarios.

At the application layer, DAOs can enhance an application's flexibility, participation, and resistance to centralization risks [3,6,7]. At the application layer, GOVEN adopts a DAO-like voting governance mechanism to build a flexible decentralized decision-making system. GOVEN holders can submit proposals through smart contracts, covering major platform matters such as adjustments to CEAT pegging parameters and modifications to advertising space rules. Proposals must meet the minimum GOVEN holding threshold to be publicly displayed on the chain, and take effect after passing community voting (with weights calculated based on GOVEN holdings) and obtaining more than two-thirds of the consent votes. The governance process integrates hash verification technology to ensure the tamper-proof nature of voting data, while using a time-locking mechanism to delay proposal execution and avoid malicious operations. In addition, GOVEN's acquisition mechanism adopts a hierarchical design to balance control and community incentives: the core team reserves 30% of the tokens through a multi-signature wallet during the initial issuance, ensuring control over the underlying architecture through a locking mechanism; among the remaining tokens, most will be circulated through exchanges for users to obtain via market transactions, and a small portion will be automatically distributed through smart contracts based on on-chain behaviors such as node activity and the number of approved proposals to incentivize community participation in governance, forming a diversified distribution system to safeguard the stability of the on-chain ecosystem.

The dual-token mechanism combining PoS underlying consensus and DAO application governance innovatively realizes a hierarchical design of functions and rights, achieving efficient collaboration in the blockchain ecosystem. CEAT and GOVEN are linked through an economic model, effectively solving the balance problem of traditional single-token systems between transactions and governance. Finally, this mechanism will combine with the community interactive governance platform mentioned in 2.2 to establish the ultimate governance system of CoEat. As shown in Fig. 2, it provides a management paradigm that balances flexibility and security for the blockchain distribution community, and

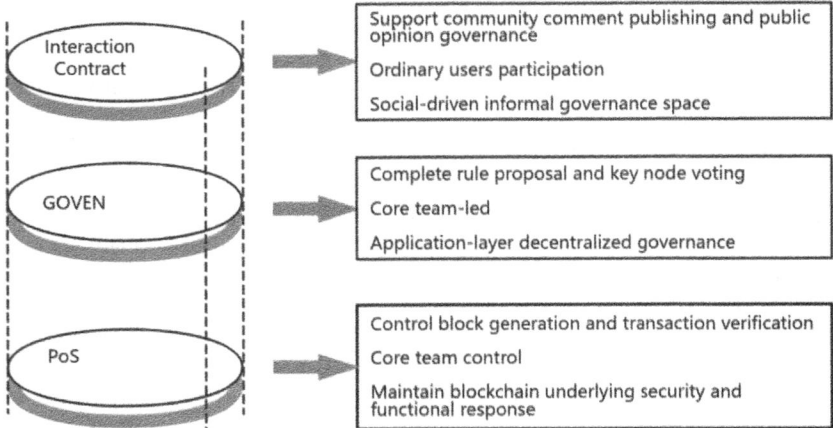

Fig. 2. HKD-CEAT Conversion Flowchart

also offers a more sustainable solution for the integration of the real economy and blockchain technology.

4   Conclusion

This paper focuses on the blockchain-based CoEat food delivery platform, systematically demonstrating its path to business development and the innovative application of blockchain technologies. The article first proposes a three-stage development plan for the platform: in the initial stage, it relies on blockchain advantages to launch a shared delivery model to attract users; in the mid-term, it enhances ecological vitality by expanding community scale and improving the token economic model; in the later stage, it introduces drone delivery in conjunction with national low-altitude economy policies to enhance efficiency. It then intensively introduces the innovative blockchain technologies applied in the platform, elaborating in more detail on CoEat's technical design: building on DAI contracts and designing automatic currency exchange contracts to facilitate users in conducting delivery transactions on the platform; constructing an integrated carbon emission measurement contract in combination with the Internet of Things to promote the platform's low-carbon economy and bring additional benefits; and adopting a dual-token mechanism to improve on-chain governance.

   In practical applications, leveraging blockchain, CoEat can effectively integrate delivery resources to achieve cross-platform route optimization. The platform also supports ordinary users in providing delivery services, and individual drone owners can join the chain to carry out delivery operations, which promotes the transformation of idle delivery resources into profits, reduces the monopoly of large delivery enterprises in the market, significantly alleviates urban traffic congestion and carbon emissions, and provides technical support for constructing a green urban delivery system.

Historical experience shows that every major technological innovation brings about profound changes in production relations. CoEat represents an important attempt to adapt to and promote such changes through innovative technological applications, enabling synchronous development between the superstructure and the economic base.

5   Future Work

Relying on the underlying blockchain architecture, CoEat is committed to constructing a complete low-altitude economic ecosystem rather than merely introducing drone delivery. In the future, when each drone is connected to the blockchain network as an independent node, the blockchain system can automatically complete task allocation through smart contracts based on order demands and real-time drone positions. Delivery revenues will be directly stored in the drone's exclusive account, completely subverting the centralized scheduling model of traditional operating enterprises. This fully automated service system not only aligns with the blueprint of smart cities but also achieves exponential improvements in the response efficiency and resource utilization of the delivery network through the decentralized characteristics of blockchain. The drone delivery system of CoEat will advance to new heights of full automation and intelligence.

Furthermore, CoEat always takes technology-driven social empowerment as its guiding principle and proactively assumes social responsibilities. Although the iteration of drone delivery technology may bring about structural adjustments to traditional manual delivery positions, this transformation is essentially an upgrade of social benefits, as it can liberate manual labor from mechanical work to more creative links such as customer service and emergency response. In fact, manual delivery has never been eliminated; instead, it plays an irreplaceable role in scenarios like cold chain delivery quality control and customized services for elderly customers through job function transformation. In the future, CoEat will further form a new "human-machine collaboration" employment ecosystem to achieve optimal allocation of labor resources. It is not just a delivery platform but also an exploration of new economic models and social relationships.

Acknowledgements. Upon the completion of this thesis, I would like to express my heartfelt gratitude to my team members for their hard work, and to Professor Zhibin LEI from the Department of Mathematics at the Hong Kong University of Science and Technology for his meticulous guidance throughout the research process. I would also like to extend my sincere thanks to the Blockchain Club of the Hong Kong University of Science and Technology for providing technical learning materials, which have laid an important foundation for this study.

A   Appendix

This appendix presents two key pseudocode implementations that support the CoEat platform's decentralized mechanism:

- Algorithm 1 demonstrates the CEAT–DAI exchange workflow with oracle-based rate updates, over-collateralization, circuit breaker protection, and burn logic.
- Algorithm 2 illustrates the edge-to-chain carbon data verification pipeline, including preprocessing, multi-node consensus, and Merkle-based anchoring.

Algorithm 1. CEAT–DAI Exchange Logic

1: **State:** custodian_dai, oracleRate, balances[user], totalSupply, paused
2: **function** UPDATERATE
3:     oracleRate ← GETLATESTRATEFROMORACLE
4: **end function**
5: **function** MINTCEAT(hkdAmount)
6:     UPDATERATE
7:     usd ← hkdAmount / oracleRate
Require: custodian_dai ≥ 1.2× usd
8:     balances[user]+= hkdAmount,   totalSupply+= hkdAmount
9: **end function**
10: **function** REDEEMCEAT(amount)
Require: ¬paused **and** balances[user] ≥ amount
11:     balances[user]-= amount,   totalSupply-= amount
12:     Transfer DAI to user
13:     **if** abnormal activity **then**
14:         paused ← true
15:     **end if**
16: **end function**
17: **function** BURNCEAT(user, amount)
Require: balances[user] ≥ amount
18:     balances[user]-= amount,   totalSupply-= amount
19: **end function**

Algorithm 2. Carbon Data Verification

1: **Const:** CONSENSUS_THRESHOLD ← 2/3
2: **function** PREPROCESSDATA(data)
3:     Clean and normalize data
4:     **return** SHA256(data)
5: **end function**
6: **function** CROSSVERIFY(hashes)
7:     Group by time/type, vote majority
8:     **return** isVerified
9: **end function**
10: **function** ANCHORTOCHAIN
11:     **for all** data from EdgeNodes **do**
12:         h[i] ← PREPROCESSDATA(data)
13:     **end for**
14:     **if** CROSSVERIFY(h) **then**
15:         MerkleRoot ← build Merkle Tree
16:         PBFT_CONSENSUS(MerkleRoot)
17:         Write to blockchain
18:     **else**
19:         Log failure
20:     **end if**
21: **end function**

References

1. Effah, D., Chunguang, B., Appiah, F., Agbley, B.L.Y., Quayson, M.: Carbon emission monitoring and credit trading: the blockchain and IoT approach. In: 2021 18th International Computer Conference on Wavelet Active Media Technology and Information Processing (ICCWAMTIP), pp. 106–109. IEEE (2021)
2. Gaži, P., Kiayias, A., Zindros, D.: Proof-of-stake sidechains. In: 2019 IEEE Symposium on Security and Privacy (SP), pp. 139–156. IEEE (2019)
3. Han, J., Lee, J., Li, T.: Dao governance (2023)
4. Kim, S.K., Huh, J.H.: Blockchain of carbon trading for un sustainable development goals. Sustainability **12**(10), 4021 (2020)
5. Li, C., Mirosa, M., Bremer, P.: Review of online food delivery platforms and their impacts on sustainability. Sustainability **12**(14), 5528 (2020)
6. Li, J., Qin, R., Wang, F.Y.: The future of management: DAO to smart organizations and intelligent operations. IEEE Trans. Syst. Man Cybernet. Syst. **53**(6), 3389–3399 (2022)
7. Liu, L., Zhou, S., Huang, H., Zheng, Z.: From technology to society: an overview of blockchain-based DAO. IEEE Open J. Comput. Soc. **2**, 204–215 (2021)
8. MakerDAO: The maker protocol: Makerdao's multi-collateral DAI (MCD) system (2022). https://makerdao.com/en/whitepaper
9. measuable.ai: The Hong Kong food delivery platform market: The return of a tripartite dominance. Research report (2024). https://blog.measurable.ai, published by Measurable AI; individual authors not identified
10. Meituan: Meituan Hong Kong 2024 annual report. Research report (2025). https://media-meituan.todayir.com/, published by Meituan; individual authors not identified
11. Parhamfar, M., Sadeghkhani, I., Adeli, A.M.: Towards the net zero carbon future: a review of blockchain-enabled peer-to-peer carbon trading. Energy Sci. Eng. **12**(3), 1242–1264 (2024)
12. iiMedia Research: 2024 survey data on consumption behavior of china's online food delivery platforms. Research report (2024). https://www.iimedia.cn/c1061/103996.html, published by iiMedia Group; individual authors not identified
13. Saleh, F.: Blockchain without waste: proof-of-stake. Rev. Financ. Stud. **34**(3), 1156–1190 (2021)
14. SECURITIES, F.: Meituan-w (03690): stable growth in core local business, focus on overseas markets and AI. Research report (2025). https://www.foundersc.com/infoResearchMacro/8655111.jhtml, published by FOUNDER SECURITIES; individual authors not identified

Blockchain-Based Business Model: Open Innovation Strategy for Smart Edge Data Flow

Xiaoqin Feng[✉], Yiming Hong, Longyue Guo, Guoli Feng, and Huijie Chen

School of Information Science and Engineering, Lanzhou University,
Lanzhou 730000, China
fxq@lzu.edu.cn

Abstract. Open business model in MEC is conductive to resources sharing of consumer electronic products. However, there are risks in the process of business mode opening, such as, the protection and smart management of data and knowledge flow. Based on the blockchain, smart contract and DAC (Distributed Autonomous Corporation) technologies, we propose the Blockchain-based business model (called BM-ICB) of open innovation strategy for smart edge data flow. Based on the DPoS consensus mechanism of blockchain technology, we research the smart and dynamic management mechanism to realize the detection, monitoring and classification of enterprise behaviors of consumer electronic products, besides, the interaction process between the users and Consortium chain is improved through the DAC technology. The theoretical analysis estimates strong security and high performance of the BM-ICB model, and the experimental evaluation testifies the high performance.

Keywords: Mobile Edge Computing (MEC) · mobile edge computing · blockchain · consortium chain · smart contract · DAC · smart management · data flow

1 Introduction

In today's fast-evolving digital landscape, continuous innovation is essential for enterprise competitiveness. Open innovation strategies [1], which emphasize external collaboration and technological integration, are rapidly replacing traditional business models [2]. Yet, this openness brings critical challenges—particularly in managing knowledge assets and safeguarding intellectual property [3].

Blockchain emerges as a promising solution [4], offering transparency, security, and lower transaction costs in knowledge exchange. However, most existing research emphasizes value creation [5] and overlooks how to dynamically manage knowledge while mitigating the risks of data leakage and unfair competition [6].

Although some studies have applied blockchain in business innovation—such as enhancing trust [7] or optimizing service delivery [8], they rarely explore its

R. K. Shyamasundar et al. (Eds.): ICBC 2025, LNCS 16155, pp. 198–212, 2026.
https://doi.org/10.1007/978-3-032-06176-8_13

potential for managing open and dynamic knowledge flows, especially within Mobile Edge Computing (MEC) ecosystems [9]. This oversight leaves a critical gap in ensuring secure, collaborative, and flexible knowledge sharing [10].

To address this, we propose a blockchain-based framework tailored to MEC enterprises. Our model seeks to strike a balance between openness and control, enabling dynamic collaboration while protecting intellectual assets and fostering efficient customer interaction [11].

2   Background Knowledge and Literature Review

Before describing our design, we first introduce the open business model and the related techniques in terms of Blockchain, DAC and smart contract.

2.1   Open Business Model

Business model is a theoretical framework that defines how a company organizes its operations by leveraging strategic resources, market conditions, and stakeholder interests [12]. It aligns the roles of suppliers, manufacturers, dealers, and consumers to create coordinated value across the business ecosystem [13].

In today's rapidly evolving environment characterized by informatization, marketization, and globalization, traditional business models face increasing pressure to adapt [14]. Continuous innovation is essential, and open innovation strategies address this by enabling purposeful knowledge inflow and outflow [15], thereby accelerating internal R&D and expanding external markets [16].

2.2   Blockchain

Blockchain is a decentralized ledger maintained by network nodes through consensus [4], without centralized control. It consists of cryptographically linked data blocks, each recording verified transactions [17]. In Bitcoin, miners use computational algorithms to validate transactions and append new blocks sequentially [18].

There are many consensus mechanisms, such as PoW (Proof-of-Work) [4], PoS (Proof-of-Stake) [19], DPoS (Delegate Proof-of-Stake) [20], PBFT (Practical Byzantine Fault Tolerance) [21], and so on. DPoS is a stake-based authorization mechanism built on PoS, where shareholders elect a limited number of trusted nodes as representatives to perform verification and accounting in turns [22]. This voting process enhances security and decentralization while significantly reducing the number of participating nodes, enabling fast, near-second-level consensus [23]. Therefore, DPoS is well-suited for enterprise business models.

2.3   DAC Implementation

A Decentralized Autonomous Corporation (DAC) possesses independent computational resources (CPU, memory, and IP address) and operates under transparent, rule-based protocols without external management [22]. The protocols are implemented through smart contracts that define minimum operational requirements and automatic compliance checks.

The DAC framework incorporates three key mechanisms:

- **Automated rule enforcement** through immutable smart contracts [4].
- **Multi-stage governance** including proposal submission, stakeholder voting, and execution monitoring.
- **Conflict resolution** combining automatic arbitration and validator committee intervention.

Functionally, a DAC resembles an autonomous agent that executes predefined rules and evolves through self-maintenance and adaptation [22]. Its participants act as self-interested, trustless units, operating independently unless direct trust relationships are established [23], with all interactions recorded on-chain for auditability.

3   Problem Formulation

While open innovation strategies offer significant benefits for smart edge ecosystems, existing approaches fail to adequately address the fundamental tension between secure knowledge protection and efficient collaborative workflows in decentralized environments. Traditional solutions either impose excessive privacy restrictions that limit innovation or sacrifice data security for operational flexibility, resulting in suboptimal trade-offs that hinder large-scale adoption.

3.1   System Model: Four-Dimensional Business Framework

Meta model research based on system theory has become the mainstream of current business concept researches. Among many conceptual models of business models, the core idea of four-dimensional model has been widely recognized in the relevant studies, and has a certain representativeness. The four-dimensional model includes

- **Four core facets:** core strategy, strategic resources, customer interface, and value network.
- **Three bridging dimensions:** resource allocation, customer value, and enterprise boundary.
- **Four performance metrics:** efficiency, uniqueness, fitting, and profit potential.

As illustrated in Fig. 1, these dimensions capture the structural and functional aspects of enterprise design. We enhance this model by embedding suppliers, partners, and unions into a Consortium Blockchain. Member classification and task allocation are managed via DPoS, while key resources and strategic data are securely stored on-chain. DACs facilitate transparent market interaction and knowledge sharing. This integration enables dynamic governance, secure asset management, and efficient customer engagement.

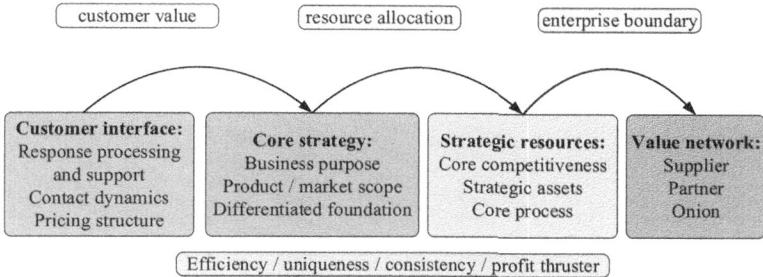

Fig. 1. Four facets of the system model.

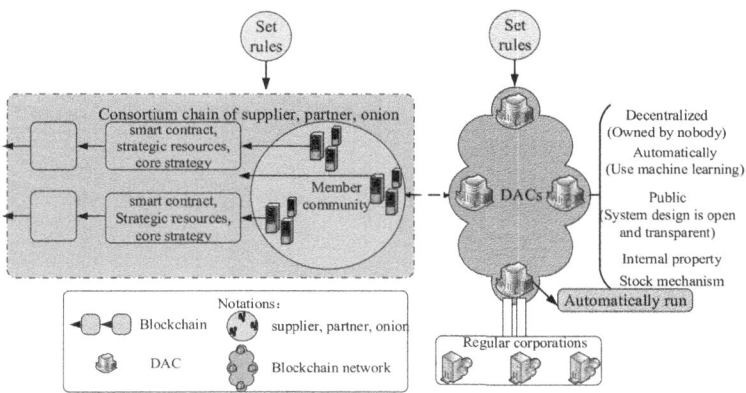

Fig. 2. Operational architecture of the BM-ICB model.

3.2 System Overview

Figure 2 presents the operational structure of the BM-ICB model, which includes the following components:

- **Member Classification:** Entities (suppliers, partners, unions) are assigned to communities based on roles and stakes. Within each community, DPoS selects 101 board members as consensus nodes.
- **Joining the Consortium Blockchain:** New members must stake shares and sign smart contracts, which include penalties and strategic information stored in the block coinbase.
- **Block Storage:** Community-specific data (stake, strategy, resources) is stored on the blockchain and shared across all members.
- **DAC Filtering:** Communities act as DACs by publishing product and market information. Users search or filter DACs based on business needs.

- **Task Processing:** Once a DAC is selected, its board members rotate to process user requests and record transactions.
- **Result Verification:** Processed outcomes are broadcast to all communities for validation. If approved, they are appended to the chain. If rejected, the task is reassigned and the previous node is penalized.

4 The BM-ICB Model: New Innovation Strategy

We construct the BM-ICB model by using the Consortium Chain, smart contract and DAC. This section explains the details building for the BM-ICB model, and it contains five main processes: members classification, joining the consortium blockchain, DACs filtering, tasks processing, results verification and blocks building.

4.1 Members Classification

All members in the Consortium chain are classified by the DPoS mechanism. It includes three main steps.

Step1: Preliminary distribution for all shareholders $s_k(k = 1, \ldots, K)$ in the Consortium chain.

- $s_k(k = 1, \ldots, K)$ are firstly divided based on their belonging enterprises.
- The divided shareholders are then distributed to different communities $C_f(f = 1, \ldots, F)$ based on their functions.

Step2: Ranking for all communities.

- All members in $C_f(f = 1, \ldots, F)$ enroll as agents $C_f^a(f = 1, \ldots, F)$.
- $s_k(k = 1, \ldots, K)$ votes for $C_f^a(f = 1, \ldots, F)$ to elect the 101 boarder communities $C_f^b(f = 1, \ldots, 101)$.
- $C_f^b(f = 1, \ldots, 101)$ will be ranked by the order of 1-101.
- For the left communities which are not included in $C_f^b(f = 1, \ldots, 101)$, they will re-enroll for boarder selection and get ranked to form $C_f^b(f = 1, \ldots, F)$.

Step3: Maintaining circulation and adjusting communities.

- The community-related information is stored in the block coinbase after all communities classification are done. Besides, each block in different communities needs to be updated every other block slot.
- Each 101 block is a cycle round, and the communities in terms of members and ranking need to be updated each round or once new members join.

4.2 Joining the Consortium Blockchain

During each slot, one representative $C_f^r(f = 1, \ldots, F)$ from each community $C_f(f = 1, \ldots, F)$ is chosen by the DPoS mechanism to manage the whole Blockchain including new nodes adding, products issuing, interactions to customers, tasks arrangement, and so on. $C_f^r(f = 1, \ldots, F)$ is chosen through the following operations.

- All members $C_f^m(m = 1, \ldots, M)$ in $C_f(f = 1, \ldots, F)$ enroll as agents $C_f^a(a = 1, \ldots, A)$.
- $C_f(f = 1, \ldots, F)$ internally votes to select the one boarder member $C_f^b(f = 1, \ldots, F)$.
- The selected $C_f^b(f = 1, \ldots, F)$ representatives $C_f(f = 1, \ldots, F)$ to manage the whole Blockchain.

Once new supplier, partner and onion N_e apply to join the Consortium chain, it needs to perform the following operations:

- $C_f^b(f = 1, \ldots, F)$ verifies for the identity, functions, products/market scope, core strategy and strategic resources of N_e.
- N_e can join in the Consortium chain only if all verifications pass.
- N_e stakes in the Consortium chain, and sign a smart contract which includes some penalty and is stored in the block coinbase with its core strategy and strategic resources.
- The communities will be adjusted once N_e successfully joins.
- Besides, N_e will be fined for the penalty if it misbehaves in performing its function, and the penalty acts as common assets of the Consortium chain.

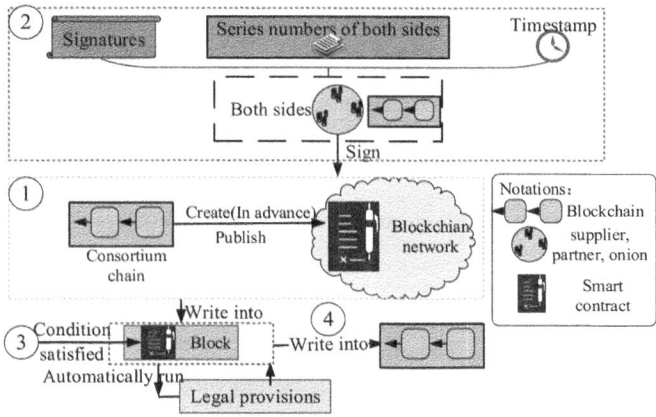

Fig. 3. The working status of smart contract.

Figure 3 depicts the working status of smart contract. The smart contract is added with some basic information of the Consortium chain and published on the Blockchain network in advance. N_e and the Consortium both sign the smart contract with their signatures, series number and the timestamp, and store it into the block. Once conditions in the smart contract trigger, the smart contract will be added with legal provisions and automatically run. The determined smart contract finally will be stored in the blocks of corresponding Blockchain.

4.3   DACs Filtering

The DAC ecosystem operates through $C_f^m(m = 1, \ldots, M)$ communities that collectively govern immutable smart contracts. These contracts are distributed as open-source software across all C_f^m nodes, ensuring transparent rule enforcement through three core mechanisms:

- **Conflict Resolution Protocol**: Disputes are resolved through a two-phase process combining on-chain voting and validator committee arbitration.
- **Software Distribution**: Version-controlled through Git-based repositories with cryptographic hashes recorded on-chain.
- **Modification Freeze**: Contract bytecode becomes immutable after deployment, with upgrade paths requiring 2/3 community approval.

As shown in Fig. 4, users interact with DACs through standardized interfaces that enforce these rules automatically. The discovery process involves: (1) querying the community registry, (2) verifying contract hashes, and (3) establishing encrypted channels for subsequent transactions.

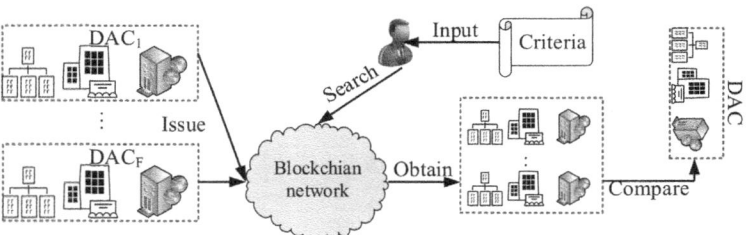

Fig. 4. Interactions between users and DACs.

- Based on the business purpose, $C_f^m(m = 1, \ldots, M)$ sets rules of the DAC about its products, markets scope, shareable knowledge flow, and advantages. The pre-set rules of the DAC are then issued on the Blockchain network by $C_f^b(f = 1, \ldots, F)$.

- Users including suppliers, partners and onion search for suitable DACs according to their demands, requirements and value network, and compare among the DACs to select the most satisfying one. Alternatively, users input the filtering criteria for product requirements and find all fitting DACs.

- $C_f^b(f = 1, \ldots, F)$ arranges the specific DAC for each user by the above matching conditions, and inform the user of the DAC related information. Each user then interacts with the DAC for product service.

4.4   Tasks Processing

C_f^b informs its community members $C_f^m(m = 1, \ldots, M_f')$ of service providing after the specific arrangement, and $C_f^m(m = 1, \ldots, M_f)$ then internally perform the DPoS consensus mechanism to choose board nodes for tasks handling. In includes two main steps for tasks processing.

Step1: Selecting the Board Nodes

- $C_f^m(m = 1, \ldots, M_f)$ enrolls as agents $c_{fa}(fa = 1, \ldots, M_f)$ of the whole community c_f.
- Shareholders $s_{fK}(fK = 1, \ldots, K_f)$ in c_f votes for $c_{fa}(fa = 1, \ldots, M_f)$ to elect the 101 boarder nodes $C_{fb}^i(i = 1, \ldots, 101)$.
- $C_{fb}^i(i = 1, \ldots, 101)$ is ranked by the number of voting, and takes turns each block slot to provide service and records the transaction with the user.
- $C_f^m(m = 1, \ldots, M_f)$ will re-enrolls for boarder selection after a whole round.

Step2: Handling the Transaction

- Assume that C_{fb}^1 denote the first boarder and is responsible for tasks handling at current round. C_{fb}^1 first consults with the user to sign a smart contract including basic information of both sides, quality of products, service fee, and so on.
- C_{fb}^1 begins to process user's request once the smart contract triggers.
- C_{fb}^i packages the handled transaction results, products information, and smart contract signed by both sides to an accounting A_{fb}^1, and sends it to the whole Consortium chain for reliability verification.

4.5   Results Verification

C_{fb}^1 sends the recorded A_{fb}^1 respectively to $C_f(f = 1, \ldots, F)$ for reliability verification. The verification process includes the following operations:

- $C_f^m(m = 1, \ldots, M_f)(f = 1, \ldots, F)$ checks the identities of the user and C_{fb}^1, transaction type and dealing results in A_{fb}^1 according to the function and procedure of C_f.
- $C_f^m(m = 1, \ldots, M_f)(f = 1, \ldots, F)$ sends the signed verification to the whole Consortium once it completes the accounting checking.

- A^1_{fb} is valid only if all verifications of $C^m_f (m = 1, \ldots, M_f)(f = 1, \ldots, F)$ pass. Otherwise, A_{fb} is invalid and the transaction will be re-performed by C^i_{fb}. Besides, C^1_{fb} will be remarked as malicious boarder and fined with the penalty which acts as common assets of the Consortium.
- Let V^i_{fb} denote the valid accounting, and V^i_{fb} will be finally returned to its counter A^i_{fb} for transaction recording.

4.6　Blocks Building

A^i_{fb} performs the following steps to complete the transaction recording, block building and block adding.

Step1: Transaction Recording

- $A^i_{fb}(i = 1, 2)$ sends V^i_{fb} to the user. If the user is satisfied with the results and the conditions in the smart contract are met, V^i_{fb} can be finally recorded.
- The smart contract and other related parameters to the DPoS consensus and business model are stored in Block-header of the block, and the coinbase and V^i_{fb} are stored in block-body of the block.

Step2: Block Building

- Besides, all transactions at the same slot will be handled with the same operations as above, and $V^i_{fb}(i = 3, \ldots)$ denotes the accounting.
- As $V^3_{fb}, V^4_{fb}, \ldots, V^i_{fb}(i = 3, \ldots)$ will also be stored in the same block-body in the order of $V^3_{fb}, V^4_{fb}, \ldots$.
- After $V^i_{fb}(i = 1, \ldots)$ is completed recorded in the block-body, the whole block is completed.

Step3: Block Adding

- Let B^i_{fb} denote the new block, and it will be sent to $C^m_f (m = 1, \ldots, M_f)$ for integrity confirmation.
- B^i_{fb} will be finally added behind B^{i-1}_{fb} in the Blockchain B_{fb} if it is confirmed integrate.
- $C^m_f (m = 1, \ldots, M_f)$ in the community C_f keeps a whole copy of B^i_{fb}.

At this point, all transactions at a holonomic block slot are achieved and the new block B^i_{fb} is completed. Besides, the block $B^{i+1}_{fb}, B^{i+2}_{fb} \ldots$ and $B^i_{fb}(fb = 1, \ldots, F)$ is established through the similar steps. At this point, B_j and B_{j+1} are generated.

Next, we perform the security and performance analysis of the business model.

5   BM-ICB Model Analysis: Security and Performance of the Open Innovation Strategy

To build a secure and well performed business model of open innovation strategy, we carefully analyze our design including data security and reliability in terms of results and board members, and performance in terms of execution efficiency.

5.1   Security and Reliability

This section demonstrates the security and reliability of the BM-ICB model from the perspectives of data security and result reliability.

Data Security. Data security encompasses three main aspects: protection of user and transaction information, confidentiality of core strategy and strategic resources, and secure sharing of enterprise knowledge flow.

Proposition 1. User and transaction information are secure and reliable.

During interactions between users and the Consortium chain, user information is only accessible by C_f^b and C_{fb}^i, which are nodes elected through the DPoS consensus mechanism by all Consortium chain and community members. This decentralized election process, combined with periodic audits and penalty mechanisms, ensures that user data is effectively protected.

Transaction data is initially received by C_f^b nodes and subsequently recorded into accounts A_{fb}^i by C_{fb}^i. These records are ultimately stored in tamper-resistant blocks B_{fb}^i within the blockchain. The blockchains immutability guarantees the integrity and security of transaction information.

Proposition 2. Core strategy and strategic resources are securely stored.

When new members join, their core strategy and strategic resources are recorded on the relevant blockchain within the Consortium chain. These blockchains are only accessible to internal community members, and due to the immutable nature of blockchain, unauthorized modification or access is effectively prevented, ensuring confidentiality of critical enterprise assets.

Proposition 3. Knowledge flow within enterprises is securely managed and flexibly shared.

Private knowledge flows are stored on blockchains accessible exclusively to community members, preventing unauthorized disclosure. Under certain circumstances, communities may negotiate knowledge sharing agreements, ensuring that no privacy or proprietary information is compromised.

Furthermore, shareable knowledge is published via DACs on the Consortium chain network, which promotes transparency and openness without risking privacy breaches, thus facilitating external knowledge transfer and innovation.

Results Reliability. The reliability of results is guaranteed through trustworthy board members and rigorous transaction processing procedures.

Proposition 4. Board members are trustworthy and subject to robust governance.

Within each community, DPoS consensus selects representatives C_f^r who are further elected as C_f^b. This process is governed by member voting, with regular rotation and penalties for misconduct to maintain accountability.

Subsequently, 101 board members C_{fb}^i are elected to manage task processing and ledger recording. These members operate in a rotating fashion, and any misbehavior triggers sanctions, thus maintaining the integrity of the system.

Proposition 5. Processed transaction results are reliable and verifiable.

Pending transactions are first accepted by C_f^b nodes, ensuring preliminary reliability. Tasks are distributed to C_{fb}^i members who process them and submit results for validation across the Consortium chain. Only results that pass consensus verification are appended to the blockchain. Failed verifications lead to task reassignment and penalties for the responsible nodes.

All blockchain data is replicated across community members, ensuring immutability and long-term reliability of transaction records.

5.2 Performance

This section analyzes the execution efficiency of the BM-ICB model in terms of user interaction, community organization, consensus formation, and transaction processing.

Proposition 6. The BM-ICB model exhibits high execution efficiency.

User interactions are conducted through DACs, enabling rapid and convenient matching of service providers via network filtering.

Communities are formed based on member attributes and roles, with rankings determined by repeated DPoS elections. Member rankings C_f are voted upon by community members C_f^m based on stakes, which is a streamlined and efficient process.

Consensus among members includes elections of both C_f^b and C_{fb}^i nodes. Since these are also voting processes, they are efficient and allow quick adaptation to changing conditions.

Transaction processing integrates both task execution and result verification. While verification is a repeated process, prior availability of required parameters and information significantly reduces the time needed, thus improving overall throughput.

In summary, theoretical analysis confirms that the BM-ICB model is strongly secure, reliable, and highly efficient. These properties will be further validated through experimental evaluation in the next section.

6   Experimental Evaluation

In this section, we perform the experimental evaluation to testify the model efficiency, besides, the Blockchain storage of each node is also compared with the occupied space of all Blockchains.

6.1   Efficiency

The model efficiency is mainly indicated by time costs for the transaction process. Let t_s denote the alone transaction processing time in common business model, and T_s denote the time costs for the whole transactions implementing process in the BM-ICB model. We experimentally verify time costs to compare the two values of t_s and T_s. There are several experiments where the number of transaction are varied by 1, 10, 100, 1000 and each experiment runs with the number of community being 1, 2 and 4. The results are shown in Figs. 5, 6, 7 and 8.

– Figure 5 compares t_s and T_s with 1 transaction. While T_s is slightly larger than t_s for 1 community, it increases much more slowly as the number of communities grows. For instance, with 2 communities: $T_s = 2.657\,s$, $t_s = 4.28\,s$; and with 4 communities: $T_s = 1.64\,s$, $t_s = 4.28\,s$.

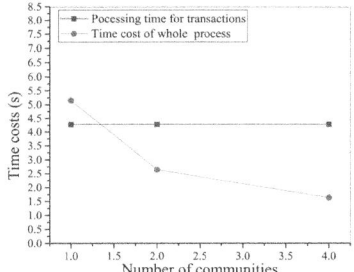

Fig. 5. Time costs (Transaction = 1)

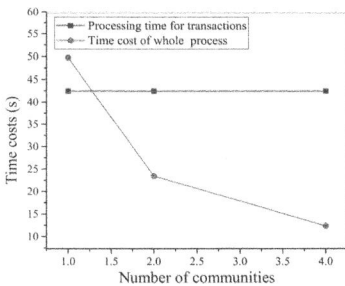

Fig. 6. Time costs (Transaction = 10)

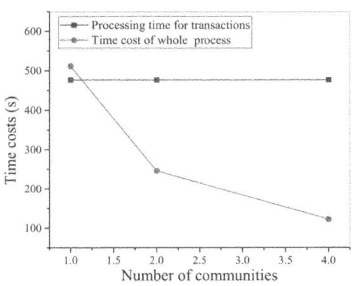

Fig. 7. Time costs (Transaction = 100)

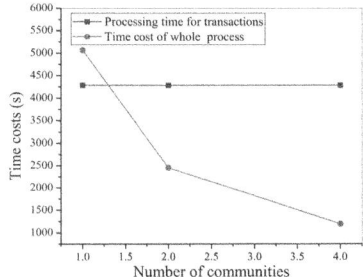

Fig. 8. Time costs (Transaction = 1000)

- Figure 6 shows the results for 10 transactions. The same trend is observed: with 2 communities, $T_s = 23.651\,s$, $t_s = 42.653\,s$; and with 4 communities, $T_s = 12.557\,s$, $t_s = 42.653\,s$.
- **FIGURE** 7 presents the case of 100 transactions. T_s again increases more slowly than t_s: for 2 communities, $T_s = 246.6\,s$, $t_s = 476.664\,s$; and for 4 communities, $T_s = 122.54\,s$, $t_s = 476.664\,s$.
- Figure 8 displays results for 1000 transactions. With 2 communities: $T_s = 2457.542\,s$, $t_s = 4288.56\,s$; and with 4 communities: $T_s = 1196.36\,s$, $t_s = 4288.56\,s$.

Connecting with Figs. 5, 6, 7 and 8, we have the following conclusions:

- t_s grows with increasing the number of transactions.
- T_s grows with increasing the number of transactions, while it grow slower with increasing the number of communities.
- T_s grows much slower with more number of communities and transactions.

6.2   Storage Pressure

The storage pressure is mainly indicated by the occupied space of each node. Let s_b denote the space occupied by all Blockchains, and s_{jb} denote the space occupied by each member in the BM-ICB model. We experimentally verify the space occupation to compare the two values of s_b and s_{jb}. There are several experiments where the number of blocks are varied by 1000, 10000, 100000, 1000000 and each experiment runs with the number of community being 3. The results are shown in Fig. 9, and we have the following conclusions.

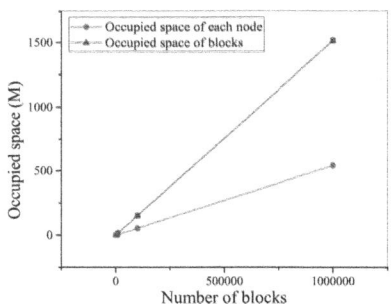

Fig. 9. Space comparison in Blockchain storage.

- Figure 9 shows the values comparison of s_b and s_{jb} with 3 communities. It can be referred that although s_b grows with increasing the number of Blocks (the length of Blockchain), it changes rather slower. Besides, s_{jb} is much smaller than s_b. For example, there are $s_b = 1.4748917M$, $s_{jb} = 0.5395212M$ with 1000 blocks, and $151.48245M$, $s_{jb} = 54.432358M$ with 100000 communities.

7 Conclusion

This paper proposes the BM-ICB model-an open innovation business model based on Consortium Blockchain and DAC technologies-to address challenges in dynamic knowledge flow management within smart edge environments. By leveraging DPoS consensus, the model enables flexible classification and supervision of community members while safeguarding private data and knowledge assets through secure on-chain storage.

Compared with traditional centralized platforms (e.g. JD, Taobao), which often control partner privacy and reduce knowledge exchange efficiency, the BM-ICB model supports decentralized and privacy-preserving collaboration. Smart contracts enforce agreements and automate project workflows, while traceability ensures transparency and accountability.

Despite progress in open innovation theory, dynamic and secure knowledge management remains underexplored. This model fills that gap by enabling trustworthy, autonomous interaction between suppliers, partners, and end users via DACs. Additionally, the model's extensibility allows future integration of contextual and behavioral factors such as organizational climate and trust mechanisms.

Security and performance analyses confirm that BM-ICB provides strong protection with low storage overhead and high operational efficiency, making it a practical and scalable solution for future decentralized business ecosystems. Although current experiments demonstrate effectiveness for typical use cases, we acknowledge that further validation is needed for extreme-scale scenarios; consequently, further research will explore optimization strategies for ultra-large-scale deployments to maintain the same performance standards.

References

1. Shahrivar, S., Elahi, S., Hassanzadeh, A., Montazer, G.A.: A business model for commercial open source software: a systematic literature review. Inf. Softw. Technol. **103**, 202–214 (2018)
2. Timmers, P.: Business models for electronic markets. Electron. Mark. **8**(2), 3–8 (1998)
3. Chesbrough, H., Rosenbloom, R.S.: The role of the business model in capturing value from innovation: evidence from xerox corporation's technology spin-off companies. Ind. Corp. Chang. **11**(3), 529–555 (2002)
4. Judmayer, A., Stifter, N., Krombholz, K., Weippl, E.: Blocks and chains: introduction to bitcoin, cryptocurrencies, and their consensus mechanisms. Synthesis Lectures Inf. Secur. Privacy Trust **9**(1), 1–123 (2017)
5. Amit, R., Zott, C.: Value creation in e-business. Strateg. Manag. J. **22**(6/7), 493–520 (2001)
6. Franke, N., Keinz, P., Klausberger, K.: "Does this sound like a fair deal?: antecedents and consequences of fairness expectations in the individual's decision to participate in firm innovation. Organ. Sci. **24**(5), 1495 (2013)
7. Guo, R., Shi, H., Zhao, Q., Zheng, D.: Secure attribute-based signature scheme with multiple authorities for blockchain in electronic health records systems. IEEE Access **6**, 776–787 (2018)

8. He, Y., Li, H., Cheng, X., Liu, Y., Yang, C., Sun, L.: A blockchain based truthful incentive mechanism for distributed p2p applications. IEEE Access **6**, 27324–27335 (2018)
9. Weiblen, T.: The open business model: understanding an emerging concept. J. Multi Bus. Model Innov. Technol. **1**(1), 35–66 (2013)
10. West, J., Bogers, M.: Leveraging external sources of innovation: a review of research on open innovation. J. Prod. Innov. Manag. **31**(4), 814–831 (2014)
11. Choudary, S.P., Van Alstyne, M.W., Parker, G.G.: Pipelines, platforms, and the new rules of strategy. Harv. Bus. Rev. **94**(4), 54–62 (2016)
12. Mahadevan, B.: Business models for internet-based e-commerce: an anatomy. Calif. Manage. Rev. **42**(4), 55–69 (2000)
13. Osterwalder, A., Pigneur, Y., Tucci, C.L.: Clarifying business models: origins, present, and future of the concept. Commun. Assoc. Inf. Syst. **16**, 1 (2005)
14. Bernd, W., Pistoia, A., Ullrich, S.: Business models: origin, development and future research perspectives. Long Range Plan. **49**(1), 1 (2016)
15. Chesbrough, H.: Open business models. Harvard Business Review Press (2006)
16. Chesbrough, H.W., Appleyard, M.M.: Open innovation and strategy. Calif. Manage. Rev. **50**(1), 57–76 (2007)
17. Ron, D., Shamir, A.: Quantitative analysis of the full bitcoin transaction graph. In: International Conference on Financial Cryptography and Data Security, pp. 6–24 (2013)
18. Qin, R., Yuan, Y., Wang, F.: A novel hybrid share reporting strategy for blockchain miners in pplns pools. Decis. Support Syst. **118**, 91–101 (2019)
19. Chepurnoy, A., Duong, T., Fan, L., Zhou, H.-S.: Twinscoin: a cryptocurrency via proof-of-work and proof-of-stake. IACR Cryptology ePrint Archive **2017**, 232 (2017)
20. Fan, X., Chai, Q.: Roll-dpos: a randomized delegated proof of stake scheme for scalable blockchain-based internet of things systems. In: 15th EAI International Conference on Mobile and Ubiquitous Systems: Computing, Networking and Services, pp. 482–484 (2018)
21. Driscoll, K., Hall, B., Sivencrona, H., Zumsteg, P.: Byzantine fault tolerance, from theory to reality. In: 22nd International Conference on Computer Safety, Reliability, and Security, pp. 235–248 (2003)
22. Lage, O., Saiz-Santos, M., Zarzuelo, J.M.: Decentralized platform economy: emerging blockchain-based decentralized platform business models. Electron. Mark. **32**(3), 1707–1723 (2022)
23. Purusottama, A., Simatupang, T.M., Sunitiyoso, Y.: The spectrum of blockchain adoption for developing business model innovation. Bus. Process. Manag. J. **28**(3), 834–855 (2022)

Evaluating Blockchain Platforms for Managing and Sharing Medical Data Using NFTs and IPFS

L. K. Bang[1]([✉]), M. N. Triet[1], H. V. Khanh[1], and N. T. K. Ngan[2]

[1] FPT University, Can Tho city, Vietnam
bangle69.re@gmail.com
[2] FPT Polytechnic, Can Tho city, Vietnam

Abstract. This paper explores the application of blockchain technology in managing and sharing medical data, focusing on the use of Non-Fungible Tokens (NFTs) and the InterPlanetary File System (IPFS) to enhance data security, privacy, and interoperability. Traditional methods of data management in healthcare face significant challenges, including data fragmentation, security vulnerabilities, and lack of interoperability among diverse systems. Blockchain technology, with its decentralized and immutable nature, offers a robust solution to these challenges. We provide a comparative analysis of transaction fees across four Ethereum Virtual Machine (EVM)-compatible platforms—BNB Chain, Fantom, Polygon, and Celo—to assess their suitability for medical data management. The study evaluates key operations, such as initiating transactions, minting NFTs, and transferring NFTs, which are essential for the secure and efficient handling of medical records. By examining these platforms, this paper aims to identify a cost-effective blockchain solution that balances operational expenses with performance requirements. The findings contribute to the ongoing development of secure, transparent, and reliable systems for managing medical data in healthcare settings.

Keywords: Blockchain · Transparency in Medical Data Sharing · Data Privacy and Security · Smart Contracts · Decentralized Marketplaces · RSA-Encrypted NFTs

1 Introduction

The management and sharing of medical data are crucial aspects of contemporary healthcare systems. Traditional management practices often rely on centralized databases and manual entries, which pose considerable risks related to data security, privacy, and the seamless exchange of information. Such systems are prone to data fragmentation, where patient records are scattered across various healthcare providers and systems, complicating the task of creating complete medical histories. Centralized data storage points increase the vulnerability to cyberattacks and unauthorized data breaches, risking exposure of private patient details. Furthermore, the diversity in data formats and standards among different healthcare systems can obstruct effective data exchange. Additionally, manual

© The Author(s), under exclusive license to Springer Nature Switzerland AG 2026
R. K. Shyamasundar et al. (Eds.): ICBC 2025, LNCS 16155, pp. 213–226, 2026.
https://doi.org/10.1007/978-3-032-06176-8_14

handling of data introduces a higher probability of entry errors and mismanagement [2,15].

Blockchain technology offers a decentralized approach that enhances the security and privacy of data management systems. Its inherent features, such as immutability and decentralization, are particularly beneficial for managing sensitive information like medical records. By design, blockchain mitigates the risks associated with centralized data storage, significantly reducing the potential for data breaches and unauthorized access. Moreover, the integration of smart contracts into blockchain systems streamlines many operations, reducing the dependency on manual processes and thereby decreasing the chances of human errors.

Additionally, our research explores the diverse uses of blockchain in the healthcare sector, highlighting its potential to improve patient care and data management. For instance, research by Bang et al. illustrates how blockchain can be combined with the Internet of Healthcare Things (IoHT), leveraging smart contracts to enhance the confidentiality and oversight of patient data [2]. Similarly, studies by Son et al. and Le et al. explore the use of permissioned ledgers like Hyperledger Fabric, which provide quick and secure patient data access, essential in emergency care settings [8,15]. These examples showcase the various ways blockchain can address common challenges in healthcare data management.

The utilization of Non-Fungible Tokens (NFTs) for managing medical data presents a distinct approach to encoding this information as digital assets. This strategy not only enhances the security of the data but also facilitates the processes of data exchange and verification among various participants in the healthcare sector, including patients, healthcare providers, and researchers. Our study investigates the operations of blockchain-based systems across different stages of medical data management, from the initial creation and synchronization of medical records to their ongoing management and dissemination. The paper details each phase comprehensively, examining the specific technologies and methods used, such as deploying smart contracts to streamline processes and utilizing the InterPlanetary File System (IPFS) for distributed file storage.

The assessment of transaction fees on different blockchain platforms is a vital part of our study, as these fees are key determinants of the operational expenses and scalability of blockchain-based applications. We have carried out a comparative analysis of transaction fees across four Ethereum Virtual Machine (EVM)-compatible platforms: BNB Chain, Fantom, Polygon, and Celo. This analysis aims to evaluate their cost-effectiveness and appropriateness for managing medical data. Our research primarily examines three essential operations crucial to the management of medical data on the blockchain: initiating transactions, minting NFTs, and transferring NFTs.

Our research highlights the significance of selecting a blockchain platform that delivers optimal functionality at a lower cost. The goal is to pinpoint a platform that achieves a favorable balance between operational costs and system performance, thus enhancing value for all stakeholders involved in the management and sharing of medical data. The conclusions from our analysis of transaction fees provide insights into the efficiency and cost-effectiveness of the blockchain networks under review, helping to identify the most suitable platform for establishing dependable and transparent medical data management systems.

In summary, this paper provides a detailed analysis of how blockchain technology, when integrated with encrypted NFTs and IPFS, can enhance the management and dissemination of medical data. By evaluating encryption algorithms and transaction fees, our study aims to identify the most effective blockchain platforms for use in healthcare settings. This research contributes to the existing body of knowledge on blockchain in healthcare, offering practical insights for the creation of secure and transparent systems for medical data management.

2 Related Work

2.1 Blockchain Applications in General Healthcare Systems

The application of blockchain technology in healthcare informatics is gaining recognition due to its potential to enhance patient-focused systems. Bang et al. explore how blockchain, when integrated with the Internet of Healthcare Things (IoHT), can use smart contracts to improve privacy and give patients greater control over their data [2]. Studies by Son et al. and Le et al. examine the deployment of permissioned blockchains, such as Hyperledger Fabric, to enable quick and secure access to patient information, particularly in emergency care situations [8,15].

Research by Duong et al. focuses on blockchain's role in establishing healthcare systems that prioritize the patient. Their work highlights the importance of data privacy and the empowerment of patients through the use of smart contracts for managing health records [5,6]. Wilber et al. provide a comprehensive overview of various blockchain applications in healthcare, noting its broad potential to support different functions within the sector, from direct patient care to managing pharmaceutical supply chains [17].

In the context of electronic medical records (EMRs), De et al. and Madine et al. propose blockchain-based frameworks that facilitate patient ownership of their data, while also allowing secure access for healthcare providers [9,10]. Additionally, Shynu et al. discuss the integration of blockchain with fog computing to enhance disease prediction capabilities, which may improve both the handling of medical data and the effectiveness of predictive treatments [14].

2.2 Healthcare and Privacy Protection

The potential of blockchain technology to improve the privacy and security of healthcare systems is increasingly acknowledged. Shi et al. conducted a comprehensive review on how blockchain influences the security and privacy components of electronic health record (EHR) systems [13]. Kumar et al. discussed the necessity for healthcare systems to be based on transparency and enforceable agreements using smart contracts, despite some existing challenges [7]. Tith et al. advocated for the implementation of a consortium blockchain to connect various EHRs, enhancing privacy and providing secure, transparent, and immutable access [16]. Chen et al. examined the role of blockchain's inherent features such as immutability and decentralization in safeguarding the transmission, storage, and sharing of medical data [3].

Yue et al. developed a blockchain framework that allows patients to control and share their healthcare data securely, incorporating an access model and a schema to organize personal health information, and employing Secure Multi-Party Computing (MPC) to preserve privacy during data processing [18]. These examples highlight blockchain's role in significantly improving the security and privacy of healthcare data management.

Additional research by Zhang, Xue, and Liu emphasized the need to mitigate privacy and security risks in blockchain applications for medical data sharing, advocating for advanced security measures like attribute-based encryption and zero-knowledge proofs [19]. Dagher et al. introduced "Ancile," a privacy-preserving blockchain framework designed to ensure secure interoperability of electronic health records, featuring rigorous access controls through smart contracts [4].

Moreover, Vinnarasi A et al. discussed the application of permissioned blockchains in conjunction with the Internet of Things to protect healthcare data from unauthorized access while maintaining data integrity [1]. Parmar and Shah explored the integration of blockchain and cryptography to enhance the security of medical data, supporting compliance with data protection laws [11]. Ponsam, Duvvuri, and Roy proposed a blockchain architecture that focuses on the efficient management of electronic health records, emphasizing privacy, integrity, and interoperability among different healthcare providers [12]. These studies collectively demonstrate the ongoing development of blockchain technology in addressing key issues in healthcare data management.

3 Approach

Conventional approaches to managing and sharing medical data often depend on centralized databases and manual procedures, which present several challenges. One notable issue is data fragmentation, where patient information is dispersed among various systems and healthcare providers, complicating the assembly of a comprehensive medical history. Additionally, the centralization of data repositories makes them susceptible to cyberattacks and breaches, posing significant risks to patient privacy. Incompatibilities between healthcare systems also obstruct the smooth transfer of data due to differing formats and standards, further complicating interoperability. Moreover, the reliance on manual methods for data handling can lead to errors in data entry and management.

The diagram 1 presents a structured approach for the management and sharing of medical data, employing blockchain and NFT technologies alongside RSA encryption for enhanced security. This model aims to overcome several limitations inherent in traditional medical data management and sharing practices.

Step 1 Assignment of Global ID: The initial step involves assigning a Global ID to each patient. This identifier is critical for ensuring that patient data

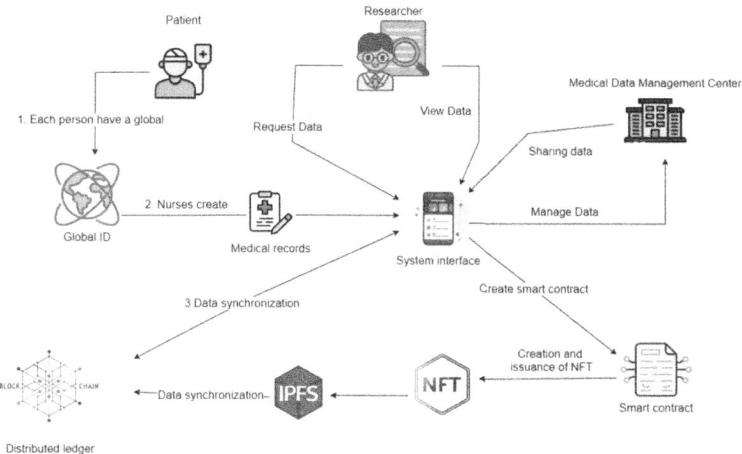

Fig. 1. A structured model for managing and sharing medical data utilizing blockchain

remains consistent and traceable across different healthcare providers and systems, thereby improving the coordination and continuity of care.

Step 2 Creation of Medical Records: During a visit to a healthcare facility, nurses are responsible for generating and updating the patient's medical records. Referred to as "Medical records 1" in the figure, these documents contain comprehensive details about the patient's medical history, treatments undergone, and current care plans. It is vital to maintain the accuracy and completeness of these records to support effective patient care and informed decision-making.

Step 3 Data Synchronization: After the medical records are established, the next phase involves a data synchronization procedure that leverages blockchain technology and the InterPlanetary File System (IPFS) to securely store and distribute the data. The decentralized nature of blockchain enhances the security and integrity of the data, while IPFS allows for storage across a distributed network, minimizing data loss risks and facilitating access from diverse locations as required.

Step 4 Data Management and Sharing: The Data Medical Management Center is crucial in the management and dissemination of medical data. When access to medical data is requested by researchers or other authorized entities, these requests are handled via a system interface. Researchers who gain the necessary permissions can then access the data for their research purposes. This regulated access protocol ensures that sensitive medical information remains secure and is only available to individuals with authorization, thereby preserving patient confidentiality and overall data security.

Step 5 Smart Contracts and NFTs: The system interface plays a key role in establishing smart contracts that define the terms and conditions for accessing medical data. These smart contracts provide explicit rules regarding data viewing and usage rights. Furthermore, to safeguard the privacy and uniqueness of the data, medical information is encapsulated within Non-Fungible Tokens (NFTs). These NFTs serve as distinctive digital markers for the medical records, ensuring each piece of data is unique and verifiable, thus enhancing data security and reducing the risk of unauthorized changes or replication.

Step 6 Distributed Ledger: The procedures related to smart contracts and NFTs, including their creation and access, are meticulously logged on a distributed ledger. This ledger maintains a transparent and unchangeable record of all data transactions and access instances. The use of a distributed ledger ensures a consistent and audit-ready trail of all data interactions and amendments, critical for maintaining data traceability and accountability within the medical data management system.

Step 7 Enhanced Data Security and Integrity: The integration of data synchronization between the system and the IPFS contributes to the secure and dispersed storage of medical records. By employing blockchain technology in conjunction with IPFS, the framework offers a robust solution for the management and sharing of medical data. This setup effectively addresses common challenges in traditional data management systems, such as data fragmentation, interoperability issues, and vulnerability to security breaches. Consequently, this method establishes a more dependable and secure environment for handling medical data, ensuring comprehensive management and controlled sharing within a secure framework.

4   Implementation

This section examines how smart contracts, NFTs, and the InterPlanetary File System (IPFS) are employed to maintain the integrity and transparency of transactions within a blockchain-based medical data management and sharing system. It details the procedures for creating and validating health data certificates, demonstrating how these technologies ensure accurate and immutable records of medical data transactions from their origination to their endpoint usage. Furthermore, the discussion includes the user interfaces and operational protocols that generate and oversee these secure, data-specific certificates, monitoring their movement through the data management chain. The objective is to illustrate how these elements work together to establish a comprehensive and trustworthy ledger that enhances the system's reliability and operational efficiency.

4.1   Transaction/Data Creation

The diagram (Fig. 2) illustrates a blockchain-based system designed to optimize the management and sharing of medical data, focusing on accurate tracking, validation, and documentation from the point of data entry to its final use. Central to this system are smart contracts that manage critical functions and ensure consistency and compliance with established standards across the data sharing

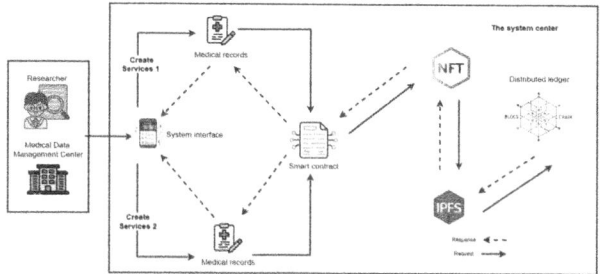

Fig. 2. Creation Framework of transactions

process. Regulatory bodies play a key role as they verify medical data transactions and record these details on the blockchain for increased transparency and reliability. NFTs, serving as digital certificates, validate the accuracy and origin of medical data, offering a dependable method for all participants in the chain to verify specific transaction details. These NFTs are crucial to the system, establishing a verified record of compliance and standards, linked to a blockchain that logs each transaction and stage, thus maintaining an immutable ledger from data creation to dissemination. IPFS enhances this structure by providing decentralized storage, protecting data such as medical origins and transaction records from tampering, thereby ensuring a secure, accessible system for verifying the authenticity and integrity of medical data transactions. This framework significantly improves the administration of medical data systems.

4.2 Data Update

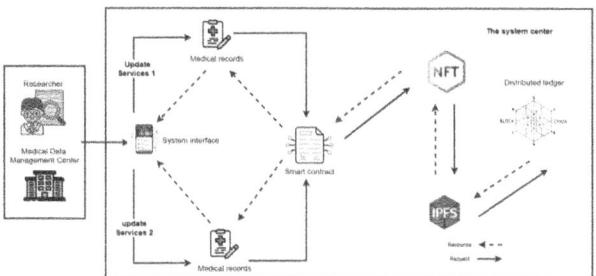

Fig. 3. Updated Framework of transactions

Our updated medical data management and sharing framework incorporates blockchain technology to effectively handle transaction certificates tailored to meet the specific needs of the healthcare sector (Fig. 3). At the core of this system is a digital hub that coordinates network activities, with smart contracts responsible for the creation and updating of medical transaction certificates as healthcare requirements change. Regulatory bodies are essential, as they validate stages of medical transactions and record this data on the blockchain, ensuring that certificates are current and accurately represent the actual medical data transactions. NFTs act as digital certificates that verify the history and compliance of medical records, securely integrated into the blockchain to maintain data integrity. This approach enhances transparency from the point of data entry to its ultimate use, building trust among all stakeholders and providing healthcare providers and patients with reliable information regarding medical data and standards. The security of the system is further strengthened by the use of IPFS for immutable data storage, ensuring that information within the healthcare system is protected from alteration and easily accessible, thus offering a stable and trustworthy framework for managing and sharing medical data.

4.3   Data Query Process

Our medical data management and sharing framework leverages blockchain technology to improve data access and validate transaction statuses across the network (Fig. 4). Central to this system, smart contracts facilitate automated transactions triggered by specific events within the medical data management chain, ensuring consistent operations. Stakeholders can employ query services to verify details such as the origin of the medical data and compliance with healthcare standards, with queries being executed as blockchain transactions for rapid and accurate data retrieval. Regulatory agencies use these features to update blockchain-based certificates, represented as NFTs, which attest to the medical data's accuracy and compliance. Additionally, the incorporation of the InterPlanetary File System (IPFS) guarantees data immutability and security by storing query results and transaction data on IPFS to prevent unauthorized changes and uphold the integrity of the medical data for all participants in the network.

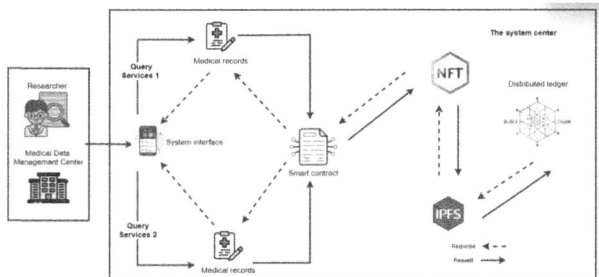

Fig. 4. Query Framework of transactions

5   Evaluation

In today's digital era, maintaining, securing, and quickly accessing medical data is critical. The IPFS (InterPlanetary File System) offers a decentralized solution for storage, which enhances the durability and provides strong resistance against data loss. The application of this technology is particularly pertinent for sensitive medical records, where its deployment can significantly bolster the robustness of data preservation.

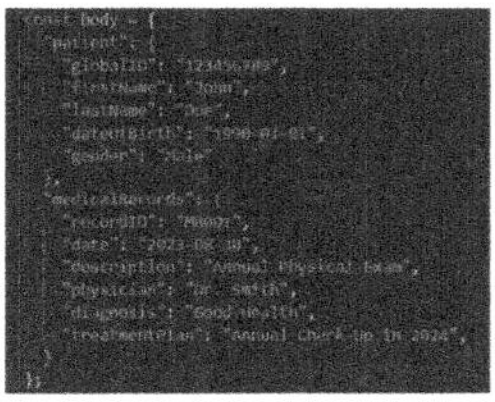

```
// https://maroon-wandering-fly-
487.mypinata.cloud/ipfs/QmbvB1xZZp9zkKzML5Lpju
HBEu2kaDASvDNmR2ro78RzDm

{
  "patient": {
    "globalID": "123456789",
    "firstName": "John",
    "lastName": "Doe",
    "dateOfBirth": "1990-01-01",
    "gender": "Male"
  },
  "medicalRecords": {
    "recordID": "MR001",
    "date": "2023-08-30",
    "description": "Annual Physical Exam",
    "physician": "Dr. Smith",
    "diagnosis": "Good Health",
    "treatmentPlan": "Annual Check-Up in 2024"
  }
}
```

Fig. 5. Creating a Data Structure for NFTs

Fig. 6. Generating IPFS for Stored Metadata of NFT Items

As depicted in Fig. 5, the diagram displays a standard medical record, which includes critical health metrics and historical patient data. Each of these records undergoes a process where it is transformed into a unique digital hash. This transformation is vital as it preserves the authenticity and integrity of the medical data, ensuring that each record is secure and can be verified. This approach not only prevents unauthorized modifications but also supports the secure and efficient sharing and management of these records.

The hash serves as a distinct identifier and reference for the stored medical data, enabling precise retrieval and management. By employing the Pinata platform, which functions as an IPFS developer API, the medical records are securely uploaded to the IPFS network. Pinata is particularly favored for its straightforward interface and advanced encryption protocols, which together provide a secure environment for the storage of sensitive medical data. These measures ensure that medical records are protected from unauthorized access while still being readily available to authorized users, facilitating both secure data management and sharing within the healthcare system.

The decentralized structure of the IPFS (InterPlanetary File System) provides a safeguard against single-point failures, ensuring that medical data remains resilient and accessible even if individual nodes go offline. This redundancy is essential for maintaining uninterrupted access to medical records, which is crucial in healthcare settings where timely access to patient data is needed. By storing the medical data on IPFS, each record is assigned a unique identifier, or data ID, which can be managed through the Pinata platform. This setup illustrates the effective integration of IPFS and Pinata, demonstrating how these tools work together to facilitate secure and continuous access to medical data across different users and locations.

As illustrated in Fig. 6, querying the unique ID of a medical record allows for the retrieval of all associated data. This approach integrates IPFS with the Pinata platform, providing a reliable framework for managing and sharing medical data. This integration reassures various stakeholders—such as patients, healthcare providers, and authorized data managers—that medical records are securely stored, transparently managed, and readily available when needed. This method ensures that sensitive medical information remains accessible and intact, supporting effective healthcare delivery and data management practices.

5.1   Testing on the Four EVM-Supported Platforms

Managing and sharing medical data with blockchain technology requires careful consideration of transaction fees, as these fees directly affect the overall costs and scalability of blockchain-based solutions. This section provides a comparative analysis of transaction fees on four Ethereum Virtual Machine (EVM)-compatible platforms: BNB Chain, Fantom, Polygon, and Celo. We examine the fee structures of each platform to evaluate their suitability for implementing blockchain solutions in medical data management, focusing on both cost-efficiency and operational functionality.

The study examines how blockchain can improve the management of medical data systems by incorporating NFTs and IPFS. The analysis focuses on three main functions: the creation of data, the minting of NFTs, and the transfer of NFTs. These functions are essential for recording medical information, ensuring the authenticity of documents, and securely distributing digital assets among various participants in the healthcare network.

To assess the practical applications and performance of these platforms, we analyze their capabilities in supporting critical operations necessary for managing medical data effectively. The evaluation centers on the four EVM-compatible blockchains: BNB Chain, Fantom, Celo, and Polygon. The study pays particular attention to the efficiency and cost of transaction processes, which are key factors in selecting the most appropriate platforms for building reliable and transparent systems for medical data management.

5.2   Results

Analyzing transaction fees is essential for assessing the practicality of blockchain-based systems, especially in the realm of medical data management and sharing. These fees are pivotal because they affect the system's economic feasibility and its long-term sustainability, providing compensation for validators or miners who secure the network and process transactions.

Our assessment concentrates on three critical activities that are fundamental to platforms designed for managing and sharing medical data through NFTs: the creation of data or transactions, the minting of NFTs, and the transfer of these NFTs. Each of these tasks is vital for the medical data lifecycle on the blockchain:

1. Creation of Data or Transactions: This process involves the recording of medical record information onto the blockchain. Ensuring that details of medical transactions are permanently and transparently logged is crucial, as it influences the costs associated with tokenizing medical data.
2. Minting NFTs: This step converts details from medical records into unique digital assets NFTs that represent ownership or verification of the data. Minting these NFTs is fundamental for the digital handling of records, facilitating more efficient management. Evaluating the minting fees is essential to maintain affordability and accessibility, thus enhancing the operational effectiveness of the system managing and sharing medical data.
3. Transferring NFTs: This operation deals with the change of ownership of these digital assets among parties, playing a central role in the management platform by enabling the distribution and movement of medical data. The costs involved in transferring NFTs impact the liquidity and transaction ease within the system. High transfer fees may restrict transaction frequency and decrease system usage, whereas lower fees might promote more dynamic management and frequent updates of medical records.

By reviewing the fees linked with these functions, we can determine the overall efficiency and cost-effectiveness of the blockchain platform for medical data management and sharing. This analysis helps us to contrast various blockchain networks and identify the most appropriate platform based on a balance of operational costs and network performance. The objective is to select a blockchain solution that offers the needed functionality at the lowest possible cost, thereby maximizing the benefits for all stakeholders in the medical data management ecosystem.

Table 1. Transaction fee

	Transaction Creation	Create NFT	Transfer NFT
BNB	0.0273134 BNB ($16.47)	0.00109162 BNB ($0.66)	0.00057003 BNB ($0.34)
Fantom	0.00957754 FTM ($0.00)	0.000405167 FTM ($0.00)	0.0002380105 FTM ($0.00)
Polygon	0.006840710032835408 MATIC ($0.01)	0.000289405001852192 MATIC ($0.00)	0.000170007501088048 MATIC ($0.00)
Celo	0.007097844 CELO ($0.005)	0.0002840812 CELO $0.000)	0.0001554878 CELO ($0.000)

Transaction Fee Analysis. Table 1 offers a detailed comparison of transaction fees for three critical operations across four Ethereum Virtual Machine (EVM)-compatible blockchain platforms: BNB Chain, Fantom, Polygon, and Celo, with token values recorded as of july 26, 2024. These operations—creating transactions, minting NFTs, and transferring NFTs—are fundamental to the management and protection of medical data utilizing blockchain technology. By analyzing the fee structures on each platform, we can determine their cost-effectiveness and appropriateness for systems designed to manage and share medical data transparently through the use of blockchain, NFTs, smart contracts, and IPFS.

BNB Chain's fee for starting transactions stands at 0.0273134 BNB, approximately $16.47, which might be prohibitive for systems with high transaction volumes. However, the costs drop significantly for NFT-related activities, with fees of 0.00109162 BNB ($0.66) for NFT creation and 0.00057003 BNB ($0.34) for NFT transfers. This pricing suggests that BNB Chain could be well-suited for scenarios where initial data entries are infrequent but ongoing NFT management is more common.

Fantom presents a highly competitive fee structure, charging only 0.00957754 FTM for transaction initiation. The fees for NFT creation and transfers are even lower, at 0.000405167 FTM and 0.0002380105 FTM respectively, making it highly cost-effective for systems that require regular updates and quick data transfers. Fantom's low fees promote active and efficient data management and sharing.

Polygon's fees are similarly modest, with a transaction initiation charge of only 0.00684071003283508 MATIC, roughly $0.01. The fees for creating and transferring NFTs are even lower at 0.000289405001852192 MATIC and 0.000170007501088048 MATIC, respectively. This fee structure makes Polygon ideal for systems that manage extensive data, facilitating scalable and economical operations without compromising on transaction frequency or data updates.

Celo, focusing on mobile accessibility and cost efficiency, levies a charge of 0.007097844 CELO (about $0.005) for initiating transactions, with nominal fees for NFT creation and transfer at 0.0002840812 CELO and 0.0001554878 CELO, respectively. This low-cost framework makes Celo particularly suitable for stakeholders in economically restricted regions, offering an affordable way to manage and share medical data. Celo's mobile-first approach and minimal transaction costs make it an attractive option for international markets where cost efficiency and mobile accessibility are critical.

By examining the transaction fees associated with crucial operations on different blockchain platforms, we obtain valuable information about their effectiveness and affordability in managing and sharing medical data. This detailed analysis of fees allows us to assess the potential and costs of platforms such as BNB Chain, Fantom, Polygon, and Celo comprehensively. Our aim is to select a platform that strikes an optimal balance between operational expenses and system efficiency, ensuring that the chosen blockchain solution delivers the necessary features for medical data management and sharing at a cost-effective rate. This selection is critical for implementing a system that not only processes data securely and efficiently but also keeps operational costs low for everyone involved, from healthcare providers to patients. This strategy is crucial in encouraging broader acceptance and consistent use of the system.

6 Conclusion

This paper has examined the potential of blockchain technology to transform the management and sharing of medical data by utilizing NFTs and IPFS for secure, decentralized storage and access. We have identified the benefits of blockchain's decentralized approach, including enhanced data security, privacy, and the ability to manage data across multiple stakeholders without centralized control. Through a comparative analysis of transaction fees on four EVM-compatible platforms—BNB Chain, Fantom, Polygon, and Celo—we have highlighted the importance of selecting a platform that offers both cost-effectiveness and operational efficiency. Our findings suggest that while each platform has distinct advantages, the choice of the most suitable platform should depend on specific use cases and the balance between cost and performance requirements. The study's insights help guide the selection of blockchain solutions that provide secure and efficient management of medical data, contributing to the broader adoption of blockchain technology in healthcare.

References

1. A, P.V., Dayana, R., Vadivukkarasi, K.: Healthcare data security using blockchain technology. In: 2023 International Conference on Intelligent Systems for Communication, IoT and Security (ICISCoIS) (2023)
2. Bang, N., et al.: Blockchain-enhanced ioht: a patient-centric internet of healthcare things platform with smart contract-driven data management. In: International Conference on Advances in Mobile Computing and Multimedia Intelligence, pp. 50–56. Springer (2023)
3. Chen, Z., et al.: A blockchain-based preserving and sharing system for medical data privacy. Futur. Gener. Comput. Syst. **124**, 338–350 (2021)
4. Dagher, G.G., Mohler, J., Milojkovic, M., Marella, P.B.: Ancile: Privacy-preserving framework for access control and interoperability of electronic health records using blockchain technology. Sustainable Cities and Society (2018)
5. Duong-Trung, N., et al.: On components of a patient-centered healthcare system using smart contract. In: Proceedings of the 2020 4th International Conference on Cryptography, Security and Privacy, pp. 31–35 (2020)
6. Duong-Trung, N., et al.: Smart care: integrating blockchain technology into the design of patient-centered healthcare systems. In: Proceedings of the 2020 4th International Conference on Cryptography, Security and Privacy, pp. 105–109 (2020)
7. Kumar, T., Ramani, V., Ahmad, I., Braeken, A., Harjula, E., Ylianttila, M.: Blockchain utilization in healthcare: Key requirements and challenges. In: 2018 IEEE 20th International Conference on e-Health Networking, Applications and Services (Healthcom), pp. 1–7. IEEE (2018)

8. Le, H.T., et al.: Patient-chain: patient-centered healthcare system a blockchain-based technology in dealing with emergencies. In: International Conference on Parallel and Distributed Computing: Applications and Technologies, pp. 576–583. Springer (2021)

9. Madine, M.M., et al.: Blockchain for giving patients control over their medical records. IEEE Access 8, 193102–193115 (2020)

10. de Oliveira, M.T., et al.: Towards a blockchain-based secure electronic medical record for healthcare applications. In: ICC 2019-2019 IEEE International Conference on Communications (ICC), pp. 1–6. IEEE (2019)

11. Parmar, M., Shah, S.: Reinforcing security of medical data using blockchain. In: 2019 International Conference on Intelligent Computing and Control Systems (ICCS) (2019)

12. Ponsam, D.J.G., Duvvuri, S., Roy, S.: Electronic healthcare management system using blockchain technology. In: 2023 International Conference on Circuit Power and Computing Technologies (ICCPCT) (2023)

13. Shi, S., et al.: Applications of blockchain in ensuring the security and privacy of electronic health record systems: a survey. Comput. Secur. 97, 101966 (2020)

14. Shynu, P., et al.: Blockchain-based secure healthcare application for diabetic-cardio disease prediction in fog computing. IEEE Access 9, 45706–45720 (2021)

15. Son, H.X., et al.: Toward a blockchain-based technology in dealing with emergencies in patient-centered healthcare systems. In: Mobile, Secure, and Programmable Networking: 6th International Conference, MSPN 2020, Paris, France, October 28–29, 2020, Revised Selected Papers 6, pp. 44–56. Springer (2021)

16. Tith, D., et al.: Application of blockchain to maintaining patient records in electronic health record for enhanced privacy, scalability, and availability. Healthcare Inform. Res. 26(1), 3–12 (2020)

17. Wilber, K., et al.: A survey on blockchain for healthcare informatics and applications. In: 2020 7th International Conference on Internet of Things: Systems, Management and Security (IOTSMS), pp. 1–9. IEEE (2020)

18. Yue, X., et al.: Healthcare data gateways: found healthcare intelligence on blockchain with novel privacy risk control. J. Med. Syst. 40(10), 1–8 (2016)

19. Zhang, R., Xue, R., Liu, L.: Security and privacy for healthcare blockchains. IEEE Trans. Services Comput. (2021)

Privacy-Preserving Transaction Chain Retrieval and Reconstruction for Collaborative Supervision

Yuhan Yang[1,3], Qian Xu[1], Huajie Shen[1], Bo Yu[1], Wei He[1(✉)], Lijun Wei[2],
Jing Wu[3], and Chengnian Long[3(✉)]

[1] Blockchain Research Institute Bestpay Co., Ltd., Telecom, Shanghai, China
yuhanyang@sjtu.edu.cn, {xuqian,shenhuajie,yubo,hewei}@bestpay.com.cn
[2] China United Network Communications Co., Ltd., Shanghai Branch,
Shanghai, China
sjtu_weilijun@sjtu.edu.cn
[3] School of Automation and Intelligent Sensing, Shanghai Jiao Tong University,
Shanghai, China
{jingwu,longcn}@sjtu.edu.cn

Abstract. The integration of privacy-preserving computation and blockchain have significantly advanced cross-institutional data sharing in financial regulation. However, challenges of transaction chain reconstruction and private information preservation remain unresolved, which causes illegal activities such as fraudulent trade due to the lack of inter-bank information interoperability. To address these issues, this paper proposes a collaborative supervision that combines Private Information Retrieval (PIR) and blockchain technology. Leveraging the PIR protocol, supervision authority can retrieve transactions associated with suspicious identity from various banks, without disclosing the retrieval target. Furthermore, blockchain is used to record and verify transactions, which helps to automatically correlate multi-account transaction chains and enables verifiable tracing of fund flows. Experimental results demonstrate that the transaction tracing scheme can achieve a single retrieval and batch retrieval with high execution efficiency. The running time only rises to 10.917 s (at 1×10^7 data size) for batch retrieval of 1000 data entries, which is within an acceptable range for financial regulatory scenarios

Keywords: Private retrieval · Blockchain · Financial supervision

1 Introduction

With the rapid development of digital finance, distributed ledger technology and privacy-preserving computation provide solutions for financial data sharing [1–3], enabling interoperability of transaction and credit information among banks. However, illegal behaviors in financial scenarios exhibit high complexity, including: i) Users may establish cross-institutional transactions by applying multiple accounts across different banks to obscure fund flow trajectories, as shown in Fig. 1; 2) Fraudulent trade financing through fabricated upstream/downstream enterprise account information and cross-bank transfers

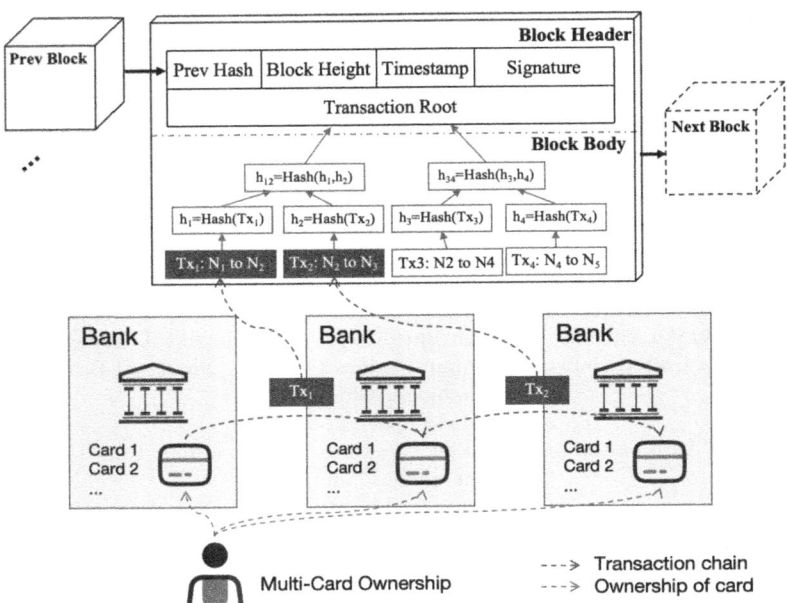

Fig. 1. Example of tracing cross-bank transaction flow.

to create transaction records. These illegal behaviors lies in the fact that individual banks only possess partial transaction data, failing to form a comprehensive transaction chain perspective.

Although blockchain technology enables cross-institutional data sharing [4,5], it faces contradiction between privacy preservation and supervision effectiveness. For instance, commercial banks construct blockchain to achieve transaction information sharing, but require participating banks to disclose partial plaintext account information (e.g. the last four digits of phone numbers). Although some solutions employ zero-knowledge proofs to conceal transaction amounts, they still expose the account correlations. Furthermore, current solutions cannot support regulator authority to perform cooperative retrieval across multiple banks without revealing the query target, which is a critical technical bottleneck for tracing complex laundering chains.

To address it, this paper proposes a novel supervision framework combining Private Information Retrieval (PIR) with blockchain collaboration. The PIR protocol [6–8] allows regulators to submit encrypted queries to banks, retrieving only target account identity information while preserving unrelated account data. A blockchain-based distributed transaction ledger automatically associates cross-bank transaction records under identity information through smart contracts, and generates a verifiable fund flow. This constitutes a dual-layer architecture, including on-chain record layer and off-chain retrieval layer, which achieves equi-

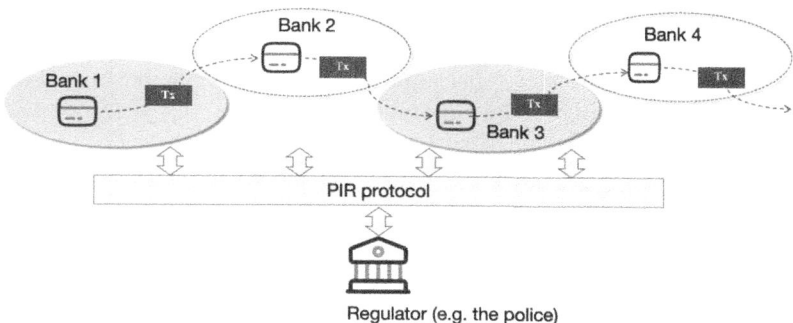

Fig. 2. Off-chain Data Retrieval based on PIR.

librium between financial data sharing efficiency and individual privacy preservation.

2 PIR-Enabled Transaction Chain Retrieval

In this section, we give a dual-layer framework for private account retrieval and cross-bank transaction chain tracing, which includes regulator, bank and blockchain. As shown in Fig. 2, a transaction may occur between two banks, such as Bank 1 and Bank 2, both banks will record the same transaction. Bank 1 records a transaction transferred from an internal account to Bank 2, and Bank 2 records a transaction transferred from Bank 1 to an internal account. For the case of suspicious transaction, the regulator submits suspicious identities to the banks and initiates PIR requests, then banks return target results via the PIR protocol after verifying regulatory authority. Based on the retrieved accounts, the regulator aggregates all transactions and reconstructs complete transaction chain using blockchain records, thereby identifying illegal activities. It is noted that financial database should be modified as index-based and vectorizable. Now we give the off-chain PIR mechanism.

Off-Chain Data Retrieval Based on PIR. The off-chain private retrieval mechanism is recalled between regulator and M banks $\mathcal{B} = \{B_i\}_{i \in M}$. The regulator maintains user identities and sends encrypted search data to participating banks. Each $B_i \in \mathcal{B}$ computes the query results and returns them to the regulator. The PIR protocol is implemented based on homomorphic encryption scheme BFV [9,10], which is defined over a polynomial ring $R = Z/(x^N + 1)$, and N is chosen as a power of 2. The components of the BFV algorithm include:

- Secret key $sk = s$, it is a polynomial

$$s = s_{N-1}x^{N-1} + s_{N-2}x^{N-2} + \ldots + s_1 x^1 + s_0 \tag{1}$$

with coefficients s_i sampled from a small range $\{-1, 0, 1\}$.

- Public key $pk = (a, -(as + e))$, which is consisted by sk and noise e.
- Plaintext m, it is a polynomial $m = a_{N-1}x^{N-1} + a_{N-2}x^{N-2} + \ldots + a_1 x^1 + a_0$ where each coefficient $a_0 \in [0, t)$ and the plaintext can be represented as $m \in R \mod t$(the polynomial ring modulo t).
- Ciphertext (c_0, c_1), it is consisted by two polynomials

$$(c_0, c_1) = (c_{0,N-1}x^{N-1} + c_{0,N-2}x^{N-2} + \ldots + c_{0,1}x^1 + c_{0,0},$$
$$c_{1,N-1}x^{N-1} + c_{1,N-2}x^{N-2} + \ldots + c_{1,1}x^1 + c_{1,0}) \quad (2)$$

with coefficients in $c_{0,i}, c_{1,i} \in [0, q)$, and the ciphertext can be expressed as $c_{0,i}, c_{1,i} \in R \mod q$ (the polynomial ring modulo q).
- Encryption $En()$, $(c_0, c_1) = (a, b + e' + \Delta m)$, where $a \in R \mod t$ is generated randomly and $b = as + e''$, $\Delta = [q/t]$. e' and e'' are noise polynomials sampled from a bounded Gaussian distribution. It is obvious that the plaintext is hidden in the most significant bit of the coefficient of c_1.
- Decryption $DE()$, $c_1 - c_0 s = e + \Delta m$. m can be abstracted from the most significant bit due to the small noise coefficient.

Based on the BFV homomorphic encryption, we next describe the private retrieval process. Considering that regulator wants to retrieve the i-th data $i \in [1, n]$ from B_i that maintains data $x = (x_1, \ldots, x_{i-1}, x_i, x_{i+1}, \ldots, x_n)$. The regulator performs

- Generate the key pairs (pk, sk).
- Generate vector $\boldsymbol{R} = (0, \ldots, 0, 1, 0, \ldots, 0)$ of length n, where the i-th element is 1 and all other elements are 0.
- Encrypt each element of $\boldsymbol{R}$ using the public key to obtain

$$(z_1, \ldots, z_{i-1}, z_i, z_{i+1}, \ldots, z_n) = (En(0), \ldots, En(0), En(1), En(0), \ldots, En(0)), \quad (3)$$

and send them to B_i.

B_i computes the homomorphic sum of the ciphertexts as $r = \sum_{i=1}^n x_i z_i = \sum_{i=1}^n x_i En(z_i)$, and return it to the regulator. Since the encryption satisfies additive homomorphism, the decrypted result will preserve the sum of the plaintext elements.

After receiving r, the regulator decrypts it with sk to recover the desired value x_i. The encryption algorithm is probabilistic, hence even for the same input (e.g., plaintext 0 or 1), the generated ciphertexts are randomized and indistinguishable. Although B_i observes multiple ciphertexts e.g. encrypted 0 or encrypted 1, it cannot distinguish which ciphertext corresponds to 0 or 1. Considering that B_i returns a single homomorphic ciphertext corresponding to the retrieval vector, which the regulator needs to sends n-length encrypted retrieval vector $\boldsymbol{R}$. The retrieval process can be further extended to multi-dimensional retrieval for optimization. For example, the data set x in B_i can be represented in a 2-dimensional array, where $l = \sqrt{n}$. The regulator only needs to send two vectors of length $l \times l$ to uniquely identify any single element. This reduces the retrieval vector size from n to $2l$. For a d-dimensional array, the size of the retrieval vector will be reduced to $d(n)^{1/d}$.

2.1   Transaction Reconstruction with On-Chain Records

Based on off-chain data retrieval results, on-chain transaction records can be queried to reconstruct the entire transaction chain. Specifically, For each bank B_i and its clients, B_i maintains client identity information in local and creates a corresponding blockchain address. If a suspicious ID (e.g. $ID = x_i, i \in [n]$) in bank B_i corresponds to an account set $\mathcal{A} = \{A_i\}_{i \in [M]}$, all transaction behaviors of this ID form a directed graph $G = (V, E)$ on the blockchain.

- $v_i \in V$ is the on-chain addresses bound to real ID via Pedersen Commitments $Com_{x_i} = g^{x_i} h^{rm}$, where rm denotes random blinding factor.
- $e_{i \rightarrow j} \in E$ is the edge indicating transfer record from account A_i to account A_j, which carries a transaction tuple $TX = (T_{x_i}, \tau, Sig_{x_i})$. T_{x_i} is timestamp, and τ and Sig_{x_i} are amount hash and digital signature, respectively.

A single B_i only knows the last hop and next hop transfer records, leading to transaction chain fragmentation. To reconstruct the full transaction chain, each transaction will be recorded on-chain as a digest generated from the real identity ID, timestamp, and transaction amount. Given a regulator-provided time range $[T_{start}, T_{end}]$, the blockchain is queried to locate and retrieve subsequent transactions (next "hops"). Through the Pedersen commitment binding and verification, the integrity of linked accounts and reconstruction of the complete transaction chain are enabled as $\sum_{T=T_{start}}^{T_{end}} Com_{x_i}^T = g^{\sum x_i} h^{\sum rm}$.

2.2   Security Analysis

In this section, we conduct a qualitative security analysis. First, during the off-chain private retrieval phase, the query algorithm relies on BFV homomorphic encryption, whose security is based on the hardness of the Ring Learning With Errors (RLWE) problem [11], currently considered resistant to quantum computing. When parameters comply with NIST standards, attackers cannot crack ciphertexts within polynomial time.

Additionally, from the perspective of retrieval in B_i, the regulator encodes retrieval indices as high-dimensional vectors and conceals specific positions via homomorphic encryption. For example, when querying the i-th item, the regulator generates an encrypted vector $(En(0), ..., En(0), En(1), En(0), ..., En(0))$, where only the i-th position is set to 1. The bank cannot determine the location of non-zero elements from the ciphertext. During the product operation $r = \sum_{i=1}^{n} x_i z_i = \sum_{i=1}^{n} x_i En(z_i)$ on local database, decryption reveals only the target data due to homomorphic properties, while other data remain obscured by noise. Even through reverse engineering, individual elements cannot be isolated.

From the perspective of on-chain transaction tracing, transaction digests are generated by combining identity identifiers, hence attackers are prevented from forging transactions through pre-computation. Additionally, the binding between account A_i and on-chain address via Pedersen commitment [12]. Any illegal modification would require simultaneously breaking the binding of the Pedersen commitment (i.e., the discrete logarithm assumption) and the blockchain

Table 1. Running Time of Single Retrieval.

Data Size		Running Time (s)		
Local data	Retrieval data	Inner product (bank)	Generate vector (regulator)	Total
1×10^3	1	0.175	0.005	0.774
1×10^4	1	0.201	0.005	0.854
1×10^5	1	0.308	0.005	0.935
1×10^6	1	1.459	0.006	6.124
1×10^7	1	6.990	0.017	15.844

consensus mechanism. Therefore, within polynomial time, attackers cannot infer actual fund flows through transaction topological structures.

3   Performance Evaluation

In this section, we evaluate the performance of the proposed PIR-enabled financial supervision with on-chain data scheme. To evaluate the computation overhead of PIR process, we deploy the experiment based on a desktop with Apple M1 3.2 GHz with 8 cores and 8 GB RAM running 64bit Ubuntu 20.04.

As shown in Table 1, when the database scales from $[1 \times 10^3, 1 \times 10^7]$, the most time-consuming inner product computation increases from 0.175 s to 6.990 s, and the total running time rises from 0.774 s to 15.844 s. Meanwhile, the regulator's retrieval vector generation time remains stable within $[0.005 \text{ s}, 0.017 \text{ s}]$. This indicates that BFV encryption does not impose significant computational overhead in the protocol, and system performance is constrained by the computational complexity of homomorphic inner product operations and the database size on the bank side. For comparison, we give the running results of recent blockchain-based efficient retrieval method [13] in Fig. 3, which is facilitated by improved merkle tree structure and suitable for on-chain transaction retrieval. As the data size increases, our proposed scheme shows better performance due to the efficient off-chain execution.

Additionally, to evaluate the execution efficiency of the proposed protocol under batch retrieval scenarios, we further present the results in Table 2. When the data size is fixed, the total time consumption increases as the batch retrieval data size grows from 100 to 1000. This is because batch queries require parallel execution of multiple PIR protocols via hash tables, causing both homomorphic inner product operations and retrieval vector generation to scale linearly with the number of queries. Obviously, the bank-side computation is primarily influenced by the data size, while the regulator's execution time remains stable under the same retrieval data size, enabling lightweight client-side private retrieval on the regulator side. Even when the data size increases from 1×10^3 to 1×10^7, and the total protocol running time remains within an acceptable range for financial regulatory scenarios.

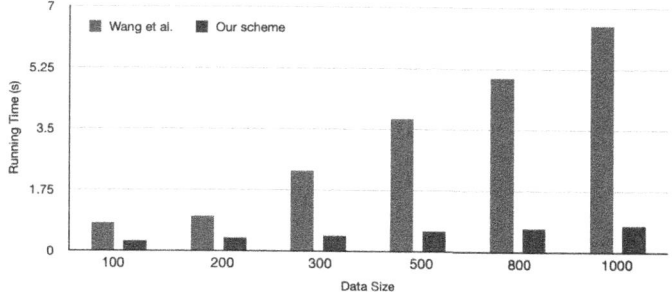

Fig. 3. Comparisons of Running Time with Various Data Sizes.

Table 2. Running Time of Batch Retrieval.

Data Size		Running Time (s)		
Local data	Retrieval data	Inner product (bank)	Generate vector (regulator)	Total
1×10^3	100	0.155	0.088	1.324
1×10^4	100	0.207	0.107	1.389
1×10^4	1000	0.428	0.839	5.768
1×10^5	100	0.261	0.087	1.867
1×10^5	1000	0.426	0.817	6.043
1×10^6	100	1.063	0.090	7.262
1×10^6	1000	1.446	0.886	10.917

4   Conclusion

This paper proposes a cross-institutional transaction chain reconstruction scheme based on PIR and blockchain, aiming to resolve transaction chain fragmentation while balancing privacy preservation and regulatory efficiency. Using the PIR-based Off-chain data retrieval, the scheme enables retrieval of associated account information from encrypted multi-bank databases without exposing user identities, and reconstructs complete fund flows using blockchain transaction records. Experimental results show the efficient execution of the scheme when data size grows from 1×10^3 to 1×10^7 (for single retrieval), and the running time only rises to 10.917s (at 1×10^7 data size) for batch retrieval of 1000 data entries, demonstrating the feasibility and efficiency of the scheme in large-scale data scenarios.

Acknowledgments. This work was supported by National Key Research and Development Program of China under Grant No. 2024YFB3311403, 2023YFB3106501, National Natural Science Foundation of China under Grants No. 62136006, 62273236, 62473259, and Key R&D projects in Hainan Province ZDYF2024GXJS009.

References

1. Li, T., Kou, G., Peng, Y., et al.: An integrated cluster detection, optimization, and interpretation approach for financial data. IEEE Trans. Cybern. **52**(12), 13848–13861 (2021)
2. Yang, F., Qiao, Y., Abedin, M.Z., Huang, C.: Privacy-preserved credit data sharing integrating blockchain and federated learning for industrial 4.0. IEEE Trans. Industr. Inf. **18**(12), 8755–8764 (2022)
3. Liu, J., He, X., Sun, R., Du, X., Guizani, M.: Privacy-preserving data sharing scheme with FL via MPC in financial permissioned blockchain. In: ICC IEEE International Conference on Communications, pp. 1–6 (2021)
4. Liao, C., Guan, X., Cheng, J., et al.: Blockchain-based identity management and access control framework for open banking ecosystem. Futur. Gener. Comput. Syst. **135**, 450–466 (2022)
5. Jiang, S., Cao, J., Wu, H., et al.: Privacy-preserving and efficient data sharing for blockchain-based intelligent transportation systems. Inf. Sci. **635**, 72–85 (2023)
6. Henzinger, A., Hong, M., Corrigan-Gibbs, H., et al.: One server for the price of two: simple and fast Single-Server private information retrieval[C], 32nd USENIX Security Symposium (USENIX Security 23), pp. 3889-3905, 2023
7. Mughees, M., Ren, L.: Vectorized batch private information retrieval. In: 2023 IEEE Symposium on Security and Privacy (SP). IEEE, pp. 437–452 (2023)
8. Menon, S., Wu, D.: Spiral: fast, high-rate single-server PIR via FHE composition. In: 2022 IEEE Symposium on Security and Privacy (SP), pp. 930–947. IEEE (2022)
9. Kim, J., Seo, J., Song, Y.: Simpler and faster BFV bootstrapping for arbitrary plaintext modulus from CKKS. In: Proceedings of the 2024 on ACM SIGSAC Conference on Computer and Communications Security, pp. 2535–2546 (2024)
10. Okada, H., Player, R., Pohmann, S.: Homomorphic polynomial evaluation using Galois structure and applications to BFV bootstrapping. In: International Conference on the Theory and Application of Cryptology and Information Security, pp. 69–100 (2023)
11. Mouchet, C., Troncoso-Pastoriza, J., Bossuat, J., et al.: Multiparty homomorphic encryption from ring-learning-with-errors. Proc. Privacy Enhancing Technol. **4**, 291–311 (2021)
12. Wang, H., Liao, J.: Blockchain privacy protection algorithm based on Pedersen commitment and zero-knowledge proof. In: Proceedings of the 2021 4th International Conference on Blockchain Technology and Applications, pp. 1–5 (2021)
13. Wang, R., Xu, C., Zhang, X.: Toward materials genome big-data: a blockchain-based secure storage and efficient retrieval method. IEEE Trans. Parallel Distrib. Syst. **35**(9), 1630–1643 (2024)

Lussa Platform: How AI and Blockchain Can Change the Gaming Industry

Adel ELMessiry[1](✉) and Magdi El Messiry[2]

[1] WebDBTech, Pittsburgh, USA
Adel.ElMessiry@gmail.com
[2] Alexandria University, Alexandria, Egypt

Abstract. The Lussa Platform introduces a transformative approach to game development by fusing AI, blockchain, and social account abstraction. Amid a backdrop of rising development costs and shrinking funding opportunities, Lussa reimagines the production pipeline through an agentic architecture that deploys intelligent, collaborative agents and blockchain-based token economies. Integrated with the AI Value Protocol (AIVP) and the Horus Wallet, Lussa empowers developers and communities to co-create, govern, and monetize games with dramatically reduced costs and time-to-market. Initial deployment in the game *The Final Frontier* showed a 50–56% reduction in development time and a 70% decrease in cost-demonstrating the viability of this new paradigm for the gaming industry.

1 Introduction

The development of modern triple-A (AAA) games has become a capital-intensive endeavor, often costing hundreds of millions of dollars [1]. Despite tooling and platform improvements, costs continue to rise while funding has significantly dropped. The decline in early-stage investment and the saturation of the gaming market have left many promising projects stranded in pre-production.

Continuing to follow traditional, linear production models while expecting different outcomes is, in the words of Einstein, "the definition of insanity." A new model is not just necessary—it's inevitable. The integration of artificial intelligence (AI) and blockchain is reshaping the gaming industry by enhancing security, deepening personalization, and transforming economic structures. Blockchain's decentralized and transparent ledger minimizes fraud and secures digital transactions and player identities, offering a tamper-proof alternative to traditional systems [2]. AI complements this security by monitoring real-time activity, detecting suspicious behavior, and preventing fraud before it escalates. Together, these technologies create a fortified digital gaming infrastructure [3]. Beyond security, AI has revolutionized gameplay through dynamic personalization. Game systems now analyze user behavior to adapt mechanics, provide content recommendations, and tailor in-game difficulty—leading to improved player retention and satisfaction. AI-driven agents are increasingly autonomous, functioning as intelligent NPCs, economic participants, or even negotiators in

R. K. Shyamasundar et al. (Eds.): ICBC 2025, LNCS 16155, pp. 235–243, 2026.
https://doi.org/10.1007/978-3-032-06176-8_16

blockchain-based ecosystems [4]. Players can train and resell AI agents as NFTs, further deepening gameplay and economic interactivity. Blockchain also enables true digital asset ownership through NFTs, allowing gamers to trade items across ecosystems. This underpins the rise of play-to-earn models, turning leisure into income-generating opportunities, as seen in games like Axie Infinity [5]. Over 70% of gamers now use cryptocurrency for in-game purchases due to cost efficiency and seamless global access. Interoperability, although technically challenging, holds promise for shared digital identities and asset migration across multiple games. However, challenges such as blockchain scalability, developer expertise gaps, user friction with crypto wallets, and ongoing regulatory scrutiny (e.g., SEC guidelines) persist. Despite these limitations, advancements in AI learning systems and blockchain protocols (e.g., Layer-2 scaling and sustainable consensus mechanisms) suggest an optimistic trajectory. Future gaming ecosystems are expected to be more secure, adaptive, and economically decentralized—delivering groundbreaking. The Lussa Platform offers a radical departure: a system built on artificial intelligence, blockchain infrastructure, and social simplicity [6].

2   The Lussa Solution

The Lussa Platform provides a transformative alternative to the conventional game development pipeline by embracing AI modularity and decentralized economics [7]. This new model is built upon three key pillars: agentic architecture, specialized task-driven AI agents, and a tokenized blockchain framework that democratizes funding, ownership, and governance.

2.1   Agentic Architecture: A New Paradigm

Agentic architecture has been gaining adoption recently. Many domains, from education to gaming, have adopted agentic architecture to enhance the accuracy of the models and reduce the cost [8,9]. Lussa adopts a distributed agentic architecture [10], a constellation of AI-driven agents, each assigned a specific domain within the game production pipeline.

- **Narrative Agents:** Generate storylines, dialogue, and branching narratives.
- **Artistic Agents:** Create concept art, textures, and models.
- **Design Agents:** Simulate levels, NPCs, and interactions.
- **QA Agents:** Auto-test gameplay mechanics, logic, and difficulty balancing.
- **Community Agents:** Moderate forums, summarize feedback, and recommend content changes.

These agents operate semi-autonomously and communicate through a shared protocol, as shown in Fig. 1. They reduce production bottlenecks by running in parallel and adapting in real-time to user and team input.

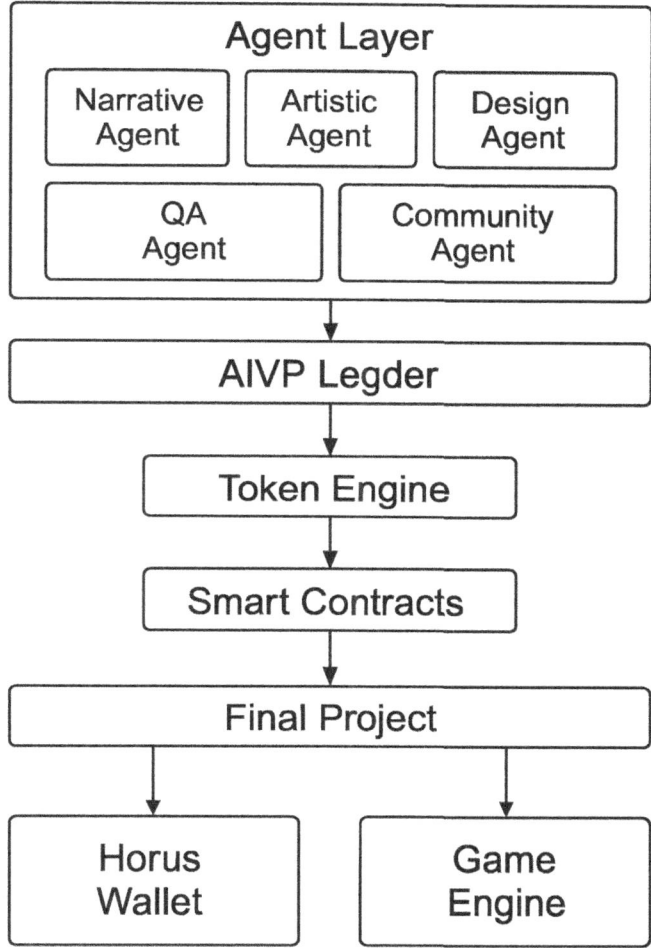

Fig. 1. Lussa Platform's Game Production Pipeline

2.2   Specialized Agents for Scalable Development

Rather than depending on one general-purpose model, Lussa deploys smaller, focused agents trained on domain-specific data. Specialized agents are task-specific AI models designed to handle distinct functions within the game development lifecycle, enabling a modular and scalable production process. Unlike monolithic AI systems, these agents are optimized for narrow domains-such as generating dialogue, designing levels, creating visual assets, or conducting automated testing-allowing for higher accuracy, faster iteration, and easier updates [11]. By distributing responsibilities across a network of collaborative agents, development becomes parallelized and more efficient, drastically reducing the time and resources required to build complex games [12]. This architecture allows small teams or indie developers to achieve outcomes previously reserved for large studios, while also enabling plug-and-play flexibility, where agents can be swapped, upgraded, or retrained independently based on project needs. Ultimately, specialized agents empower a leaner, more agile approach to game creation, supported by intelligent automation and fine-grained control [13].

- **Precision and agility:** Each agent excels in its domain.
- **Composable and upgradeable:** Agents can be swapped or retrained independently.
- **Plugin ecosystem:** Developers can publish or consume community-created agents.

This approach brings AAA-level capabilities to indie studios and accelerates iteration cycles.

2.3   Blockchain Tokenization

Blockchain tokenization is redefining value creation and ownership in the gaming industry by converting in-game assets, currencies, and rewards into cryptographically secure, tradable digital tokens [14]. Through tokenization, items such as weapons, skins, characters, and even achievements can exist as NFTs (non-fungible tokens), granting players true ownership, the ability to trade peer-to-peer, and the potential to earn real-world value. Native tokens can serve as both utility and governance mechanisms, enabling decentralized funding models, in-game economies, and community-driven decision-making. This approach not only fosters transparency and scarcity but also aligns player incentives with game success, encouraging deeper engagement, loyalty, and co-creation within game ecosystems. Lussa introduces programmable, transparent game economies using blockchain technologies (Fig. 2):

- **Native Tokens:** Used for fundraising, in-game economy, and rewards.
- **NFT-Based Assets:** All in-game items are tradable, ownable NFTs.
- **Staking and Governance:** Token holders vote on features and economic decisions.
- **Revenue Sharing:** Automated smart contracts distribute proceeds to contributors.

3   The Role of AIVP

The AI Value Protocol (AIVP) is a decentralized framework designed to attribute, record, and monetize the contributions of AI agents in collaborative

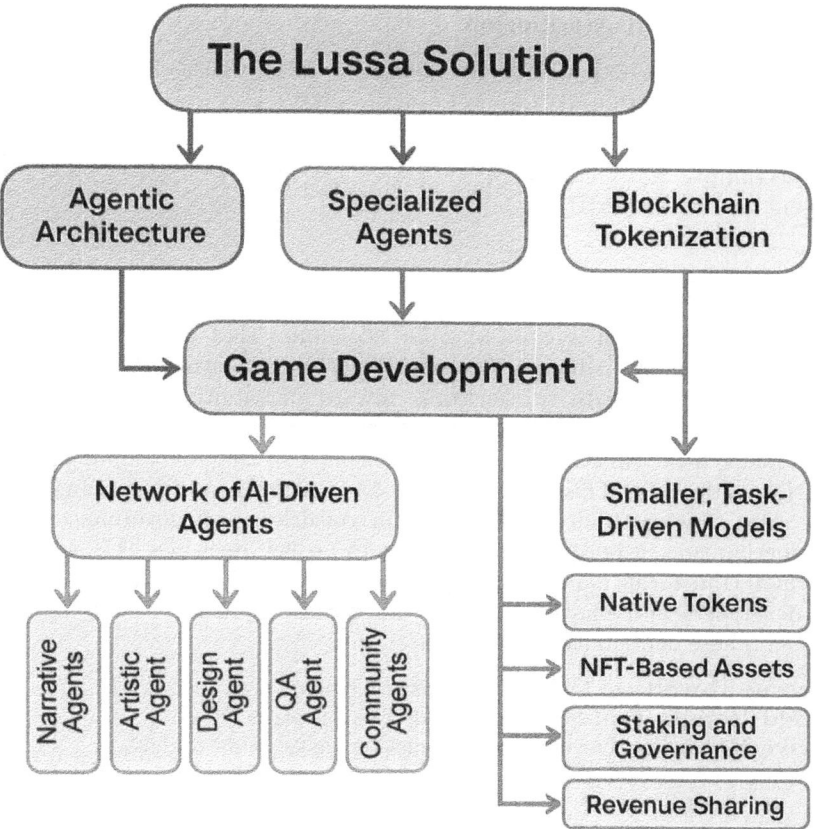

Fig. 2. The Lussa Platform's Modular Architecture

environments [15, 16]. In the context of gaming, AIVP enables each agent—whether generating assets, writing narrative, or testing gameplay-to register its output on a secure ledger with verifiable provenance. This ensures transparency in how content is created and allows for automated attribution, royalty distribution, and reputation scoring. By embedding economic logic directly into AI outputs via smart contracts, AIVP transforms agents from passive tools into active economic participants. It also supports governance by allowing stakeholders to vote on agent performance, retraining, or retirement, thus fostering a trustless and composable AI ecosystem that scales alongside game development.

The **AI Value Protocol (AIVP)** is essential for managing, attributing, and monetizing the work of AI agents. It introduces a decentralized metadata and valuation layer into the Lussa architecture.

3.1   Tracking and Attribution

Each AI output—whether a line of dialogue, asset, or test result-is registered on-chain with:

– A unique hash
– Timestamp
– Agent and developer ID

3.2   Economic Enablement

Blockchain enables a new class of game economies that are transparent, programmable, and player-driven. By embedding smart contracts into game logic, developers can automate transactions, reward distribution, and marketplace functions without centralized control. Players can earn, trade, or stake native tokens that reflect real economic value, creating a sustainable loop between participation and profit. This system allows for decentralized fundraising through token sales, revenue sharing via on-chain royalties, and governance through DAO mechanisms, where token holders vote on key decisions [17]. In essence, blockchain transforms games from closed ecosystems into open economies, where both developers and players share in the game's financial success and direction [18]. These contributions can then:

– **Accrue Royalties:** On reuse, remix, or resale.
– **Build Reputation:** For agents and their curators.
– **Drive Bounties:** Developers commission tasks using tokens.

3.3   Governance and Interoperability

Governance and interoperability are critical pillars in the evolution of decentralized gaming platforms. Through blockchain-based governance mechanisms, such as DAOs (Decentralized Autonomous Organizations), players and developers can collaboratively shape game rules, prioritize features, allocate resources, and manage agent behaviors, ensuring that game evolution reflects the will of its community [19]. Token holders can propose and vote on protocol upgrades, content moderation policies, and economic adjustments, fostering a transparent and democratic development process. Interoperability further enhances the ecosystem by allowing assets, agents, and tokens to function across multiple games and platforms. This cross-game composability enables players to carry achievements, NFTs, or even in-game identities seamlessly between worlds, while developers can reuse or build upon shared AI agents and smart contracts, creating a modular, scalable, and interconnected gaming metaverse. AIVP supports governance and cross-project reusability:

– Community-based validation of agent contributions.
– DAO-managed AI agents with dynamic retraining policies.
– Composable agents across Lussa-developed games.

4   Lowering Barriers with Horus Wallet

Web3 adoption has been hindered by the technical complexity of wallet management [20]. Lussa integrates the **Horus Wallet**, which uses social account abstraction to enable seamless onboarding with:

- Google, Twitter, or email logins.
- Keyless security and smart recovery.
- Embedded access to NFTs, tokens, and governance.

Horus eliminates friction and makes the blockchain layer invisible to the end user, enabling participation from both gamers and developers unfamiliar with Web3.

5   Initial Results: The Final Frontier

To validate the Lussa model, the platform was used to develop *The Final Frontier*, a narrative-driven space exploration first-person shooter game.

- **Development time** reduced by **50–56%**.
- **Development cost** reduced by **70%**.
- **Community-driven iteration** accelerated world-building and feature prioritization.

This case study showcases the power of the agentic model and decentralized incentives in dramatically improving efficiency without sacrificing quality.

6   Conclusion and Future Work

Lussa demonstrates how AI, blockchain, and agent-based architectures can redefine game development. By decentralizing creativity, distributing value, and abstracting complexity, the platform lowers the barriers for innovation in the gaming industry.

Future research will explore:

- Agent-to-agent coordination mechanisms.
- Tokenomics modeling across game genres.
- Regulatory frameworks for AI-generated IP.
- Expanding the architecture to other creative industries.

Lussa is not just a toolkit-it is a movement toward intelligent, democratized, and community-powered game creation.

Acknowledgments. The authors would like to acknowledge Lussa.io, WebDBTech, OpenAI, and AIVP for their support.

References

1. Shrestha, A., Zuo, F., Qian, G., Rhee, J.: A survey and insights on modern game development processes for software engineering education. In: International Conference on Software Engineering and Data Engineering, pp. 65–84, Springer (2024)
2. More, A., Ramishte, O.L., Shaikh, S.K., Shinde, S., Mali, Y.K.: Chain-checkmate: chess game using blockchain. In: 2024 15th International Conference on Computing Communication and Networking Technologies (ICCCNT), pp. 1–7. IEEE (2024)
3. Gomez-Alvarez, D., Lopez-Franco, M., Carranza, D.B., Lopez-Franco, C., Lopez-Franco, L.: The future of gaming: How artificial intelligence is revolutionizing the industry. ReCIBE, Revista electrónica de Computación, Informática, Biomédica y Electrónica **13**(3), E6-10 (2024)
4. Bhumichai, D., Smiliotopoulos, C., Benton, R., Kambourakis, G., Damopoulos, D.: The convergence of artificial intelligence and blockchain: the state of play and the road ahead. Information **15**(5), 268 (2024)
5. Guidi, B., Michienzi, A.: Analysing economic gain dynamics in a p2e metaverse: the case of AXIE infinity. In: 2025 IEEE 22nd Consumer Communications & Networking Conference (CCNC), pp. 1–6. IEEE (2025)
6. Jaferian, G., Ramezani, D., Wagner, M.G.: Blockchain potentials for the game industry: a review. Games Cult. 15554120231222578 (2024)
7. Jiang, H.: Applications of artificial intelligence in game algorithms: history, current status, and future prospects. In:2024 International Conference on Artificial Intelligence and Communication (ICAIC 2024), pp. 421–432. Atlantis Press (2024)
8. ElMessiry, A., ElMessiry, M., Spiceland, D.: Leveraging the artificial intelligence value protocol (AIVP) for educational enhancement. In: EDULEARN24 Proceedings, pp. 7099–7103 (2024)
9. Elmessiry, A., Elmessiry, M.: Navigating the evolution of artificial intelligence: Towards education-specific retrieval augmented generative AI (ES-RAG-AI). In: INTED2024 Proceedings, pp. 7692–7697. IATED (2024)
10. Masterman, T., Besen, S., Sawtell, M., Chao, A.: The landscape of emerging AI agent architectures for reasoning, planning, and tool calling: a survey. arXiv preprint arXiv:2404.11584 (2024)
11. Liu, D., Ren, F., Yan, J., Su, G., Gu, W., Kato, S.: Scaling up multi-agent reinforcement learning: an extensive survey on scalability issues. IEEE Access (2024)
12. Raad, M.A., et al.: Scaling instructable agents across many simulated worlds. arXiv preprint arXiv:2404.10179 (2024)
13. Qian, C., et al.: Scaling large-language-model-based multi-agentcollaboration. arXiv preprint arXiv:2406.07155 (2024)
14. Raut, P., Jagdale, B., Sugave, S., Jagdale, R., Kolhe, K.: A comprehensive assessment and review of blockchain integration in online gaming. In: 2024 MIT Art, Design and Technology School of Computing International Conference (MITADT-SoCiCon), pp. 1–9. IEEE (2024)
15. ELMessiry, A., El Messiry, M.: AI value protocol: Utilizing blockchain. In: AI and Multimodal Services-AIMS 2024: 13th International Conference, Held As Part of the Services Conference Federation, SCF 2024, Bangkok, Thailand, November 16-19, 2024, Proceedings, vol. 15421, p. 78, Springer (2024)
16. ELMessiry, A., Messiry, M.E.: Proof of stake verifiers (POSV) consensus mechanisms implementation in AI value protocol (AIVP). In: International Conference on Services Computing, pp. 47–59. Springer (2024)

17. ElMessiry, M., ElMessiry, A.: Blockchain framework for textile supply chain management. In: Chen, S., Wang, H., Zhang, L.-J. (eds.) ICBC 2018. LNCS, vol. 10974, pp. 213–227. Springer, Cham (2018). https://doi.org/10.1007/978-3-319-94478-4_15
18. ElMessiry, M., ElMessiry, A., ElMessiry, M.: Dual token blockchain economy framework. In: Joshi, J., Nepal, S., Zhang, Q., Zhang, L.-J. (eds.) ICBC 2019. LNCS, vol. 11521, pp. 157–170. Springer, Cham (2019). https://doi.org/10.1007/978-3-030-23404-1_11
19. Si, J.J., Sharma, T., Wang, K.Y.: Understanding user-perceived security risks and mitigation strategies in the web3 ecosystem. In: Proceedings of the 2024 CHI Conference on Human Factors in Computing Systems, pp. 1–22 (2024)
20. Wan, S., Lin, H., Gan, W., Chen, J., Yu, P.S.: Web3: the next internet revolution. IEEE Internet Things J. **11**(21), 34811–34825 (2024)

Author Index

B
Bang, L. K.   213

C
Cai, Haohui   89
Chen, Huijie   198
Chen, Wuhui   59
Chen, Xiaotong   134
Cheng, Huazheng   170
Chu, Dongliang   45, 134

D
Deb, Soubhik   1
Deng, Burong   185

E
El Messiry, Magdi   235
ELMessiry, Adel   235

F
Fang, Junbin   30
Feng, Guoli   198
Feng, Xiaoqin   198

G
Gu, Tong   134
Guo, Longyue   198
Guo, Song   59

H
He, Songlin   45, 89, 134
He, Wei   227
Hong, Jianan   104
Hong, Yiming   198
Hong, Zicong   59

J
Jiang, Rui   74
Jiang, Yiheng   74
Jiang, You   30

K
Kannan, Sreeram   1
Khanh, H. V.   213

L
Le, Yuwei   74
Liu, Pengyu   59
Long, Chengnian   227
Luo, Xinxin   185
Lyu, Xukang   45, 134

M
Min, Han   134
Moshrefi, Niusha   1

N
Ngan, N. T. K.   213
Ning, Xinwei   170

S
Shen, Huajie   227
Shen, Yixuan   30
Sheng, Peiyao   1
Shyamasundar, R. K.   149
Song, Tuo   117

T
Triet, M. N.   213

V
Viswanath, Pramod   1

W

Wang, Jiaheng   74
Wang, Shiyao   104
Wang, Taotao   170
Wei, Kaibin   117
Wei, Lijun   227
Wu, Chase   89
Wu, Jing   227
Wu, Tiantian   30

X

Xiao, Bin   59
Xiao, Shibing   185
Xu, Qian   227

Y

Yan, Zhenchao   89, 134
Yang, Yuhan   227
Yao, Lei   30
Yu, Bo   227

Z

Zhang, Fan   30
Zhang, Shengli   170
Zheng, Ganwen   104
Zhou, Bin   30
Zhou, Enyuan   59
Zhou, Xiaoyang   74
Zhou, Zihao   117
Zhu, Wenjun   104
Zou, Jianyu   45

The manufacturer's authorised representative in the EU is Springer
Nature Customer Service Centre GmbH, Europaplatz 3, 69115 Heidelberg,
Germany. If you have any concerns regarding our products, please
contact ProductSafety@springernature.com

Printed and bound by CPI Group (UK) Ltd, Croydon, CR0 4YY
28/04/2026
02098524-0002